Fortify and Empower Yourself at Thirty: Rewriting the Life Success Script

By: Mustafa Nejem

Table of Contents

Chapter 1

Thirty is a number that invites reflection

***

Your emotions may be mixed up when you reach the age of thirty. This could mean being excited and anxious at the same time. It's also about following societal expectations. These are difficult because they lead to much confusion and pressure as people move from twenty something into thirty something years old. Every one of us has our own notions of what is "successful" or "stable." But sometimes these thoughts make us lose confidence in ourselves or compare ourselves with each other.

In this section, we shall discuss how society perceives turning 30 years old. We will delve into common pressures and expectations. By examining these external forces, it will be easier for us to guide ourselves through life. Moreover, we can better understand our emotional experiences and desires.

It's essential for us to consider how we feel about reaching this stage in life. It's different for everyone; just know it! Accepting and enjoying your individual journey is important here. When we spend some time reflecting on where we were, what which milestones we passed so far towards where our dreams are taking us next, things become clearer to see once more again as well as self-confidence during this critical period.

This book will provide tips and information that will help strengthen oneself during such an important period in their lives. We should redefine what success means at 30 years of age. Here we can choose our own kind of victory at last though there is no universal definition for success especially since life has its own rhythm which operates naturally according to its own timelines. So let's come forward with hope, strength & new goals to embrace the thirties together.
About Our Fears

Your thirtieth birthday is around the corner? Nervous? Well you're not alone! The idea of growing old scares some people but they say age is just a number right? It doesn't refer solely to body changes or the passage of time, but instead to one's personal development as they live in the moment.

Feeling pressured by society's "thirty checklist"? Such as a good job, stable relationship or family? Just know that your journey is for you. There isn't a perfect definition for success. Life is happening at its own pace. Trust your timing.

Do you ever feel like you are lagging behind, while others have achieved more? Remember this: never compare yourself with others. By comparing yourself to others you are only robbing yourself of joy. You have your own path and unique timeline more important than common standards.

Look, it can be comforting and understandable we address worries early on. The point of this book is simple: there is no one-size-fits-all approach to success. Everybody has their own individual journey in life. It seeks to prepare people for their thirties bravely. Being open-minded and believing in oneself is the key, which unlocks numerous opportunities for growth and self-improvement leading to a happy prosperous future worth celebrating. Let's discuss spotting opportunities and potentials:

The 30s are fun years – they're about personal growth, knowing oneself better and new beginnings again. Your twenties say goodbye leaving behind a treasure chest full of wisdom from lessons already learnt about life during those last ten years that become great foundations for the rest of our lives.

Thirty means looking back on what you may have learned from being young adults in your twenties. That decade usually involves many significant changes such as entering into employment relations ship building networks or seeking a place in society resulting into who we are now today because through them we obtained knowledge skills strength.

With all these things understood better now, your self-awareness grows deeper every day. At least I know what I want and need now more than ever before when I am well over thirty years old which offers space & time to learn about oneself. More so, it's about getting to know your passion, values and life principles on a deeper level. It is crucial for you to evaluate what matters most in your life so that you can make choices based on who you really are.

Your thirties are marked by increasing confidence and consistency. You've encountered different challenges and conquered them. You've come to know your strengths and weaknesses better. Such awareness helps you approach new opportunities with clarity and determination.

This stage also gives you a fresh start to chase after new dreams and objectives. This could mean trying out a new profession, starting a business, or furthering your education. There are many opportunities to rebuild the career self in his or her 30s. What has been learnt in the twenty-something years should be used in making wiser decisions based on risks taken.

Besides, thirty some-things is an exceptional time for forming deep personal relations as well as nurturing vital ties. Either you have managed to create a strong support system or identified friendships that empower and nourish you. Use these insights from your twenties to build healthier relationships during this decade of your life. These relationships should be anchored on mutual respect, common values and genuine connection.

Embrace what your 30s offer you! It is a decade of growth, empowering experiences, unlimited possibilities and potentialities. Therefore, by looking into past lessons with open eyes while preserving current opportunities you will create for yourself the most comfortable future where everything will make sense. Your 30s are a chance to embark on an exciting journey of self-discovery through change. Goals for the Thirties:

In your thirties things change. It's an opportunity for growth. Let us look at some ways we can make these years count.

1. Setting Goals: Think about what comes next for you? In the next ten years what could happen? Choose goals that are important to you then do something about them.
2. Self-development: Make use of this period to acquire knowledge or skills; other than school think about such activities like sports which needs practice so much that one may not necessarily be good at it but learns over time'.
3. Changes: Big changes will come because they always do. See change being a good thing. Change in life enables one to learn from their past experiences and be better in future. Be open to changes.
4. Trust Yourself: Make choices of life that show whom you are. Trust your intuition. Trust yourself;" always be yourself'. Flock with the good birds only and say no to bad circumstances.
5. Try a Growth Mindset: Believe in your potential to improve, keep trying hard and persisting at something until it finally pays off. Look at challenges as an opportunity for growth and learning. Keep positive about setbacks as those are necessary steps to success.

Create Goals for Your 30s the action takes will foster more growth, happiness, and self-acceptance. Be ready for chances that come by, open-mindedness about new things or even different views on the same subject matter. Focus together with optimism can take you far at this crucial stage of your life. Fortify and Empower Yourself at Thirty: Rewriting Your Life Success Script is here to help you out. This book is filled with tools meant for readers who go through the ups-and-downs of being thirty-something years old. In its chapter we can find a number of aspects which are particularly pertinent in this important decade of our lives.

This book sets out to teach, inspire, and provide practical guidance so that readers can lead fulfilling lives during their 30s onwards till death do us part. There is also useful information about personal development, career advancement, relationships improvement, health matters, finance …and others.

Every single section of it has been designed to provide valuable advice and simple instructions, based on real-life stories. Readers are prompted to reflect on their lives, set goals for their 30s, and write a guide to their own success. Its major objective is to assist the audience in managing problems, gaining resilience, developing good mannerisms and achieving maximum potential. This book serves as an invaluable companion for anyone who is about to hit thirty years. If readers need guidance on advancing their careers, building strong relationships or making self-care non-negotiable this text attempts at giving them the tools and knowledge they need to bloom in this important decade.

Chapter 2
Self-Reflection: Assessing Your Journey So Far
*****

The Importance of Reflecting on Your Twenties and How It Can Contribute to Personal Growth and Future Success

In our fast-paced world, we get so caught up in the hustle and bustle of everyday life that we often don't take time out to reflect on our experiences. Reflection is a powerful tool for personal growth and development, especially as it pertains to the transformative decade that is our twenties. By looking back on the lessons learned and experiences had during this time period, we can gain valuable insights that will guide us into our thirties.

Reflection allows you to celebrate your accomplishments and recognize how far you've come. Take a moment to acknowledge the goals you've achieved, challenges you've overcome, milestones you've reached. Whether it's landing your dream job, completing your education, starting a business or building meaningful relationships, these are all things worthy of celebration. Not only do they give us confidence in ourselves but also serve as reminders of what success looks like for us.

On the other hand, celebrating successes without acknowledging setbacks is incomplete reflection. Your twenties probably featured instances where things didn't go according to plan or obstacles seemed insurmountable at first glance. Those moments are equally valuable learning opportunities. Look back at those situations and pinpoint what was learned from them as well as how they shaped who you are today. Remember that setbacks are not failures but essential steps towards personal growth.

Reflection will allow you to identify areas where there's room for growth and improvement.. Self-awareness plays an integral role in personal development so assess your strengths and weaknesses accordingly. Think about how each strength has served you well throughout your twenties then see how you can further strengthen them. Similarly, evaluate areas where improvements need to be made or if there's a skillset which needs acquiring before entering your thirties.

Finally, reflecting on this past decade empowers us with goal setting abilities for the future . The knowledge gained from reflection can be used to set tangible, meaningful goals for our thirties. Now armed with an understanding of how far we've come and what it took to get here, setting realistic expectations becomes a lot easier. Whether it's advancing in your career, nurturing relationships, finding balance or pursuing personal passions, make sure the path you take aligns with your values and aspirations.

In conclusion, taking the time out to reflect on your twenties is an essential part of personal growth and future success. Celebrating successes, learning from setbacks, assessing areas for growth and setting goals for the future lay the groundwork for living your best life in "Fortify and Empower Yourself at Thirty."

Take a moment to consider the goals you had in your twenties. Did you accomplish any of them? Maybe you nabbed your dream job, got around to traveling to those new countries, or finished a personal project that was important to you. Whether big or small, these triumphs are worthy of recognition.

Acknowledging and celebrating accomplishments can lead to an increase in self-esteem and confidence as we move into our thirties. Doing this reminds us what we're capable of achieving and how strong we can be when it counts. Celebrating also allows for us to truly appreciate all the work put into reaching these goals and the growth that came with it.

It's important not to compare our success with others as well since everyone has their own definition of what it looks like. What matters most is feeling proud about what was accomplished. With so much going on in life, sometimes it can be hard to stop and really think back on what happened so consider jotting down a list of them in your journal or notebook. Putting it down somewhere concrete means it'll always be there as a reminder of progress made which could come in handy when faced with future obstacles.

By celebrating accomplishments from your twenties, a solid foundation is laid for the next chapter in life. Take advantage of being able to build off past successes and continue pushing towards personal growth and fulfillment now that you'll be entering your thirties

As you look back on the failures of your twenties, also celebrate the progress you've made in overcoming them. Acknowledge the strength and resilience it took to push through those dark days. By doing so, you'll build confidence in your ability to tackle any challenge that comes your way in this decade and beyond.

In the next section, we will explore how to identify areas for growth based on your reflections and use them to set goals for your future.

Helping readers identify areas where they can grow is a key aspect of self-awareness and self-reflection. When readers take time to reflect on their twenties, they gain valuable insights into patterns or behaviors that may have held them back or prevented them from reaching their full potential.

In this part of the chapter, we delve into various aspects of life such as personal relationships, career development, health and well-being, financial habits management, and personal values and beliefs.

We ask readers questions like: Were your friendships deep enough? Healthy partnerships? Are there toxic or unhealthy patterns that need attention? Opportunities for deeper connections with loved ones? In terms of career development: Reflect on what you've done so far. Can you identify areas where more skills or experience would benefit you? Do new educational opportunities exist? Can networking help?

Taking care of physical and mental health is also important. We ask if they were prioritized at all. If not now's a good chance to start making changes with exercise routines or nutrition practices etc,.

Financial habits are another critical area for reflection. What are some things that could be improved with how money is being spent? Are saving habits good? Is long-term planning strong?

Lastly we want readers to take a moment to think about their personal values and beliefs. Have these changed over time at all? And if so do they still align with how they want their lives to play out in their thirties?

By engaging in this type of self-reflection and identifying areas for growth, readers can get a better idea about where they want to direct their efforts in their thirties. This self-awareness acts as a foundation for the rest of the book. So when readers sit down to set goals and navigate different aspects of their lives with intention and purpose, they'll have some clarity on how to move   forward.

Chapter **3**

Life Reboot:
Setting New Goals
******

Setting Goals for the Future:

Now that you have reflected on your twenties and gained valuable insights from your experiences, it's time to set goals and intentions for your thirties. The lessons learned and opportunities identified during this reflection process will serve as a solid foundation for creating a roadmap towards personal growth and success in the next decade of your life.

Here are some steps to guide you in setting meaningful goals for the future:

1. Identify Your Values: Begin by clarifying your core values – what truly matters to you in life? Consider aspects such as career, relationships, health, personal development, and contribution. Aligning your goals with your values will give you a sense of purpose and direction.

2. Define Your Vision: Envision the life you want to create for yourself in your thirties. What does success look like to you? Take into account various areas of your life, including career, relationships, health, and personal fulfillment. Your vision should inspire and motivate you to take action.

3. Set SMART Goals: Make your goals Specific, Measurable, Achievable, Relevant, and Time-bound (SMART). Break down your long-term vision into smaller, manageable goals that are clear and actionable. For example, if your vision includes a successful career, a specific goal could be to achieve a promotion within the next two years.

4. Prioritize and Focus: Determine which goals are the most important to you and prioritize them accordingly. Trying to tackle too many goals at once can lead to overwhelm and lack of progress. Focus on one or two key goals at any given time to maintain focus and momentum.

5. Create Action Steps: Break each goal down into actionable steps that will help you move closer to its achievement. These steps should be specific, measurable, and time-bound. For instance, if your goal is to improve your physical fitness, action steps could include joining a gym, scheduling regular workouts, and tracking progress.

6. Track Your Progress: Regularly review and track your progress towards your goals. This will help you stay accountable and make necessary adjustments along the way. Celebrate milestones and achievements to maintain motivation and momentum.

7. Stay Flexible and Adapt: Life is unpredictable, and circumstances may change. Be open to adjusting your goals as needed while staying true to your overall vision. Embrace any opportunities or challenges that come your way, viewing them as potential catalysts for growth and learning.

Remember, setting goals is not only about achieving specific outcomes but also about the personal growth and fulfillment that comes with the journey. Be kind to yourself, embrace flexibility, and enjoy the process of striving towards your aspirations in your thirties. By setting meaningful goals that align with your values and reflecting on your progress regularly, you'll be well on your way to rewriting the life success script that is uniquely tailored to you Reflecting on the past decade is an essential step in setting intentions for the future. Take the time to carefully review your accomplishments and milestones from the previous decade. Celebrate your successes, no matter how big or small, and acknowledge the hard work and effort you put into achieving them.

Identify key lessons learned from various experiences and challenges you faced. Reflecting on these lessons will allow you to grow and develop as a person. Consider what worked well for you and what didn't, and use this knowledge to make informed decisions moving forward.

During this reflection, it's important to also acknowledge the challenges you overcame. Recognize the strength and resilience you demonstrated when faced with difficult situations. This will boost your confidence and provide a solid foundation as you set new goals and intentions for the next decade.

Remember, reflecting on your past achievements and lessons learned is not about dwelling on the past or comparing yourself to others. It is a valuable exercise that allows you to gain insights into your own journey and chart a course for future success.

By taking the time to reflect on your past experiences, you can draw upon valuable insights that will guide you as you set intentions for the decade ahead. Use this opportunity to celebrate your successes, learn from your challenges, and pave the way for a fulfilling and successful future Define Your Vision for the Next Ten Years:

In this section, we will focus on defining your vision for the next decade. This is an important step in setting intentions and goals that align with your aspirations and dreams. As you embark on your thirties, take time to visualize where you want to be in various aspects of your life, including career, relationships, health, and personal development.

Consider what success looks like to you. What do you envision for your professional life? Are you working in a fulfilling career that brings you joy and allows you to make a difference? Visualize the type of work environment, position, or industry you want to be a part of. Think about the skills and experiences you want to acquire and how they align with your long-term goals.

When it comes to relationships, think about the kind of connections you want to foster. Are you seeking a committed partnership or marriage? Do you want to build a family or expand your social circle? Visualize the qualities and values you desire in your relationships and how they contribute to your overall happiness and growth.

Consider your health and well-being. Imagine yourself leading an active, balanced lifestyle. How do you prioritize self-care and maintain physical and mental wellness? Visualize yourself engaging in activities that bring you joy and promote optimal health. Consider how taking care of yourself will positively impact other areas of your life.

Personal development is also an essential aspect to consider. How do you envision growing as an individual over the next ten years? Think about the skills, knowledge, and experiences you want to cultivate. Consider any hobbies or passions you want to explore and how they contribute to your personal growth and fulfillment.

Once you have taken time to reflect on each area, write down your vision statement. Your vision statement should encapsulate your aspirations and dreams for the next ten years. It should be a clear representation of the life you want to create for yourself, incorporating all the aspects we have discussed.

Remember, this is your vision and it should be aligned with who you truly are and what you desire. Be ambitious, but also realistic. Your vision statement will serve as a guiding light as you navigate this transformative decade. It will inspire and motivate you to take action towards achieving your goals and living a purposeful life.

Now, take a moment to write down your own vision statement. Give it careful thought and let it reflect your true desires and aspirations for the next ten years. In order to turn your long-term vision into a reality, it is crucial to break down your goals into smaller, actionable steps. This will help you stay motivated and focused, as well as provide a clear roadmap for achieving your objectives.

Start by taking your overall vision for the next decade and identifying the specific goals that will contribute to its realization. These goals should be SMART: specific, measurable, attainable, relevant, and time-bound.

Specificity is key when setting goals. Rather than saying "I want to advance in my career," define exactly what that means to you. For example, "I want to secure a management position within my current company within the next five years."

Measurability ensures that you can track your progress and determine whether or not you have achieved your goal. Establish concrete metrics or milestones that will indicate success along the way. For instance, "I will complete two professional development courses every year to enhance my skills and knowledge."

Make sure your goals are attainable, meaning they are within reach given your resources, abilities, and circumstances. Setting overly ambitious goals can lead to frustration and disappointment. Set yourself up for success by considering what is realistic and feasible.

Relevance is about ensuring that your goals align with your overall vision and values. Ask yourself why each goal is important to you and how it contributes to your long-term aspirations. This will provide a sense of purpose and motivation throughout the journey.

Lastly, set time-bound deadlines for achieving each goal. Without a timeframe, it's easy to procrastinate or lose focus. Determine when you would like to accomplish each milestone or objective and hold yourself accountable to those timelines.

Once you have established SMART goals, create a roadmap or action plan that outlines the specific steps needed to achieve each one. Break them down further into smaller tasks or sub-goals that can be tackled on a daily, weekly, or monthly basis.

Regularly review your progress, adjust your plan as necessary, and celebrate each milestone you achieve along the way. Breaking down your goals into actionable steps will provide clarity, motivation, and a greater sense of direction as you navigate your thirties and work towards rewriting your own personal success script. Prioritize and Align Your Goals with Core Values: setting intentions for the decade ahead, it's crucial to evaluate your core values and beliefs that guide your decision-making. Your values serve as the foundation of your goals and aspirations, shaping the direction you want to take in life. By ensuring that your goals align with your values, you create a sense of purpose and fulfillment that can sustain you throughout your thirties.

Take the time to reflect on what truly matters to you. Consider the principles and ideals that hold significance in your life. Are you driven by creativity, growth, compassion, or adventure? By understanding your core values, you gain clarity about what you want to achieve and where you want to invest your time and energy.

Once you have identified your core values, rank your goals based on their importance. Determine which goals deserve more focus and attention, considering how each aligns with your values. Some goals may naturally resonate more closely with your core values, while others may require reevaluation or adjustment.

Remember that aligning your goals with your core values is crucial for long-term fulfillment. When your goals are in harmony with what truly matters to you, they become more meaningful. You will have a strong sense of purpose driving you forward, making it easier to stay committed and motivated even when faced with challenges.

Ensure that the goals you prioritize are authentic to who you are and what you believe in. Don't be swayed by external pressures or societal expectations. Your own values should guide your decision-making process, allowing you to create a path that is true to yourself.

By prioritizing and aligning your goals with your core values, you set yourself up for a meaningful and fulfilling journey through your thirties. Remember, success is not just about achieving external milestones; it's about living a life that is aligned with who you are at the core.

Developing a Plan of Action is a crucial step in setting intentions for the next decade. It involves creating an actionable plan by outlining the specific steps needed to accomplish each goal.

Firstly, take the time to identify potential obstacles that may hinder your progress towards achieving your goals. By recognizing these challenges early on, you can develop strategies to overcome them. This could include seeking additional support or resources, acquiring new skills, or adjusting your approach when faced with setbacks.

Next, it is important to set deadlines for each milestone along the way. By establishing clear timelines, you create a sense of urgency and accountability for yourself. This helps to keep you focused and motivated as you work towards your goals.

In order to stay on track and hold yourself accountable, it can be helpful to establish measures of accountability. These could include regularly checking in with a mentor or accountability partner, joining a group or community that shares similar goals, or utilizing technology tools such as apps or habit trackers.

By creating an actionable plan, identifying potential obstacles, setting deadlines, and establishing accountability measures, you lay the foundation for success in achieving your goals. This step ensures that your intentions remain concrete and that you have a clear roadmap for navigating the next decade of your life.

Remember, the key to success lies not only in setting intentions but also in taking consistent action towards those intentions. With a well-developed plan of action, you will be better equipped to overcome challenges, stay motivated, and ultimately achieve the fulfilling life you envision for yourself Understanding the Importance of Self-Awareness.

Self-awareness is an integral aspect of personal growth and development. It involves having a deep understanding of oneself, including one's thoughts, emotions, values, strengths, weaknesses, and behavioral patterns. By becoming more self-aware, individuals can gain valuable insights into their own motivations, beliefs, and biases. This increased self-understanding can lead to improved decision-making, enhanced emotional intelligence, and stronger relationships with others.

One of the key benefits of self-awareness is its ability to improve decision-making. When individuals have a clear understanding of their values, priorities, and long-term goals, they can make choices that align with these aspects of themselves. Self-awareness helps individuals to recognize what truly matters to them and enables them to make decisions that are in line with their authentic selves.

Additionally, self-awareness plays a crucial role in building emotional intelligence. Emotional intelligence refers to the capacity to understand and manage one's own emotions as well as the emotions of others. By being aware of our own emotions, we can better understand how they influence our thoughts and behaviors. This awareness allows us to regulate our emotions effectively and engage in more empathetic and constructive interactions with others.

By fostering self-awareness, individuals can also strengthen their relationships with others. Understanding our own triggers, communication styles, and needs enables us to communicate more effectively and empathetically with those around us. Furthermore, self-awareness helps us recognize patterns in our relationships and identify any unhealthy dynamics or recurring conflicts. This awareness empowers us to take responsibility for our part in these patterns and make positive changes.

Developing self-awareness requires intentional effort and practice. There are various techniques that can aid in this process, such as journaling, meditation, or seeking feedback from trusted individuals. Journaling allows for reflection and introspection by providing a space to explore thoughts, feelings, and experiences. Meditation cultivates mindfulness, which enhances self-awareness by bringing attention to the present moment and promoting introspection. Seeking feedback from trusted individuals can provide valuable insights into blind spots and help shed light on areas where self-awareness is needed.

Incorporating regular self-reflection practices into daily routines is essential for maintaining and deepening self-awareness. This could involve setting aside dedicated time each day for self-reflection, engaging in mindfulness exercises, or journaling regularly. By carving out time for self-reflection, individuals can create space for introspection and gain a clearer understanding of themselves.

In summary, self-awareness is a powerful tool for personal growth and development. Its significance lies in its ability to improve decision-making, enhance emotional intelligence, and strengthen relationships. By understanding ourselves more deeply, we can lead more authentic and fulfilling lives

Reflecting on Personal Values:

To truly understand yourself and lead a fulfilling life, it is crucial to identify and clarify your core values. Your values serve as guiding principles that shape your beliefs, choices, and behaviors. They are the driving force behind your actions and decisions.

Take some time to reflect on what truly matters to you. What principles do you hold dear? What qualities do you admire in others? Consider different areas of your life, such as relationships, career, personal growth, and community involvement. What values resonate with you in each of these areas?

Some common core values include integrity, honesty, compassion, respect, courage, and perseverance. However, everyone's values are unique to their own experiences and beliefs. It's important to identify the values that personally resonate with you and align with who you aspire to be.

Once you have identified your core values, take a moment to reflect on how they currently show up in your life. Do your actions reflect your values? Are there any areas where there may be a disconnect? This self-reflection can provide valuable insights into whether you are living in alignment with your true self.

Understanding the impact of your values on your choices and behaviors allows you to make more intentional decisions that align with who you truly are. It helps you navigate through life with a sense of purpose and authenticity. By consciously living in line with your core values, you can cultivate a strong sense of self-awareness and create a life that is meaningful and fulfilling to you.

Throughout this book, you will find various exercises and strategies to further explore and integrate your values into different aspects of your life. Embracing self-awareness and understanding the power of your values is the first step towards rewriting your own personal success script at the age of thirty Examining Belief Systems.

Our beliefs shape the way we perceive the world around us and influence our thoughts, emotions, and actions. Many of these beliefs are deeply ingrained in our subconscious mind, often developed during childhood or through repeated experiences. However, not all beliefs serve us positively. Some beliefs may be limiting, holding us back from reaching our full potential.

In this chapter, we will dive into the examination of belief systems and understand how they impact our lives. By delving into our subconscious beliefs, we can identify any negative or limiting beliefs that may be hindering our personal growth and success. Through self-reflection and introspection, we can challenge and reframe these beliefs to create a more empowering belief system.

When examining our belief systems, it is essential to approach this process with curiosity and openness. Take some time to reflect on the following questions:

1. What are your core beliefs about yourself?
- Are there any beliefs that hold you back from pursuing your dreams or taking risks?
- Do you believe in your ability to overcome challenges and achieve success?

2. What are your core beliefs about others?
- Do you have a positive or negative outlook on human nature?
- Are there any biases or stereotypes that you hold about certain groups of people?

3. What are your core beliefs about the world?
- Do you believe that the world is a friendly or hostile place?
- Do you feel like you have control over your own destiny?

As you reflect on these questions, pay attention to any recurring patterns or themes in your beliefs. Notice if any of your beliefs are self-limiting or if they may no longer serve you in your current life stage.

Once you have identified any limiting beliefs, it's time to challenge and reframe them. Here are some strategies to help you in this process:

1. Question the evidence: Examine the evidence supporting your belief. Is there any concrete proof that supports this belief? Are there alternative perspectives or experiences that contradict it?
2. Find alternative explanations: Consider alternative interpretations or explanations for the situations that reinforce your limiting beliefs. Is there a different way to interpret these experiences that is more empowering and supportive?
3. Seek counterexamples: Look for examples in your own life or in the lives of others that contradict your limiting belief. This can help you realize that your belief may not be universally true.
4. Gather evidence against your belief: Actively seek out evidence and information that contradicts your limiting belief. This can help you challenge its validity and see other possibilities.
5. Reframe your belief: Once you have challenged your limiting belief, replace it with a more empowering belief. Choose a belief that aligns with your values, supports your goals, and inspires confidence.

Remember, changing long-held beliefs takes time and effort. Be patient with yourself throughout this process and celebrate each step of progress. By examining and reframing our belief systems, we can create new empowering narratives that support our personal growth and success

The Power of Self-Awareness: Uncovering Your Values and Beliefs

In this section, we will explore different techniques for cultivating self-reflection practices that can enhance your self-awareness. These practices are invaluable tools for gaining deeper insights into your values, beliefs, and inner workings. By incorporating these practices into your daily routines, you can foster a greater sense of self-awareness and live a more authentic life.

1. Journaling:

Writing in a journal allows you to reflect on your thoughts, feelings, and experiences.

Set aside time each day to write freely without judgment or censorship.

Use prompts or questions to guide your reflections and explore different aspects of your life.

Review your journal periodically to identify patterns or recurring themes.

2. Meditation:

Meditation is a powerful practice that helps calm the mind and cultivate self-awareness.

Dedicate a few minutes each day to sit in silence and focus on your breath or a specific mantra.

Observe your thoughts and emotions without getting caught up in them.

Notice any patterns or insights that arise during meditation.

3. Seeking feedback from trusted individuals:

Reach out to people who know you well and ask for their honest opinions and observations about your strengths, weaknesses, and blind spots.

Be open to feedback, even if it may be uncomfortable or challenging to hear.

Reflect on the feedback you receive and consider how it aligns or conflicts with your own self-perception.

4. Mindful reflection:

Incorporate moments of mindfulness throughout your day.

Pause and take a few deep breaths before responding to a situation or making a decision.

Check in with yourself regularly to assess how you are feeling physically, emotionally, and mentally.

Notice any thoughts or beliefs that arise in different situations and examine their origin or impact on your behavior.

By engaging in these self-reflection practices, you can deepen your self-awareness and gain valuable insights into your values, beliefs, and true desires. Regularly integrating these techniques into your life will help you align your actions with your identified values and beliefs, leading to greater authenticity and fulfillment The Power of Self-Awareness: Uncovering Your Values and Beliefs : Bridging the Gap between Values and Actions.

In this section, we will explore how to bridge the gap between your identified values and beliefs and your actions. It's one thing to understand what you value and believe, but it's another to consistently align your actions with those principles.

Aligning your actions with your values and beliefs requires conscious effort and a willingness to make changes in your life. Here are some strategies to help you bridge this gap:

1. Identify areas of misalignment: Take some time to reflect on your current actions and behaviors. Are there any aspects of your life where you notice a disconnect between your values and how you actually behave? This could be in your personal relationships, work, or even in your self-care routines. Identifying these areas is the first step towards creating alignment.

2. Set clear intentions: Once you've identified areas of misalignment, set clear intentions for how you want to align your actions with your values. For example, if you value honesty and integrity, make a commitment to always speak the truth, even when it's difficult. By setting clear intentions, you create a roadmap for how you want to show up in the world.

3. Create new habits: Aligning your actions with your values often requires creating new habits or breaking old ones. Start by focusing on small changes that are manageable and sustainable. For example, if you value health and well-being, commit to incorporating daily exercise into your routine or making healthier food choices. Over time, these small changes will add up and contribute to a more aligned life.

4. Seek support: Changing deeply ingrained behaviors can be challenging, so don't be afraid to reach out for support. Share your values and goals with trusted friends or family members who can help hold you accountable. Consider joining a support group or seeking guidance from a coach or therapist who can provide guidance and encouragement along the way.

5. Embrace self-compassion: Remember that change is a process, and it's important to be kind and patient with yourself. If you stumble or fall off track, don't beat yourself up. Instead, practice self-compassion and view setbacks as learning opportunities. Adjust your approach if needed and keep moving forward towards aligning your actions with your values.

By bridging the gap between your values and actions, you create a life that is more authentic, meaningful, and fulfilling. It takes time and effort, but the rewards are well worth it. Stay committed, stay focused, and remember that each small step towards alignment brings you closer to living a life that reflects who you truly are reflecting on Personal Values: Begin by exploring your core values and beliefs to establish a foundation for defining success. Take the time to delve deep within yourself and identify what truly matters most to you in various areas of life such as your career, relationships, health, and personal growth.

Consider the aspects of your life that bring you the greatest sense of fulfillment and joy. What values do you hold dear? Is it integrity, authenticity, or compassion? Reflect on these qualities and how they align with your goals and aspirations.

When assessing your career, think about what kind of work brings you satisfaction and a sense of purpose. Is it making a difference in people's lives, challenging yourself intellectually, or contributing to a cause you are passionate about? Knowing what drives you professionally will help you determine what success looks like in this aspect of your life.

Next, evaluate your relationships. What qualities do you value in your friendships and romantic partnerships? Is it trust, loyalty, or shared interests? Consider the level of connection and support that is important to you, as well as the depth of emotional intimacy you seek.

In terms of health and well-being, reflect on what it means to you to be physically and mentally healthy. Is it having an active lifestyle, nourishing your body with wholesome foods, or finding inner peace through mindfulness practices? Understanding what health means to you will guide your pursuit of a balanced and fulfilling lifestyle.

Lastly, delve into personal growth. Identify the areas in which you want to develop, whether it is expanding your knowledge and skills, cultivating emotional intelligence, or exploring new interests and hobbies. Reflect on the type of person you aspire to become and how this aligns with your overall definition of success.

By reflecting on your core values and beliefs across these different areas of life, you can establish a strong foundation for defining success on your own terms. This self-reflection will provide clarity and help guide your decision-making process as you navigate your thirties and beyond. Remember, success is a deeply personal and individualized concept, and by aligning your goals with your values, you can create a life that truly feels fulfilling and meaningful to you.

Shifting Perspectives on Success: Challenge traditional notions of success and embrace a more holistic and individualized definition. In this chapter, we will explore the importance of redefining success on your own terms. It's time to break free from societal expectations and consider what truly matters to you.

When it comes to defining success, it is essential to look beyond external achievements like wealth or status. While these may be important factors for some individuals, they do not encompass the full spectrum of success. Instead, consider factors like fulfillment, happiness, and work-life balance.

Start by reflecting on your personal values and beliefs. What matters most to you in different areas of life? Is it making a meaningful impact in your career? Cultivating fulfilling relationships? Nurturing your physical and mental well-being? Defining success is a deeply personal process that requires self-awareness and introspection.

Challenge the societal pressures that often dictate our perception of success. Recognize that your journey may be different from others, and that's perfectly okay. Embrace a more holistic approach that takes into account your unique circumstances, aspirations, and priorities.

Consider what brings you true fulfillment and joy. Is it pursuing your passions? Making a positive impact on others? Achieving a healthy work-life balance? Align your definition of success with these core values and desires.

Remember, success is not a one-size-fits-all concept. Each person has their own path to follow and their own set of goals to achieve. By shifting your perspective on success, you reclaim the power to define it for yourself.

In the following chapters, we will delve deeper into creating meaningful goals that align with your values and vision of success. We will also explore strategies for measuring progress and celebrating milestones along the way. Get ready to embark on a journey of self-discovery as we redefine success on our own terms Creating Meaningful Goals: Learn how to set meaningful goals that align with your values and vision of success. Developing a strategic plan to achieve these goals is essential, as it helps you stay focused and motivated.

1. Reflect on Your Values: Before setting goals, take the time to reflect on your values and what truly matters to you. What are your passions? What brings you joy and fulfillment? By understanding your core values, you can set goals that align with your authentic self.

2. Define Your Vision of Success: Consider what success means to you personally. Is it financial stability, a fulfilling career, strong relationships, or personal growth? Visualize what your ideal life looks like and use this vision as a guide when setting goals.

3. Identify Specific and Measurable Goals: When setting goals, make sure they are specific and measurable. For example, instead of saying "I want to be healthier," set a specific goal such as "I will exercise for 30 minutes five times a week." This allows you to track your progress and hold yourself accountable.

4. Break Goals Down into Actionable Steps: Breaking larger goals into smaller, manageable tasks makes them more achievable. Create an action plan by outlining the steps needed to reach each goal. Assign deadlines to these steps to help you stay on track.
5. Set Realistic Timelines: Consider the time frame in which you want to achieve your goals. Be realistic about what is attainable within that timeframe, taking into account any external factors or commitments that may influence your progress.
6. Focus on Both Short-term and Long-term Goals: While long-term goals provide a sense of direction, it's crucial to have short-term goals as well. These smaller milestones keep you motivated and provide opportunities for celebration along the way.
7. Regularly Evaluate and Adjust Your Goals: Review your goals periodically to ensure they still align with your values and vision of success. Circumstances may change, and it's essential to adapt your goals accordingly. Be open to adjusting timelines or even reevaluating the goals themselves.

By setting meaningful goals that align with your values and vision of success, you will be better equipped to navigate your thirties with purpose and fulfillment. Remember, success is personal and unique to each individual. Embrace the journey of defining success on your own terms and celebrate every step of progress along the way Measuring Progress and Celebrating Milestones: It is essential to establish ways to measure your progress towards your goals and celebrate the milestones you achieve along the way. By doing so, you can stay motivated and maintain a sense of accomplishment, reinforcing your belief in your own success.

To measure your progress effectively, consider breaking down your goals into smaller, more manageable tasks or objectives. This allows you to track your progress incrementally and gives you a clear sense of advancement. Set specific deadlines or timelines for completing these tasks to stay accountable.

One useful tool for measuring progress is creating a goal tracker or journal. This can be a physical notebook or a digital document where you record your goals, milestones, and accomplishments. Use this as a visual representation of how far you have come and how close you are to achieving your desired outcomes.

In addition to measuring progress, it is equally important to celebrate the milestones you reach along the way. Celebrating milestones not only provides an opportunity for self-reflection and acknowledgment but also fosters motivation and a positive mindset. Taking time to recognize and appreciate your achievements reinforces your sense of success and boosts your confidence for future endeavors.

When celebrating milestones, consider engaging in activities that bring you joy and fulfillment. Treat yourself to something special, such as a small indulgence or a meaningful experience that aligns with your values. Share your accomplishments with loved ones and allow them to celebrate with you, creating a supportive network that encourages your continued growth.

Remember that success is not solely defined by achieving big, final goals. It is the accumulation of small victories and milestones achieved along the way. By measuring your progress and celebrating each step forward, you build momentum and confidence, ultimately leading to the fulfillment of your larger aspirations.

Note: This part focuses specifically on measuring progress and celebrating milestones, without repeating concepts discussed in other parts of the book Embracing Evolution and Adaptability: As we journey through life, our definition of success may evolve over time. It's important to recognize that success is not a static destination but an ongoing process of growth and self-discovery. With each new experience and chapter in our lives, our goals and values may shift, requiring us to adapt and reevaluate what success means to us.

By embracing evolution and adaptability, we allow ourselves the freedom to explore new opportunities, perspectives, and passions. We become open to the possibility of changing our course and pursuing different paths that align with our evolving values and aspirations. This flexibility enables us to navigate the ever-changing landscape of our lives with grace and resilience.

The key to embracing evolution and adaptability is remaining curious and open-minded. It involves actively seeking out new experiences, challenging our beliefs, and being receptive to feedback and learning opportunities. By doing so, we create space for personal growth and development, allowing us to continuously refine our understanding of success.

Reevaluating our goals and values is an essential part of this journey. As circumstances change, what once aligned with our vision of success may no longer hold true. It's important to periodically assess whether our goals still reflect our passions, values, and aspirations. This self-reflection allows us to stay true to ourselves and make adjustments when necessary.

In this process of reevaluating our goals and values, we must also recognize that setbacks and failures are not indicators of personal failure or lack of success. They are opportunities for growth and learning. By embracing the lessons they offer, we can adapt our strategies and forge ahead with newfound wisdom and resilience.

Finally, it's crucial to cultivate self-compassion as we embrace evolution and adaptability. Change can be uncomfortable and challenging at times, but it's important to remember that it's all part of the journey towards a more authentic and fulfilling version of success. Be patient with yourself, celebrate your progress, and continue to embrace the unknown with optimism and courage.

As you embark on this chapter of redefining success on your own terms, remember to remain open to the possibilities that lie ahead. Embrace the evolution of your goals and values, and adapt accordingly. By doing so, you will continue to grow and discover new paths towards a successful and fulfilling life.

Chapter 4

The Power of Mindset: Cultivating a Growth Mindset - Life as Continuing Education

****

Understanding the concept of a growth mindset is essential when trying to cultivate lifelong learning and personal development. A growth mindset is a belief that abilities and intelligence can be developed through dedication, effort, and learning from mistakes. The polar opposite of this, a fixed mindset, believes that qualities such as intelligence and talents are set in stone.

Once someone takes on a growth mindset, they open themselves up to new possibilities and challenges. They understand that their abilities aren't set in stone but instead can be improved with time and effort. This mental shift allows them to embrace opportunities to learn new things, take risks comfortably, and overcome obstacles with resilience.

A growth mindset isn't only beneficial for personal use. In the professional world, people who have adopted this way of thinking are more likely to want to continuously learn more. This helps them adapt easier with change which leads them to embracing workplace challenges. Instead of seeing failures as setbacks, they view them as opportunities for improvement which boosts innovation and creativity.

Studies have shown many times over that people who believe in a growth mindset are more motivated in achieving success in various areas of life. Once one has fully grasped the concept of it along with actively working towards implementing it into their everyday life; they will unlock their full potential.

Identifying limiting beliefs is one of the first steps when trying to achieve this for lifelong learning. Reflecting on what we believe will help us see how we're potentially holding ourselves back both personally and professionally. Listed below are some strategies anyone could use if they want to develop a positive outlook:

1. Self-reflection: Use time you get by yourself wisely by reflecting on any recurring negative thoughts or beliefs you may have that's been holding you back.

Example questions would include "What do I believe about my abilities?" or "What fears or doubts do I have about learning something new?"

2. Challenge your beliefs: After identifying these self-destructive patterns; challenge them head-on. Look for evidence that goes against what you believe then eventually look at it from a different perspective. Ask yourself questions such as "Is this belief based on fact or perception?" or "Could there be another way of looking at this situation?"

3. 3.Reframe negative thoughts: When you catch yourself in these negative thought patterns, try and see the positive side of things. This might feel forced at first but it will eventually come naturally.

4. Example would be changing "I'm not good enough" to "I am capable of learning and growing."

5. Practice positive self-talk: Be mindful of how you speak to yourself and replace self-critical thoughts with encouraging ones. Remind yourself of the strengths, achievements, and potential you have for growth.

6. Surround yourself with positivity: Being around those who think like-mindedly is always helpful when trying to enforce a new mindset. Start by seeking out friends, mentors or communities who share your interest in personal development and foster a positive mindset.

7. Set realistic goals: Small accomplishments here and there can work wonders on boosting motivation. Set smaller goals within larger ones so they become more manageable. Most importantly, celebrate each accomplishment along the way.
8. Embrace failure as an opportunity for learning: Try seeing failure as something valuable rather than negative.
9. Turning mistakes into lessons helps refine your approach over time which leads to even more growth.

Remember that it takes time and consistent effort to develop a growth mindset. However, by challenging your limiting beliefs and practicing every day, you can create a more positive way of thinking. One that supports lifelong learning and personal growth

Failures are learning opportunities. In order to cultivate a growth mindset, you must accept that fact. It's important to stop viewing those failures as enormous setbacks, but rather stepping stones to success. And plenty of successful individuals have done just that throughout history. Just take Thomas Edison for example. He famously said, "I have not failed." then went on saying "I've just found 10,000 ways that won't work," after countless attempts at creating the electric light bulb. Instead of seeing his failures as an obstacle he saw each one as a lesson bringing him one step closer to achieving his goal.

Another example is J.K Rowling. The author of Harry Potter faced many rejections before finding success. Multiple publishing houses rejected her manuscript before Bloomsbury Publishing finally took a chance on her work. Her persistence in the face of rejection shows how resilient she was.

By reframing our perspective we can start viewing failure as an opportunity for growth and self-improvement We can see them as valuable lessons that teach us what doesn't work while guiding us towards what does Our failures provide insight into our strengths and weaknesses and help us develop resilience and perseverance

To embrace failure as a learning opportunity we must adopt something called a 'growth mindset' where abilities are seen as something developed through hard work When people with this mindset face obstacles or setbacks they know they're only temporary hurdles They know they can be overcome with effort and the right mindset

If you want to cultivate this kind of perspective it would be helpful to:
1. 1.Reframe failures: Stop associating failure with inadequacy Failure is never personal but rather something that pushes us forward Remind yourself over and over again that your worth is not dictated by your failures
2. 2. Analyze failures: Take a moment to think about the mistakes you made, and what led to failure what went wrong? What could you have done differently? Inspecting your failures will help you avoid repeating them again
3. 3.Learn from successful people: Look into the lives of individuals who've faced failure and achieved great things You'll find that their stories are inspiring, and full of valuable lessons They show how important resilience and perseverance really is
4. 4.Embrace a growth mindset: Believe that abilities and intelligence can be developed through hard work See failures as opportunities to learn instead of as limitations

By changing our perspective towards failure, we can overcome our fear this allows us to use it in order to unlock new possibilities for personal growth.

Chapter 5

Continuous Education: Becoming a Lifelong Learner

*****

Cultivating a dee-p passion for continuous learning is vital for both personal advanceme-nt and professional progress. Here-, we will delve profoundly into dive-rse techniques of life-long studying, offering guidance on nurturing inquisitivene-ss and nourishing an ardor for erudition that endures a life-time. Whether e-xploring novel subjects that spark fresh inte-rest or advancing understanding of familiar topics, an eage-rness to expand one's knowle-dge and horizons through learning yields be-nefits that are boundless. By instilling habits that foste-r learning each day, eve-n amid life's busyness, we e-mpower ourselves to grow in wisdom and fulfillme-nt through every season. Though the- path may not always be smooth, small steps fuele-d by curiosity soon lead to great strides

There- are numerous constructive strate-gies for continuing one's learning throughout life-. One particularly fruitful approach involves regularly de-dicating time to absorbing information and perspective-s from written works. The published colle-ction of knowledge known as books holds an abundance of data and unde-rstandings spanning countless themes. Establishing a consiste-nt routine where a portion of e-ach day or week is rese-rved for leisurely e-xploring volumes that capture your fascination can serve- as an impactful method for cultivating your intellect and vision. Both non-fiction title-s connected to your caree-r path that enhance your expe-rtise and imaginary fiction novels that stimulate ne-w ideas have immense- potential to widen your worldview and amplify your compre-hension of humanity through exposure to fre-sh viewpoints and insightful details. While books cove-ring practical subjects directly rele-vant to your occupation can fortify your qualifications, imaginative stories allow your mind to envision ne-w possibilities. Overall, making reading a habit has lasting value- in actively learning throughout one's life-time.

While books alone- can expand your knowledge, active-ly immersing yourself in relate-d events provides price-less value. Kee-p an eye out for upcoming workshops, seminars, and confe-rences locally that fit within your intere-sts or career goals. These- types of gatherings promise to not only give- you a chance to gain insights directly from leade-rs in the field but also welcome- chances to connect with others who share- your passions. Meeting others with comparable- motivations provides prospects to motivate e-ach other as well as to respe-ctfully debate new pe-rspectives. Real-time- discussions with industry veterans and pee-rs offer inspiration as well as challenge-s to assumptions, helping you grow intellectually in a supportive- community. Therefore, do conside-r carving out time within your schedule to participate- in relevant learning opportunitie-s beyond books alone that can further e-nrich your understanding and networks.

Taking online course-s provides a flexible and acce-ssible avenue for continuous le-arning. The proliferation of technology has e-nabled numerous virtual platforms to offer instruction on an imme-nse variety of subjects. If your obje-ctive is to cultivate novel compe-tencies applicable to your vocation or to casually imme-rse yourself in an intriguing pastime, online- learning environments judiciously accommodate- pursuing knowledge at your convenie-nce. Through engaging in online classe-s, you can expand your understanding and skillset anywhe-re with an internet conne-ction. Whether see-king career-rele-vant expertise or informal e-nrichment, technology has revolutionize-d the way people le-arn throughout life. The bounty of online e-ducational offerings allows lifelong learning to fit practically any sche-dule or context.

To cultivate curiosity and foste-r a deep passion for continual learning, it is impe-rative that we come to ne-w topics with receptive minds. We- should embrace the role- of a lifelong scholar, constantly pursuing understanding and fresh vie-wpoints. Take an inquisitive stance re-garding the environment around you, inquire- freely, and participate active-ly in discussions that encourage intelle-ctual evolution. Question assumptions, connect unre-lated ideas, and explore- concepts from varied angles. Conside-r how certain findings challenge e-stablished notions or shed light in unexpe-cted areas. Such an approach nourishes le-arning at its roots and energizes the- discovery of unforesee-n linkages and implications.

Furthermore-, make learning an interactive- process by actively impleme-nting what you've absorbed in functional manners. Pursue- chances to disseminate your wisdom with othe-rs through conversations, demonstrations, or guiding. Educating others re-inforces your own comprehension and offe-rs you the opportunity to solidify your understanding while assisting some-one else to incre-ase. Try organizing study groups or discussion sessions where- you can discuss complex topics with peers. Share- online summaries of important concepts on social me-dia or create short lesson plans that othe-rs can use to test their knowle-dge. Find ways to test your abilities by taking on le-adership roles in student organizations or online-communities. Actively see-king paths to spread insights will strengthen your e-xpertise while aiding the- learning of others.

Above all, ke-ep in mind that gaining knowledge is not limite-d to conventional avenues. We-lcome informal chances to expand your unde-rstanding like podcasts, nature films, or insightful prese-ntations on a diversity of topics available online. Se-ek out a variety of formats and uncover which style-s resonate strongest with your inte-rests and preferre-d ways of absorbing new information. Whether through audio, visual, or othe-r mediums, pursuing learning outside traditional boundarie-s can complement formal education and e-nrich your perspectives.

As you continuously see-k new information and experie-nces, welcoming opportunities to broade-n your perspectives, you cultivate- a lively, inquisitive spirit. Nurture your natural curiosity by making e-ducation an endless adventure- - approach each new subject with wonde-r, questioning preconceptions to gain de-eper understandings. In this way, you ste-adily augment comprehension while- strengthening adaptability, equippe-d to react fluidly when life pre-sents fresh challenge-s. Rather than stagnating once formal lessons e-nd, feed your enthusiasm for e-xploring fresh ideas. Let fascination prope-l you through each new phase with optimism, re-cognizing how much awaits discovery on life's engaging journe-y of self-improvement.

A Guide to Using Continuous Learning in Your 30s for Success

Reaching your 30s is a big deal. It's a great time to keep learning to do well in life. Learning new things can help you stay ahead, change with the times, and reach your goals. Here's a guide on how to keep learning for success in your 30s.

Step 1: Check Yourself and Set Goals

Look at what you're good at and what you need to work on. Set goals for what you want to achieve. For example, if you work in marketing, you might want to get better at digital marketing to do well in your job.

Look at websites like Coursera, Udemy, and LinkedIn Learning. They offer courses to help you learn new things.

Step 2: Find Areas to Improve

If you work in tech, it's good to keep up with the latest in programming or software. This can make a big difference in your career.

You can learn about programming and tech stuff on websites like Codecademy, Udacity, and Pluralsight.

Step 3: Pick How You Want to Learn

Go to workshops or seminars related to your job. For example, if you work in finance, you can learn about things like financial modeling and analysis.

You can find workshops and seminars on money stuff from places like the Financial Modeling Institute and local business schools.

Step 4: Make a Plan

Set aside some time each week to learn new things. You can do this by taking an online course. Websites like Khan Academy, Skillshare, and MasterClass offer lots of things to learn that fit into your schedule.

Step 5: Use Technology and Learn Online

There are lots of apps and websites where you can learn new things. For example, if you want to learn a new language, you can use apps like Duolingo and Babbel.

TED Talks, FutureLearn, and Open Culture have all kinds of educational stuff you can check out.

Step 6: Meet People and Get Help

Join groups or find someone who can help you out. If you know people in the same field as you, they can help you learn new things.

You can find people to help you on websites like LinkedIn and at local meetups and events.

Step 7: Get Special Certifications

If you work in project management, getting a certification like the Project Management Professional (PMP) can make a big difference in your job.

You can learn about getting the PMP certification from the Project Management Institute (PMI).

Step 8: Use What You Learn

Put what you learn into practice. For example, if you learn new skills in Excel, you can use them to do better at work.

You can try out new things you've learned from websites like Harvard Business Publishing and MIT Sloan Executive Education.

Step 9: Stay Informed

Keep up with what's happening in your field. Read things, go to events, and join webinars.

You can find out what's happening in your field from news websites and on Eventbrite and Meetup.com.

Step 10: Reflect and Change

Think about how your learning is going. If you've learned new leadership skills, think about how they've helped you at work.

You can think about your learning and make changes by using tools and workshops that help you reflect on your progress.

Step 11: Balance Work and Life

It's important to have a good balance between work and everything else. Make sure you have time for fun and relaxing.

You can find things to do outside of work on apps and at local clubs and centers.

Step 12: Help Others

Share what you know with others. You can do this by writing, teaching, or volunteering.

You can find places to volunteer on websites like Volunteer Match and at local community centers.

Learning new things in your 30s can help you do better in life. By using this guide, you can learn new things that can help you in your job and make you a better person. Keep learning and you can do well in your 30s and beyond.

Chapter 6

The Resilience Factor: Bouncing Back from Adversity

****

Cultivating resilience and perseverance is a crucial aspect of developing a growth mindset for lifelong learning. This section focuses on understanding the role of resilience in overcoming challenges and setbacks, as well as providing strategies for building resilience.

Resilience is the ability to bounce back from adversity, setbacks, or failure. It is a quality that allows individuals to navigate through difficult times and continue moving forward towards their goals. Developing resilience is essential for maintaining a growth mindset because it enables individuals to view challenges as opportunities for growth and learning.

One strategy for cultivating resilience is through self-reflection. Taking the time to reflect on past experiences can provide valuable insights into how you have overcome obstacles in the past. By examining your previous successes and identifying the strategies and strengths you utilized, you can gain confidence in your ability to face future challenges. Reflecting on your personal growth journey can also help you recognize patterns or behaviors that may hinder your progress and develop strategies to overcome them.

Seeking support is another important aspect of building resilience. Surrounding yourself with a strong support system of friends, family, mentors, or trusted colleagues can provide emotional support during challenging times. These individuals can offer guidance, encouragement, and different perspectives that may help you navigate obstacles more effectively. Additionally, seeking professional support, such as therapy or coaching, can provide valuable tools and techniques for enhancing resilience and improving overall well-being.

Maintaining a positive mindset is also crucial for cultivating resilience. Focusing on the positives and reframing negative experiences as opportunities for growth can help shift your perspective during challenging times. Embracing a positive outlook allows you to approach setbacks as temporary roadblocks rather than permanent failures, empowering you to persevere and find solutions.

By developing resilience, individuals can cultivate a growth mindset that embraces challenges as opportunities for learning and personal development. This mindset allows for continuous growth and adaptation, fostering a love for lifelong learning. So, embrace resilience and adopt a growth mindset to overcome challenges, persevere, and continue on the path of lifelong learning.

Understanding the Importance of Failure:

Failure is often seen as a negative and undesirable outcome, but it is an inherent part of life and personal growth. In society, there can be a stigma and fear associated with failure, leading many individuals to avoid taking risks or pursuing their goals fully. However, it is important to recognize that failure is not an indicator of personal worth or capability, but rather an opportunity for learning and growth.

By exploring the concept of failure as a natural part of life, we can begin to shift our perspective and embrace its transformative power. Failure provides valuable lessons and insights that cannot be gained through success alone. It teaches us about our limitations, areas for improvement, and helps us develop resilience in the face of adversity.

Rather than fearing failure, we should view it as a stepping stone towards success. Many successful individuals have experienced multiple failures before achieving their goals. Thomas

Edison famously stated, "I have not failed. I've just found 10,000 ways that won't work." This mindset allows us to reframe failures as opportunities for growth and innovation.

In embracing failure, we open ourselves up to new possibilities and experiences. It encourages us to step outside of our comfort zones, take calculated risks, and learn from our mistakes. Failure provides the necessary feedback for self-reflection and self-assessment, allowing us to identify patterns or behaviors that may be hindering our progress.

Furthermore, failure can cultivate resilience and the ability to bounce back stronger. By facing failures head-on, we develop coping mechanisms and strategies to overcome setbacks. It challenges us to push through adversity and build the mental strength needed to navigate future challenges.

It is crucial to approach failure with self-compassion and positive self-talk. We must separate our sense of self-worth from the outcome of our endeavors. By treating ourselves with kindness and understanding, we can learn from failure without succumbing to negative self-judgment.

Embracing failure as an opportunity for personal growth empowers us to leverage our experiences and use them as fuel for success. Through reflection and self-assessment, we can identify our strengths and weaknesses, allowing us to set new goals and recalibrate our approach.

By understanding the importance of failure and embracing it as a valuable teacher, we open ourselves up to endless possibilities and pave the way for personal and professional growth. Remember, failure is not the end, but rather a stepping stone towards greater success

Shifting Perspectives on Failure:

In this section, we will delve into the importance of shifting our perspectives on failure and embracing it as a stepping stone to success. Instead of viewing failure as something negative or to be feared, we can reframe it as an opportunity for growth and learning.

Throughout history, there have been numerous examples of individuals who turned their failures into remarkable opportunities. Thomas Edison famously said, "I have not failed. I've just found 10,000 ways that won't work" when talking about his numerous attempts to invent the lightbulb. His mindset and perseverance allowed him to see failure as a necessary part of the journey towards success.

By adopting this mindset, we can reframe our failures as learning experiences. Each setback provides us with valuable feedback and insights into what went wrong and how we can improve. Instead of dwelling on our mistakes or feeling discouraged, we can use failure as a springboard to propel us forward.

One effective way to shift our perspective on failure is to focus on the lessons learned rather than the outcome. Celebrate the fact that you had the courage to try and learn from your experiences. Ask yourself, "What did I gain from this failure? How can I apply these lessons to future endeavors?"

Another helpful approach is to view failure as an opportunity to build resilience. Each time we encounter failure and bounce back, we become stronger and more resilient. It is through facing adversity and overcoming challenges that we grow as individuals.

Reframing our failures as learning experiences also allows us to detach our self-worth from external outcomes. Instead of defining ourselves based on successes or failures, we can develop a sense of intrinsic self-worth that comes from knowing we are constantly growing and learning.

In the next section, we will explore practical strategies for learning from failure and using it as a catalyst for personal growth. By embracing failure and shifting our perspectives, we open ourselves up to new possibilities and pave the way for future success.

Strategies for Learning from Failure:

Identifying personal patterns or behaviors that may contribute to repeated failure:

In order to grow and learn from failure, it is essential to identify any underlying patterns or behaviors that may be contributing to repeated setbacks. Take the time to reflect on past failures and consider if there are any commonalities or recurring themes. This could include habits, attitudes, or approaches that may not be serving you well. By recognizing these patterns, you can begin to make conscious efforts to change them and prevent future failures.

Introducing techniques for reflection and self-assessment post-failure:

After experiencing a failure, it is important to engage in a process of reflection and self-assessment. This involves taking an honest and objective look at the situation, your actions, and the outcomes. Ask yourself questions such as: What did I do well? What could I have done differently? What lessons can I take away from this experience? By actively reflecting on your failures, you can gain valuable insights and identify areas for improvement.

Discussing the importance of taking responsibility and accountability for failures:

Taking ownership of your failures is a crucial step in learning from them. Rather than blaming external factors or making excuses, accept responsibility for your actions and their consequences. Acknowledge that failure is a natural part of the learning process and that you have the power to use it as an opportunity for growth. By taking accountability for your failures, you empower yourself to make positive changes and move forward with resilience and determination.

Remember, learning from failure is a continuous process. It requires self-awareness, humility, and a willingness to explore your mistakes with an open mind. Through the strategies outlined above, you can develop a mindset that embraces failure as an opportunity for growth

Building Resilience and Bouncing Back:

Developing resilience is crucial for navigating through failures and setbacks. In this section, we will explore various tools and techniques that can help you build resilience and bounce back stronger than ever before.

1. Embrace self-compassion: When facing failure, it's easy to fall into self-criticism and negative self-talk. Instead, practice self-compassion by treating yourself with kindness and understanding. Recognize that failure is a natural part of life and an opportunity for growth. Be gentle with yourself and remind yourself that everyone makes mistakes.

2. Cultivate a growth mindset: Adopting a growth mindset allows you to see failure as a chance to learn and improve. Understand that failure does not define your worth or abilities, but rather provides valuable lessons and insights. Embrace challenges, persevere through setbacks, and believe in your ability to grow and develop.

3. Seek support: Surround yourself with a strong support system that includes family, friends, mentors, or a support group. Share your experiences with trusted individuals who can provide guidance, encouragement, and perspective. Lean on these relationships during challenging times to gain strength and resilience.

4. Practice positive self-talk: Monitor your internal dialogue and challenge negative thoughts or beliefs about failure. Replace self-defeating statements with positive affirmations and realistic perspectives. Focus on your strengths, previous successes, and the progress you have made. Remember that setbacks are temporary and can offer valuable lessons.

5. Learn from failure: Take time to reflect on your failures and identify the lessons they hold. Ask yourself what went wrong, what factors contributed to the outcome, and how you can approach similar situations differently in the future. Use failure as an opportunity to reassess your goals, strategies, and priorities.

6. Set realistic expectations: Failure often arises from unrealistic expectations or setting goals that are too ambitious. Set realistic and achievable goals that align with your abilities, resources, and circumstances. Break down larger goals into smaller, manageable steps to boost your confidence and sense of accomplishment along the way.

7. Practice resilience-building activities: Engage in activities that promote resilience, such as regular exercise, mindfulness meditation, journaling, or engaging in hobbies that bring you joy and relaxation. These activities can help alleviate stress, improve emotional well-being, and enhance your ability to bounce back from failure.

Remember, failure is not a reflection of your worth or potential. Building resilience allows you to face failures with courage, learn from them, and come out stronger on the other side. Embrace the challenges that come your way and view them as opportunities for growth and personal development.

Understanding the Importance of Self-Discipline

Self-discipline is a powerful tool for achieving success in all areas of life. By cultivating self-discipline, individuals can develop the ability to stay focused and motivated, make better choices, and overcome obstacles on their path to reaching their goals.

One of the key benefits of self-discipline is the ability to maintain consistency in actions and behaviors. Whether it's sticking to a workout routine, following a healthy eating plan, or studying diligently for personal or professional development, self-discipline ensures that these actions become regular habits rather than sporadic efforts. Consistency is essential for long-term success and creating lasting positive change.

Self-discipline also allows individuals to identify areas where improvement is needed. By recognizing their weaknesses or areas of resistance, they can take proactive steps to address and overcome them. This level of self-awareness is crucial for personal growth and development.

Furthermore, self-discipline plays a critical role in achieving goals. It helps individuals stay committed to their objectives, even when faced with challenges or setbacks. Without self-discipline, it becomes easy to give up at the first sign of difficulty or to become distracted by short-term gratification. With self-discipline, individuals can push through obstacles, maintain focus, and ultimately achieve their desired outcomes.

In order to harness the power of self-discipline, it is important to cultivate a mindset that values long-term rewards over immediate gratification. This means resisting temptations and distractions that may hinder progress towards goals. By prioritizing important tasks and responsibilities, individuals can allocate their time and energy more effectively, leading to increased productivity and progress.

By understanding the importance of self-discipline, individuals can begin to assess areas in their own life where discipline may be lacking. Through a commitment to self-improvement and the adoption of strategies covered in this chapter, individuals will be able to strengthen their self-discipline skills and create the foundation for achieving success in all aspects of life

Strategies for Developing Self-Discipline:

Setting clear and realistic goals to foster self-discipline:

One of the most important steps in developing self-discipline is setting clear and realistic goals. By defining what you want to achieve, you provide yourself with a target to work towards. It's crucial to ensure that your goals are specific, measurable, attainable, relevant, and time-bound (SMART). Breaking your larger goals into smaller, manageable tasks can make them more achievable and help you stay motivated along the way. Remember to prioritize your goals based on their importance and urgency to maintain focus and drive.

Implementing effective time management techniques:

Time management plays a significant role in cultivating self-discipline. Learning how to manage your time efficiently allows you to allocate your resources effectively and avoid unnecessary distractions or procrastination. Begin by creating a schedule or using a planner to outline your daily tasks and activities. Be mindful of how you spend your time and identify any activities or habits that hinder your productivity. Set aside dedicated blocks of time for focused work and minimize interruptions, such as turning off notifications on your phone or closing distracting tabs on your computer. Additionally, consider utilizing techniques like Pomodoro Technique (working in short bursts with frequent breaks) or time-blocking (allocating specific time slots for different tasks) to optimize your productivity.

Creating daily routines and habits that support self-discipline:

Consistency is key when it comes to developing self-discipline. Creating daily routines and habits that support your goals can greatly enhance your ability to stay disciplined. Start by identifying habits that align with the behaviors you want to cultivate and incorporate them into your daily routine. For example, if you aim to exercise regularly, establish a workout routine at a consistent time each day. By making these behaviors a part of your routine, they become automatic and require less willpower to maintain. Consider starting small and gradually expanding your routines as you build momentum. Remember, self-discipline is like a muscle that strengthens over time, so be patient and persistent in practicing your routines.

Mastering Time Management: Operating with Efficiency

*****

Effective Time Management Techniques:

Here, we will look at different strategies to help you manage your time better and get more work done. With what you learn here, you'll be able to prioritize tasks based on importance and urgency. The goal is to optimize how much you get done with the time that's given.

1. Prioritizing tasks and responsibilities:

One of the best ways to manage time is to prioritize things. Start by identifying which tasks are important enough to need immediate attention over others on your list.

Your long-term goals should also be considered when prioritizing. How important a task is should align with your values and contribute to your success.

2. Utilizing time management tools:

There are plenty of online tools that can help you stay organized and on top of things. Calendars and planners can be invaluable tools for organizing your schedule and setting reminders for important deadlines or appointments.

They're simple yet effective solutions when it comes to keeping track of commitments throughout the day, week, month or even year.

3. Implementing strategies for managing distractions:

It's easy for us to be distracted by what's around us or in our heads while working or studying. Unfortunately, this takes valuable time away from what needs your focus most now.

The first step in managing distractions is recognizing them and figuring out how they come about. Once recognized, you'll notice that it's easier than ever before to reduce them altogether. Another great strategy is using a technique known as "time blocking". This involves dedicating specific blocks of time during the day for certain tasks or activities. By doing this, not only are distractions greatly minimized but deep focus on one thing becomes second nature as well.

Productivity Tools:

With the internet becoming a staple of everyday life, it's no surprise that there are countless apps and tools to help you stay focused and motivated. There are a lot of popular ones like Trello, Asana, Todoist and Notion. They all provide different twists on how to best organize your tasks, but generally speaking they work through lists or boards where you can set deadlines, manage tasks and even get others involved in projects. These tools also have notifications and reminders to help keep you accountable.

Time tracking apps like Forest or Rescue Time can be extremely useful for managing your day as well. If you're someone who gets easily distracted or loses track of time (we're all guilty of it), these apps will let you see what activities are eating away at your time throughout the day. Helps identify patterns so that adjustments can be made accordingly.

Don't worry about feeling overwhelmed by the number of different apps out there! It truly just comes down to personal preference. Find one that appeals most to you aesthetically or has the most features you know you'll use.

Procrastination is universal; everyone struggles with it at some point in their lives. The first step towards overcoming procrastination is understanding why we procrastinate in the first place.

Why do we Procrastinate?

Fear:

One of the primary reasons people procrastinate is fear; fear of failure, fear of judgment, fear of disappointing themselves or others…the list goes on. We often put off starting or completing a task because we're afraid that our performance won't meet expectations or because we'd rather not face negative feedback if things don't go as planned.

Perfectionism:

Though perfectionism may seem like a desirable trait at face value, it can significantly hinder productivity and lead to procrastination. This occurs when individuals become obsessed with achieving perfection, leading them to delay starting or finishing a task until everything aligns "perfectly". The problem is that nothing is ever perfect, and we end up wasting valuable time and energy striving for the unattainable.

Lack of Interest:

Sometimes, we simply don't find a task interesting or enjoyable, making it much harder to complete. We tend to put off these things as long as possible until they're absolutely necessary. This ties into our human nature because humans are naturally inclined to seek pleasure and avoid discomfort.

Overwhelm:

Certain tasks may appear intimidating because they're daunting or involve multiple steps. When we don't know where to start or how to go about something, we often choose not to start at all in order to avoid failure or confusion. We push it off until later when maybe we'll feel more mentally prepared.

What is Productivity?

Before diving into strategies on how to overcome procrastination and boost productivity, let's first establish what productivity truly means. According to Merriam-Webster, productivity can be defined as "the quality or state of being productive". Very helpful definition indeed…

1. Connect Your Work with Your Values: Take a moment to think about what you find important and how your work aligns with it. When it does, you'll naturally be motivated and determined to push through.
2. Goals Give You Drive: Goals give you a clear path and purpose for your work. They need to be specific, achievable, and meaningful. Then, break them down into smaller steps that are easy to manage.
3. Find out Why You're Doing What You're Doing: Sit back and understand the reasons behind your actions. Ask yourself why it matters, who it impacts, and what difference it makes in the world around you. This purpose will help you stay driven.
4. Set a Schedule: Having some structure is important too. Create a routine that involves when you'll start working, when you'll take breaks (both short and long), as well as activities for self-care — most importantly.
5. Train Your Mind: Stay in the present moment while completing tasks so they can have your full attention — no multitasking! Fully engage with what's at hand because doing so enhances both productivity and quality of work.
6. Pat Yourself on The Back: Celebrate small wins along the way by granting yourself rewards when milestones are reached or when tasks are completed in general.
7. Picture It: Imagine how success looks for whatever goal you have in mind — visualize every little detail of the satisfaction after finishing tasks, reaching goals, etc… Letting this image navigate can keep motivation consistent even during tough times

Remember that this journey takes time; discipline isn't an overnight thing but instead requires constant learning from yourself as well as effort.

Overwhelm can lead to procrastination. So when it feels like you're drowning in tasks, make a list and get things in order. Do the most urgent or important tasks first. Or break down the larger ones into smaller ones.

Doing all this makes it easier to manage your workload which should alleviate overwhelm. Now decision fatigue is another reason for procrastination. The more decisions we make throughout the day, the harder it is to continue making high-quality calls.

But by establishing routines and systems that minimize decision-making, you've found a way around this problem. For example, plan your week in advance, create meal plans, or establish a consistent morning routine.

External support and accountability are also super helpful:

You'll be surprised at how much more productive you become with just a little bit of outside help. And let's face it… sometimes we really just need someone there who can give us that push to keep going.

Find someone who shares similar goals or values and establish a system of regular check-ins or progress updates with them. This way you'll always have someone looking out for you when times get rough.

And finding a mentor would be even better! They'll guide you on your journey so that you don't have to go through the same struggles they did when they were starting up.

So address perfectionism and fear of failure, manage overwhelm and decision fatigue, seek support and accountability and you'll be well on your way to banishing procrastination forever – boosting productivity as an added bonus!

Chapter 7

Building Greater Resilience and Maintaining Self-Discipline
******

Growing tougher and never giving up is key in developing a mindset for ongoing learning. Here, we're looking at the importance of resilience in handling bumps in the road and offering ways to boost it.

Resilience means bouncing back from troubles or mistakes. It's a trait letting us move on, even when times get tough, and follow our goals. Building this strength is key for a mindset towards growth, because it lets us see struggles as chances to learn and grow.

One way to grow resilience is being self-reflective. Think back on past moments. This can shed light on how you've tackled past hurdles. Studying your past wins and noting the methods and strengths you employed, boosts your confidence for future troubles. Reflecting on personal growth can point out habits that might slow your progress. It can help create ways to tackle them.

Another important part of growing resilience is support. Having a tight network of friends, family, mentors, or colleagues provides a shoulder to lean on in tough times. These people can give guidance, positivity, and fresh views helping you maneuver around barriers more effectively. Plus, reaching out for pro help, like from therapists or life coaches, can provide useful tips and skills for growing resilience and well-being overall.

Staying positive is key to building resilience. Highlighting the good parts and seeing negative experiences as growth chances can change your view during tough times. With a positive lens, you see problems as bumps in the road and not as major failures. This helps you stay strong and find solutions.

Building resilience helps people develop a growth mindset. They see difficulties as opportunities for learning and personal growth. This mindset supports constant improvement and encourages a lifetime love of learning. Embrace resilience and foster a growth mindset. This way, you can push through adversity and tread on the lifelong learning path.

The Real Value of Failure:

Failure usually gets a bad rap. It's seen as unwanted and negative. But it's just part of life and personal growth. People are often scared of failing because society sees it as bad. This makes many avoid taking risks or chase their dreams. But, it's crucial to understand that failing doesn't make you less worthy or capable. It's actually a chance to learn and grow.

Reflecting on failure as a natural life event can help us see it differently, and understand its power. Failure offers unique lessons and insights that success alone can't give. It shows us our weak points, areas needing improvement, and nurtures resilience against hardships.

Rather than fearing failure, we should view it as a stepping stone towards success. Many successful individuals have experienced multiple failures before achieving their goals. Thomas Edison famously stated, "I have not failed. I've just found 10,000 ways that won't work." This mindset allows us to reframe failures as opportunities for growth and innovation.

In embracing failure, we open ourselves up to new possibilities and experiences. It encourages us to step outside of our comfort zones, take calculated risks, and learn from our mistakes. Failure provides the necessary feedback for self-reflection and self-assessment, allowing us to identify patterns or behaviors that may be hindering our progress.

Furthermore, failure can cultivate resilience and the ability to bounce back stronger. By facing failures head-on, we develop coping mechanisms and strategies to overcome setbacks. It challenges us to push through adversity and build the mental strength needed to navigate future challenges.

It is crucial to approach failure with self-compassion and positive self-talk. We must separate our sense of self-worth from the outcome of our endeavors. By treating ourselves with kindness and understanding, we can learn from failure without succumbing to negative self-judgment.

Embracing failure as an opportunity for personal growth empowers us to leverage our experiences and use them as fuel for success. Through reflection and self-assessment, we can identify our strengths and weaknesses, allowing us to set new goals and recalibrate our approach.

By understanding the importance of failure and embracing it as a valuable teacher, we open ourselves up to endless possibilities and pave the way for personal and professional growth. Remember, failure is not the end, but rather a stepping stone towards greater successShifting Perspectives on Failure:

In this section, we will delve into the importance of shifting our perspectives on failure and embracing it as a stepping stone to success. Instead of viewing failure as something negative or to be feared, we can reframe it as an opportunity for growth and learning.

Throughout history, there have been numerous examples of individuals who turned their failures into remarkable opportunities. Thomas Edison famously said, "I have not failed. I've just found 10,000 ways that won't work" when talking about his numerous attempts to invent the lightbulb. His mindset and perseverance allowed him to see failure as a necessary part of the journey towards success.

By adopting this mindset, we can reframe our failures as learning experiences. Each setback provides us with valuable feedback and insights into what went wrong and how we can improve. Instead of dwelling on our mistakes or feeling discouraged, we can use failure as a springboard to propel us forward.

One effective way to shift our perspective on failure is to focus on the lessons learned rather than the outcome. Celebrate the fact that you had the courage to try and learn from your experiences. Ask yourself, "What did I gain from this failure? How can I apply these lessons to future endeavors?"

Another helpful approach is to view failure as an opportunity to build resilience. Each time we encounter failure and bounce back, we become stronger and more resilient. It is through facing adversity and overcoming challenges that we grow as individuals.

Reframing our failures as learning experiences also allows us to detach our self-worth from external outcomes. Instead of defining ourselves based on successes or failures, we can develop a sense of intrinsic self-worth that comes from knowing we are constantly growing and learning.

In the next section, we will explore practical strategies for learning from failure and using it as a catalyst for personal growth. By embracing failure and shifting our perspectives, we open ourselves up to new possibilities and pave the way for future successStrategies for Learning from Failure:

Identifying personal patterns or behaviors that may contribute to repeated failure:

In order to grow and learn from failure, it is essential to identify any underlying patterns or behaviors that may be contributing to repeated setbacks. Take the time to reflect on past failures and consider if there are any commonalities or recurring themes. This could include habits, attitudes, or approaches that may not be serving you well. By recognizing these patterns, you can begin to make conscious efforts to change them and prevent future failures.

Introducing techniques for reflection and self-assessment post-failure:

After experiencing a failure, it is important to engage in a process of reflection and self-assessment. This involves taking an honest and objective look at the situation, your actions, and the outcomes. Ask yourself questions such as: What did I do well? What could I have done differently? What lessons can I take away from this experience? By actively reflecting on your failures, you can gain valuable insights and identify areas for improvement.

Discussing the importance of taking responsibility and accountability for failures:

Taking ownership of your failures is a crucial step in learning from them. Rather than blaming external factors or making excuses, accept responsibility for your actions and their consequences. Acknowledge that failure is a natural part of the learning process and that you have the power to use it as an opportunity for growth. By taking accountability for your failures, you empower yourself to make positive changes and move forward with resilience and determination.

Remember, learning from failure is a continuous process. It requires self-awareness, humility, and a willingness to explore your mistakes with an open mind. Through the strategies outlined above, you can develop a mindset that embraces failure as an opportunity for growth Building Resilience and Bouncing Back:

Developing resilience is crucial for navigating through failures and setbacks. In this section, we will explore various tools and techniques that can help you build resilience and bounce back stronger than ever before.

1. Embrace self-compassion: When facing failure, it's easy to fall into self-criticism and negative self-talk. Instead, practice self-compassion by treating yourself with kindness and understanding. Recognize that failure is a natural part of life and an opportunity for growth. Be gentle with yourself and remind yourself that everyone makes mistakes.

2. Cultivate a growth mindset: Adopting a growth mindset allows you to see failure as a chance to learn and improve. Understand that failure does not define your worth or abilities, but rather provides valuable lessons and insights. Embrace challenges, persevere through setbacks, and believe in your ability to grow and develop.

3. Get help: Build a strong team - family, friends, mentors, or a support group. Share stories with people you trust. They offer advice, cheer you on, and give you a different view. Tough times are easier with them by your side.

4. Be your own biggest fan: Check your thoughts. Stand up to any negative ones about failure. Use positive words and keep realistic views. Focus on your abilities, wins, and how far you've come. Letdowns are just bumps in the road, teaching us important stuff.

5. Discover lessons in failure: Look at failures closely. Find the lessons they hide. Understand what went sour, the causes, and how to do things differently next time. Failure is a chance to rethink your goals, game plan, and what matters most.

6. Plan with realism: Failure often comes from chasing pipe dreams. Set achievable goals that match your skills, assets, and situation. Split bigger targets into bite-sized pieces. This builds your faith in yourself, giving you a sense of success blow by blow.

7. Strengthen your bounce-back ability: Do things that build resilience. Exercise regularly, try mindful meditation, keep a journal, or enjoy hobbies that make you happy. They help to reduce stress, improve your emotions, and increase your ability to deal with failure.

Remember, failure is not a reflection of your worth or potential. Building resilience allows you to face failures with courage, learn from them, and come out stronger on the other side. Embrace the challenges that come your way and view them as opportunities for growth and personal development Understanding the Importance of Self-Discipline.

Self-discipline is a powerful tool for achieving success in all areas of life. By cultivating self-discipline, individuals can develop the ability to stay focused and motivated, make better choices, and overcome obstacles on their path to reaching their goals.

One of the key benefits of self-discipline is the ability to maintain consistency in actions and behaviors. Whether it's sticking to a workout routine, following a healthy eating plan, or studying diligently for personal or professional development, self-discipline ensures that these actions become regular habits rather than sporadic efforts. Consistency is essential for long-term success and creating lasting positive change.

Self-discipline also allows individuals to identify areas where improvement is needed. By recognizing their weaknesses or areas of resistance, they can take proactive steps to address and overcome them. This level of self-awareness is crucial for personal growth and development.

Furthermore, self-discipline plays a critical role in achieving goals. It helps individuals stay committed to their objectives, even when faced with challenges or setbacks. Without self-discipline, it becomes easy to give up at the first sign of difficulty or to become distracted by short-term gratification. With self-discipline, individuals can push through obstacles, maintain focus, and ultimately achieve their desired outcomes.

In order to harness the power of self-discipline, it is important to cultivate a mindset that values long-term rewards over immediate gratification. This means resisting temptations and distractions that may hinder progress towards goals. By prioritizing important tasks and responsibilities, individuals can allocate their time and energy more effectively, leading to increased productivity and progress.

By understanding the importance of self-discipline, individuals can begin to assess areas in their own life where discipline may be lacking. Through a commitment to self-improvement and the adoption of strategies covered in this chapter, individuals will be able to strengthen their self-discipline skills and create the foundation for achieving success in all aspects of life Strategies for Developing Self-Discipline:

Setting clear and realistic goals to foster self-discipline:

One of the most important steps in developing self-discipline is setting clear and realistic goals. By defining what you want to achieve, you provide yourself with a target to work towards. It's crucial to ensure that your goals are specific, measurable, attainable, relevant, and time-bound (SMART). Breaking your larger goals into smaller, manageable tasks can make them more achievable and help you stay motivated along the way. Remember to prioritize your goals based on their importance and urgency to maintain focus and drive.

Implementing effective time management techniques:

Handling time well is crucial for self-command. To do this well, you need to chart out your daily chores and tasks. Spot anything that may slow down your work, then set blocks of time for focused tasks. Ways to cut down on distractions could be turning off your phone notifications or closing unneeded tabs on your computer. Try methods like the Pomodoro Technique where you work in short spurts with regular breaks to boost your output.

How to build daily habits to help your self-governance:

Being routine is a solid base for self-regulation. Form daily habits that help you reach your targets boosts self-command. Start by observing habits that go along with what you seek to foster. Then, weave them into your daily life. For instance, if you want to train regularly, pick a set workout time each day. By forming these routines, it feels more natural and takes less effort to continue. Start small and progressively grow your routines as you gain momentum. Remember, self-governance gets stronger with time, just like a muscle. So, stay patient and keep at it with your routines.

Chapter 8

Career Catalyst: Advancing Professionally in Your 30s

*****

Understanding Why Career Transitions Matter

Dramatic leaps in your career can indicate personal growth and development. These changes happen for many reasons, such as wanting a new challenge, finding better work-life balance, or embracing an entirely new perspective on life. It's important to realize that change is part of the natural flow of life and by accepting it you may open yourself up to opportunities that will bring you excitement and overall job satisfaction.

Tackling the Reasons For Career Transitions Head-On

If you think about making a huge career decision, then taking time to self-reflect is key. Here are some common motivations for why people tend to make this transition.

1. **Professional Growth:** There's always more room at the top! Seeking out new challenges, skill development, or even just advancement opportunities indicates a person with a growth mindset. This means they're looking to expand their knowledge base and constantly learn things they don't currently know.

2. **Getting Your Time Back:** A lot of people try hard to strike up a solid balance between their personal life and professional life. You should too! When you do both your mind will be at ease knowing neither one is dragging the other down. Making transitions gives people the chance to re-prioritize what they have going on outside of work.

3. **Love What You Do Every Day:** If someone tells you "I love my job", then consider yourself lucky as most don't get to experience this feeling daily… Most hate it in fact… But those who've made huge career moves find themselves working jobs that align better with their lifestyle and values. Jobs like these aren't always easy to find but once found it offers maximum fulfillment whenever they clock into work.

4. **It's About the Money:** Sometimes money talks… Changes in markets or stability might force people into thinking about moving careers or transitioning into something else related that has higher earning potential than what they currently do.

Understand the Pros of Career Transitions

The good almost always comes with the bad and risks will need to be taken. This doesn't mean you should shy away from these changes as the pros greatly out way the cons.

1. Personal Growth: There's no hiding in your comfort zone when making a career transition. In fact there's not enough room for it! Stepping into new territory brings out personal growth by stimulating adaptability, resilience, and new skills that were never used before.

2. More Connections: Huge moves in careers usually involve connecting with professionals who come from different industries or backgrounds. Building connections like this are great because they offer opportunities for mentorship, collaboration, and professional development… All things that sound fancy on paper but can actually take someone's whole career to another level if they're serious about their work.

3. Job Satisfaction At Its Finest: When you have passion for something you naturally tend to put more effort into it, right? Well obviously… So why wouldn't you want a career that aligns with both your interests and values?! When people fall into positions like these their happiness skyrockets 10x which leads them to putting out high quality work that makes other notice them more often than ever before.

4. Increased Skill Set: Taking leaps in your career might require learning new skills or even knowledge depending on what path you decide to go down. The benefit of gaining all these extra lessons is how versatile it'll make you look compared to those who decided to stick around in one space for too long without exploring anything else.

In order to approach transitions correctly and confidently you must have an open mind combined with a willingness to embrace change... Understanding why these changes happen along with the benefits they bring can help greatly flexibility needed during this process while keeping your goal of being fulfilled professional journey alive!

Finding Your Purpose through Skills and Values

Being confident starts with knowing yourself first! To do this think about the skills you have right now and how you can apply them to new roles that aren't like what you've become accustomed to.

Furthermore, take this chance to evaluate your passions and see how they'd line up with potential career options. What genuinely interests you? What subjects or activities do you naturally gravitate towards? Knowing your passions will help guide you towards fulfilling and enjoyable careers. With a mix of passion and your new career path, opportunities that match your interests should present themselves.

While evaluating skills and passions is important, values are another key factor in decision making for most people during the transition process. Some guiding principles might be: what's most important to you? What do you value in a professional environment or workplace? To make decisions that align with what truly matters to you, it's crucial to understand your own values. Finding satisfaction as well as fulfillment from work can be better guaranteed if your career path aligns with those values.

Always remember: transitioning careers is an opportunity for self discovery and personal growth. Reflecting on what really sparks joy within yourself is just one way to evaluate what motivates and excites you. By assessing skills, passions, and values there should be enough confidence built up to explore new paths without fear.

Researching different industries, roles, and companies that fit into goals or interests requires diligence too. When done correctly though it'll provide valuable insights needed for informed decisions about potential career paths.

Utilizing online resources like websites or job boards is a great way gather information on different industries or companies. In order to progress forward there needs to be some understanding of trends within certain fields so don't hesitate on this step.

Aside from researching through websites or job boards don't forget about professionals who are currently working exactly where you see yourself one day too! Informational interviews will give out firsthand insights into the challenges, responsibilities, as well as rewards of specific careers. They're also perfect for building connections with likeminded individuals so don't skip reaching out through LinkedIn or networking events.

Ever heard of the saying "If there's a person who's been through it before, why not follow their advice"? It applies to this scenario too. If you can locate someone who's worked in the industries or roles you want more information on reach out to them for guidance. They might even be able to connect you with contacts and opportunities that'll help your career take off.

Remember though that researching and exploring new things isn't a linear process. It'll require an open mind, flexibility, as well as being willing to learn and adapt. Opportunities will only be found if sought after so make sure to do so!

As all of the information starts rolling in from research, interviews, or guidance from others take time to reflect on how well each potential career aligns with skills, passions, and values. Pay close attention to growth opportunities plus work life balance because these are big factors in job satisfaction as well as fulfillment. Don't forget about salary expectations either!

By conducting thorough research, utilizing online resources, engaging in informational interviews, and seeking guidance from mentors or career counselors, you will be better equipped to explore new career options with confidence. The insights gained through this process will enable you to make informed decisions that align with your interests, goals, and values

Developing a Transition Plan:

One of the key elements in successfully navigating a career transition is creating a comprehensive and well-thought-out plan. This plan will serve as your roadmap, guiding you through each phase of the transition and ensuring that you stay on track towards your desired career path. In this section, we will explore the essential steps involved in developing a transition plan.

1. Reflect on Your Goals and Priorities:

Begin by clarifying your goals and priorities for your new career. What do you hope to achieve? What values and passions do you want to align with your work? Reflecting on these questions will help you create a clear vision for your future and set meaningful goals to guide your transition.

2. Identify Necessary Skills and Qualifications:

Research your desired career path and identify the skills and qualifications that are required or valued in that field. This could include formal education, certifications, or specific technical skills. Understanding these requirements will help you develop strategies to acquire any necessary qualifications.

3. Assess Your Current Skills and Experience:

Evaluate your current skill set and work experience to determine how your existing strengths can be applied to your new career path. Identify transferable skills that can bridge the gap between your current role and your desired field. Consider any relevant experiences, even if they were not obtained through formal employment.

4. Set Realistic Timelines:

Setting realistic timelines for each phase of your transition is crucial for staying organized and motivated throughout the process. Break down your transition plan into smaller milestones, such as completing certain courses or certifications, networking with professionals in your desired field, or gaining relevant experience through internships or volunteering. By setting achievable timelines, you can keep yourself accountable and maintain momentum towards your goals.

5. Create a Step-by-Step Action Plan:

Once you have identified the necessary skills and qualifications and set realistic timelines, it's time to create a detailed action plan. Outline the specific steps you need to take to acquire the required skills, such as enrolling in courses, attending workshops, or gaining practical experience. Break down your plan into actionable tasks and assign deadlines to each one.

6. Seek Additional Learning and Development Opportunities:

In addition to acquiring the necessary skills and qualifications, consider seeking out additional learning and development opportunities that can enhance your knowledge and make you a more competitive candidate. This could involve attending industry conferences, participating in webinars, or joining professional associations related to your desired career field. Emphasize continuous learning and growth throughout your transition journey.

7. Leverage Your Network:

Utilize your professional network to gain insights and advice from individuals who have successfully transitioned into similar careers. Reach out to mentors, former colleagues, or professionals in your desired field for informational interviews or guidance. Networking can also help you discover hidden job opportunities and connect with potential employers

Transitions in your career aren't always a straight line. You're likely going to run into bumps and problems along the way, but that's only natural. It's important that you stay adaptable and keep an open mind. Be ready to change your plan on a dime while keeping your long-term goals in focus. By having this well-developed transition plan, you're putting yourself in a better position to feel confident and prepared as you make your way down the road of new career.

Chapter 9

Networking Nuances:
Cultivating Professional Relationships
*****

Building a Support Network

Engaging with professional ne-tworks and communities related to your ne-w career path allows you to tap into invaluable re-sources, gain fresh perspe-ctives, and make useful contacts that can aid your journe-y navigating career transitions. Interacting with othe-rs in your desired industry through rele-vant associations provides opportunities to cultivate a riche-r knowledge of that field from those- within it, uncovering nuances you may not discover othe-rwise. The insights and introductions available through such ne-tworks also help potentially create-prospects down the line as you look to e-nter your new profession. While- change can be difficult, taking advantage of the- connections in circuits aligned with where- you wish to head makes understanding your de-stination clearer and ease-s the transition there through the-helpful guidance of others who have- traveled that route be-fore.

Beginning your re-search into professional groups, trade associations, and online- communities applicable to your fresh care-er route can prove use-ful. You'll find these platforms regularly host ne-tworking occasions, workshops, and online discussions enabling you to interact with like--minded professionals, gain from their journe-ys, and keep informed on e-volving industry patterns. By tapping into relevant organizations, you ope-n doors to build connections with others in your chosen fie-ld while expanding your knowledge- on current trends and opportunities that may be-nefit your career goals.

In addition to professional ne-tworks, actively pursuing mentorship or guidance from individuals who have- already navigated comparable care-er changes can be e-xceptionally useful. Mentors can offe-r invaluable advice, recount the-ir own journeys, and give encourage-ment as you face the difficultie-s and ambiguities of shifting careers. Look for me-ntors within your present connections or think about contacting profe-ssionals in your wished-for area who motivate you. The-ir guidance may help provide fre-sh perspectives to conte-mplate various options during your transition period. Reach out and ask about le-ssons learned from their e-xperiences changing paths, as we-ll as recommendations for resource-s to explore next ste-ps in your new direction.

Surrounding yourself with a supportive network of friends, family, and colleagues is equally important. These individuals can provide encouragement, offer a fresh perspective, and provide emotional support as you embark on this new journey. Share your career goals and aspirations with them, and don't hesitate to ask for their input or assistance when needed.

When de-veloping a support system, kee-p in mind that it involves both giving and receiving assistance——being available to aid others just as the-y aid you. Consider assisting those within your network by offe-ring guidance, suggestions, or a compassionate e-ar. Creating relationships goes both ways, so nurturing me-aningful connections through assistance provided as we-ll as received may le-ad to unforeseen prospe-cts later on.

By engaging with professional networks and surrounding yourself with a supportive community, you will have access to valuable resources, insights, and connections that can help you navigate your career transition with confidence. Embrace the power of networking and build relationships that will support you throughout your professional journeyAssessing your current career path is an essential step in finding purpose and meaning in your work. Take the time to reflect on your current job and evaluate whether it aligns with your values, passions, and overall sense of purpose. Consider how satisfied you are in your current role and identify any areas of dissatisfaction or disconnect. This reflection will help you identify potential changes or adjustments that could bring more fulfillment to your work.

During this assessment, ask yourself what aspects of your job resonate with you and bring you joy. Consider whether your current role allows you to utilize your strengths and talents. If there are areas where you feel unfulfilled, think about how you can incorporate your passions and interests into your work.

Kee-p in mind that discovering significance in your work goes furthe-r than the job title or the re-sponsibilities you carry out. It includes coordinating your principles and e-nthusiasm with the effect you have- on others through your work. Consider how your occupation adds to a more e-xtensive objective- or vision inside your association or industry sector. Think about the positive- effect you have on custome-rs or clients and how you change lives for the- better. While your re-sponsibilities may be focused around particular tasks, se-arch for how the work you do each day connects to he-lping or serving others in a meaningful way. This will he-lp you find fulfillment and maintain motivation even during challe-nging times.

While it is prude-nt to regularly examine your care-er trajectory and how well it matche-s with your core interests, motivations, and se-nse of purpose, truly appreciating your work involve-s a deeper re-flection. Evaluating any aspects that cause dissatisfaction or fe-el misaligned can reve-al opportunities to cultivate more significance- in your professional journey. Some possibilitie-s to explore may include adapting ce-rtain duties, adjusting your focus, taking on a new role within your curre-nt field, or considering an alternate- career path entire-ly. The ultimate goal is uncovering ways to infuse- richer purpose and fulfillment e-ach working day.

A Step-by-Step Guide to Networking for Career Growth in Your 30s

Making connections and growing your network is essential for advancing in your career, especially in your 30s. Here's a simple guide to help you navigate the world of networking and propel your career forward.

Step 1: Self-Reflection and Goal Setting

Reflect on your career goals and the type of connections that can help you achieve them.

Set clear networking goals, such as expanding your professional circle or finding a mentor in your field.

Step 2: Identify Networking Opportunities

Research industry events, professional meetups, and conferences relevant to your career aspirations.

Leverage online platforms like LinkedIn to identify potential contacts and industry-specific groups.

Step 3: Develop Your Personal Brand

Craft a compelling and professional online presence, including a polished LinkedIn profile and, if applicable, a personal website showcasing your expertise.

Ensure consistency across your professional and social media profiles to present a cohesive brand image.

Step 4: Engage in Informational Interviews

Reach out to professionals in your industry for informational interviews to gain insights and expand your network.

Ask thoughtful questions and express genuine interest in their experiences and career paths.

Step 5: Attend Networking Events

Participate in industry-specific networking events, both in person and virtually, to connect with like-minded professionals.

Actively engage in conversations and seek to build meaningful relationships rather than focusing solely on self-promotion.

Step 6: Offer Help and Support

Be willing to offer assistance or share your expertise with others in your network without expecting immediate returns.

Contributing value to your connections can foster long-term, mutually beneficial relationships.

Step 7: Seek Out a Mentor

Identify individuals whose career paths and experiences resonate with your aspirations and approach them about mentorship.

A mentor can provide guidance, support, and valuable insights as you navigate your career growth.

Step 8: Utilize Online Networking Platforms

Actively participate in industry forums, groups, and discussions on platforms like LinkedIn, Reddit, or industry-specific online communities.

Share your knowledge, engage in meaningful conversations, and establish yourself as a valuable contributor in your field.

Step 9: Follow Up and Stay Connected

After networking events or initial interactions, follow up with a personalized message to express gratitude and reinforce the connection.

Stay engaged with your network by periodically reaching out, sharing relevant content, and offering support when possible.

Step 10: Embrace Diversity in Your Network

Seek to diversify your network by connecting with individuals from varied backgrounds, industries, and perspectives.

Embracing diversity can enrich your network and provide new opportunities for learning and collaboration.

Step 11: Contribute to Industry Conversations

Write articles, participate in panel discussions, or speak at industry events to establish yourself as a thought leader in your field.

Contributing to industry conversations can elevate your professional profile and attract new connections.

Step 12: Pay It Forward

As you grow in your career, be open to assisting and mentoring others who are earlier in their professional journey.

Paying it forward can strengthen your network and contribute to a thriving professional community.

Networking is a vital component of career growth, especially in your 30s. By following this step-by-step guide, you can effectively expand your professional network, seek mentorship, and position yourself for success in your chosen field. Remember, genuine connections and a willingness to contribute to your network are key to fostering lasting and impactful professional relationships.

Chapter 10

Exploring your
Strengths and Passions at Work

Exploring your strengths and passions:

In order to find purpose and meaning in your work, it is essential to start by conducting a thorough self-assessment of your core strengths and talents. Reflect on the skills that come naturally to you and bring you a sense of accomplishment. These strengths can include anything from problem-solving abilities to excellent communication skills or creative thinking.

Additionally, consider your hobbies, interests, and activities that bring you joy and energize you outside of work. These personal passions can often be indicators of what truly inspires and motivates you. Think about the aspects of these activities that you enjoy the most and how they can be translated into your professional life.

Once you have identified your strengths and passions, it's time to explore how you can leverage them in your current job or even consider new career paths that align with them. Look for opportunities within your organization where you can apply your strengths and bring value. This might involve taking on additional responsibilities, collaborating with different teams, or seeking out projects that align with your passions.

If it becomes clear that your current job does not provide the opportunity to utilize your strengths and pursue your passions, you can start exploring other career options that align more closely with what truly drives you. This could involve researching different industries or roles that align with your interests and seeking out networking opportunities or informational interviews with professionals in those fields.

Let's talk about your work journey. It's a path of discovery. It aims to connect your job with what you love, letting you feel purpose-filled. Discover new options, accept risks, chase chances fitting your skills and loves. It'll lead you to rewarding work, bubbling with daily purpose. Paving your path also involves setting purposeful goals. Should you ask, 'What's success for me?' Answer thoughtfully. Think about your own beliefs, desires, and grandest dreams. Chew over what truly makes work rewarding and satisfying for you.

Now, once you grasp your personal success definition, time to set some goals. They should sync with your own values and passions. Break up big aims into bits, real steps you can take a bit at a time. This helps keep you on track and bursting with inspiration in your work-journey. Maybe your goal is to brighten others' world with your work. You can target specific marks, like:

1. Craft a guiding program in your team, pushing newer coworkers toward growth.
2. Lend a hand in projects or drives that match your beliefs and lead to a greater cause.
3. Write and refer to a personal work mission to remind you of the change you hope to bring through your role.

Set specific goals. It's like drawing a map for yourself. You'll always work on finding meaning in your work. Keep checking your goals. Make sure they match your changing values and desires. You must grow your skills. It's a key factor in finding meaning in your work. If there are skills you lack in your current or dream career, discover them. Then, take steps to learn them to boost your professional growth.

Start by checking your abilities. Find areas where you don't know enough. Think about the skills you need in your job or industry. Do you need any technical abilities, software skills, or industry-specific knowledge? Finding these gaps will help you focus on what you must learn.

After you've found the skills you want to develop, find learning opportunities. Look for suitable training programs, workshops, online classes, or mentorship programs. These provide the knowledge and expertise you need. Seek advice from professionals in your network. They offer helpful tips and guidance.

Also, get some real-life experience along with formal learning. Try doing new tasks or roles at work. They will give practical experience in the areas where you want to improve. You could volunteer on different teams or chase assignments that challenge you to learn something new. Don't stop learning for your career. Always be on the lookout for new trends. Keep yourself updated with the latest tech happening in your field. Always take time for self-study, like reading articles about your industry, going to Webinars or conferences, even joining online groups for your field.

Learning new things isn't just useful, it's also fun. It makes you feel more confident at work. Also, it makes you an important part of your company. Love learning. Never let a chance to learn something new pass by. By learning more, you prepare yourself for a bright future in your chosen career. Always remember, when you learn more for yourself, you are doing your future a big favor. Understand the power of your job in making the world a better place. Not only is it about doing your job but how doing it makes others happier. Understand how it makes you feel important.

Think about how your work is helpful to others. Maybe you are helping the customers reach their goals. Maybe you're making their life better. Or even changing their lives in a big way. By knowing these things, you can do your work happier because you know it helps.

Remember, it's key to see how your work fits with your group's big dreams. Think about your company's mission and values. How does your job help them? Knowing where your work fits into the big plan can give your job meaning and direction.

Note that finding a deeper meaning in your job doesn't have to be huge. Even the little things, like being nice or connecting with people, can matter a lot. When you look at the good parts of your job and see the worth in what you do, you can build a sense of meaning and purpose at work.

Know that finding purpose in your work is a process. It changes. So, keep your eyes open for new chances. Think about what you care about, what you love. Be ready to change things up. When you look for a deeper meaning beyond your job title, you can find more joy and pleasure in your career.

Chapter **11**

Leadership and Influence: Becoming a Person of Impact
****

Exploring Leadership:

Here- we are, diving dee-p into the world of leadership, a major ke-y to furthering your career. If you're- in your thirties, honing your leadership skills is absolute-ly crucial. These skills can stee-r a team or entire company towards succe-ss. In this conversation, we'll highlight differe-nt styles, facets, and characteristics of le-adership. Our aim is to help you thoroughly understand what make-s a leader truly effe-ctive.

Leadership comes in different forms like autocratic, democratic, transformational, and servant leadership. By examine these styles, you get to discern which one fits your values and aspirations best. There's also a section about leadership flexibility, given the varying demands of different circumstances.

We're also looking into traits that make leaders successful. Attention will be on attributes like integrity, resilience, empathy, and good communication. Familiarity with these attributes lets you self-evaluate and refine areas needing improvements as you build leadership ability.

Finally, self-awareness counts in good leadership. Knowing your strong points, weak spots, and values helps you lead with sincerity. It lets you make decisions that agree with your personal convictions. You can better your self-awareness and form a personal leadership style through exercises in self-reflection or via feedback from others.

This section serves as a foundation for the subsequent chapters on building leadership skills. By providing a thorough understanding of leadership theories and concepts, readers will be well-prepared to embark on their journey towards becoming effective leaders in their thirties Building Self-Awareness: In this section, readers will embark on a journey of self-discovery as they explore the importance of self-awareness in effective leadership. By developing a deep understanding of their own strengths, weaknesses, and personal values, readers will be empowered to align their leadership style with their authentic self.

To enhance self-awareness, readers will engage in practical exercises designed to cultivate introspection and reflection. These exercises may include journaling prompts, mindfulness practices, or guided meditation exercises. Through these activities, readers will gain insight into their unique qualities, enabling them to leverage their strengths and address areas for improvement.

Additionally, seeking feedback from others is an invaluable tool for enhancing self-awareness. The book provides guidance on how to request and receive constructive criticism from colleagues, mentors, and trusted individuals in one's professional network. By actively seeking feedback and considering different perspectives, readers can gain a more comprehensive understanding of their leadership style and its impact on others.

By nurturing self-awareness, readers will be better equipped to lead with authenticity and make informed decisions that align with their personal values. This self-awareness will not only benefit their own professional growth but also contribute to creating an inclusive and supportive work environment for their team members.

Reading this chapter helps you know yourself better, especially your leadership qualities. You'll see how your unique talents uplift your team and inspire them to excel. Fostering self-awareness, you'll stay on the path of growth and success professionally. Good communication is vital for strong leadership. In this part, we're looking at how key communication is to leadership, and we're checking out effective ways to communicate.

A major part of leadership communication is active listening. This means really tuning into others when they talk, catching their words, how they say it, and what their body language says. When we listen intently to our team, coworkers, and bosses, we show them respect. They feel heard and important. This builds trust and tightens relationships, which sets the stage for effectual teamwork and collaboration.

Body language counts in leadership communication, too. What we do with our bodies, faces, and hands sends strong signals. Knowing what our bodies say and controlling these signals help us display confidence, attentiveness, and curiosity. Plus, keeping an eye on others' non-verbal clues lets us read their feelings or issues even before they put them into words.

Leaders need the skills to persuade and inspire people. This needs clear thoughts, strong reasoning, passion, and belief. With these, we can encourage our teams, build support for projects, and share our goals effectively.

Being influential goes hand-in-hand with great leadership communication. Such leaders can spark action and gather support for a common dream. To gain influence, we need to be reliable, nurture strong bonds, and use persuasion well. This way, we spark positive change, drive team work, and reach better outcomes.

As we aim to become good leaders, it's key to improve our communication. This means active listening, using non-verbal signals, good persuasion, and gaining influence. Doing this boosts our leadership communication and helps us make a positive difference. Emotional intelligence is also a key leadership quality. It means understanding and managing personal feelings, as well as respecting others' emotions.

To grow emotional intelligence, the following areas are key:

1. Self-Regulation: It's about handling our feelings, urges, responses. It demands discipline and calmness in tough times. Techniques like mindfulness, deep-breathing exercises help us.
2. Empathy: Empathy means feeling what others feel. It needs us to listen carefully, understand others' views, show real care. If we step in others' shoes, empathy increases, relationships get stronger, the work place gets supportive.
3. Social Awareness: It means staying alert to others' emotions, needs. It calls for reading social clues, understanding group vibes, changing our behavior accordingly. By observing, listening well, we understand their drives, worries, strengths.

Improving these emotional intelligence skills can help us connect better with team members, earn trust, promote teamwork. It helps establish positive work atmosphere where everyone feels important, backed.

To boost emotional intelligence, think about:

1. Practice active listening: Listen actively when others speak, aim to understand their view without bias.
2. Here's how to level up your emotional skills: Step into someone else's shoes. See the world from their perspective. Be there for them. Understand what they feel and why.
3. Know what sets you off emotionally. Learn healthier ways to manage that. Take a breather when things get tough. This will help you cope better with stress.
4. Be open to what others think of you. Get feedback from coworkers and superiors. They'll give you a glimpse of how they see your emotional behavior. Treat their opinions as constructive tips for improving your emotional skills.

Your journey in emotional intelligence won't end. Keep learning and growing. Expand your knowledge with various resources such as books and online courses.

Strong emotional intelligence can make you a better leader. You can motivate your team effectively and handle tough situations with understanding. You'll also build stronger relationships. It's a key skill for being successful in any leadership role. Plus, it will help you grow professionally.

Want to make a stronger impact as a leader? Start by building a solid leadership presence. This goes beyond just being a leader. It involves having genuine confidence and behaving like a true executive.

Bolster your presence with confidence. Confidence can inspire trust. To feel more confident, recognize your strong points. Make a list of your successes. Use these as motivation. Visualize yourself as a confident leader in various situations. This way, when these situations arise, you'll be ready to take them on.

Leadership presence ties with authenticity. If you stay real and constant, folks 'round you can see and trust your honesty. Real leaders pull folks together because they're relatable. They provoke loyalty. Take time to discover your values, views, and rules. Line up your actions with these parts of your identity. Be honest with your team about your plans and decisions.

Next, leadership presence also connects with the skill to pull others' attention and sway them. Your body language matters. It shows your sureness and command. Stay straight, keep good posture, and look others in the eyes when you chat or listen. Use welcoming and positive movements, like leaning in when chatting or nod upward to show you're actively listening.

Your voice tone affects leadership presence as well. Speak clearly and firmly, and with conviction. Practice mixing up your tone, loudness, and speed to share your message and catch everyone's attention. Consider your voice's rise and fall, emphasize key points, and pause for emphasis.

Finally, how you dress can boost your leadership presence. Looking professional shows your respect for your role. Dressing well helps your confidence and influences others' impressions of you as a leader. Think about your work or industry's dress rules and expectations. Aim to look sharp and organized.

Growing your leadership strength helps earn respect, boost trust, and bring positive shifts within your team and company. Remember, improving leadership abilities is a continuous journey that needs self-reflection, practice, and ongoing growth. Accept your distinct traits, converse genuinely, and display your leadership skills to unlock your greatest leadership success. Mixing Ambition and Wellness:

Recognizing Ambition's Effect on Wellness:

This part digs into the complex connection between ambition and wellness. While ambition can push individual and work growth, balancing it to sustain overall wellness is key. Understanding ambition's influence, identifying imbalance and burnout signs, and learning effective techniques to set limits can guide us on the ambition journey more mindful and caring for ourselves.

Healthy ambition can shoot us toward achievement and satisfaction. But, if ambition goes too far, it can harm our wellness. It's crucial to spot imbalance signs caused by unchecked ambition, like nonstop stress, tiredness, and overwhelming feelings. These signals are bright red alarms to review our priorities and readjust for balance.

Setting limits is important to control ambition's effect on our wellness. By marking clear limits around work time, personal promises, and self-care habits, we free up time for rest, renewal, and real connections outside our ambitions. Being able to say no to too much and managing expectations, both our own and others', lets us focus on our wellness without sacrificing our ambitions.

By integrating self-care practices into our daily lives, we strengthen our well-being amidst ambitious endeavors. Self-care is a foundational aspect of maintaining balance, vitality, and mental resilience. It encompasses various practices such as mindfulness meditation, exercise, proper nutrition, adequate rest, and engaging in activities that bring joy and relaxation.

To ensure that our ambitions align with our personal values and priorities, regular reflection is essential. Take time to evaluate whether your current ambitions truly resonate with your core values. If there is a misalignment, consider adjusting your goals or redefining success according to what truly matters to you. By aligning our ambitions with our values, we can pursue meaningful goals that contribute to our overall well-being and bring a sense of fulfillment.

Effective time management strategies play a crucial role in balancing ambition and well-being. Prioritizing tasks, setting realistic expectations, and creating schedules that allow for breaks and self-care activities are essential steps in maintaining a sense of balance. It's also important to recognize when it's necessary to delegate tasks or seek support from others to prevent overwhelm and burnout.

Lastly, cultivating a supportive environment is vital in maintaining a healthy balance between ambition and well-being. Surrounding ourselves with individuals who understand the importance of balancing ambitions with personal well-being can provide guidance, encouragement, and accountability. Creating boundaries in both professional and personal relationships ensures that we protect our well-being while pursuing our aspirations.

Gaining insight into ambition's effects on well-being helps avoid burnout and foster resilience. This is a journey, not a sacrifice, to balance effort and self-care. It's about achieving goals and nurturing our multiple aspects simultaneously. Consider Self-care.

Self-care is vital, especially in your thirties. Getting lost in goals can impact your health. However, valuing self-care can prevent exhaustion, keep you healthy, and aid in reaching your goals.

Create a self-care routine that matches your values. Reflect on what actions nourish your mind, body, and soul. Perhaps it's meditation, writing, or a hobby. Including these activities in your routine can reduce stress and promote balance.

Experiment with self-care choices. Mindful exercises, such as deep breaths or gratitude, can keep you grounded and lower stress. Physical exercise also helps enhance mood and well-being. Find an exercise that suits you, and prioritize it.

In addition to mindfulness and exercise, relaxation techniques can help you unwind and recharge. This may involve taking regular breaks throughout the day to engage in activities that help you relax, such as reading a book, taking a bath, or listening to calming music. Prioritizing quality sleep is also crucial for well-being. Establish a bedtime routine that promotes restful sleep and allows you to wake up feeling refreshed and ready to tackle your ambitions.

Remember that self-care is not selfish; it is an essential investment in yourself. By prioritizing self-care, you are ensuring that you have the energy, focus, and emotional well-being to pursue your ambitions effectively. Take the time to identify your self-care needs and create a routine that allows you to nurture yourself. When you prioritize self-care, you are setting the foundation for achieving both personal fulfillment and success in your thirtiesAligning Ambitions with Personal Values goes beyond the conventional definition of success and encourages readers to reflect on their fundamental beliefs and values. By understanding how personal values align with career ambitions, individuals can make informed decisions that lead to greater satisfaction and fulfillment. This section explores strategies for assessing and adjusting goals and ambitions to ensure they are in harmony with personal values.

Reflecting on personal values and how they relate to career ambitions is an essential first step in the journey towards balance and well-being. Take the time to introspect and identify your core values. What truly matters to you? Is it making a positive impact on others? Pursuing creative endeavors? Achieving financial stability? Each individual's values will differ, and it is important to honor your unique aspirations.

Identifying your values is the first step. Next, check your current aspirations. Do they match your essential beliefs? Or are you following a path carved out by society's expectations? Think about what your underlying ambitions say about your true self and your primary values.

If your aspirations don't fit with your values, you might need to alter your course. This can mean reassessing your goals, revising your definition of success, or changing your direction. Tweaking your aspirations to match your values will bring a deeper sense of purpose and satisfaction.

Remember, it's not a one-time thing. It is an ongoing process. As your life changes, your values might too. So, check in with yourself often. Are your aspirations in sync with your current values? By making conscientious decisions that respect your core beliefs, you can ensure your pursuits are worthwhile and contribute positively to your mental and emotional health.

Remember, success doesn't solely lie in societal standards or external achievements. True success is leading a life aligned with your values. When you balance your aspirations and values, you'll experience a deeper sense of fulfillment surpassing surface-level achievements. Effectively managing your time plays a vital role in this balance. Poor time management can leave you overwhelmed and burnt out. Here we give you some strategies to enhance your time management skills and find the perfect balance between your aspirations and well-being.

Prioritizing tasks is a crucial part of time management. It helps you spot the vital and urgent tasks and rank them. This helps you avoid less important things. You can spend your time and energy cleverly. This ensures you focus on the most valuable tasks.

Besides prioritizing, keeping expectations real is vital too. Ambitious people often have high expectations. They might want to do everything at once. But, this can lead to stress and harm overall well-being. So, keep your expectations realistic, know your limits. This way, you can dodge being overwhelmed and keep a healthy work-life balance.

One more approach to balancing ambition and well-being is to seek help or delegate when you need to. Understand, you don't need to do everything. It's okay to ask for help. Let others help or assign them tasks. This can lessen your load and let you focus on tasks that suit your abilities and interests. By sharing tasks, you can lessen stress. You can find time for relaxation and self-care.

Recall, efficient time management is not about doing more work. It's about working smartly. By ranking tasks, keeping realistic expectations, and delegating, you can find a better balance. The balance between your goals and well-being. This balance not only boosts your productivity but also can make you happier and successful. Remember to Cultivate a Supportive Environment.

Maintaining a balance between drive and life means surrounding yourself with positive influences. This helps you keep your health in check while staying ambitious. Form meaningful bonds with people who also value balance in life. This positive network supports, embraces, and hypes your journey.

When shaping this positive space, find folks who can guide you and inspire you. Seek out mentors or idols who've managed to juggle ambition and life successfully. Their advice and stories can be priceless as you map out your own path.

It's also crucial to set boundaries in this positive space. Define a clear divide between work and personal life. This keeps your mental health safe as you chase your dreams. This may mean setting a cap on work hours or setting boundaries with loved ones so you save time for self-nurturing and relaxation.

Remember, shaping this positive space isn't for applause or approval. It's about finding individuals who understand your goals and maintain their own balance. Together, you build a neighborhood that backs each other up. This aids the threading of the needle between drive and life Understanding the power of Networking:

In this chapter, we will delve into the significance of networking and its role in professional growth. Networking is the process of establishing and nurturing relationships with individuals who can provide valuable support, guidance, and opportunities throughout your career journey. By actively participating in networking activities, you can expand your circle of professional contacts, gain access to new resources and information, and increase the visibility of your skills and expertise.

One of the key benefits of building a strong network is the potential for career advancement. Through networking, you can connect with professionals in your field who may be able to offer mentorship, recommend you for job openings, or provide insights into industry trends and opportunities. These connections can open doors to new experiences, collaborations, and promotions that may not have been possible otherwise.

Networking also plays a crucial role in personal and professional development. Interacting with individuals from diverse backgrounds and industries broadens your perspective, exposes you to new ideas and approaches, and fosters continuous learning. These interactions can spark inspiration, help you stay abreast of industry developments, and challenge your existing knowledge and assumptions.

Moreover, networking offers a platform for showcasing your skills and expertise. By sharing your knowledge and insights with others, you can establish yourself as a thought leader in your field. This can lead to speaking engagements, writing opportunities, and invitations to participate in industry events or conferences. Building a reputation as an expert in your area of focus enhances your professional credibility and can attract new career opportunities.

Additionally, networking provides a valuable support system throughout your career. By cultivating relationships with like-minded professionals, you create a network of individuals who understand the challenges you face and can offer guidance and encouragement. Your network can serve as a sounding board for ideas, provide feedback on important decisions, and offer support during times of uncertainty or change.

Recognizing the impact of networking on career opportunities and advancement is essential in today's competitive job market. By actively engaging in networking activities, you can harness the power of these connections to propel your professional growth and open doors to exciting new possibilities. In the following sections, we will explore effective networking strategies, nurturing professional relationships, online networking on social media platforms, and strengthening business relationships Effective Networking Strategies:

Networking is an essential component of professional growth and success. It offers opportunities for career advancement, mentorship, and access to valuable resources. In this section, we will explore some effective strategies to maximize your networking efforts and build strong business relationships.

Identifying Key Networking Opportunities and Events:

When it comes to networking, it's crucial to identify the key opportunities and events relevant to your industry. Research local meetups, conferences, workshops, or industry-specific gatherings where like-minded professionals gather. These events provide a platform to connect with individuals who share similar interests and goals.

How to Create a Lasting First Impression:

A positive first impression is important in networking. Here are some tips to stand out:

1. Dress well: Professional attire suggests confidence and regard for the event.
2. Prepare a good elevator pitch: A short, impactful intro that outlines your skills, experiences, and aspirations. It aids in communication and leaves a strong impact.
3. Make eye contact and listen actively: Keep eye contact in conversations to reveal true interest. Listen closely and reply meaningfully to what the person says.
4. Be welcoming and cheerful: Smile, have a firm handshake, and genuinely want to know others. A friendly attitude makes you more approachable.

The Art of Engaging in Depth Talks and Building Real Connections:

Building true connections underpins networking success. Here's how to enhance your talks:

1. Ask open questions: Prompt others to share their thoughts and experiences with open questions. This sparks deeper talks and exhibits real interest.

2. Listen actively and show empathy: Show you're listening by nodding, holding eye contact, and recapping main points. Empathy builds trust and connection.
3. Put your knowledge to use: Guide others by sharing lessons or tools that can help them. Becoming a source of knowledge brands you as an informed pro who adds to the dialogue.
4. Keep in touch and grow relationships: After events, be proactive and keep the connection alive with those you met. Send custom emails or join them on business

platforms like LinkedIn. Strengthen these bonds by regularly touching base and offering help when it's required.

Don't forget, good networking is not just giving out business cards or gathering contact info. It's about creating impactful relationships built on mutual trust, respect, and common interests. By pinpointing key networking moments, making a lasting impact from the start, and participating in honest talks, you can pave the way for strong business relationships which will push your career forward. Cultivating and keeping relationships with mentors, coworkers, and industry leaders is a key part of building a solid professional network. These bonds can offer irreplaceable support, guidance, and chances for growth throughout your career. Below are some core points to contemplate when caring for professional relationships:

1. **Making Real Connections:** When making new professional bonds, concentrate on crafting real connections rooted in common interests, ideals, or targets. Approach talks with an open mind and actively hear other viewpoints. Show real curiosity in their projects and lend a hand where possible.

2. **Find Guides:** Coaches often share helpful advice from their profession's history. Look for successful people in your dream areas and ask them politely. Make sure they understand what you're trying to achieve and how they can assist you. Don't forget about reversed coaching where you could teach someone less skilled than you.

3. **Be Part of Professional Groups or Squads:** Being in a professional group fastens your bond with others in your field and updates you on what's new. Go to meets, gatherings, or learning sessions where you'll see people from different places who are similar to you.

4. **Give More, Take Less:** Networking isn't just about taking--it's giving back and helping others. Lend a hand, teach someone something, or just be there without wanting something in return. When you're kind and helpful, people like you more and you'll have a lot of friends.

5. **Keep in Touch:** Friendship needs time and hard work, so talk to people often. Share your feats or ask how they're doing now and then. Regular chats keep the bond tight after you first meet.

6. **Going to Work Events:** Going to work operating events gives you a chance to meet other professionals and learn from the best. Start interesting talks, ask real questions, and switch contact details to keep the bond alive after the event ends.

7. **Be Active on Job Networks Online:** Use web platforms like LinkedIn to link with pros in your field. Post pertinent news or thoughts, take part in chats, and applaud others on their wins. Being active online aids in showcasing your professional persona and growing your contacts.

Keep in mind, forming professional bonds is a lasting task that needs true grit, mutual regard, and regular involvement. When you build a network that boosts your career objectives and give support back, you set a robust base for a successful career. Online bonds: Using Social Media Platforms:

With our present digital era, social media tools have turned into potent devices for networking and cementing work bonds. By employing platforms like LinkedIn, Twitter, and field-specific forums, you broaden your set of contacts and generate valuable links in your interest area. Let's delve into the different methods you can apply online networking to boost your job chances.

Utilizing tools like LinkedIn helps to create an appealing online persona and personal brand. Initiate by refining your profile with a professional snapshot, a well-penned summary showing your proficiency, and a comprehensive archive of your talents and experiences. Regularly updating your profile to showcase new feats or credentials is key. Presenting yourself as an informed and successful professional helps draw opportunities and links.

Get involved in online groups related to your interest. Join groups on LinkedIn or use Twitter chats that focus on your area. Take part in conversations, offer useful insights, and ask good questions. Actively participating shows your knowledge and connects you with professionals.

Online networking isn't just for promoting yourself. It's about making real relationships. Connect with others by engaging with their posts, sharing their work, or celebrating their wins. By showing interest in others' work, you can make real connections that can lead to teamwork or jobs.

You need to balance promoting yourself and helping others. Share articles, insights, or updates that might help your network. Give your advice or expertise when you can. By sharing your knowledge and tools, you make yourself valuable in your network.

Lastly, don't overlook online networking events or conferences. Many conferences are now online, hosting panels, workshops, and meet-and-greet sessions. Attending these virtual events can help you meet new people, swap ideas, and grow your network.

Using social media platforms and online communities thoughtfully helps you grow professionally. Develop a strong online presence, take part in relevant online groups, and build real relationships. This can support your career aim and uncover exciting possibilities. So, dive into the digital world and explore the opportunities for online networking.

Strong Business Relationships:

Here, we discuss why it's key to build strong relationships with clients and partners. It's a must-have for long-term professional growth and success.

Firstly, good communication is the foundation of trust and understanding your business contacts. Open, clear conversations help establish a solid working relationship. Quick responses, active listening, and maintaining communication build a strong rapport with your clients and associates.

Then, understand the unique needs of everyone you work with. Know their aims, difficulties, and expectations. That lets you offer specialized solutions. Show that their success matters to you and that you're devoted to meeting their needs. This deepens trust and loyalty.

Stay in touch and follow up - these are the building blocks of lasting business relationships. Don't wait for business needs to buzz your contacts. Regular emails, calls, or casual coffee meet-ups work fine. Be interested in their journey, step in with advice when needed, and keep them abreast of industry happenings.

Moreover, successful follow-ups solidify these relationships. This means addressing your clients or partners' worries promptly, reacting instantly to their inquiries, and fulfilling promised commitments. By sticking to your word and going beyond anticipation, you fortify your image as a reliable professional.

Remember, it's not a one-time job. Building healthy business bonds is a never-ending task needing your time and resources. It requires nurturing and adjusting per changing scenarios and requirements. Prioritize relationship building and effective communication to set the base for fruitful long-term partnerships. Understanding Communication Styles:

In this section, we dive into the world of communication styles, crucial for our relationships. By understanding the different ways of communication, we comprehend how our speech, tone, and body language influence our relationship with others.

Everyone talks differently. Your upbringing, heritage, and life directly impacts how you communicate. Understanding these styles can help conversations go smoothly.

It's vital to pick up on other people's styles. Paying attention to what they say and don't say can help you communicate better. Adaptable communication builds stronger relationships.

Empathy and active listening are big parts of good conversation skills. We need to put ourselves in their shoes and really understand them. This builds trust and deeper conversations.

Active listening is more than just hearing. It's really paying attention. This shows respect and validates their ideas and feelings. This helps conversations go well and deepens relationships.

By learning about different talking styles, you'll gain some useful know-how and tools. We'll deepen connections with empathy and active listening and transform relationships. You'll become a more effective communicator.

Talking well is key in connecting with others and forming strong pathways. We'll cover strategies that will sharpen your speech, help you express feelings, and avoid common talking slip-ups.

Improving clarity and articulation in verbal communication begins with being mindful of our words and how we deliver them. By speaking clearly and concisely, we ensure that our message is accurately understood by others. It is important to articulate our thoughts in a coherent manner, organizing them logically to maintain clarity throughout the conversation.

Assertive communication techniques are essential for expressing our thoughts and feelings effectively while respecting the perspectives of others. Assertiveness allows us to communicate our needs, desires, and boundaries without infringing upon or disregarding the rights of others. By using "I" statements and expressing ourselves in a calm and composed manner, we can convey our thoughts assertively while promoting open dialogue.

When engaging in conversations, it is important to be mindful of common communication pitfalls that can hinder effective communication. Interrupting others while they are speaking can disrupt the flow of conversation and make individuals feel unheard. Instead, practice active listening by giving others the space to express themselves fully before responding.

Dominating conversations by constantly steering the topic towards oneself can create an imbalance in communication dynamics. It is important to show genuine interest in others' perspectives and actively engage in active listening. Remember that effective communication is a two-way street, where both parties have the opportunity to contribute and be heard.

By practicing effective verbal communication skills such as improving clarity and articulation, using assertiveness techniques, and avoiding common communication pitfalls, we can foster better understanding, connection, and collaboration in our personal and professional relationships. These skills are invaluable tools that will fortify and empower you as you navigate your thirties and beyond Nonverbal communication plays a crucial role in our daily interactions, often conveying more than our words alone. Understanding and enhancing our nonverbal cues can greatly improve our ability to accurately convey messages and build strong relationships.

One important aspect of nonverbal communication is body language. Our posture, gestures, and facial expressions can speak volumes about our thoughts and feelings. For example, maintaining open body posture, making appropriate eye contact, and using hand gestures to emphasize key points can help convey confidence and engagement.

Additionally, tone of voice is another essential component of nonverbal communication. The way we say something can completely change its meaning. By being mindful of our tone and speaking with clarity and warmth, we can ensure that our intended message is accurately conveyed.

To enhance our nonverbal cues, it is important to develop awareness of our own habits. Take the time to observe how you naturally communicate nonverbally and consider if any adjustments need to be made. Practice in front of a mirror or with a trusted friend to receive feedback on your body language and tone.

Chatting with friends or delivering a speech, it's key to pay attention to what isn't being said. Watch for body language and facial expressions. They can clue you in on whether people really get what you're saying or not.

Improving how we use nonverbal cues can make our communication more impactful. Spend time building this awareness. Try using positive, clear signals when talking to othersConflict Resolution is a must-have skill. It helps keep relationships healthy. It's also key in finding a positive way to handle disagreements. In this part, we'll look at ways to deal with problems well.

Conflict is normal. It happens when people interact, whether that's in friendships, with family, or at work. Yes, conflicts can be hard. But they also offer a chance to grow, learn, and make connections stronger.

When problems arise, stay cool and open-minded. Here a few ways you can handle disagreements positively and respectfully:

1. Active Listening: This is the most important part of resolving conflicts. Make sure you understand what the other person is really saying. Try to see things from their perspective – their thoughts and their feelings. This means not judging or interrupting them.

2. Pick Your Moment and Spot: Picking the right time and location can help settle disputes. Wait until everyone is calm for a chat. A quiet, safe spot where discussions won't be interrupted is best.

3. Opt for "I" Messages: Using "I" phrases can help stop you from seeming hostile when you voice your worries. For instance, instead of "You always make me feel...", say "I feel hurt when..."

4. Find Similarities: Hunt for shared likes or agreements between you and the other person. Sharing something in common aids in communication and lays the groundwork for a resolution.

5. Keep to the Point, Not the Person: It's vital to separate the person from the problem. Steer clear of blaming or nasty comments. Focus on sorting out the exact problem instead.

6. Look at Other Views: Open discussion helps, ask the other person their thoughts. Be ready to listen to other ideas and believe in the chance of finding a solution that suits everyone.

7. Show Compassion and Try to Understand: Walk in the other person's shoes and try to feel their emotions and worries. This can help you be more understanding and settling disputes in a kinder way.

8. Hunt for Solutions for Both Parties: Aim for an outcome that helps everyone involved. Be imaginative in finding solutions that suit each person's wants and needs.

9. Seek Mediation if Necessary: In some situations, it may be helpful to involve a neutral third party to mediate the conflict. A mediator can provide an unbiased perspective and facilitate effective communication between both parties.

By understanding different conflict resolution styles and implementing these strategies, you can effectively manage conflicts and work towards mutually satisfactory resolutions. Conflict resolution is not about winning or losing; it's about finding common ground, fostering understanding, and preserving relationships. Remember, conflicts are opportunities for growth and deeper connections when approached with respect, empathy, and open-mindedness

Building Strong Relationships:

One of the keys to fortifying and empowering yourself in your thirties is by building strong relationships with those around you. Nurturing trust, respect, and rapport with others is essential for personal and professional growth. Here are some insights and strategies to deepen connections through effective communication and maintain healthy relationships:

1. Genuine Interest and Active Listening:
- Show a genuine interest in others by actively listening to their thoughts, opinions, and experiences.
- Demonstrate empathy and understanding by validating their feelings and perspectives.
- Avoid interrupting or dominating conversations, allowing space for open and reciprocal dialogue.

2. Effective Communication:
- Speak in a truthful, upfront, and clear manner to build trust and prevent confusion.
- Utilize "I" phrases to share your views and emotions without blaming others.
- Pay attention to how you sound, your body movements, and your face. They should match what you intend to say.

3. Disagreements WITH Respect:
- Realize that clashes and differences of opinion are normal in any connection.

- Face disagreements with an open attitude, aiming to find mutual understanding and solutions over winning debates.
- Listen attentively during disputes, acknowledging the other person's point of view before sharing yours.

4. Setting Limits:
- Ensure mutual respect and emotional health by setting clear limits in your relationships.
- Express your needs, bounds, and desires openly to others.
- Be ready to set limits when needed, even if it involves saying "no" or moving away from harmful relationships.

5. Time Well-Spent and Common Experiences:

Invest energy in forming purposeful relationships through shared experiences.

Take part in shared activities or hobbies, nurturing mutual interests and delight.

Make quality time with those close to you a priority, creating space for open chats and bonding.

Remember, establishing strong relationships is a continuous process requiring effort, patience, and understanding. By fostering trust, esteem, and connection with others, you can build a support network that boosts and supports you throughout your thirties and beyond.

Understanding Your Worth

To bargain better when discussing your salary, raises, and benefits, first, find out your real value. This means, understand your skills, work history, and what you're worth in the job market. You need this to argue well for yourself in the talks.

First, think about your skills and knowledge. What special abilities or talents do you have? Look at how your past work experiences have helped you grow. Notice any special training or certifications you own. By knowing what you're good at, you can boldly explain why you're valuable in the talks.

Also, you should explore the standard pay rates and wage scale in your field of work. Get to know the usual trends in the job market and what people in your field usually get paid. You'll discover what most bosses offer for jobs like yours. Use websites, industry surveys, and chats with colleagues in similar positions to get this information.

Although you should compare with industry standards, always remember what you've contributed to your company. Think about the unique ways your work has changed things in your job. Think about any success stories, like surpassing goals, finding ways to save money, or winning projects. By showing off these successes in the talks, you prove that you have something no one else can offer.

Remember, understanding your worth is not just about monetary compensation but also encompasses recognition and appreciation for your contributions. Take pride in your skills, experiences, and accomplishments, recognizing that they are valuable assets in any negotiation

Preparing for Negotiation:

When it comes to negotiating salaries, raises, and benefits, preparation is key to success. In this chapter, we will explore the essential steps to take before entering into a negotiation, ensuring that you are well-equipped and confident in advocating for what you deserve.

1. Setting clear goals and objectives for the negotiation process:

Before entering any negotiation, it is crucial to define your goals and objectives. Take some time to reflect on what you hope to achieve from the negotiation. Are you seeking a higher salary, better benefits, or both? Consider your priorities and what is most important to you in terms of compensation. By having a clear understanding of your objectives, you can better navigate the negotiation process.

2. Gathering evidence of your accomplishments and contributions:

To support your case during negotiations, gather tangible evidence of your accomplishments and contributions within your role or organization. This can include quantifiable results, positive feedback from clients or colleagues, or any awards or recognition you have received. By presenting this evidence, you can demonstrate your value and the impact you have made within your position.

3. Anticipating potential objections or counteroffers and preparing responses:
In any negotiation, it is important to anticipate potential objections or counteroffers that may arise. Put yourself in the shoes of your employer and consider any concerns they may have regarding your requests. By proactively preparing responses to these objections, you can address them confidently and alleviate any doubts or hesitations. This shows that you have thoroughly considered all aspects of the negotiation and are prepared to provide solutions or alternatives if needed.

Remember, preparation is key to successful negotiations. By setting clear goals, gathering evidence of your accomplishments, and anticipating potential objections or counteroffers, you can enter into negotiations with confidence and increase your chances of achieving a favorable outcome Effective Communication Techniques:

Articulating your value proposition confidently and clearly:
In order to negotiate salaries, raises, and benefits effectively, it is crucial to master the art of articulating your value proposition confidently and clearly. Begin by thoroughly understanding your own strengths, skills, and accomplishments. Take time to reflect on your past achievements and how they have contributed to the success of your organization. This self-awareness will give you the confidence to communicate your value to potential employers or supervisors.

When articulating your value proposition, it is important to be concise and focused. Highlight specific examples of how your work has made a positive impact, whether it be through increased revenue, cost savings, improved efficiency, or successful project completions. Use quantifiable data whenever possible to demonstrate the tangible results you have delivered.

Additionally, make sure to tailor your message to the needs and values of the organization or individual you are negotiating with. Research their priorities and challenges beforehand to understand what they value most. By aligning your value proposition with their goals and objectives, you can position yourself as a valuable asset that can contribute significantly to their success.

Using persuasive language and powerful storytelling:
In negotiations, it's not just about presenting facts and figures; it's about conveying them in a compelling manner. To persuade others of your worth, use persuasive language that emphasizes the benefits and outcomes associated with your contributions. Instead of simply stating what you've done, focus on explaining how your accomplishments have positively impacted the organization.

Storytelling can be a powerful tool in negotiation. Craft a narrative that showcases your journey, challenges overcome, and lessons learned along the way. Share anecdotes that highlight your problem-solving abilities, leadership skills, and resilience. By framing your experiences as stories of growth and success, you can captivate the attention of those you are negotiating with and make a memorable impression.

Remember to tailor your message to the recipient's communication style. Some individuals may respond better to logical, data-driven arguments, while others may be more influenced by emotional appeals or anecdotes. By adapting your approach to the preferences of the person you are negotiating with, you can increase the effectiveness of your communication.

Hearing and knowing what bosses want:
Good talk is a two-way thing. In pay talks, you need to really hear what bosses want and get it. You'll be thinking about your needs, sure. But knowing what they want can make things better for both of you.

Give them your full focus. Don't butt in. Ask things if their point isn't clear. Listen to their words but watch their face and body. This way, you can find out stuff like what they want most, what they're worried about.

Get it. Show that you get their point. Help them trust you. Say you know what they're up against. Say you're ready to think out of the box to help both of you. Working together like this can mean better talks, a better chance of a deal that works for both.

In short, good talk is key when discussing pay, perks, and raises. Be proud and clear when talking about the good stuff you've done and how it's helped the company. Use strong words to sell your case. Hear them. Understand them. This way, you can hit it off and work together better during talks about pay.

One of the most important aspects of any job negotiation is the discussion of salary. Whether you are seeking a raise in your current position or negotiating the salary for a new job offer, it's crucial to approach this conversation with confidence and preparation.

To begin, it is essential to present a compelling case for why you deserve a salary increase or your desired initial salary offer. This involves highlighting your accomplishments and contributions within your role. Gather evidence of your achievements, such as specific projects you've successfully completed, positive feedback from clients or colleagues, or any measurable results you've achieved.

During the negotiation process, it's important to navigate salary discussions tactfully and assertively. Be prepared to discuss your expectations and be clear about your desired salary range. However, it's also essential to listen actively and understand the employer's perspective. Keep in mind that negotiations typically involve compromises from both sides, so be open to finding common ground.

Recognizing when to compromise and when to stand firm on your desired salary is crucial. While it's important to be flexible, it's equally important to value yourself and your skills. If you believe that your desired salary reflects your worth in the market and aligns with industry standards, don't be afraid to stand firm. However, if there are other negotiable aspects, such as benefits or perks, that could contribute to overall job satisfaction, be willing to consider alternatives that may still meet your needs.

Remember, effective negotiation is a skill that can be developed with practice. By presenting a strong case, navigating discussions with confidence, and knowing when to compromise versus standing firm, you can increase your chances of achieving a successful outcome in salary negotiations Beyond Salary: Negotiating Benefits and Perks:

In addition to salary negotiations, it's important to consider the non-monetary aspects of your compensation package. While a higher salary is certainly appealing, other benefits and perks can greatly enhance your overall job satisfaction and work-life balance. By strategically negotiating these additional elements, you can create a comprehensive package that aligns with your personal and professional needs.

Firstly, take the time to understand the importance of non-monetary aspects in your compensation. While money is undeniably important, benefits and perks can have a significant impact on your overall well-being and job satisfaction. These additional offerings can range from healthcare coverage and retirement plans to flexible work arrangements, professional development opportunities, bonuses, or additional time off. Recognize that these benefits contribute to your overall compensation package and can make a substantial difference in your quality of life.

Identifying the specific benefits and perks that are most valuable to you is crucial before entering into negotiations. Consider what aspects would best support your personal life and long-term career goals. For instance, if work-life balance is a priority, negotiating for flexible work hours or the option to work remotely could greatly enhance your overall job satisfaction. Alternatively, if professional growth is a priority for you, discuss opportunities for training, continuing education, or mentorship programs.

Think about which extras matter most to you when discussing benefits. Show how they'll help your work and the business. This emphasizes how the added benefits aid your personal and professional growth, helping you pitch your case better.

Enter these talks with a flexible mindset but firm needs. Don't forget, companies often have strict rules around benefit plans. So, be ready for potential trade-offs. Focus on the extras that matter most to you, and be open to bargaining to secure a win-win deal.

By assigning worth to perks beyond cash, recognizing which extras best suit your needs, and efficiently negotiating for these, you can craft a well-rounded package that caters to your personal and professional health. Consider that pay is not everything. By incorporating the importance of both benefits and perks, you can optimize your overall compensation.

Chapter 12

Personal Finance Mastery: Securing Your Financial Future

*****

Investing can seem like a huge, confusing mountain to climb. But if you want to succeed financially later on in life, you have no choice but to give it your all and climb that mountain anyway. This chapter will help you get the fundamentals so that you actually know what you're doing when investing your money.

One of the most important things you'll learn here is about risks and returns. Investing is an inherently risky thing to do with your money, but at the same time it's also one of the best ways to grow wealth. It might seem counterintuitive but once you understand how risk works when it comes to investments, then you can make calculated decisions that align with how much risk appetite you have.

Along with that, we're going to be discussing a whole bunch of different investing options; Stocks, bonds, mutual funds and real estate just to name a few. Every option has its own level of risk and potential rewards (and sometimes losses). You should understand each option very well before putting any money into them.

You'll also see why diversification is super important for successful investing. The last thing anyone wants is having everything they own dissapear because one company went under or some other negative event occurred in the market. By spreading out your assets across many different investment options, not only are you more likely able to ride out any hard times. But by doing this methodically and strategically enough, your portfolio over time will actually become really stable and safe.

Lastly, we've got compound interest talk. Without boring you too much with math let's just say compound interest makes it so that no matter how small something seems at first glance - It adds up quick over time as long as consistency is there.

So by following along here and being fully aware of these principles from here on out.. You'll be able to build a strong investment strategy for yourself.

Remember to update your investment plan when life changes. The plans we make for ourselves are based on the circumstances we're in at a given time and they can grow outdated easily. Regularly reviewing goals and adjusting the plan will help you stay on track.

While creating a financial plan can be done independently, it may also be beneficial to seek professional advice from a financial advisor or investment manager. Working with an expert in the field can provide valuable insights and guidance tailored to your specific needs. They can help analyze your current financial situation, evaluate risk tolerance, and recommend appropriate investment options.

Investing in your future self is a journey that requires careful planning and consideration. By creating a solid financial plan, you can set yourself up for success and make informed investment decisions that align with your goals and aspirations. Remember, investing is a long-term commitment, so stay focused, monitor your progress regularly, and adjust your plan as needed

Building an Investment Portfolio:

Building a successful investment portfolio is crucial for securing your financial future. By diversifying investments across different asset classes, risks are minimized while returns are maximized.

Diversification: One of the golden rules of investing is to not put all your eggs in one basket. By spreading investments out among stocks, bonds, real estate & commodities risk is reduced.

Asset Allocation: The right mix of assets depends on factors like risk tolerance, goals & time horizon.

Liquidity: How easy it is to convert an investment into cash without significant loss of value should always be considered.

Volatility & Returns: Higher returns generally come with increased volatility which also means more risk

Periodic Rebalancing: As markets fluctuate so does the value of different investments in our portfolio so it's important to buy low & sell high

Remember that building an investment portfolio is a dynamic process that requires regular monitoring and adjustments. Stay informed about market trends, economic indicators and changes in your personal circumstances. By diversifying wisely and maintaining a well-balanced portfolio, you can enhance your chances of achieving financial success and security in the years to come.

Managing Investment Risk:

Understanding the concept of risk tolerance is crucial when it comes to making investment decisions. Everyone has a different comfort level when it comes to taking risks with their money. Some individuals are more conservative and prefer low-risk investments, while others are more willing to take on higher risks in search of potentially greater returns.

By understanding your risk tolerance, you can make informed decisions about the types of investments that align with your personal preferences and financial goals. It's important to consider your investment timeline and financial situation when determining your risk tolerance. If you have a longer time horizon and stable financial circumstances, you may be more comfortable with higher-risk investments. On the other hand, if you have a shorter time horizon or are more risk-averse, you may opt for lower-risk investments.

Implementing risk management strategies is another important aspect of investing. Dollar-cost averaging is a popular strategy that involves regularly investing a fixed amount of money into an investment, regardless of its price. This approach reduces the impact of short-term market fluctuations and allows you to buy more shares when prices are low and fewer shares when prices are high.

Stop-loss orders are another useful tool for managing investment risk. A stop-loss order is a predetermined price at which you will sell an investment if it falls below that threshold. This strategy helps protect against significant losses by automatically triggering the sale of an investment if it experiences a steep decline in value.

Staying informed about market trends and economic indicators is crucial for managing investment risk effectively. By staying updated on the latest news and developments that can impact the financial markets, you can make more informed decisions about your investments. Keep an eye on factors such as interest rates, inflation, geopolitical events and industry-specific news that may affect the performance of your investments.

Remember that managing investment risk is an ongoing process. As your financial situation changes and market conditions fluctuate, it's important to reassess your risk tolerance and adjust your investment strategy accordingly. Regularly reviewing your portfolio and seeking professional advice when needed can help ensure that your investments align with your risk tolerance and financial goals

Seeking Professional Advice:

When it comes to investing in your financial future, seeking professional advice can provide valuable insights and guidance. Working with a financial advisor or investment manager brings many benefits that can optimize your portfolio and help you make informed decisions.

Firstly, evaluate the benefits of working with a financial advisor or investment manager. These professionals have in-depth knowledge and expertise in the world of investments. They stay up-to-date with market trends, economic indicators, and investment strategies. By leveraging their expertise, you can gain access to their wealth of knowledge and experience.

Researching and choosing the right advisor is key. They need to align with your investment goals, so ask for recommendations from friends, family or other trusted sources. Look into their qualifications and certificates. You want them to have relevant experience in the financial industry. Meet with multiple advisors to find someone who understands your unique financial situation along with sharing your values.

Once you've found the perfect advisor then leverage their expertise. Because they will assist in analyzing your financial goals, risk tolerance and time horizon. Using this information they will create an investment plan catered towards you.

They can also provide ongoing support and help monitor investments too. They'll keep an eye out for any changes in market conditions. Alongside suggesting adjustments to portfolios as needed, helping rebalance assets periodically too.

Remember that while professional advice is helpful always maintain open communication with your advisor. Regularly review investment strategies together, discuss changes in financial circumstances or objectives as well as address concerns or questions.

Professional advice is valuable which means you should take advantage of their expertise throughout your entire journey!

The importance of retirement planning cannot be overstate when it comes to long-term financial security. In this chapter we will discuss the importance of early retirement planning as well as the benefits of starting early on saving and investing (never too early). We'll also go over what consequences could arise if you neglect it.

Retirement might seem like a distant milestone when you're still in your thirties but it's never too soon to prepare for it. One really important reason why early retirement planning is essential is because of compound interest power . By starting early means giving more time for compounding returns to occur thus growing investments much faster even if small contributions were made initially when you're younger

Being able take advantage of long-term investment strategies is another crucial aspect of early retirement planning since more time equals higher percentage allocation of portfolio to growth oriented assets which are historically known for providing higher returns than more conservative investment options. By starting early you can also weather market ups and downs and potentially have a lot of wealth accumulation.

Neglecting retirement planning can result in serious consequences for your future financial well-being. Without any type of plan in place might mean you'll rely solely on Social Security benefits which may not be sufficient to maintain your desired lifestyle during retirement. Delaying saving for retirement also means having to save larger sums later on in life thus potentially causing strain on finances and limiting ability to enjoy retirement years fully

By understanding the importance of early retirement planning, you can take proactive steps towards securing your financial future. It's never too early to start saving and investing for retirement, and by doing so, you set yourself up for long-term financial stability. In the following sections of this chapter, we will explore different retirement savings options and provide guidance on creating a personalized retirement savings strategy. Remember that the sooner you begin, the greater your chances of achieving a comfortable and fulfilling retirement

This is a crucial step in planning for retirement and building wealth. Think of it as conducting a thorough assessment to better understand where you currently stand financially.

Start by setting goals for your desired lifestyle during retirement. Consider things like what age you want to retire at along with specific activities or hobbies you might be interested in trying out as well as any travel plans or leisure activities that come to mind.

Once that's established, estimate how much money will be needed when supporting such a lifestyle throughout your entire retirement. This will be key when it comes time to create your plan.

Evaluate living expenses, healthcare costs, travel expenses, inflation and all other possible unexpected expenses waiting around the corner.

Gather all necessary information like bank statements, investment account balances, outstanding debts along with any sources of income from today. Calculate net worth by subtracting liabilities from assets.

Next is analyzing income sources which may change throughout retirement years. Things like pension plans or social security benefits should be considered but don't forget about future income from investments or interest received.

Finalize with evaluating current spending habits so adjustments can be made if necessary in order to save more money now instead of later on when it'll have much less value.

Always review past decisions that were made every now and then because our circumstances constantly change whether we realize it or not. Keep track events such as changing jobs or getting married because they could impact our goals specifically related to our personal finance journey.

So get an understanding for where you stand financially, set goals for your desired lifestyle, estimate how much money is required to achieve said lifestyle and finally, make adjustments to keep pushing forward.

Exploring Various Retirement Saving Options

When it comes to planning and accumulating wealth for retirement, it is important to explore the various options available when saving for retirement. In this chapter, we will go over several different retirement saving vehicles such as 401(k)s, IRAs, and pensions. I will highlight some key advantages and disadvantages of each option so you can make an educated decision on which one best suits your needs.

1. 401(k) - A 401(k) is a popular type of retirement savings plan that employers commonly offer. This allows employees to contribute a percentage of their salary pre-tax; meaning those contributions are subtracted from your income before taxes are applied. One huge perk about a 401(k) is that many companies match their employee's contribution up to a given percent of their salary. Essentially this means they're offering you free money which greatly increases the amount in your nest egg. However, most times there are limitations on how and when these funds can be accessed without being penalized.

2. Individual Retirement Accounts (IRAs) - Another common option for retirement savings is an IRA; short for Individual Retirement Account. There are two subcategories within an IRA called Traditional IRAs and Roth IRAs. Traditional IRAs allow you to contribute pre-tax dollars similar to a 401(k), thus lowering your taxable income in the year you make contributions but taxing withdrawals during retirement. On the other hand, Roth IRAs require post-tax dollars meaning you don't receive any deduction upfront; however qualified withdrawals made during retirement years come out tax-free.

3. Pensions - Pensions are less common than they were in the past but some employers still provide them today – mainly found within public sectors or large corporations. This type of plan offers defined benefits depending on factors such as how long you were employed and what your salary history looked like while employed by them was like. Most times pension plans offer consistent amounts of income during retirement years. If your employer does offer a pension plan then it's important to understand the requirements for eligibility, the terms and conditions as well as the benefits you should expect.

As you go over these different saving options in your head it is extremely beneficial to assess your individual circumstances such as – what your current income level is, your goals, and most importantly how much risk you can tolerate. A financial advisor will be able to provide personalized guidance based on these factors. Just remember that while each option has their advantages and disadvantages there isn't one option that fits all.

1. Asses your money situation: Review what you already have, savings, investments, stuff like that. See how much you make compared to how much you spend. This will give you a good idea of where you're at.
2. Have a target: Decide how much money you want to save for retirement. Remember that the longer you wait the more expensive it gets so don't take forever.
3. Maximize contributions: If your job has any savings programs use them! Any help is better than nothing so always contribute the maximum amount allowed.
4. Investigate other accounts: Not all jobs have these saving things so if yours doesn't then look at some others! Traditional IRAs offer tax-deferred growth on contributions while Roth IRAs provide tax-free withdrawals in retirement.
5. Spread it out: There's plenty of investment options out there so don't just stick to one thing!
6. Keep updating your plan as life goes on: You won't know which direction is right until after it's over but as long as you are moving forward everything should be fine.

By following these steps and adopting a disciplined approach to saving and investing, you can create a retirement savings strategy that sets you up for a financially secure future. Remember, the key is to start early, contribute consistently, and regularly reassess your plan to ensure you're on track to meet your retirement goals.

Emphasizing the importance of regularly reviewing and adjusting your retirement savings plan, this section highlights the need for ongoing monitoring to ensure that you stay on track towards your retirement goals. Here are some tips for effectively tracking your progress and adapting your plan based on changes in personal circumstances or market conditions:

1. Regularly review your retirement savings plan: Take the time to assess your retirement savings plan at least once a year. This will help you stay informed about the performance of your investments and make any necessary adjustments.
2. Track your contributions and investment growth: Keep a record of the amount you contribute to your retirement savings each month or year. Additionally, monitor the growth of your investments over time to see if they align with your expectations.
3. A financial advisor can help: If you're not sure how to monitor and adjust your plan effectively, consider working with a qualified financial advisor. They can offer tailored advice based on your specific circumstances and provide guidance to help you make sound decisions.
4. Stay informed about personal changes: Life is unpredictable, and unforeseen events can throw a wrench into your retirement plans. Be watchful of any changes in income, expenses or family status that could necessitate adjustments to your savings strategy.
5. Keep an eye on market conditions: Pay attention to the broader economic landscape, and be aware of any significant shifts that could affect your investments. Remember that it's normal for markets to fluctuate and that doing so may require adjusting the allocation of assets in your portfolio.
6. Diversify your investments: By spreading risk across different asset classes, a well-diversified portfolio helps protect against volatility. Reassess the allocation of your investments regularly, considering further diversification if necessary.
7. Adjust contributions as needed: The amount you contribute toward retirement savings may need adjustment as circumstances change over time — perhaps increasing or decreasing depending on your financial situation — so keep this mind.
8. Revisit goals periodically: Aspirations for life shift over time, including those for retirement. Periodically reassess yours and make any needed adjustments accordingly.

Just remember that monitoring and adjusting are two actions that require consistent effort and attention; by remaining proactive and adaptable, you can ensure that your plan stays in line with shifting circumstances while still helping you achieve a financially secure future.

Chapter **13**

Financial Adventures: Exploring Passive Income
****

Financial Adventures: Exploring Passive Income in your 30's

In this chapter, we will embark on an exciting journey into the world of passive income and how it can transform your financial landscape in your 30's. We will explore various strategies, tips, and ideas to help you achieve financial growth and freedom through passive income streams.

Imagine being able to generate income while you sleep, travel, or pursue your passions. That's the power of passive income. Whether you're looking to supplement your current earnings, build wealth for the future, or achieve financial independence, exploring passive income opportunities is a game-changer.

Join us as we delve into the concept of passive income, understand the different types of passive income streams available, and build the mindset required for success. We will guide you through the process of creating a personalized passive income plan tailored to your goals and explore strategies that are particularly relevant for individuals in their 30's.

Additionally, we will address the risks and challenges associated with passive income and provide valuable tips for navigating them. We'll also dive into the importance of scaling and diversifying your passive income streams to maximize your financial potential. And finally, we'll explore how achieving financial freedom through passive income is not only attainable but also within reach.

So, get ready to embark on this thrilling chapter of your financial journey. Let's dive in and start exploring the world of passive income in your 30's!

Understanding the Concept of Passive Income

Before we dive into the practical aspects of generating passive income, let's first gain a clear understanding of what passive income really means. Passive income refers to the earnings you receive from sources that require minimal effort to maintain. Unlike active income, which involves trading your time and skills for money, passive income allows you to generate revenue even when you're not actively working.

Passive income is a game-changer in the world of personal finance. It offers the potential for financial freedom, allowing you to break free from the traditional paycheck-to-paycheck cycle. By leveraging the power of passive income, you can create a sustainable income stream that continues to grow over time.

So, how does passive income differ from active income? While active income is earned through direct participation in tasks or employment, passive income is generated through investments, businesses, or assets that work for you. Rather than trading your time for money, you focus on building and managing income streams that generate cash flow on autopilot.

Exploring Different Types of Passive Income

When it comes to generating passive income, there is no shortage of options to explore. From rental income to dividend investments and affiliate marketing, there are various avenues you can pursue to create a steady stream of income without actively trading your time for money.

Rental Income: Investing in real estate properties and renting them out is a popular and time-tested way to earn passive income. By becoming a landlord, you can leverage the power of real estate to generate cash flow on a monthly basis.

Dividend Investments: Dividend-paying stocks can be a great source of passive income. By investing in companies that regularly distribute dividends, you can earn a share of the company's profits without having to actively manage the business.

Affiliate Marketing: If you have a website, blog, or a strong social media presence, affiliate marketing can be a lucrative passive income opportunity. By promoting other people's products or services and earning a commission for each sale or lead generated, you can monetize your online platform and earn passive income while you sleep.

Online Course or eBook Sales: If you have specialized knowledge or expertise in a particular field, you can create and sell digital products like online courses or eBooks. Once the initial work is done, these digital assets can continue to generate passive income through sales, even when you're not actively promoting them.

Peer-to-Peer Lending: Platforms like Lending Club and Prosper enable you to lend money to individuals or small businesses in exchange for interest payments. By diversifying your lending portfolio, you can earn passive income through the interest generated from your loans.

Royalties: If you're a creative individual, you can earn passive income through royalties. This can include royalties from books, music, patents, or even licensing your intellectual property to others.

Digital Products and Services: From stock photos to software applications, selling digital products and services online can be a lucrative way to generate passive income. Once the initial work is done to create and set up these products, you can earn money while they continue to be purchased or used by customers.

These are just a few examples of the different types of passive income streams you can explore. It's important to note that each passive income opportunity has its own set of pros and cons, and what works for one person may not work for another. As you delve deeper into the world of passive income, take the time to research and identify the options that align with your interests, skills, and goals.

Building a Passive Income Mindset

Generating passive income requires more than just financial knowledge and investment strategies. It requires a mindset shift—a way of thinking that opens up possibilities and allows you to embrace the power of passive income. Building a passive income mindset is crucial in order to navigate the challenges and fully maximize the potential of this wealth-building tool.

So, how can you cultivate a passive income mindset?

1. **Believe in the Possibility:** First and foremost, believe that passive income is achievable. Understand that it is not reserved for a select few but is accessible to anyone with the right mindset and determination. Believe that you have the ability to create multiple streams of income that work for you even when you're not actively working.

2. **Embrace Long-Term Thinking:** Passive income is a long-term game. It requires patience, persistence, and a willingness to delay gratification. Shift your focus from short-term gains to the long-term benefits that passive income can bring. Embrace the idea of building a solid foundation that will support you financially in the future.

3. **Adopt a Growth Mindset:** A growth mindset is essential for success in any endeavor, including passive income. Embrace challenges as opportunities to learn and grow. View failures as stepping stones to progress. Believe that your abilities and skills can be developed through dedication and hard work.

4. **Emphasize Financial Education:** Educate yourself about passive income strategies, investment options, and financial literacy. The more you know, the better equipped you'll be to make informed decisions and seize opportunities. Stay curious and stay hungry for knowledge in the ever-evolving world of passive income.

5. **Overcome Limiting Beliefs:** Identify and challenge any limiting beliefs you may have about money, success, and wealth. Replace negative thinking with positive affirmations and empowering beliefs. Surround yourself with like-minded individuals who inspire and motivate you on your passive income journey.

6. **Stay Committed and Flexible:** Building a passive income mindset requires commitment. Stay the course even when faced with setbacks or obstacles. Be open to adjusting your strategies if needed but remain dedicated to your long-term vision. The road to passive income may have twists and turns, but with the right mindset, you can navigate them with confidence.

By developing a passive income mindset, you lay the foundation for financial abundance and freedom in your 30's and beyond. Stay focused, embrace the journey, and believe in the power of passive income.

Creating a Passive Income Plan

Achieving passive income requires careful planning and strategic decision-making. In this section, we will help you craft a personalized passive income plan tailored to your financial goals and lifestyle. By following the steps below, you'll be on your way to building a reliable and sustainable income stream.

1. Goal-Setting

Start by clearly defining your financial objectives. Do you want to pay off debt, save for retirement, or achieve financial independence? Setting specific and measurable goals will give you a sense of direction and help you stay focused throughout your passive income journey.

2. Financial Analysis

Take a deep dive into your current financial situation. Assess your income, expenses, and existing assets. Calculate your debt-to-income ratio and evaluate your risk tolerance. This analysis will help you determine the level of passive income you need to achieve your goals.

3. Identifying Passive Income Streams

Explore different passive income options that align with your interests, skills, and resources. Consider real estate investments, stock market dividends, online businesses, peer-to-peer lending, or creating digital products. Research each opportunity to understand the potential returns and associated efforts required.

4. Developing an Action Plan

Outline the specific steps you need to take to generate passive income. Break down your plan into manageable tasks, set deadlines, and track your progress. This structured approach will keep you organized and motivated as you work towards your passive income goals.

5. Implementing and Monitoring

Once you have your passive income plan in place, it's time to put it into action. Start building your income streams, whether it's buying rental properties, creating an e-commerce store, or investing in dividend stocks. Regularly review and adjust your plan as needed, taking advantage of new opportunities and making necessary improvements.

By following these steps, and with dedication and patience, you can create a passive income plan that will pave the way for financial freedom and a more secure future.

Passive Income Strategies for your 30's

When you're in your 30's, you have a unique opportunity to start building passive income streams that can set you up for financial success in the long run. By implementing the right strategies, you can create a solid foundation for a passive income portfolio that will continue to grow and generate revenue well into the future.

One effective passive income strategy for individuals in their 30's is to invest in real estate. This can be done through rental properties or real estate investment trusts (REITs). By purchasing properties and renting them out, you can generate a steady stream of rental income that can provide financial stability and build wealth over time. Additionally, investing in REITs allows you to diversify your real estate holdings without the hassle of property management.

Another strategy to consider is starting an online business. With the ever-growing digital landscape, there are numerous opportunities to create passive income streams through e-commerce, affiliate marketing, or online courses. By leveraging your skills and expertise, you can build a scalable online business that generates income while you focus on other aspects of your life.

Additionally, you can explore dividend investing as a passive income strategy. By investing in dividend-paying stocks, you can earn regular cash payments from the companies you have invested in. This can be a great way to create a passive income stream while also benefiting from the potential capital appreciation of your investments.

Furthermore, leveraging your existing skills and assets can be a powerful way to generate passive income in your 30's. Whether it's offering consulting services, monetizing your hobbies, or turning your home into a vacation rental, there are countless ways to tap into your strengths and create income-generating opportunities.

As you embark on your passive income journey in your 30's, it's essential to keep a long-term perspective and be patient. Building passive income takes time and effort, but the rewards can be significant. By implementing a combination of strategies that align with your goals and interests, you can unlock the potential for financial stability and freedom in the years to come.

Tips for Navigating Risks and Challenges

While passive income offers numerous advantages, it is also important to understand and address the associated risks and challenges. By taking proactive steps, you can mitigate potential pitfalls and protect your financial investments in the long run.

Mitigating Risks

When it comes to passive income, navigating risks requires a thorough understanding of the specific investment or income stream. Ensure you conduct comprehensive research and due diligence before committing your resources. Diversify your portfolio to spread risks across different assets and industries. This helps minimize the impact of any potential downturns or changes in market conditions.

Overcoming Challenges

Challenges are an inevitable part of any financial venture. It's crucial to develop resilience and adaptability to overcome these hurdles. Stay informed about the latest trends, regulations, and industry developments relevant to your passive income streams. Be prepared to adjust your strategies and adopt new approaches when necessary.

Building a solid network can also help you navigate challenges more effectively. Connect with like-minded individuals, attend industry conferences, and engage in online communities. Surrounding yourself with knowledgeable peers can provide valuable support, insight, and potential collaboration opportunities.

Long-Term Sustainability

To ensure the sustainability of your passive income, it is essential to have a realistic perspective and set achievable expectations. Avoid falling for get-rich-quick schemes or unrealistically promising opportunities. Understand that passive income requires consistent effort, continuous learning, and a long-term mindset.

Educate yourself about taxation, legal obligations, and any regulations that may impact your passive income streams. Consult with financial advisors or professionals who specialize in passive income to ensure you are on the right track. Regularly review and reassess your strategies to identify areas for improvement and capitalize on emerging opportunities.

By proactively addressing risks, overcoming challenges, and focusing on long-term sustainability, you can navigate the often unpredictable landscape of passive income with confidence and maximize your chances of financial success.

Scaling and Diversifying Passive Income Streams

Maximizing the benefits of passive income requires more than just creating a single source of revenue. To truly unlock its potential, you need to scale and diversify your income streams. This not only increases your earning potential but also safeguards against potential risks and market volatility.

Scaling Passive Income:

Scaling passive income involves expanding your existing income streams to generate more revenue. One effective strategy is to reinvest your passive income earnings into new opportunities. For example, if your rental property is generating steady income, you can use the profits to acquire additional properties or invest in real estate investment trusts (REITs) for further diversification.

Another way to scale passive income is by leveraging your expertise. Consider creating an online course or e-book sharing your knowledge in a specific subject area. This allows you to reach a wider audience and generate passive income through sales and royalties.

Diversifying Income Streams:

Diversifying your income streams is essential for long-term sustainability and mitigating risks. By spreading your investments across different asset classes, industries, and markets, you can reduce the impact of any single failure or downturn.

Investing in dividend-paying stocks, bonds, or peer-to-peer lending platforms can provide additional streams of passive income while diversifying your investment portfolio. You may also explore income opportunities in real estate, such as vacation rentals or commercial properties.

Furthermore, consider the potential of online businesses. Affiliate marketing, digital product sales, and e-commerce ventures offer diverse revenue streams that can be scaled and automated over time.

Capitalizing on Emerging Opportunities:

The world of passive income is constantly evolving, with new opportunities emerging regularly. Stay informed about market trends, technological advancements, and consumer behavior to identify emerging opportunities to capitalize on.

For instance, the rise of the gig economy has opened doors for freelancers and independent contractors to create passive income through platforms like Upwork, Fiverr, and Airbnb Experiences. Exploring these new channels can help diversify your income streams and potentially increase your overall passive income.

Remember, scaling and diversifying passive income streams requires careful planning, research, and a willingness to adapt. By implementing these strategies, you can enhance your financial stability, increase your wealth-building potential, and ultimately achieve greater financial freedom.

Achieving Financial Freedom through Passive Income

Are you dreaming of a life of financial freedom, where you have the flexibility to pursue your passions and enjoy the things that truly matter to you? Passive income can be the key to turning that dream into reality. By generating income streams that require minimal effort to maintain, you can free yourself from the constraints of a conventional 9-to-5 job and build a solid foundation for a prosperous future.

Managing your passive income effectively is crucial for attaining long-term financial freedom. It's important to have a clear understanding of your income sources, track your earnings, and create a budget that aligns with your goals. By establishing good financial habits, such as reinvesting your passive income and saving for emergencies, you can establish a strong financial foothold and create a pathway to true independence.

Setting realistic expectations is another key aspect of achieving financial freedom through passive income. While passive income streams can provide a consistent and reliable source of earnings, it's important to remember that they require time and effort to establish. Patience and perseverance are essential as you work towards building your passive income portfolio, but the rewards are well worth the journey.

As you start reaping the benefits of your passive income journey, it's vital to embrace the fruits of your labor. Whether it's taking that dream vacation, pursuing a new hobby, or donating to meaningful causes, financial freedom gives you the opportunity to live life on your own terms.

Remember to savor the moments and enjoy the newfound freedom that passive income can provide.

Chapter 14

The Side Hustle:
Turning Passions into Profits

****

The Side Hustle: Turning Passions into Profits in your 30's

Welcome to the chapter where we delve into the exciting world of side hustles. In this chapter, we will explore the art of managing a career while pursuing your passions and turning them into profitable ventures. Balancing your passions with profit is not just a dream, but an attainable goal.

Many individuals today find themselves yearning for an avenue to express their creativity, explore their interests, or bring their innovative ideas to life. However, with the demands of a full-time career, it can be challenging to find the time and resources to turn these aspirations into reality.

That's where side hustles come in. A side hustle is a passion project that allows you to pursue your interests and make money outside of your primary job. Whether it's photography, writing, graphic design, or baking, your side hustle can become a fulfilling way to express yourself and supplement your income.

But managing a career and a side hustle simultaneously can be daunting. How do you strike the right balance? How can you ensure that both your primary job and your passion project receive the attention they deserve? These are the questions we will answer in this chapter.

We will guide you through the process of identifying your true passion and finding the perfect side hustle that aligns with your skills and interests. We will also provide insights into effective time management, setting achievable goals, building a support system, and marketing your side hustle to attract clients or customers.

So, if you've been yearning to pursue your passions outside of your career and turn them into profitable endeavors, join us as we embark on this exciting journey together. It's time to balance your passions with profit and discover the joy of managing a career and a side hustle.

Why Pursue a Side Hustle?

Are you looking for additional income streams or a way to turn your passions into profits? A side hustle might be the answer you're seeking.

There are numerous reasons why pursuing a side hustle can be beneficial, both personally and professionally. Let's explore some of the benefits that come with having a side hustle alongside your career.

Financial Security

A side hustle provides an excellent opportunity to increase your income and improve your financial stability. By diversifying your revenue streams, you can become less dependent on a single source of income and create a safety net for unexpected expenses.

Personal Fulfillment

Pursuing a side hustle allows you to follow your passion and indulge in activities that bring you joy and fulfillment. Whether it's starting a blog, launching an online store, or offering freelance services, you have the freedom to explore and engage in work that aligns with your interests and values.

Skills Development

A side hustle can serve as a platform for personal and professional growth, providing the opportunity to learn new skills or expand on existing ones. By stepping outside of your comfort zone and taking on new challenges, you can enhance your skill set and develop valuable expertise that can benefit your primary career as well.

Networking and Collaboration

A side hustle can create connections with individuals who share similar passions or professional goals. Engaging in a side hustle opens doors to networking opportunities, collaboration with like-minded individuals, and the chance to build a supportive community that can inspire and motivate you.

Creative Outlet

A side hustle allows you to express your creativity and explore your ideas freely. Whether it's through writing, designing, or creating unique products, having a side hustle offers you a creative outlet to unleash your imagination and find fulfillment through your work.

In conclusion, pursuing a side hustle provides a multitude of benefits. From financial security and personal fulfillment to skills development and networking opportunities, having a side hustle can complement your career and enhance your overall professional and personal growth.

Finding Your Passion

When it comes to starting a side hustle, one of the most important factors to consider is finding your passion. Identifying what truly excites and motivates you will not only make your side hustle more enjoyable but also increase your chances of success.

So how do you go about identifying your passion? It starts with self-reflection and exploring your interests, values, and skills. Think about the activities that bring you joy and fulfillment, the things you could spend hours doing without getting bored.

Take some time to brainstorm and make a list of your interests. Consider your hobbies, areas of expertise, and any topics that you find yourself constantly gravitating towards. This will help you understand what truly sparks your enthusiasm.

Once you have a list of potential passions, take the time to research and explore opportunities within those areas. Look for side hustles that align with your interests and skills, and that have the potential for profitability.

Keep in mind that your passion doesn't have to be something completely unique or revolutionary. It could be as simple as offering a service or creating a product that solves a common problem in a way that resonates with you.

Be open to experimentation and trying out different side hustles. It may take some time and exploration to find the perfect fit, and that's okay. Treat the process as a learning experience and embrace the opportunity to grow and evolve along the way.

Remember, finding your passion is about combining what you love with what you're good at. So, take the time to identify your true passion and choose a side hustle that allows you to pursue it. When you do what you love, success will naturally follow.

Balancing Time and Priorities

Successfully managing a career and side hustle requires careful time management and prioritization. Juggling the responsibilities of both can be challenging, but with the right strategies, you can find a harmonious balance between the two and ensure they both receive the attention they deserve.

One key aspect of effective time management for side hustles is setting clear boundaries and creating a schedule that accommodates both your primary job and your side hustle. This may involve blocking off specific times during the week for your side hustle activities and allocating dedicated time to focus on your career as well.

1. Prioritize Tasks

When you have limited time available, it's crucial to prioritize your tasks effectively. Identify the most important and time-sensitive tasks for both your career and your side hustle. By focusing on these priorities first, you can ensure that you make progress in both areas and avoid feeling overwhelmed.

2. Delegate and Outsource

Consider delegating or outsourcing certain tasks that can be handled by others. This can free up valuable time for you to concentrate on the core aspects of your career and side hustle that require your specific expertise and attention.

3. Utilize Time-Management Techniques

Explore various time-management techniques such as the Pomodoro Technique or time-blocking to maximize your productivity and efficiency. By setting specific time intervals for focused work and incorporating regular breaks, you can make the most of your available time and avoid burnout.

4. Maintain Work-Life Boundaries

While managing a career and side hustle, it's essential to maintain boundaries between work and personal life. Prioritize self-care and recreation to prevent burnout and ensure overall well-being. By setting aside dedicated time for relaxation and leisure activities, you can recharge and stay motivated.

By implementing these time management strategies and prioritizing your career and side hustle effectively, you can navigate the demands of both and find success in your endeavors.

Building a Support System

When it comes to managing a career and side hustle, having a strong support system is essential. Building a network of mentors, like-minded individuals, and professionals who understand the challenges and rewards of a side hustle can provide you with valuable guidance, inspiration, and resources to help your side hustle thrive.

Networking with other side hustlers can offer numerous benefits. By connecting with people who are also pursuing their passions alongside their primary careers, you can learn from their experiences, gain new insights, and even collaborate on projects or opportunities.

One effective way to build a support system for your side hustle is to join relevant networking groups, both online and offline. These groups can connect you with individuals who share your interests and can offer support and advice. Attend local industry events, conferences, and meetups to meet with professionals in your field and expand your network.

In addition to networking, seeking out mentors can be tremendously beneficial. Mentors can provide valuable guidance and share their expertise, helping you navigate the challenges you may encounter in your side hustle journey. Look for experienced professionals who have succeeded in a similar field or have expertise in areas relevant to your side hustle.

Elevate Your Side Hustle with a Support System

With a strong support system in place, you'll have access to a group of individuals who can offer guidance, support, and resources to help you overcome obstacles and seize opportunities. They can serve as a sounding board for ideas, provide constructive feedback, and keep you motivated on your side hustle journey.

Building a support system takes time and effort, but the benefits are well worth it. Don't hesitate to reach out to like-minded individuals, attend networking events, and seek mentorship. Remember, you don't have to navigate the world of side hustles alone.

Setting Goals and Milestones

Setting clear and measurable goals is essential for the success of your side hustle. By establishing specific objectives, you can track your progress, stay focused, and evaluate your achievements. Here are some techniques to help you set effective goals and milestones:

1. Set SMART Goals

Follow the SMART framework when defining your goals: Specific, Measurable, Achievable, Relevant, and Time-Bound. For example, instead of setting a vague goal like "increase sales," make it more specific by aiming to "increase monthly sales by 15% within six months." This way, you have a clear target to work towards.

2. Break Down Your Goals

Large goals can seem overwhelming, so break them down into smaller, more manageable milestones. This helps to keep you motivated and allows you to celebrate progress along the way. For instance, if your goal is to launch an e-commerce website, break it down into tasks like selecting a platform, designing the layout, and adding products.

3. Track Your Progress

Regularly track your progress against your goals and milestones. This keeps you accountable and lets you make adjustments if needed. Use tools like spreadsheets, project management software, or online goal-tracking platforms to stay organized and monitor your progress visually.

4. Celebrate Milestones

When you achieve a milestone, take a moment to celebrate your success. Reward yourself or your team for reaching important milestones along the way. Celebrating your achievements boosts morale and motivates you to keep pushing forward.

5. Stay Flexible

As you navigate your side hustle journey, be open to adjusting your goals and milestones based on new opportunities or unforeseen challenges. Flexibility allows you to adapt to changing circumstances and ensures your goals remain aligned with the evolving needs and demands of your side hustle.

Remember, setting goals and milestones creates a roadmap for your side hustle's success. By following these techniques, you can measure your progress and stay motivated as you work towards achieving your dreams.

Financial Management

Managing your finances is a crucial aspect of running a successful side hustle. With the right budgeting and financial management strategies, you can ensure that your venture remains profitable and sustainable.

Effective Budgeting

Creating a budget specifically for your side hustle is essential for keeping track of your income and expenses. Start by listing all your sources of income and estimating how much you expect to earn from your side hustle each month. Then, identify your fixed expenses, such as rent, utilities, and loan payments. Finally, allocate funds for variable expenses, such as marketing, supplies, and any other costs associated with your side hustle.

By budgeting effectively, you can prioritize your spending and make informed decisions to maximize your profits. Review your budget regularly and make adjustments as necessary to ensure that you're staying on track and meeting your financial goals.

Expense Tracking

Tracking your expenses is crucial for understanding where your money is going and identifying areas where you can cut costs. There are several tools and apps available that can help you easily track your expenses and categorize them. By keeping a close eye on your spending, you can make informed decisions about which expenses are necessary and which ones can be reduced or eliminated.

Maximizing Profits

One of the goals of managing your finances in a side hustle is to maximize your profits. Look for opportunities to cut costs without sacrificing the quality of your products or services. Consider negotiating better deals with suppliers or finding more cost-effective ways to market your side hustle, such as utilizing social media platforms or leveraging word-of-mouth referrals.

Additionally, explore ways to increase your revenue. This can include identifying new target markets, expanding your product or service offerings, or implementing strategic pricing strategies. Continuously monitor your sales and revenue to identify trends and opportunities for growth.

By effectively managing your finances, budgeting wisely, tracking your expenses, and maximizing your profits, you can achieve financial stability and growth in your side hustle. With a solid financial foundation, you'll be well on your way to entrepreneurial success.

Marketing and Branding

When it comes to your side hustle, effective marketing and branding are key to attracting customers or clients and achieving success. In this section, we will explore essential marketing strategies and techniques that will help you promote your side hustle and stand out from the competition.

One of the most powerful tools in your marketing arsenal is social media. Platforms like Instagram, Facebook, and Twitter allow you to reach a wide audience and engage with potential customers. Create a strong online presence by sharing carefully curated content, posting regularly, and interacting with your followers. Leverage the power of hashtags to increase your visibility and attract a targeted audience. Remember to always maintain a consistent brand image across all your social media channels.

Creating a Personal Brand

Personal branding is an important aspect of marketing your side hustle. It allows you to establish yourself as an expert or authority in your niche. Start by defining your unique selling proposition (USP) - what makes your side hustle special and different from others. Use this USP to craft your brand message and communicate your value to potential customers.

Develop a brand identity that reflects your values, personality, and the essence of your side hustle. This includes elements such as your logo, color palette, typography, and overall visual style. Consistency is key - use these brand elements across all your marketing materials, including your website, social media, and packaging.

A strong personal brand goes beyond visual elements. Build credibility by sharing your expertise and knowledge through blog posts, videos, or podcasts. Seek opportunities to speak at industry events or provide guest content for relevant publications. Engage with your audience by responding to comments and messages and nurturing relationships with your customers or clients.

In conclusion, by implementing effective marketing strategies and creating a strong personal brand, you can significantly enhance the visibility and success of your side hustle. Embrace the power of social media, define your unique selling proposition, and build a consistent and compelling brand image. With these techniques, you'll attract customers or clients who resonate with your side hustle and help it thrive.

Overcoming Challenges and Obstacles

Running a side hustle comes with its own set of challenges and obstacles that can sometimes hinder your progress. However, with the right strategies and problem-solving skills, you can overcome these hurdles and ensure the long-term success of your side hustle.

One of the common challenges in side hustles is managing your time effectively. Balancing your primary career and side hustle can be demanding, and it's essential to find ways to prioritize tasks and allocate time efficiently. Consider creating a schedule or using productivity tools to optimize your time management.

Another challenge in side hustles is finding a steady flow of customers or clients. This obstacle can be addressed by implementing effective marketing strategies and building a strong personal brand. Utilize social media platforms, network with like-minded individuals, and actively promote your side hustle to attract potential customers.

Financial management can also be a challenge when running a side hustle. It's crucial to track your expenses, set a budget, and ensure that your side hustle is financially viable. Consider seeking professional advice or using financial management apps to help you stay on top of your finances.

Inevitably, setbacks and obstacles will arise during your side hustle journey. It's essential to adopt a problem-solving mindset and stay resilient. Embrace failure as a learning opportunity and develop strategies to overcome challenges, adapt to new circumstances, and keep moving forward.

Remember that every successful side hustle has faced its own challenges and obstacles. By proactively identifying potential challenges and implementing problem-solving techniques, you can navigate through setbacks and ensure the growth and sustainability of your side hustle.

Scaling Your Side Hustle

If your side hustle starts to gain traction and generates consistent profits, it's a clear sign that it's time to think about scaling it up. Scaling a side hustle means expanding it to reach a wider audience and increase its profitability. It's an exciting phase for any entrepreneur, but it also comes with its own set of challenges. However, with careful planning and strategic execution, you can successfully take your side hustle to the next level while still effectively managing your career.

One method for scaling your side hustle is to analyze your current operations and identify areas where you can optimize and streamline processes. Look for opportunities to automate tasks, outsource non-essential activities, or leverage technology to improve efficiency. By minimizing time-consuming tasks and optimizing your workflow, you can free up more of your valuable time to focus on business growth.

Expanding a profitable side hustle also requires careful financial planning. Evaluate your revenue streams and expense breakdown to determine which areas are generating the most returns and where you can potentially invest more. Consider seeking professional advice from an accountant or financial advisor to help you develop a solid financial strategy that aligns with your scaling goals.

Additionally, networking and forming strategic partnerships can play a crucial role in scaling your side hustle. Connect with individuals in your industry who have complementary skills or resources that can help you expand your reach and tap into new markets. Collaborating with like-minded entrepreneurs and businesses can provide valuable insights, access to new customers, and opportunities for cross-promotion.

Remember to keep a customer-centric approach when scaling your side hustle. Focus on providing exceptional customer service and incorporating feedback from your existing customers. Satisfied customers are more likely to refer your side hustle to others, helping to drive organic growth.

As you scale your side hustle, it's important to continuously monitor and analyze key performance indicators. Regularly evaluate your progress against your goals and objectives, and make any necessary adjustments to your strategies and operations. Stay agile and adaptable to market changes, and be willing to pivot your approach if needed.

In conclusion, scaling your side hustle is an exciting and rewarding journey that allows you to expand your profits and reach. By optimizing processes, managing finances wisely, networking strategically, and staying customer-focused, you can successfully scale your side hustle while still effectively managing your career.

Finding Work-Life-Side Hustle Balance

Managing a career and a side hustle can be overwhelming, but finding a balance is crucial for your overall well-being. Achieving a healthy work-life-side hustle balance allows you to pursue your passions, excel in your career, and still have time for personal fulfillment.

One strategy for finding balance is effective time management. Prioritize your tasks and allocate specific time blocks for your career, side hustle, and personal life. By setting boundaries and sticking to a schedule, you can ensure that each aspect of your life receives the attention it deserves.

Another important aspect of work-life-side hustle balance is self-care. Take time for yourself to recharge and relax. Whether it's engaging in hobbies, exercising, or spending quality time with loved ones, making self-care a priority helps prevent burnout and ensures you have the energy to excel in both your career and side hustle.

Additionally, don't be afraid to delegate or ask for help. Building a support system of mentors, friends, or fellow side hustlers can provide valuable guidance and support. By sharing responsibilities and leveraging the expertise of others, you can alleviate some of the pressure and create more time for yourself.

Chapter 15

Eco-conscious living:
Sustainable Lifestyle Choices
******

Welcome to our chapter on eco-conscious living! In this chapter, we will explore various ways to incorporate eco-friendly changes into your daily life. By understanding your environmental impact and making sustainable lifestyle choices, you can reduce your carbon footprint and contribute to a greener planet.

Are you ready to make a difference? Let's dive in and discover practical tips for eco-friendly living, starting with understanding your environmental impact. Together, we can create a more sustainable future.

Why Make Eco-Friendly Changes?

In today's world, it has become increasingly important to make eco-friendly changes in our lives. The environmental impact of our actions is becoming more evident, and sustainability has become a pressing concern. By embracing a more eco-friendly lifestyle, we not only contribute to the well-being of our planet, but also enjoy a range of benefits that enhance our daily lives.

One of the key reasons to make eco-friendly changes is to minimize our environmental impact. Our actions, such as excessive energy consumption, waste generation, and reliance on non-renewable resources, directly contribute to pollution, climate change, and habitat destruction. By making conscious choices, we can reduce our carbon footprint and preserve the planet for future generations.

Additionally, transitioning to a sustainable lifestyle brings about a host of benefits. By adopting eco-friendly practices, we can improve our own health and well-being. For example, switching to organic and locally sourced food reduces exposure to harmful chemicals and supports healthier agricultural practices. Similarly, using energy-efficient appliances not only reduces our carbon emissions but also saves money on utility bills.

Embracing eco-friendly living can also foster a sense of connection and fulfillment. By aligning our values with sustainable practices, we become part of a global movement that aims to create a more equitable and livable world. By actively participating in environmental initiatives, we contribute to the collective effort towards a greener future.

In the following sections, we will explore practical tips for eco-friendly living, as well as specific changes that can be made in areas such as home, transportation, food choices, fashion, and more. Let's dive in and discover the wonderful possibilities that eco-friendly living has to offer.

Understanding Your Environmental Impact

As individuals, it is crucial to understand our environmental impact in order to make informed decisions and contribute to a sustainable future. Two key concepts that help measure our impact are the carbon footprint and the ecological footprint.

The carbon footprint refers to the total amount of greenhouse gases, particularly carbon dioxide, emitted as a result of our activities and lifestyle choices. This includes the carbon emissions produced by our transportation, energy consumption, and daily habits. By measuring our carbon footprint, we can assess the extent of our contribution to climate change and take steps to mitigate it.

The ecological footprint, on the other hand, takes into account not only carbon emissions but also other resources that are used or impacted by our actions. It measures the amount of land and water needed to sustain our lifestyles, including food production, energy consumption, and waste generation. Understanding our ecological footprint helps us comprehend the broader impact we have on the planet's ecosystems and biodiversity.

Measuring our environmental impact involves evaluating various components, such as energy use, water consumption, waste generation, and transportation choices. There are online calculators and tools available that can assist in quantifying our carbon footprint and ecological footprint. These tools take into consideration factors like household size, travel habits, and consumption patterns to provide an estimate of our environmental impact.

By measuring our carbon and ecological footprints, we can gain insights into the areas where our actions have the greatest impact. This knowledge empowers us to make more sustainable choices and prioritize efforts to reduce our environmental footprint. Whether it's through energy conservation, waste reduction, or adopting eco-friendly transportation alternatives, every small step counts in creating a greener and more sustainable world.

Practical Tips for Eco-Friendly Living

If you're looking to make a positive impact on the environment, incorporating sustainable habits and making green choices is essential. Living an eco-conscious lifestyle doesn't have to be complicated or overwhelming. By adopting a few simple practices, you can significantly reduce your environmental footprint and contribute to a more sustainable future.

Sustainable Habits

Developing sustainable habits is key to living an eco-friendly life. Start by reducing your energy consumption by turning off lights and appliances when not in use. Consider investing in energy-efficient appliances and switch to LED light bulbs, which last longer and use less electricity.

Another essential habit is reducing water waste. Fix any leaks in your home, install low-flow showerheads and faucets, and be mindful of your water usage. Additionally, practice mindful shopping by avoiding single-use plastic products and opting for reusable alternatives like cloth bags, metal straws, and refillable water bottles.

Green Choices

When it comes to making green choices, consider the products you use and the impact they have on the environment. Choose eco-friendly cleaning products, toiletries, and cosmetics made from natural and biodegradable ingredients. Look for certifications like USDA Organic, Fair Trade, or Forest Stewardship Council (FSC) to ensure the products meet sustainable standards.

Supporting local and organic food producers is another green choice. Shop at farmer's markets or join community-supported agriculture (CSA) programs to access fresh, locally grown produce. By opting for organic and sustainably farmed foods, you can reduce the use of harmful chemicals and support environmentally friendly farming practices.

Eco-Conscious Lifestyle

Living an eco-conscious lifestyle means being mindful of how your choices impact the environment. Consider adopting a plant-based diet or reducing your meat consumption to minimize greenhouse gas emissions associated with animal agriculture. Embrace minimalism and reduce waste by purchasing only what you need and donating or recycling items you no longer use.

Get involved in your community and support environmental initiatives. Join local cleanup events, participate in tree-planting activities, or volunteer with environmental organizations. By spreading awareness and educating others about the importance of sustainable living, you can inspire more people to make eco-friendly choices.

Incorporating sustainable habits, making green choices, and living an eco-conscious lifestyle is within reach for everyone. By implementing these practical tips, you can play a part in creating a more sustainable future for generations to come.

Eco-Friendly Changes at Home

When it comes to making eco-friendly changes, your home is a great place to start. By implementing environmentally conscious practices, you can turn your house into a green home. This not only benefits the planet but also contributes to your overall well-being.

One of the key aspects of creating a green home is investing in energy-efficient appliances. These appliances are designed to consume less energy while maintaining the same level of functionality. By replacing older, energy-guzzling appliances with their energy-efficient counterparts, you can significantly reduce your carbon footprint and save on utility bills.

Additionally, waste reduction strategies play a crucial role in making your home more eco-friendly. Implementing practices such as recycling, composting, and reducing single-use plastics can greatly minimize the amount of waste produced in your household. These small changes can have a big impact on the environment.

Creating a green living space is another important step towards eco-conscious living. This involves incorporating sustainable materials and practices into your home's design and décor. Opt for eco-friendly building materials, such as bamboo flooring or reclaimed wood, and consider using low VOC (volatile organic compound) paint for a healthier indoor environment.

By making eco-friendly changes at home, you not only contribute to a greener planet but also create a sustainable and healthy living space for you and your family. Let's explore more ways to embrace eco-conscious living in the following sections.

Eco-Friendly Changes in Transportation

When it comes to making eco-friendly changes, transportation plays a crucial role in our daily lives. By adopting sustainable commuting practices, utilizing public transportation, and embracing the rise of electric vehicles, we can significantly reduce our carbon footprint and contribute to a greener future.

Sustainable Commuting

Sustainable commuting refers to the use of environmentally-friendly modes of transportation for our daily travel needs. This includes walking, cycling, carpooling, and using electric scooters or bicycles. By opting for these alternatives, we can minimize greenhouse gas emissions, reduce traffic congestion, and improve air quality in our cities.

Moreover, incorporating sustainable commuting into our routine promotes an active lifestyle and provides multiple health benefits. Walking or cycling to work can improve cardiovascular fitness, reduce stress levels, and enhance overall well-being.

Public Transportation

Public transportation is a key component of sustainable commuting. Taking buses, trains, trams, or subways not only helps reduce individual carbon emissions but also contributes to the overall reduction in traffic congestion and fuel consumption.

Public transportation systems are designed to accommodate a large number of passengers, making them a cost-effective and efficient way to travel. By utilizing public transportation, we can save money on fuel, parking, and maintenance costs associated with private vehicles.

The Rise of Electric Vehicles

Electric vehicles (EVs) have gained popularity in recent years as a greener alternative to traditional gasoline-powered cars. EVs produce zero tailpipe emissions, significantly reducing air pollution and dependency on fossil fuels.

The advancement of technology has enhanced EV performance and availability, making them a viable option for sustainable transportation. With improved battery range and charging infrastructure, electric vehicles are becoming more accessible and convenient for everyday use. Additionally, governments and policymakers worldwide are providing incentives and promoting the adoption of electric vehicles to accelerate the transition to a cleaner transportation system.

In conclusion, by embracing sustainable commuting practices, utilizing public transportation, and considering electric vehicles, we can contribute to a more environmentally-friendly transportation system. These eco-friendly changes in transportation not only benefit the planet but also enhance our personal well-being and create a more sustainable future for generations to come.

Sustainable Food Choices

In today's world, making sustainable choices extends beyond just reducing waste and conserving energy. It also encompasses the food we eat and the impact it has on our planet. Adopting a plant-based diet, supporting local and organic produce, and actively reducing food waste are all crucial steps towards creating a more eco-conscious lifestyle.

The Benefits of a Plant-Based Diet

One of the most impactful sustainable food choices you can make is transitioning to a plant-based diet. By reducing or eliminating meat and animal products from your meals, you significantly reduce your carbon footprint. The livestock industry is a leading contributor to greenhouse gas emissions, deforestation, and water pollution. Embracing a plant-based diet not only helps combat these environmental issues but also promotes healthier eating habits.

Supporting Local and Organic Produce

Choosing local and organic produce is another essential element of sustainable food choices. When you buy from local farmers or farmers' markets, you support your community and reduce the carbon emissions associated with long-distance transportation. Additionally, opting for organic produce reduces exposure to harmful pesticides and promotes sustainable farming practices that prioritize soil health and biodiversity.

Strategies for Reducing Food Waste

Food waste is a significant environmental concern, contributing to greenhouse gas emissions and squandering valuable resources. By implementing strategies to reduce food waste, you can make a meaningful contribution towards a sustainable food system. Planning meals, storing food properly, and repurposing leftovers are just a few simple tactics that can help minimize waste and save money.

By making sustainable food choices, you actively participate in the global movement towards a more environmentally friendly and ethically conscious society. The power lies in your hands to shape a future where the food we consume nourishes both our bodies and our planet.

Sustainable Fashion and Shopping

In today's world, where our choices have a significant impact on the environment, embracing ethical fashion, secondhand shopping, and minimalism can play a crucial role in reducing consumer waste and promoting sustainability.

Ethical Fashion: Making a Positive Impact

Ethical fashion encompasses a range of practices that prioritize social and environmental responsibility. By supporting brands that prioritize fair wages, safe working conditions, and sustainable production methods, you can contribute to a more ethical and sustainable fashion industry. Additionally, ethical fashion encourages transparency in the supply chain, ensuring that the products we purchase are produced in an environmentally and socially conscious manner.

Secondhand Shopping: Giving New Life to Pre-Loved Pieces

Secondhand shopping is an excellent way to reduce our environmental footprint. By opting for pre-loved items, we can extend the lifecycle of clothing and accessories, minimizing the need for new production. Thrift stores, consignment shops, and online platforms offer a wide selection of unique and well-maintained pieces that allow us to express our individual style while being mindful of the planet.

Minimalism: Less is More

Minimalism is a mindset that promotes intentional living and reducing excessive consumerism. By adopting a minimalist approach to our wardrobe, we can focus on quality over quantity, investing in timeless pieces that withstand trends and transcend seasons. Owning fewer items also means creating less waste and reducing the demand for fast fashion, which often comes at the expense of ethical production practices.

By embracing ethical fashion, secondhand shopping, and minimalism, we can make sustainable choices that have a positive impact on both the fashion industry and the environment. Together, let's create a more conscious and responsible approach to fashion and shopping.

Becoming an Eco-Advocate

In today's world, environmental activism plays a crucial role in creating positive change. By becoming an eco-advocate, you can make a difference in your community and contribute to the well-being of our planet.

One of the key ways to become an eco-advocate is through community engagement. By actively participating in local environmental initiatives, joining groups and organizations dedicated to sustainability, and attending community events, you can connect with like-minded individuals, share ideas, and collaborate on impactful projects.

Spreading awareness is another powerful tool for driving change. Use your voice, both online and offline, to educate others about environmental issues and the importance of making eco-friendly choices. Sharing informative content, organizing workshops or seminars, and even starting conversations within your social circle can help raise awareness and inspire others to take action.

Remember, every small step towards a sustainable future counts. By embracing environmental activism, engaging with your community, and spreading awareness, you can become an influential eco-advocate, igniting positive change and encouraging others to make eco-friendly choices.

Chapter 16

Digital Literacy: Keeping Up with the Tech Tide

****

In this chapter, we will explore the exciting world of learning new technologies and the importance of staying relevant in a digital world. With technology advancing at a rapid pace, it's crucial to adapt and thrive in the ever-changing digital landscape.

Are you eager to expand your horizons and acquire new skills? Do you want to stay ahead in this fast-paced digital era? Well, you're in the right place. In the following sections, we will guide you through strategies to assess your technological knowledge, identify emerging technologies, set learning goals, choose the right learning resources, build a strong learning network, embrace continuous learning, overcome challenges, apply new technologies, and future-proof your skills.

By the end of this chapter, you'll be equipped with the tools and knowledge to navigate the digital world with confidence and finesse. So, let's dive in and embark on this exciting journey of learning and staying relevant in a digital world.

The Importance of Digital Literacy

In today's ever-evolving digital landscape, digital literacy is more important than ever. It refers to the skills and knowledge required to effectively navigate, utilize, and understand digital technologies and tools. Developing digital literacy is not only essential for personal use but also critical for professional growth and success.

Digital literacy empowers individuals to confidently engage with various digital platforms, applications, and devices. It enables them to navigate the vast online landscape, access information, and communicate effectively in a digital world. Whether it's using social media, conducting research, or leveraging digital tools for work, digital literacy plays a foundational role in these activities.

Moreover, digital literacy is an invaluable skillset in a technology-driven workplace. As industries continue to evolve, organizations increasingly rely on digital technologies to streamline processes, enhance productivity, and drive innovation. Individuals who possess strong digital literacy skills are better equipped to adapt to technological changes, leverage emerging tools, and stay relevant in their careers.

Digital literacy also plays a vital role in promoting critical thinking, problem-solving, and creativity. It enables individuals to analyze and evaluate digital information, discern credible sources, and make informed decisions. In a digital era characterized by a flood of information and potentially misleading content, digital literacy serves as a shield against misinformation and promotes responsible digital citizenship.

In summary, digital literacy is a fundamental skillset that empowers individuals to navigate the ever-evolving digital landscape. It enhances personal and professional growth, promotes critical thinking and problem-solving, and ensures individuals can confidently and responsibly engage with technology. As the digital landscape continues to evolve, investing in digital literacy is a wise decision that will yield long-term benefits.

Assessing Your Technological Knowledge

In this section, we will guide you through the process of assessing your current technological knowledge. It is essential to have a clear understanding of your strengths and areas for improvement in order to effectively navigate the ever-changing digital landscape.

Assessing your technological skills allows you to identify which areas require further development and prioritize learning new technologies that align with your goals. By taking stock of your abilities, you can create a focused plan for continuous learning that maximizes your growth.

During the assessment, consider evaluating your proficiency in various technologies, such as coding languages, digital marketing tools, data analysis software, or any other relevant areas. Identify the specific skills and knowledge you possess, and be honest about areas where you may have gaps.

It's also beneficial to assess how well you can apply your technological knowledge in real-life scenarios. Reflect on your past experiences and consider if you were able to effectively utilize your skills to solve problems or achieve desired outcomes. This self-reflection will provide valuable insights into your abilities.

Once you have assessed your technological knowledge, you can use this information to develop a personalized learning plan. By focusing on areas where you have identified gaps, you can set specific learning goals and select appropriate resources to enhance your skills.

Identifying Emerging Technologies

In today's fast-paced world, staying ahead of emerging technologies is essential to remain competitive and future-proof your skills. By identifying these emerging technologies, you can position yourself as an early adopter and gain a competitive edge in your industry.

So, how can you stay updated on the latest advancements? One effective way is to explore various sources such as industry reports and technology publications. These sources provide valuable insights and information about the latest breakthroughs and advancements in technology.

Industry reports offer in-depth analysis and forecasts of emerging technologies in specific sectors. They provide valuable market intelligence and help you understand how these technologies are expected to impact various industries. By studying industry reports, you can gain a comprehensive understanding of the potential future trends and opportunities.

Technology publications are another valuable source of information. These publications feature articles, news, and analysis on the latest advancements in various technological fields. They offer insights into cutting-edge technologies, emerging startups, and industry trends. Subscribing to technology publications and staying updated on their content will allow you to keep a finger on the pulse of the ever-changing tech landscape.

In addition to industry reports and technology publications, attending conferences and technology events can provide valuable networking opportunities and firsthand exposure to emerging technologies. These events often feature keynote speeches, panel discussions, and product demonstrations, offering insights and knowledge directly from industry experts.

By diligently exploring various sources, you can identify emerging technologies that align with your interests and professional goals. Anticipating future trends and being among the first to adopt new technologies will give you a competitive advantage, enhance your skill set, and open up new opportunities in your career.

Setting Learning Goals

In order to succeed in acquiring new technology skills, it is crucial to set clear and effective learning goals. By defining specific objectives and timelines, you can structure your learning journey and measure your progress along the way.

When setting your learning goals, it's important to consider both your personal and professional aspirations. Reflect on the skills you wish to acquire and the areas where you desire improvement. This self-reflection will guide you in identifying the technology skills that are most relevant to your needs.

Start by setting realistic goals that are specific, measurable, achievable, relevant, and time-bound - commonly known as SMART goals. For example, instead of simply stating, "I want to learn programming," refine your goal to "I want to learn Python programming by the end of next month."

Chunking your goals into manageable milestones is also beneficial. Break down larger goals into smaller, actionable tasks that can be accomplished within a specific timeframe. This approach helps you stay motivated and maintain a sense of progress as you check off each milestone along the way.

Personalize Your Learning

Everyone learns differently, so it's crucial to personalize your learning experience. Consider your preferred learning style - whether you're a visual learner who benefits from videos and diagrams, an auditory learner who thrives on podcasts and discussions, or a kinesthetic learner who learns best through hands-on activities.

Explore various resources that align with your learning style, such as online courses, tutorials, books, or interactive platforms. By selecting materials that resonate with you, you'll enhance your ability to absorb and retain information effectively.

Lastly, keep in mind that setbacks and challenges are a normal part of the learning process. Be patient with yourself and celebrate small victories along the way. With perseverance and a well-defined set of learning goals, you'll be well-equipped to develop the technology skills you desire.

Choosing the Right Learning Resources

When it comes to learning new technologies, having access to the right learning resources is crucial. With the vast array of online platforms, tutorials, and courses available, it can be overwhelming to find the most suitable options. But don't worry, we're here to help you navigate through the sea of choices.

Firstly, consider your learning style and preferences. Some people prefer interactive video tutorials, while others find written guides more effective. Knowing what type of resources resonate with you will make your learning journey more enjoyable and productive.

Next, take into account the credibility and reputation of the learning resources. Look for reliable sources that are known for providing accurate and up-to-date information. Check for reviews and recommendations from trusted sources or individuals within the technology field.

Additionally, consider the level of difficulty and the depth of coverage that the learning resources offer. If you're a beginner, you may want to start with introductory courses or tutorials that provide a solid foundation. If you're more advanced, you might be interested in specialized resources that delve deeper into specific topics.

Remember to also consider the accessibility and flexibility of the learning resources. Are they available online and accessible whenever you need them? Can you learn at your own pace? These factors are essential for ensuring a seamless and personalized learning experience.

Finally, take advantage of free trial periods or sample lessons when choosing paid resources. This allows you to evaluate the quality and compatibility of the learning materials before making a commitment.

By following these guidelines and considering your learning style, preferences, credibility, level of difficulty, access, and flexibility, you can choose learning resources that best suit your needs. So get ready to embark on your learning journey with confidence and discover the most effective resources for enhancing your technological skills!

Building a Learning Network

In the fast-paced tech industry, building a learning network is essential to stay ahead of the curve. Connecting with like-minded individuals, attending industry events, and participating in online forums can provide invaluable opportunities for growth and collaboration.

By joining a learning network, you can tap into a wealth of knowledge and expertise. Engaging with fellow tech enthusiasts allows you to exchange ideas, share insights, and seek advice on navigating the ever-changing technological landscape.

Attending industry events, such as conferences and meetups, enables you to network with industry professionals and stay up-to-date on the latest trends and innovations. These events often feature keynote speakers, workshops, and interactive sessions, providing a platform for learning and forging meaningful connections.

Moreover, active participation in online forums and communities dedicated to technology can offer constant opportunities for discussion, problem-solving, and knowledge exchange. These digital spaces enable you to connect with individuals from diverse backgrounds and gain diverse perspectives on various tech-related topics.

By building a strong learning network in the tech community, you not only expand your knowledge and skills but also increase your chances of discovering new career opportunities. Networking with professionals in your field can lead to collaborations, mentorships, and job prospects.

Investing time and effort in cultivating these connections can provide valuable insights, support, and motivation throughout your learning journey. So, don't hesitate to engage with the tech community and build a strong learning network.

Embracing Continuous Learning

Technology is constantly evolving, and in order to stay ahead, it is crucial to embrace continuous learning. Adopting a mindset of lifelong learning is essential for personal and professional growth in today's fast-paced digital landscape. By continuously acquiring new skills and staying up-to-date with the latest advancements, individuals can ensure they remain relevant in their respective fields.

To integrate learning into your daily routine, consider allocating dedicated time for self-improvement. Whether it's setting aside a few minutes each day or scheduling dedicated learning sessions, maintaining a proactive approach is key. By prioritizing continuous learning, you can stay ahead of the curve and adapt to changing technologies more effectively.

One effective strategy is to explore online learning platforms that offer a wide range of courses and tutorials. These resources can help you acquire new skills and enhance your knowledge in specific areas of interest. Additionally, joining relevant professional communities and attending industry events can provide opportunities for networking, mentorship, and shared learning experiences.

Furthermore, developing a growth mindset is crucial. Embrace challenges as opportunities for growth, and don't be afraid to step out of your comfort zone. Take on projects that push your boundaries and encourage you to acquire new skills. Remember, continuous learning is not just about acquiring knowledge; it's also about applying what you've learned in practical scenarios.

By embracing continuous learning, you can future-proof your skills and ensure you remain valuable in a rapidly changing digital environment. Lifelong learning is not just a trend—it's a necessity. Stay curious, stay proactive, and keep evolving to thrive in the ever-evolving world of technology.

Overcoming Learning Challenges

Learning new technologies can be an exciting but challenging journey. It's common to encounter obstacles along the way that can make the learning process feel overwhelming. However, with the right strategies and mindset, you can overcome these challenges and adapt to technology with confidence.

Dealing with Information Overload

One of the most common learning challenges is dealing with information overload. As you explore new technologies, you may come across a vast amount of information, tutorials, and resources. To overcome this challenge, it's important to break down your learning into manageable chunks:

Focus on one technology or concept at a time.

Set specific learning goals for each session.

Organize your resources and create a learning schedule.

By following these steps, you can avoid feeling overwhelmed and ensure a more focused and effective learning experience.

Navigating Steep Learning Curves

Some technologies may have steep learning curves, making it difficult to grasp the concepts and skills quickly. To navigate these challenges, consider the following strategies:

Break down complex concepts into smaller, more manageable components.

Practice regularly to reinforce your understanding.

Seek support from online communities or forums dedicated to the technology you're learning.

Remember that persistence and patience are key when navigating steep learning curves.

Celebrate small victories along the way, as they are milestones towards your overall progress.

Embracing a Growth Mindset

Adapting to new technologies requires embracing a growth mindset. Instead of viewing challenges as roadblocks, see them as opportunities for growth and learning. With a growth mindset, you are more likely to overcome obstacles and persevere in your learning journey. Here are a few ways to cultivate a growth mindset:

Embrace failure as a learning opportunity.

Stay curious and maintain a positive attitude towards learning.

Set realistic expectations and be kind to yourself during the learning process.

By adopting a growth mindset, you can build resilience and a willingness to adapt to new technologies.

Learning challenges are a natural part of the process, but they shouldn't discourage you from pursuing your goals. By implementing these strategies and developing a proactive approach to learning, you can overcome challenges, adapt to new technologies, and thrive in the ever-changing digital landscape.

Applying New Technologies

In today's fast-paced world, learning new technologies is not enough. The true value lies in applying the skills and knowledge you have acquired. In this section, we will explore practical ways to implement new technologies in both your personal and professional life, allowing you to make the most of your newfound expertise.

When it comes to applying technologies, start by identifying areas where these innovations can have a significant impact. Consider how you can leverage these technologies to streamline processes, enhance productivity, and improve outcomes. Whether it's adopting automation tools in your workflow or utilizing data analytics to drive better decision-making, the possibilities are endless.

Moreover, don't shy away from experimenting with different technologies. Embrace a mindset of curiosity and innovation, and don't be afraid to step out of your comfort zone. Trying new things and pushing the boundaries of what is possible can lead to breakthroughs and unexpected opportunities.

In your personal life, explore how you can integrate these technologies to enhance your daily routines or pursue your hobbies. From smart home devices that make your life easier to creative applications that fuel your passion, the applications of technology extend far beyond the workplace.

Additionally, collaborative projects can be a great way to apply your new skills. Partner with colleagues or fellow enthusiasts to work on real-world projects that allow you to put your knowledge into practice. By engaging in hands-on experiences, you can solidify your understanding and gain valuable insights from others.

Remember that applying new technologies is an ongoing process. As technologies continue to evolve, it is essential to stay up-to-date and adapt accordingly. Embrace continuous learning and actively seek out opportunities to expand your technological capabilities.

Case Study: The Impact of Applying New Technologies

To illustrate the power of applying technologies, let's explore a real-life example. ABC Company, a leading manufacturer, faced challenges in their production line, resulting in inefficiencies and increased costs. By implementing robotic automation and machine learning algorithms, they were able to streamline their operations and reduce errors significantly.

The integration of these technologies enabled ABC Company to automate repetitive tasks, optimize production schedules, and predict maintenance needs, resulting in improved efficiency, reduced downtime, and higher customer satisfaction. By applying these new technologies strategically, ABC Company transformed their operations and gained a competitive advantage in the market.

By applying new technologies effectively, you can unlock countless opportunities and drive meaningful change. The key lies in identifying where these technologies can make a difference, being open to experimentation, and continuously expanding your knowledge and skills. Embrace the power of applying technologies and unlock your full potential in today's digital age.

Future-Proofing You're Skills

In today's rapidly evolving digital landscape, future-proofing your skills has become more essential than ever. As technological advancements continue to reshape industries, it is crucial to stay ahead of the curve to remain competitive in the job market.

One of the key strategies for future-proofing your skills is to anticipate and adapt to future technological advancements. Stay curious and keep a pulse on emerging technologies. By actively seeking new learning opportunities and staying updated on the latest trends, you can position yourself as a valuable asset in your field.

Remaining adaptable is another crucial aspect of future-proofing your skills. Embrace change and be open to acquiring new knowledge and abilities. By continuously expanding your skill set and being flexible in your approach, you can navigate the evolving digital landscape with confidence.

In summary, future-proofing your skills requires a proactive mindset of continuous learning and adaptability. By anticipating and adapting to future technological advancements, actively seeking new learning opportunities, and remaining flexible in your approach, you can ensure your skills remain relevant and in-demand in an ever-changing digital world.

Chapter 17

Health is Wealth: Prioritizing
Physical Well-being

*****

Understanding the Importance of Physical Well-being

As one re-aches their thirties, focusing on physical we-llness becomes e-ven more crucial. The body unde-rgoes alterations during this phase whe-re maintenance is e-ssential. By dedicating effort into one-'s physical condition, numerous advantages can materialize- that favorably affect all realms of existe-nce. While the body may not re-cover as quickly as before, staying active- and nourishing it properly can help offset such transformations. Small adjustme-nts like including more whole foods and mode-rate exercise- into a daily routine go a long way. Prioritizing well-being e-nsures continued success pe-rsonally and professionally well into the future-. Overall health allows fully engaging with re-sponsibilities as well as loved one-s.

Making physical health a top conce-rn offers various rewards exte-nding beyond just your bodily functions. Taking the nece-ssary steps to care for your physical form means you'll be-better prepare-d to cope with life's stresse-s, enhance your disposition, and fee-l more energize-d. Workouts that occur routinely cause the brain to ge-nerate endorphins, the- so-called "feel-good" che-micals that can aid the battle against anxiety and gloomine-ss. When one dedicate-s time to moving the muscles and raising the- heart rate, these- natural painkillers are rele-ased, resulting in a sense- of lightness and calmness. Overall we-llness improves as both spirit and flesh are- tended to hand in hand.

While the-re is certainly a link betwe-en exercise-, diet, and physical well-being, this re-lationship is quite complex with many intertwining factors. Consiste-ntly participating in physical activity can aid in maintaining a healthy body weight and also build up muscular and skele-tal strength over time. Workouts stre-ngthen the cardiovascular system lowe-ring risks for serious health issues like- heart disease, hype-rtension, and chronic diseases. Exe-rcise has additional perks too - it enhance-s immune function making the body more robust against common illne-sses. Moving your body routinely has widespre-ad benefits beyond physical shape- and appearance. Overall fitne-ss influences health in se-veral ways although other lifestyle- and genetic aspects still contribute- largely to wellness outcome-s.

Furthermore, physical health and mental well-being are intertwined. Research has shown that exercise can improve cognitive function, memory, and focus. By engaging in regular physical activity, you are not only taking care of your body but also benefiting your mind.

Understanding the- connection betwee-n physical condition and psychological wellness is vital in grasping why emphasizing bodily we-llbeing is indispensable in your thirtie-s. By dedicating time and effort to work out routine-ly, eat nutritious dishes, and get e-nough rest, you are laying the groundwork for a he-althier and more joyful forthcoming. While making yourse-lf and your future wellbeing a priority through re-gular exercise, nutritious e-ating, and sufficient sleep, will sure-ly aid in reducing stress leve-ls and boosting your mental state, which can otherwise-become threate-ned if such necessitie-s are ignored in the busy-ne-ss of everyday life. Prioritizing your we-llbeing now sets up favorable circumstance-s for continued health in the ye-ars ahead.

Creating he-althy habits for physical well-being require-s long-term dedication. While the-advantages may not surface immediate-ly or be distinct at first, consistently prioritizing your physical health pre-sently will construct a robust foundation supporting a lively, prosperous future-. Your body is building strength gradually over days and wee-ks through repeated e-xercise and good nutrition. Stay encourage-d by small successes along the way, like- having more energy for family time- or sleeping more soundly. Visualizing your be-st self years down the road can inspire- commitment to daily choices aiding a healthy life-style. Though progress may fee-l slow, remember that ste-ady, persistent effort is more- impactful than occasional bursts of motivation. Make physical wellness a priority that nourishe-s your entire being.

A Beginner's Guide to Prioritizing Health in Your 30s

care of your health becomes increasingly important as you enter your 30s. Here's a simple guide to help you prioritize your well-being during this significant phase of life.

Step 1: Self-Reflection and Goal Setting

Reflect on your current health status and identify areas that need improvement.

Set specific health goals, such as adopting a healthier diet, incorporating regular exercise, or managing stress more effectively.

Step 2: Assess Your Lifestyle

Evaluate your daily habits, including diet, exercise, sleep patterns, and stress levels.

Identify areas where small, positive changes can be made to improve your overall well-being.

Step 3: Adopt a Balanced Diet

Focus on incorporating a variety of nutrient-rich foods, including fruits, vegetables, lean proteins, and whole grains, into your daily meals.

Limit the intake of processed foods, sugary snacks, and excessive amounts of caffeine and alcohol.

Step 4: Establish an Exercise Routine

Find physical activities that you enjoy and can easily integrate into your schedule, such as brisk walking, yoga, or cycling.

Aim for at least 150 minutes of moderate-intensity exercise per week, as recommended by health authorities.

Step 5: Prioritize Mental Health

Practice stress-reducing activities, such as mindfulness meditation, deep breathing exercises, or engaging in hobbies that bring you joy.

Seek professional help if you are experiencing persistent feelings of anxiety, depression, or overwhelming stress.

Step 6: Schedule Regular Health Check-ups

Visit your healthcare provider for routine screenings, vaccinations, and preventive health services.

Discuss any concerns or symptoms you may have and follow through with recommended follow-up care.

Step 7: Get Sufficient Sleep

Prioritize getting 7-9 hours of quality sleep each night to support overall health and well-being.

Establish a relaxing bedtime routine and create a comfortable sleeping environment to promote restful sleep.

Step 8: Limit Sedentary Behavior

Break up long periods of sitting by incorporating regular movement and stretches throughout your day.

Consider using a standing desk or taking short walks during work breaks to reduce the impact of prolonged sitting.

Step 9: Cultivate Supportive Relationships

Surround yourself with positive influences and nurturing relationships that contribute to your mental and emotional well-being.

Seek out social connections and engage in activities that foster a sense of belonging and community.

Step 10: Practice Mindful Eating

Pay attention to your body's hunger and fullness cues, and aim to eat meals and snacks mindfully, free from distractions.

Avoid emotional eating and practice portion control to maintain a healthy relationship with food.

Step 11: Stay Hydrated

Drink an adequate amount of water throughout the day to support optimal bodily functions and overall health.

Limit the consumption of sugary beverages and opt for water as your primary source of hydration.

Step 12: Embrace Regular Self-Care

Dedicate time for self-care activities that promote relaxation and rejuvenation, such as taking a warm bath, reading a book, or engaging in a hobby.

Prioritizing self-care is essential for managing stress and maintaining a healthy work-life balance.

Prioritizing your health in your 30s sets the foundation for a vibrant and fulfilling life. By following this guide, you can take meaningful steps towards improving your physical, mental, and emotional well-being. Remember that small, consistent changes can lead to significant improvements in your overall health and quality of life.

Chapter 18

Fitness Evolution: Tailoring Your Exercise Routine

****

Designing an Effective Exercise Routine:

When it comes to creating healthy habits for physical well-being, designing an effective exercise routine is key. This section will guide you through the process of assessing your current fitness level, setting realistic goals, exploring different types of exercises, and creating a workout schedule that fits into your daily routine.

Firstly, it's important to assess your current fitness level. Take some time to evaluate your current level of physical activity, strength, and endurance. This will help you determine where you are starting from and what areas you may need to focus on.

Next, set realistic goals for yourself. Consider what you want to achieve through exercise, whether it's improving cardiovascular health, building strength and muscle tone, increasing flexibility, or simply maintaining overall fitness. By setting specific and achievable goals, you will have a clear direction and purpose for your exercise routine.

Explore different types of exercises to find what suits you best. There are countless options available, such as cardiovascular exercises like running, swimming, cycling, or group fitness classes. Strength training exercises using free weights or resistance bands can also be beneficial in building muscle tone and increasing metabolism. Additionally, consider incorporating activities that promote flexibility and balance, such as yoga or Pilates. Experiment with different activities to find those that you enjoy and that align with your fitness goals.

Once you have identified your preferred exercises, it's time to create a workout schedule that fits into your daily routine. Consider factors such as time availability, convenience, and personal preferences. Determine how many days a week you want to dedicate to exercise and how much time you can commit to each session. It can be helpful to schedule your workouts in advance and treat them as non-negotiable appointments with yourself.

Remember to start slowly and gradually increase the intensity and duration of your workouts over time. This will allow your body to adapt and reduce the risk of injury. Listen to your body and make adjustments as needed, such as incorporating rest days or modifying exercises to accommodate any limitations or injuries.

Finally, hold yourself accountable and stay motivated on your fitness journey. Consider tracking your progress through a journal or using fitness apps that can help monitor your workouts, set reminders, and provide feedback. Additionally, finding an accountability partner or joining a fitness community can provide support, encouragement, and a sense of camaraderie along the way.

By designing an effective exercise routine tailored to your needs and preferences, you will be on your way to improving your physical well-being and achieving your fitness goals.

Creating a Personalized Exercise Routine for Optimal Fitness

When it comes to establishing healthy habits for physical well-being, crafting a tailored exercise routine is crucial. This section will guide you through evaluating your current fitness level, setting achievable goals, exploring diverse exercise types, and structuring a workout regimen that integrates seamlessly into your daily life.

Assessing Your Current Fitness Level

Begin by assessing your existing level of physical activity, strength, and endurance. This evaluation will provide insight into your starting point and areas that require attention.

Setting Realistic Goals

Define achievable fitness goals based on your preferences and aspirations, whether it's enhancing cardiovascular health, building strength and muscle tone, improving flexibility, or maintaining overall fitness.

Exploring Exercise Varieties

Cardiovascular Exercises:

Beginner: Walking or cycling for 20-30 minutes, three times a week.

Intermediate: Jogging or swimming for 30-45 minutes, four times a week.

Advanced: High-intensity interval training (HIIT) sessions for 45-60 minutes, five times a week.

Strength Training:

Beginner: Bodyweight exercises (squats, push-ups, lunges) 2-3 times a week.

Intermediate: Incorporate resistance bands or free weights into a full-body workout routine 3-4 times a week.

Advanced: Weightlifting sessions targeting major muscle groups 4-5 times a week.

Flexibility and Balance Activities:

All Levels: Add yoga or Pilates sessions 1-2 times a week to enhance flexibility and core strength.

Creating a Workout Schedule

Design a weekly exercise plan that suits your availability and preferences. Here's a sample schedule for each fitness level:

Beginner:

Cardio: 3 days a week

Strength Training: 2 days a week

Flexibility: 1 day a week

Intermediate:

Cardio: 4 days a week

Strength Training: 3 days a week

Flexibility: 2 days a week

Advanced:

Cardio: 5 days a week

Strength Training: 4-5 days a week

Flexibility: 2-3 days a week

Progression and Adaptation

Gradually increase the intensity and duration of your workouts over time. Listen to your body, incorporate rest days, and modify exercises as needed.

Fitness Plan for a Man and a Woman in Their 30s

Beginner Level (0-3 Months)

Cardiovascular Exercise:

Man: Start with brisk walking or cycling for 20-30 minutes, three times a week.

Woman: Begin with moderate-intensity swimming or stationary cycling for 20-30 minutes, three times a week.

Strength Training:

Man: Bodyweight exercises (e.g., squats, push-ups, lunges) 2-3 times a week.

Woman: Incorporate bodyweight exercises and resistance band workouts 2-3 times a week.

Flexibility Training:

Both: Introduce beginner-level yoga or Pilates sessions once a week to improve flexibility and balance.

Intermediate Level (3-6 Months)

Cardiovascular Exercise:

Man: Progress to jogging or light running for 30-45 minutes, four times a week.

Woman: Increase intensity with longer swimming or cycling sessions for 30-45 minutes, four times a week.

Strength Training:

Man: Transition to resistance band or free weight exercises targeting major muscle groups 3-4 times a week.

Woman: Incorporate free weight exercises and bodyweight workouts 3-4 times a week.

Flexibility Training:

Both: Add yoga or Pilates sessions twice a week to enhance flexibility and core strength.

Advanced Level (6+ Months)

Cardiovascular Exercise:

Man: Engage in high-intensity interval training (HIIT) sessions for 45-60 minutes, five times a week.

Woman: Incorporate longer and more intense swimming or cycling sessions for 45-60 minutes, five times a week.

Strength Training:

Man: Implement weightlifting sessions targeting specific muscle groups 4-5 times a week.

Woman: Progress to more challenging weightlifting sessions 4-5 times a week.

Flexibility Training:

Both: Increase yoga or Pilates sessions to 2-3 times a week for advanced flexibility and core strength.

By customizing an effective exercise routine tailored to your individual needs and fitness level, you can progress toward optimal physical well-being and accomplish your fitness aspirations. Remember, consistency, progression, and adaptation are pivotal to realizing long-term fitness success.

Chapter 19

Nutritional Nuances:
Eating for Your Age

******

Nurturing Nutritional Habits for Optimal Health:
In this section, we dive deeper into the importance of nutrition in maintaining physical well-being and explore strategies for incorporating healthy eating habits into your lifestyle. Understanding the impact of nutrition on energy levels and long-term health is crucial in ensuring that you have the vitality and stamina to thrive in your thirties.

Balanced Diets and Portion Control:
One of the key principles of nurturing nutritional habits is maintaining a balanced diet. This means consuming a variety of nutrient-rich foods from all food groups, including fruits, vegetables, whole grains, lean proteins, and healthy fats. By having a balanced diet, you ensure that your body receives the necessary vitamins, minerals, and macronutrients it needs to function optimally.

Portion control is another important aspect of maintaining a healthy diet. It involves being mindful of the quantity of food you consume and avoiding excessive portions. Pay attention to your body's hunger and fullness cues to prevent overeating. By practicing portion control, you can maintain a healthy weight, prevent chronic diseases, and avoid feeling sluggish or bloated.

Mindful Eating:
Incorporating mindfulness into your eating habits can have a profound impact on your overall health and well-being. Mindful eating involves paying attention to the sensory experience of eating, such as the taste, texture, and smell of food. It also involves being aware of your body's hunger and fullness signals.

To practice mindful eating, take time to savor each bite, chew slowly, and fully engage with the flavors and textures of your food. Avoid distractions like screens or work while eating, as they can lead to mindless overeating. By cultivating a mindful eating practice, you can develop a healthier relationship with food, improve digestion, and make better food choices.

Incorporating Healthy Eating Habits:
In order to incorporate healthy eating habits into your lifestyle, it's important to start small and make gradual changes. Begin by setting realistic goals and focusing on one aspect of your diet at a time. It may be incorporating more fruits and vegetables into your meals, reducing your intake of processed foods, or cooking meals at home instead of relying on takeout.

Meal planning and preparation can also be helpful in maintaining healthy eating habits. Take the time to plan your meals for the week, create a shopping list, and prepare nutritious meals in advance. This reduces the reliance on unhealthy convenience foods and ensures that you have healthy options readily available.

Additionally, seeking out resources such as cookbooks, online recipes, or nutrition apps can provide inspiration and guidance on creating nutritious meals. Experiment with new flavors and ingredients to keep your meals interesting and enjoyable.

Remember that developing healthy eating habits is a journey, and it's okay to have occasional indulgences or setbacks. The key is to approach nutrition with a balanced mindset and make sustainable changes that align with your long-term health goals.

In your thirties, good eating habits can make you healthy. How? By eating balanced meals, proper portions, and focusing on what you eat can greatly boost your health. This can lead to a better quality of life. What else is important? Good sleep.

Never underestimate the power of good sleep. It helps you heal and think clearly. When you hit your thirties, regular sleep becomes vital. So, what's the deal with sleep?

First, get a sleep schedule.

Try waking up and sleeping at the same time every day. Doing it every weekend too is a smart move. This way, your body gets ready for sleep and wake up times, making you sleep better.

Next, create a sleep haven.

Your bedroom should be cool, quiet, and dark. What helps? Blackout curtains, earplugs, a white noise machine to block out the noise. A good mattress and comfy bedding can also help.

Finally, take some time to relax before bed.

Find calming activities like reading a book, doing yoga, taking a warm bath, or chilling with some smooth tracks. These can ease your mind and prepare you for a good snooze.

Avoiding Stimulants before Bedtime:

To ensure a good night's sleep, it is important to avoid stimulants such as caffeine, nicotine, and alcohol close to bedtime. These substances can interfere with your ability to fall asleep or stay asleep throughout the night. Instead, opt for calming herbal teas or warm milk if you find that you need something soothing before bed.

Minimizing Screen Time:

Electronic devices emit blue light that can disrupt your sleep patterns by suppressing the production of melatonin, a hormone that regulates sleep-wake cycles. It is advisable to limit the use of electronic devices, such as smartphones and tablets, for at least an hour before bedtime. Instead, engage in relaxing activities that do not involve screens, such as reading a book or practicing meditation.

Implementing these strategies for prioritizing sleep and rest can significantly improve your physical well-being. By establishing a consistent sleep routine, creating a sleep-friendly environment, implementing relaxation techniques, avoiding stimulants before bedtime, and minimizing screen time, you can achieve deep, restorative sleep that supports your overall health and wellness Maintaining Consistency and Accountability

In order to sustain healthy habits for physical well-being, it is crucial to develop strategies that will keep you motivated and overcome any obstacles that may arise on your journey. Consistency is key when it comes to making lasting changes in your lifestyle. Here are some effective techniques to help you maintain consistency and hold yourself accountable:

1. Make Simple Goals: Decide your health and fitness aims, like losing pounds, becoming stronger, or boosting stamina. Your aims should be SMART: Specific, Measurable, Achievable, Relevant, and Time-based. Jot them down and check them often. This keeps you driven and on track.

2. Plan Your Time: Add workouts and well-being tasks in your day-to-day or weekly plan. Consider them as fixed dates with yourself. By setting fixed workout times, you'll give them top priority, making them a regular part of your day.

3. Discover Fun Activities: Try out various exercises to find ones that you love. It could be walking, dancing, yoga, water sports, or lifting weights, choose things that make you happy. If you really enjoy what you're doing, you'll stay committed to it.

4. Follow Your Growth: Monitor your workouts, diet, and overall progress. You can do this through writing, or mobile apps that let you log your efforts and check your triumphs. Watching your growth not only holds you responsible but also gives you a feeling of success as you witness your journey.

5. Reward Your Achievements: Mark mini-goals along your fitness path to celebrate. Give yourself a treat when you hit these mini-goals, perhaps indulging in a self-care routine. These mini celebrations keep you encouraged and support the healthy habits you're building.

6. Get a Support Buddy: Find a friend, a family member, or even a fitness mate with similar health aims. A buddy checking on you can give you an extra push when you're close to slipping. Share your journey with them, the good and the bad.

7. Enter a Health Group or Exercise Class: You could start an exercise class, join group training, or even enter an online wellness group. Being around others with the same goals can give you a friendly, supportive atmosphere.

8. Reflect Often: Regular self-thinking is a must. Review your progress often. Acknowledge the good parts and the ones needing more work. Crack down on things slowing you down. With regular reflection, you can adjust and stay focused.

Remember, good habits need constant work and patience. Some days may seem hard, but don't give up on your long-term health. Using these methods, and having systems to keep check, helps you maintain good habits for many years.

Meal Plan for Men in Their 30s (2200kcal):

Day 1:

Breakfast: Scrambled eggs with whole grain toast and avocado slices
Snack: Greek yogurt with mixed berries
Lunch: Grilled chicken salad with mixed greens, cherry tomatoes, and balsamic vinaigrette
Snack: Apple slices with almond butter
Dinner: Baked salmon with quinoa and steamed broccoli

Day 2:

Breakfast: Oatmeal with sliced banana and chia seeds
Snack: Cottage cheese with pineapple chunks
Lunch: Turkey and avocado wrap with whole grain tortilla and side salad
Snack: Handful of almonds
Dinner: Lean beef stir-fry with bell peppers and brown rice

Day 3:

Breakfast: Whole grain English muffin with peanut butter and sliced strawberries
Snack: Carrot and celery sticks with hummus
Lunch: Quinoa salad with chickpeas, cucumber, and feta cheese
Snack: Mixed nuts
Dinner: Grilled shrimp with quinoa and roasted asparagus

Meal Plan for Women in Their 30s (1800 kcal):

Day 1:

Breakfast: Smoothie with spinach, banana, almond milk, and protein powder
Snack: Sliced cucumber with hummus
Lunch: Lentil soup with a side of whole grain bread
Snack: Mixed berries with a dollop of Greek yogurt
Dinner: Grilled tofu with roasted sweet potatoes and sautéed kale

Day 2:

Breakfast: Whole grain toast with mashed avocado and poached eggs
Snack: Cottage cheese with peach slices
Lunch: Quinoa and black bean salad with diced bell peppers and lime vinaigrette
Snack: Handful of walnuts
Dinner: Baked chicken breast with quinoa and steamed green beans

Day 3:

Breakfast: Overnight oats with almond milk, chia seeds, and mixed berries
Snack: Sliced bell peppers with hummus
Lunch: Grilled vegetable wrap with whole grain tortilla and side salad
Snack: Greek yogurt with honey
Dinner: Baked cod with quinoa and roasted Brussels sprouts

These meal plans are designed to provide a balance of essential nutrients, including lean proteins, healthy fats, complex carbohydrates, and a variety of vitamins and minerals, tailored to the dietary needs of men and women in their 30s.

Chapter 20

Mental Clarity:
Sustaining Your Mental Health
****

Getting a Grip on Mental Well-being in Your Thirties:
Your thirties are key to focusing more on mental health. This is a time when you face many life changes. By getting to know what mental health involves and the possible issues, you're more able to keep healthy.

What is Mental Health?:
Your mental health has to do with your feelings, thoughts, and interactions. It shapes how you deal with problems, make choices, and bond with others. It's part of sailing through life's high and low points. Putting your mental health first means constantly looking after your emotional and psychological condition for complete well-being.

Common Problems to Watch Out For:
Moving into your thirties, different things might lower your mental health. Here are some typical situations:

1. Work stress: Juggling a growing job role, handling work strains, confusion, and aiming to reach career goals could affect your mental state.
2. Changes in personal life: Starting or finishing relationships, getting married, or becoming a parent, the adjustments in personal ties during this phase can invite fulfillment and tension.
3. Social pressure: Society often sets bars for milestones like owning property, being financially secure, or settling down. Missing these societal ideals can stir feelings of lack or worry.
4. Physical changes: Hormonal fluctuations, changes in metabolism, and the impact of aging on the body can affect mental health. Accepting and adapting to these changes is crucial for maintaining well-being.

Breaking the Stigma:
Despite progress in raising awareness about mental health, stigma still surrounds seeking support for mental health issues. It's essential to break down these barriers and prioritize seeking help when needed. Remember that mental health challenges are common and treatable, and seeking support is a sign of strength rather than weakness.

Here are some strategies for breaking the stigma and seeking support:

1. Educate yourself: Learn more about mental health, different conditions, and available treatments. Understanding that mental health is a normal part of life can help reduce stigma.
2. Talk openly: Share your experiences and challenges with trusted friends or family members. By opening up, you not only break the stigma but also encourage others to do the same.
3. Seek professional help: If you're facing persistent or overwhelming mental health challenges, consider reaching out to a mental health professional such as a therapist or counselor. They can provide guidance, support, and evidence-based treatments tailored to your needs.

Remember, prioritizing mental health is a journey that requires ongoing attention and self-care. By understanding mental health, recognizing common challenges, and breaking the stigma, you can take proactive steps towards maintaining your well-being and thriving in your thirties and beyond Developing Emotional Intelligence

Emotional intelligence plays a crucial role in personal growth and overall well-being. It involves the ability to identify, understand, and manage your emotions effectively, as well as recognize and empathize with the emotions of others. Developing emotional intelligence in your thirties can greatly enhance your relationships, career success, and overall life satisfaction. To begin developing emotional intelligence, it's important to become aware of your own emotions. Take the time to reflect on how you feel in different situations and why certain emotions arise. By understanding your own emotional patterns, you can better navigate them and respond appropriately.

Next, practice managing your emotions in a healthy way. This involves recognizing when negative emotions arise and finding constructive ways to cope with them. Instead of suppressing or lashing out at these emotions, try techniques such as deep breathing, journaling, or engaging in activities that bring you joy and relaxation.

Building empathy and understanding towards others is another key component of emotional intelligence. Empathy allows you to put yourself in someone else's shoes and truly understand their perspective and emotions. This skill can greatly enhance your relationships by fostering deeper connections and effective communication.

To develop empathy, actively listen to others without judgment and strive to understand their experiences and feelings. Practice putting aside your own biases and assumptions, and genuinely seek to understand the thoughts and emotions behind someone's words or actions. This will help build trust and strengthen your relationships.

In addition to practicing empathy, it's important to cultivate self-compassion. Treat yourself with kindness and understanding when you make mistakes or face challenges. By being kind to yourself, you'll be better equipped to extend that kindness to others.

Developing emotional intelligence is an ongoing process that requires self-reflection, practice, and patience. As you navigate your thirties, prioritize strengthening your emotional intelligence skills. The benefits will extend far beyond this decade, shaping a more fulfilling and harmonious life Nurturing Mental Well-being

In this section, we will explore various self-care strategies that can promote mental well-being and enhance overall happiness and fulfillment in your thirties. It is crucial to prioritize your mental health and make conscious efforts to take care of yourself. By incorporating these practices into your daily life, you can cultivate a sense of inner peace and resilience.

1. Practice Self-Compassion:

Self-compassion involves treating yourself with kindness, understanding, and acceptance, especially during challenging times. Instead of being overly critical or judgmental towards yourself, practice self-compassion by offering yourself words of encouragement and support. Treat yourself as you would treat a dear friend or loved one.

2. Engage in Mindfulness:

Mindfulness is the practice of being fully present in the moment, without judgment. By cultivating mindfulness, you can develop a greater awareness of your thoughts, emotions, and sensations, allowing you to respond to them with composure and clarity. Incorporate mindfulness into your daily life through activities such as meditation, deep breathing exercises, or simply taking a few moments to pause and observe your surroundings.

3. Prioritize Self-Care:

Self-care refers to activities that nourish and replenish your physical, emotional, and mental well-being. It is essential to carve out time in your busy schedule for activities that bring you joy and relaxation. This could include engaging in hobbies you love, spending time in nature, practicing yoga or exercise, reading a book, or pampering yourself with a soothing bath or spa treatment. Find what brings you comfort and make it a priority.

4. Develop Healthy Coping Mechanisms:

Life can be filled with stressors and challenges, but having healthy coping mechanisms can help you navigate them with greater ease. Identify activities or practices that help you manage stress effectively. This could include journaling, talking to a trusted friend or therapist, engaging in creative outlets like painting or playing an instrument, or practicing relaxation techniques such as progressive muscle relaxation or guided imagery.

5. Set Boundaries:

Setting boundaries is crucial for maintaining mental well-being. Learn to prioritize your needs and communicate them assertively to others. Establish boundaries around the use of technology, work-life balance, and personal relationships. Remember that saying "no" when necessary and setting limits on your time and energy are not selfish acts but rather acts of self-respect.

6. Cultivate Positive Relationships:

Surround yourself with positive, supportive individuals who lift you up and bring out the best in you. Foster deep connections with friends, family, or mentors who share similar values and aspirations. Engaging in meaningful conversations and spending quality time with loved ones can greatly contribute to your mental well-being.

Remember, prioritizing your mental well-being is not a selfish act but an essential aspect of leading a fulfilling life. By nurturing your mental health through self-care practices, mindfulness, setting boundaries, and cultivating positive relationships, you can fortify yourself against stress and adversity. Make it a priority to invest in your mental well-being as you embark on this transformative decade Enhancing Resilience and Coping Mechanisms

Building resilience is crucial for navigating the challenges and setbacks that come with life in your thirties. By developing healthy coping mechanisms for stress and anxiety, you can cultivate a positive mindset to overcome adversity.

1. Acceptance and Adaptability:

Practice accepting situations that are beyond your control.

Focus on adapting to new circumstances and finding solutions instead of dwelling on the problem.

Embrace flexibility and open-mindedness to navigate unexpected changes.

2. Reframing Negative Thoughts:

Challenge negative thoughts and replace them with more positive and empowering ones.

 Use affirmations and positive self-talk to reframe your mindset.

 Cultivate gratitude by focusing on the things you are thankful for.

3. Seeking Support:

Reach out to friends, family, or support groups when facing challenges.

Building a strong support system can provide guidance, encouragement, and different perspectives.

Think about seeking therapy or counseling. It can help you handle emotional issues and learn useful coping strategies.

Spend time on self-care:

Make time for things that make you feel good and energized. Try enjoyable hobbies or exercise. Spend quality time with the people you love.

Don't forget to set boundaries. You need them to protect your mind and prevent burnout.

Next, learn how to cope in a healthy way:

Find good ways to handle stress and worry, like deep breathing or writing a journal. Try physical activities like yoga or running. These can help you relieve tension and feel happy.

You may need to talk to a professional. They can show you coping skills that will help you the most.

Focus on a learning mindset:

See challenges as chances to grow. Consider setbacks as lessons, not losses. Try to look back at past experiences and learn from them.

By learning to bounce back and finding healthy ways to cope, you'll be ready for the challenges your thirties will bring. You'll get through hard times, keep your mental health, and keep growing personally and professionally. Don't be afraid to seek professional help if you need it.

Recognizing when professional help may be beneficial is an important part of prioritizing your mental health and emotional well-being. While self-care strategies and coping mechanisms can be helpful, there are times when the support of a trained professional is necessary. Understanding the different types of mental health professionals and their specialties can guide you in finding the right form of therapy or counseling for your needs.

Psychiatrists are medical doctors who specialize in diagnosing and treating mental illnesses. They can prescribe medication to help manage symptoms and may also provide therapy. If you suspect that you have a mental illness that may require medication, consulting with a psychiatrist is essential.

Psychologists are trained professionals who provide therapy to individuals, couples, families, and groups. They are not medical doctors and cannot prescribe medication. However, they often specialize in specific areas such as cognitive-behavioral therapy (CBT), dialectical behavior therapy (DBT), or trauma-focused therapy. Psychologists can help you explore your thoughts, emotions, and behaviors to improve your mental well-being.

Licensed counselors or therapists come from various backgrounds and may hold degrees in psychology, counseling, social work, or related fields. They provide counseling services to individuals, couples, and families, focusing on emotional well-being, personal growth, and relationship issues. Depending on their training and specialization, therapists may incorporate different therapeutic approaches into their practice.

When seeking professional help, it's important to choose a provider whose expertise aligns with your specific needs. Consider factors such as their experience, approach to therapy, and any specialized training they have received. It may be helpful to schedule an initial consultation or phone call to determine if it's a good fit before committing to ongoing sessions.

Overcoming barriers to seeking therapy or counseling can be challenging but is crucial for your well-being. Common barriers include stigma, financial concerns, lack of access to resources, or fear of judgment. Remember that seeking help is a sign of strength, and there are ways to address these barriers.

Educate yourself about mental health and challenge the stigma surrounding it. Understand that seeking therapy is a proactive step towards self-improvement and personal growth. Many therapists offer sliding scale fees based on income, and there may be community mental health centers or low-cost clinics available in your area. Explore online resources or teletherapy options if you have limited access to in-person services.

Discussing your intention to seek therapy with trusted friends or family members can also provide emotional support. Sharing your experiences with others who have sought therapy can help normalize the process and alleviate any fears or concerns you may have.

Remember, prioritizing your mental health is an investment in yourself and your overall well-being. Seeking professional help can provide valuable guidance, support, and tools to navigate life's challenges and cultivate emotional resilience. Don't hesitate to reach out and take the first step towards a healthier and happier future.

Chapter 21

Family Ties: Navigating Family Dynamics
****

In the pivotal stage of one's 30's, the significance of family and friends cannot be overstated. It is imperative to delve deeper into ways to fortify and enhance these relationships in order to derive maximum benefit from them. This essay delves into the critical importance of family and friends during this phase of life and provides comprehensive insights into how these vital connections can be strengthened and improved, ultimately leading to a more fulfilling and well-supported existence.

Emotional Support and Stability
Family

Enhancing emotional support and stability from family members necessitates consistent and open communication. Regularly scheduling catch-ups, whether in person or virtually, can help maintain connections and facilitate the sharing of life's trials and triumphs.

Actively seeking advice and guidance from older family members who possess invaluable insights garnered from their own life experiences can provide a sense of stability and reassurance during challenging times.

Friends

Strengthening friendships demands active presence and attentiveness. Actively listening to your friends' concerns and reciprocating support can foster a deeper connection. Demonstrating appreciation for their presence in your life through thoughtful gestures and acts of kindness is equally essential.

Organizing regular social gatherings or activities can play a pivotal role in maintaining and deepening friendships. Shared experiences have the potential to solidify bonds and provide opportunities for mutual support.

Shared Experiences and Milestones
Family

Taking the initiative to organize family events or reunions to celebrate milestones can create lasting memories and foster a stronger sense of familial unity. These gatherings serve as an opportunity to reconnect with relatives and strengthen the familial bond.

The preservation and sharing of family traditions and stories can contribute to a sense of identity and belonging within the family unit and should be actively encouraged.

Friends

Actively participating in your friends' significant life events and milestones demonstrates genuine interest and support in their endeavors. Showing appreciation and being present in times of celebration can deepen the bond with friends.

Planning group outings or trips to create new shared experiences and memories can be instrumental in strengthening the bond with friends and providing opportunities for deeper connections.

Balancing Personal and Professional Life
Family

Seeking advice from family members who have successfully managed their personal and professional lives can provide valuable insights and help navigate challenges effectively. Their wisdom can be indispensable in striking a healthy balance between work and personal life.

Open communication with family about commitments and responsibilities is crucial. Setting clear boundaries and expectations can contribute to a healthy equilibrium between personal and professional spheres.

Friends

Engaging in open discussions with friends about work-life balance can lead to the sharing of experiences and challenges. Being receptive to their insights and advice can foster a supportive network and strengthen friendships.

Offering support and understanding to friends who are navigating similar challenges can contribute to the strength of friendships and create a supportive environment for managing life's demands.

Health and Well-being

Family

Involving family members in activities that promote health and well-being, such as outdoor excursions, exercise routines, or healthy meal preparations, can foster a supportive environment for maintaining a healthy lifestyle.

Encouraging open conversations about mental and emotional well-being within the family can create a safe space for discussing concerns and seeking support when needed.

Friends

Initiating group activities focused on health and wellness, such as workout sessions, meditation classes, or healthy cooking workshops, can promote a shared commitment to well-being. Engaging in such activities together can strengthen the bond and foster a supportive environment.

Cultivating an environment of trust and openness within your friend group, where mental health concerns can be discussed without judgment, is essential. Offering support and understanding to friends who may be struggling with their well-being can fortify the bond.

Networking and Personal Growth

Family

Leveraging family connections for professional growth and development is essential. Seeking mentorship and guidance from family members who are established in their careers can be invaluable, and active participation in family business or professional networks is recommended.

Sharing aspirations and goals with family members, seeking their support and encouragement, can provide a valuable source of motivation and accountability for personal growth.

Friends

Actively engaging in your friends' professional endeavors by offering support, networking opportunities, and constructive feedback can lead to mutual growth and advancement. Building a collaborative and supportive professional network within your friend group can be conducive to personal and professional development.

Sharing knowledge and skills with friends and seeking opportunities for learning and development within your social circle can foster an environment that encourages personal and professional growth.

Recognizing and enhancing the importance of family and friends in one's 30's is vital for personal well-being and growth. By actively nurturing these relationships, seeking support, sharing experiences, and fostering open communication, individuals can derive immense benefit from these vital connections. As individuals navigate the complexities of life in their 30's, the support and connections established with family and friends play a pivotal role in shaping their journey and overall satisfaction.

Chapter 22

Social Circle Revamp: Creating Meaningful Relationships
*****

Family isn't the only thing that matte-rs; friends are crucial too. After all, frie-nds are the ones we- choose. They expose- us to new perspective-s, share moments with us, and provide support in ways that are- different from our family. Building great frie-ndships takes effort and require-s contribution from both parties.

In making friends, look for trust, mutual respect, and common interests. Friends with the same values and goals boost our sense of fit. They offer a support group beyond our close family. We gain company in happy and tough times.

Yet, it's sometimes essential to check our friendships. Bad relationships can emotionally tire us, stunting growth. Spotting toxic signs and setting firm limits protect our welfare. Cutting ties with unhealthy friendships might be hard but serves our happiness and growth.

In our thirties, balancing family, friends, work, personal aims, and self-care gets important. Spending quality time with loved ones keeps those bonds robust and satisfying.

Fitting family and friends into busy days might mean regular meet-ups, plans for outings suiting everyone's hobbies, or chit-chats over the phone or video. Active time and effort can grow and toughen our bonds with family and friends, making our lives richer.

Next, we'll dig into ways to build stronger ties with family, make friendships richer, set limits in relationships, and juggle our many responsibilities best. Seeing the value of family and friends and knowing how good relationships can boost our happiness, helps build lasting ties that make life enjoyable.

Making Family Bonds Stronger

Developing robust links in your family is key for keeping and growing healthy bonds. By talking better, showing empathy, and solving problems well, you can improve family ties and build a helpful network that will stick around during your thirty years and even longer.

Better Family Talks:

1. Active Hearing: Try active hearing when you chat with your family. Focus on them, look them in the eyes, and avoid cutting them off or thinking about your reply before they're done. By really hearing them, you can understand them more and create a deeper bond.

2. Open and True Talks: Support open and honest chats in your family. Make a space where everyone can share their views, feelings, and worries without fear. Build a judgment-free or criticism-free zone to encourage conversations that strengthen family ties.

3. Schedule Family Gatherings: Think about having regular family get-togethers. This could be a weekly or monthly event when everyone comes together to talk about important stuff, share news, and speak up on any issues. This helps keep us close and lets everyone be heard.

4. Invest in Each Other: Try to have special moments with each family member and as a group. Organize fun things to do that also help us connect, like trips, games, or shared interests. This creates unforgettable memories and strengthens our bonds.

Fostering Empathy and Understanding in the Family:

1. Listen with Empathy: Grow empathy by imagining how your family members feel. Try to really get their points of view, feelings, and experiences without criticizing. When they talk about their highs or lows, offer understanding and backup instead of quickly saying what to do or dismissing what they feel.

2. Confirm Emotions: Be truly interested in your family members' feelings. Show you know they have feelings and tell them those feelings matter. Don't downplay or make light of their experiences. Confirming feelings promotes a safe emotional climate in the family.
3. Foster Forgiveness and Release: Harboring hard feelings or past arguments can put tension in the family. Practice forgiving and moving on from old problems to leave room for recovery and progress. Understand everyone messes up, and encouraging forgiveness helps create a more peaceful, loving setting.

How to Tackle Problems and Reach Solutions:
1. Pick Your Fights: Know that not every conflict needs an argument. Master determining the important issues to confront and when to let minor disputes go. This strategy helps keep peace and tackle bigger issues when required.
2. Use "I" Phrases: Use statements starting with "I" during disagreements to not sound blaming or combative. Instead of saying, "You always...", say, "I feel...". This method encourages understanding and prevents defensiveness.
3. Get Help if Required: If confronting issues gets tough, seek help from a mediator. Neutral third parties can encourage open talking and guide the process towards peaceful settlement.

With these tactics, you can improve relationships with your family, yielding a supportive network that offers warmth and understanding in your thirties and beyond. Nurturing these bonds calls for continuous work, patience, and comprehension from everyone.

Building Worthwhile Friendships
Nurturing meaningful friendships is crucial while empowering yourself at thirty. As priorities evolve, realizing healthy friendship traits becomes vital. It's important to find shared interests with friends and sustain these bonds.

Building strong friendships hinges on recognizing key traits. Good friends are supportive and trustworthy. They're dependable. It's beneficial to find folks who hold similar beliefs and like things you do. This commonality can create a strong base for a lasting friendship.

You can deepen bonds by finding shared interests or activities. Try hobbies or join clubs where you can find people who share your preferences. Activity-based friendships allow for shared experiences that strengthen ties.

Friends aren't made overnight. It takes a consistent effort. Your thirties bring additional responsibilities, so you must make room for pals. Scheduling regular get-togethers or special friend-time can help.

Talking is integral to friendships. Connecting regularly, via calls or messages, can foster strong ties. It's always nice to celebrate wins together and also be there during tough times.

As you journey through your thirties, priorities can shift. The lure of career progression and personal responsibilities can undermine friendships. However, resisting this and investing in friends can enhance your overall well-being and joy.

True friendships need two engaging people. Care about your friends' world, listen intently, and be there in rough times. Look for chances to create unforgettable experiences together, like planned adventures or new activities.

To wrap up, nurturing strong friendships adds strength and courage to your thirties. By understanding the elements of good friendships, finding mutual interests, and working hard to keep these bonds, you'll have relationships that give you happiness, help, and satisfaction for many years.

Creating Limits and Saying Goodbye to Harmful Friendships
Spotting harmful friendships is key for emotional health. In this part, we will learn how to set limits and disconnect from damaging friendships, guiding us towards healthier bonds.

Harmful friendships may badly affect our mental and emotional health. They often appear as never-ending criticism, tricks, domination, or disrespect. It's crucial to watch for warning signs and to listen to your instincts if something seems off.

Setting limits is vital when facing harmful friendships. Limits keep your emotional health and define appropriate behavior. Begin by deciding what you're okay with and what crosses the line. Convey these boundaries firmly and directly to the people involved.

Ditching harmful friendships is tough but essential for self-betterment and a better future. Understand that some relationships aren't forever, and putting your wellness first before a bad bond is completely fine. Check how the relationship affects you. Ask yourself if it brings more bad than good. Be with folks who cheer you up, help you grow, and bring out your greatness.

After ending toxic friendships, it's time to build healthier bonds. Find people who get your values, have similar hobbies, and truly care about you. It takes time and action to build strong friendships, so stay patient and open-minded. Grow these new bonds with trust, conversation, and equal respect.

Set your boundaries. Walking away from unhealthy connections is a gesture of self-care. When you heed to your emotional health, you make room for healthier bonds to grow. Trust in you and believe you're worthy of positive and rewarding relationships in your life.

In the coming segment of this chapter, we'll look at achieving a balance of family and friends along with important commitments during the hectic thirties.

Juggling family, friends, and other things can be tough, more so when life gets busy in your thirties. However, it's crucial to value relationships and make space for family and friends amid our packed calendar for genuine bonds.

Firstly, managing time and energy between family, friends, career, and personal life requires careful planning and prioritization. It can be helpful to create a schedule or use time management techniques to allocate specific time slots for different aspects of your life. This allows you to dedicate quality time to both family and friends without neglecting other commitments. Remember to be realistic about what you can reasonably accomplish within the time available.

When it comes to prioritizing relationships while maintaining other responsibilities, it's essential to communicate openly and honestly with your loved ones. Let them know that they are important to you and that you value the time you spend together. Setting boundaries with work or other obligations is key to ensuring that you have dedicated time for family and friends. Consider establishing specific "family nights" or "friendship dates" on a regular basis to guarantee quality time with your loved ones.

Strategies for integrating family and friends into your busy schedule can include finding activities that allow you to spend time together while also accomplishing other tasks. For example, invite a family member or friend to join you for a workout session or go grocery shopping together. This way, you can combine quality time with practical tasks.

Additionally, take advantage of technology to stay connected even when physically apart. Schedule regular video calls or phone calls with long-distance family members or friends who may not be geographically close. Use social media or group messaging apps to share updates and stay connected on a daily basis.

Quality is key in relationships, not quantity. Even with scarce time, optimize the time you can spare for better bonds. Listen well and care genuinely about your dear ones in all interactions. Small actions that show love and gratitude can help keep relationships rock solid.

To conclude, it needs deliberate action and proper focus to balance family, friends and other responsibilities. Effective time management, defining limits and smart methods to mesh loved ones in your hectic timetable safeguards relationship's quality and satisfaction throughout your thirties.

Chapter 23

Digital Detox: Managing Technology's Role in Your Life

****

The Balance of Tech: Controlling Gadgets in Your Daily Routine

Just picture this – the- average adult in the U.S. spe-nds about 11 hours a day consuming media. That's a huge chunk of time de-voted to electronic de-vices! Living in our hyper-connecte-d world, it's essential to strike a balance- between using te-chnology and maintaining our health. That's where the- concept of a digital detox comes into play.

This "detox" is taking a break from gadgets like phones, TVs, computers, tablets, and social sites. The goal is more real, offline social time, less distractions, and less stress from always being "on."

Next, we'll look at the perks of this detox and how to manage tech in your life. By finding balance and making a digital detox part of your routine, you'll likely feel better, get more done, and enjoy life more.

Why a Digital Detox May Be Good for You

Always on your phone or some other gadget? Feeling stressed by too much screen time? You might need a digital detox. Breaking up with constant tech use can be a big help to your mental and physical health.

A major reason to try a detox is to savor "me-time" without digital interruptions. By stepping away from screens, you grab back quiet moments to focus on things that make you happy and peaceful.

Excessive device use is known to add stress to our lives. Studies have shown that a significant percentage of teens feel addicted to their mobile phones, and heavy technology use has been linked to sleeping problems, depressive symptoms, and increased stress levels. By taking a step back from our devices, we can break free from the grip of technology addiction and reduce the negative impact of excessive device use on our mental and physical health.

Additionally, a digital detox can help address the potential dangers of being constantly connected. Being constantly bombarded with notifications, social media updates, and messages can create an unhealthy cycle of stress and anxiety. By disconnecting from devices, we can gain perspective, reduce stress, and find a better balance in our lives.

It's clear that a digital detox can bring about positive changes in our lives. It's time to take control of our technology use and prioritize our well-being. So why not take the first step and embark on a digital detox journey?

The Impact of Technology on Stress and Sleep

The use of technology has become an integral part of our daily lives. However, excessive use of technology can lead to increased stress levels, negatively impacting both our mental and physical well-being. Many adults report technology as a significant source of stress in their lives.

One area where technology has a particularly detrimental effect is on our sleep. Heavy device use, especially before bedtime, can interfere with sleep quality and quantity. Research shows that children who use digital devices at bedtime experience worse sleep and have an increased risk of obesity.

Furthermore, the use of social media in bed has been found to have adverse effects on sleep and mood. Individuals who check social media while in bed at night report higher levels of anxiety, insomnia, and shorter sleep duration. This in-bed electronic social media use disrupts the natural sleep cycle, making it difficult to fall asleep and stay asleep.

It is crucial to recognize the impact of technology on our stress levels and sleep patterns. By acknowledging these effects, we can take proactive steps to limit technology use, establish healthy boundaries, and improve our overall well-being.

The Impact of Technology on Mental Health

Excessive daily technology use has been associated with an increased risk for mental health problems. Among adolescents, this includes symptoms of ADHD and conduct disorder, as well as worse self-regulation. Research has also linked the use of social media sites like Facebook, Snapchat, and Instagram to decreased well-being.

Studies have found that symptoms of depression and loneliness improve when social media use is limited. The constant comparative nature of social media can contribute to negative self-perception and feelings of inadequacy. By taking a break from technology and engaging in a digital detox, individuals can reduce the negative impact of technology on their mental health and improve their overall well-being.

Balancing Work and Life with a Digital Detox

The constant connectivity provided by technology can make it challenging to establish a healthy work-life balance. Research suggests that the use of internet and mobile technologies can influence overall job satisfaction, job stress, and feelings of overwork.

A digital detox helps draw lines between work and private lives. Less tech can reduce stress and give a better work-life balance.

Effect of Social Media on Comparing Ourselves and Fear of Missing Out

Social media is part of life. It helps us be closer to loved ones and share moments. But, there are downsides. It can make us feel less than others and scared to miss out.

Looking at perfect posts breeds bad feelings and can warp our self-view. It's easy to feel less than others, with their flawless trips, love stories and successes. These feelings can make us uneasy and hurt self-worth.

A digital detox can help a lot. Pausing social media and unplugging can help us focus on what matters for us. We stop comparing ourselves and start working on growing and accepting ourselves. We have time for our desires and dreams then.

A break lets us reboot our mindset and care for us first. We relieve the need to be up-to-date and on social media. Embracing a digital detox frees up time for thinking, personal care, and real-life bonds.

It's important to remember that the lives portrayed on social media are often heavily curated and only highlight the highlights of others' lives. By taking a step back, we can gain perspective and understand that everyone experiences ups and downs. This realization can help reduce anxiety and restore our self-esteem.

Additionally, a digital detox allows us to break free from the fear of missing out (FOMO). We no longer have to constantly check our feeds to see what others are doing or attending. Instead, we can fully immerse ourselves in our own lives, fully experiencing the present moment without the distractions of digital connections.

In conclusion, social media can contribute to self-comparison and FOMO, affecting our mental well-being. However, by taking a break from social media and engaging in a digital detox, we can focus on what truly matters, improve our self-esteem, and alleviate the pressure to constantly stay connected. It's time to embrace a healthier relationship with social media and prioritize our own happiness and fulfillment.

Signs of Digital Addiction

Digital addiction, including phone addiction, is a real behavioral addiction that can have detrimental effects on our physical, psychological, and social well-being. Recognizing the signs of digital addiction is the first step towards regaining control over our device usage and breaking free from its grasp.

One common sign of digital addiction is constantly checking our phones. If we find ourselves reaching for our phones compulsively, even when there is no urgent need, it may indicate a dependency on our devices. Feeling anxious or stressed when we're without our phones or being emotionally affected by the usage of social media are additional signs of digital addiction. Being preoccupied with social media metrics, such as the number of likes, shares, or followers, may also point to an unhealthy attachment to our devices. This preoccupation can diminish our ability to fully engage in real-life interactions and experiences. Difficulty concentrating without constantly checking our phones is another sign that digital addiction may be affecting us.

By recognizing these signs and acknowledging the impact of our device use, we can take steps to regain control over our digital lives. Setting boundaries, implementing device-free time, and finding alternative activities to engage in can help reduce our dependency on screens and alleviate the anxiety associated with digital addiction. Seeking support from loved ones or professionals can also be beneficial in our journey towards breaking free from digital addiction and finding a healthier balance with device use.

Finding the Right Balance with Technology Usage

A digital detox doesn't require completely disconnecting from all devices. It's about setting boundaries and using technology in a way that promotes emotional and physical well-being. For some, a complete digital detox may be feasible, while for others, it may involve setting limits on device usage during specific times or activities. Finding the right balance for device usage is crucial to establishing a healthy relationship with technology and reaping the benefits of a digital detox.

Implementing a Digital Detox Routine

It's crucial to have a digital detox routine in our tech-dense world. Arranging set times for activities without gadgets helps maintain a healthy relationship with technology, focusing on well-being.

A digital detox plan could include fixed gadget-free periods each day. You could make mealtimes, mornings, and evenings before sleep device-free. This focus on the here and now, away from screens, allows for a full dive into the physical world, improving overall wellness. It's key to allocate specific times for things like work, hobbies, fitness, and bonding with loved ones. During these phases, shut off from digital distractions to truly experience the moment. This unplugged time nurtures deep relationships and enables pursuits that promote personal evolution and contentment.

Your digital detox pattern should pay special attention to social media usage. Studies show that limiting social media to roughly half an hour daily boosts mental health. Capping social media time can curb feelings of isolation and gloom, and re-establish your command over your digital existence.

Emphasize gadget-free periods and be faithful to your limits for a prosperous digital detox regimen. Discover a routine that suits you and preserve it. You'll recognise a positive transformation in your health and enhanced interaction with your surroundings over time.

Screen Time: Giving Mind and Body a Break

Sitting in front of a screen for too long can put both our mental and physical health at risk. Whenever we're glued to our phones, tablets, or computers for long periods, it can lead to health issues.

Tire Eyes and Poor Sleep

Eye strain is common if we spend too much time looking at screens. Our eyes may get dry, vision might blur, and discomfort can set in. Screens emit blue light which can mess up our sleep patterns. This light slows down the production of melatonin, our sleep hormone. This can make it hard to fall asleep and ruin our sleep quality.

Less Exercise, More Stress

When we spend hours in front of screens, we're not moving much. Whether we're watching TV or wasting time online, too much screen time can cut into our physical activity time. Our health depends on staying active. Failing to do so can trigger stress and lay the groundwork for chronic conditions like obesity and heart disease.

Anxiety and Loneliness

Too much screen time can also boost our stress and anxiety levels. Feeling compelled to keep up with social media or believing that we must compare to others online can make us feel inadequate and anxious. This comparison game can drain our happiness. On top of this, spending loads of time on screens can also lead to feelings of loneliness due to fewer real-life social interactions, only adding to mental health concerns.

Fortunately, by implementing a digital detox that involves managing screen time, individuals can mitigate these health risks and improve their overall well-being. Taking regular breaks from screens, setting limits on screen time, and engaging in other activities can help promote a healthier relationship with technology, reduce stress levels, and foster a sense of balance in our lives.

The Benefits of a Digital Detox

Engaging in a digital detox can have numerous benefits that positively impact your overall well-being. By taking a break from technology and disconnecting from screens, you can experience a variety of positive outcomes, including:

Stress Reduction

A digital detox allows you to step away from the constant notifications and demands of technology, helping to reduce stress levels. By creating a temporary space free from digital distractions, you can find a sense of calm and relaxation.

Improved Focus and Productivity

By removing the distractions of technology, a digital detox allows you to regain control over your attention span and enhance your focus. Without the constant interruptions from notifications and social media, you can concentrate better on tasks, leading to increased productivity.

Better Sleep Quality

Excessive exposure to screens and the blue light emitted by devices can disrupt your sleep patterns. By disconnecting from technology, especially before bedtime, you can improve the quality of your sleep and wake up feeling more refreshed.

Better Connections with People

Talking to those around you instead of constantly being on your device builds real relationships. A short screen break lets you speak up, truly listen to others, and bond with the people you care about.

More Time for Fun Stuff

You can do more of what you love without screens. Do you like hobbies, nature walks, reading, or just chilling out? Cutting down on screen time can help you enjoy these simple pleasures again.

A digital detox can enhance your life. Balance is key. Define what's healthy digital use for you.

What Works in a Digital Detox

Want to nail a digital detox? Here are a few pointers:

1. Draw the Line: Decide on when and where the screens should be off. For example, no gadgets at the dinner table or in your sleep area.
2. Go for Real Talk: Try to interact with others face-to-face. Plan regular meetups with your buddies and loved ones. Have deep chats without screens stealing your attention.

3. Get Active: Make the most of your digital break by adding exercise to your daily routine. Take a stroll, join a fitness class, or enjoy nature to rejuvenate yourself.
4. Be Mindful: Find time for mindfulness or meditation. Use this chance to live in the now, concentrate on breathing, and find tranquility.
5. Renew Hobbies: In your digital detox, revitalize activities that spark joy. From painting to playing music or gardening, partake in past-times not needing screens.

By following these steps, you'll be able to disconnect from tech and explore the many pluses of a digital detox.

Understanding the Pluses of a Digital Detox

By committing to a digital detox and reducing screen time, your mental and physical health can improve. Taking a tech hiatus helps recharge and reduce stress, leading to better well-being. Forming real connections with others deepens bonds and improves community. A digital detox may also rekindle creativity in your life, making for a more rewarding existence.

Appraising and Making it Last

When your digital break's over, it's crucial to review the experience and its effect on your well-being, stress, and productivity. Evaluating the detox benefits can guide you in making lasting tech usage changes, helping you to keep prioritizing your health.

Checking on your screen-free time helps see its good effect on your mind. Pay attention to any lift in spirits, focus, and general joy. Think about if less screen time helped lower stress and made your mind feel fresh.

Looking at how this helps your work ethic is key. Did you feel more in the zone and productive while not using gadgets? Notice any rise in getting work done and reaching goals without tech distractions.

Changing how you use tech for good is a big step after cutting down screen time. Think about how this change affected your view of technology and its place in your life. Make firm rules for tech use going forward, like setting times for checking emails or scrolling through social media.

If you feel swamped during this or find it hard to keep up these new habits, asking for help from health experts or mental health pros is advised. They can offer advice, tools, and methods to help you deal with problems and keep up your new habits.

By checking on your screen-free time and changing your tech uses for good, you can keep focusing on your mental and physical health. A well-done screen-free period can offer lasting benefits, like less stress, better productivity, and a better life overall.

The Wrap-Up

Let's circle back. Disconnecting from the digital world, even for a bit, can do wonders. Less screen time equals less stress. Better focus. Even, better sleep! Its magic trick? It gives us the chance for one-on-one conversations again. This is crucial for relationships. It also helps us find work-life balance.

This is your game. Rules? Yours to set. Find a routine. Make it your own. That's key to a successful digital detox. Cut the digital cord, at least sometimes. It results in a healthier friendship with our devices. In the end, we feel better and work smarter.

Detox isn't about saying goodbye to technology. It's about smart usage. The trick lies in balance. Free some time for fun stuff. Exercise. Meditate. Rediscover offline hobbies. Take these steps, and voila! The benefits of a digital detox, with a healthy grip on the digital world.

Chapter 24

Back to Basics: Simplifying Your Life in Your 30's

****

Did you know that the average person spends 3.2 hours a day using their phone? In the fast-paced world we live in today, people in their 30s are struggling to keep up with it. The constant noise of social media and distraction can be overwhelming and stressful to some, leaving them longing for a simple life.

This is where simplifying your life comes in handy. By focusing on what truly matters and decluttering both mentally and physically, you can gain a sense of clarity, purpose and happiness in your everyday life.

In this section, we will give you practical tips to help simplify your life in your 30s. From finding your purpose to embracing minimalism, building good habits to developing healthy relationships, we will guide you through an intentional life that'll mean something.

If you're ready to leave behind all the clutter from your chaotic lifestyle then buckle up!

The Importance of Finding Your Purpose

The first step is finding out what you love doing. Knowing who you are, what values you hold and how you want the world to see that is important. Once found you can align actions with decisions on things that matter most.

Once this part has been unlocked it provides a sense of direction in a sea full of uncertainty. It becomes obvious what's worth time or not which allows for more fulfilling moments.

Setting Goals — Realistic Ones

After unlocking the first stage just know achieving everything won't happen overnight. One step at a time works best as rushing things puts unnecessary stress on us which sets us back even further than before.

Embrace Minimalism & Declutter

Simplifying your life also includes embracing minimalism while also decluttering both mentally and physically. After being absolutely bombarded by excesses it's nice having something refreshing once in awhile that brings peace into our daily lives again.

Minimalism encourages simplicity while prioritizing experiences over possessions — I'm sure this was hard for many since most of us were raised that buying things will make us happy. The truth is, it's time to let go of whatever baggage we're holding both mentally and physically.

The Benefits of Minimalism

Adopting such a mindset comes with many perks. Embracing minimalism allows you to:

Reduce stress

Create an organized and peaceful living space

Save time by not spending hours everyday deciding what to wear or eat

Put your focus where it should be – the world needs more people like these!

Appreciate beauty in simplicity

Minimalism isn't about throwing everything away then starting from scratch. It's about being picky with what you choose to surround yourself with every day so that each item only brings joy into your life.

It's not just about the physical things, but it's also about your mind and daily routine as well. Get rid of anything that doesn't serve a purpose in your life, or anything that brings you joy. If you don't need it, get rid of it. Simple.

Decluttering your mental space is also very important. Don't let negative thoughts take up room in your head, along with limiting beliefs and emotional baggage. Be mindful and let go of things that no longer matter to you.

Don't forget to declutter on a regular basis as well. It's not just one time. It's an ongoing process.

Creating Daily Routines and Rituals

If you want to have some stability in your life then this will be very important for you. In times of trouble and uncertainty, having something like this can help a lot.

Adding things to your daily routine is also very good for the soul and mind. Whether it's starting your day with a walk or a cup of tea can do wonders for yourself.

By being consistent with these activities help keep things balanced within the day itself. They act as reminders to focus on what really matters to you.

Building daily routines can also help when trying to reach personal goals as well.

Try to be intentional yet adaptable at the same time with these two things because they could change depending on where you are in life right now.

Benefits of Daily Routines and Rituals

What they say is true, they definitely have their benefits that'll impact your life greatly:

- Increased productivity: An organized day helps make everything more efficient.
- Improved mental health: Regular rituals can promote emotional well-being.
- Enhanced focus and concentration: Less distractions means more work getting done.
- Greater self-discipline: You'll become more disciplined by following them consistently.
- Boosted creativity: They can serve as inspiration for many new ideas.
- Heightened self-awareness: Helps you learn more about yourself.

By doing these things, you'll be able to simplify your life in no time.

Mindfulness, on the other hand, is about being present and aware of everything going on inside you. The thoughts, feelings, and sensations that are all part of your everyday life. By practicing mindfulness you can get rid of that fear of the future or regret from the past. This way you're able to fully engage in the current moment.

Gratitude and mindfulness are tied together. When you show gratitude it's easier to find appreciation for what's within your own life. Mindfulness makes you more aware of things that should be appreciated as well. Making it possible to enjoy even that simplest of experiences.

In order to embrace gratitude and mindfulness in your daily lives incorporate simple rituals into your routine. Start by reflecting on three things you're grateful for every morning right when you wake up. During the day take a moment to pause and appreciate what's happening around you at least once. Finally end your day with an activity that brings joy to yourself.

Benefits:

- Reduces stress and anxiety
- Promotes fulfillment
- Increases overall well-being
- Appreciate the present moment
- Foster positive relationships and connections with others
- Improves mental clarity and focus
- Enhances resilience and inner strength
- By following these steps it will simplify not only yours but everyone's life by focusing on what truly matters at this very moment. Take a deep breath, cultivate gratitude, and embrace mindfulness while navigating towards a simpler fulfilling life.

Building good habits:

Taking care of both our physical health as well as mental health is very important when we try to make our lives simple. When we prioritize self-care activities we can cultivate healthy habits that improve us in more ways than one can count.

Start by incorporating exercise into your regular routine because doing so will release those endorphins we love so much! Not only does exercise help keep our body fit but also boosts mood which reduces stress levels also! It doesn't even have to be super intense either! Joining a fitness class, going for a walk or even a run. All are good enough!

Another way to practice self-care is by eating better and paying attention to the foods we consume. Going after that well-balanced diet that has all of our favorite fruits and vegetables in it can make us feel good too.

Just as important, maybe even more so than exercise is getting an adequate amount of sleep each night. By doing so we function at our best levels + supports our immune system and brain functions.

Building healthy habits might be hard but the benefits are amazing! Our life becomes less stressful and much much simpler. So when you make yourself a priority everything else will fall into place too.

When it comes to simplifying your life, one of the most important things you can do is be financially responsible and save money. Adopting a frugal mindset and being mindful of your spending habits can help get rid of unnecessary financial stress and create a stable future.

One way to keep track of your finances is by creating a budget. This lets you see where all your money is going and helps with identifying areas where you can cut back on spending.

Another method for saving money is looking for ways to reduce unnecessary expenses. Buying used items instead of new ones not only saves you money but also helps protect the environment. It's also worth exploring community sharing initiatives that allow you to lend or borrow items from others without having to buy them yourself.

Saving for the future is just as important as being careful with spending now. Set aside some money each month and create an emergency fund so that when unexpected expenses come up, they don't leave you financially devastated.

It may sound daunting or boring at first, but making sure your financial life is simple and secure will go a long way in freeing up mental space later on in life.

Building Fulfilling Relationships

Building relationships with people who support and uplift us brings great joy into our lives; however, we must remember to let go of relationships that waste our precious energy. Spending quality time with loved ones through open communication, shared experiences and other methods can help develop deeper connections with them.

Connection really is everything when it comes to human relationships. Make sure to make time for others so that real understanding between the two parties can be achieved. Actively listen while someone else speaks their mind, offer up support when needed and always show gratitude towards the presence others have in your own life. Both face-to-face contact and digital communication have value — make use of both methods frequently.

The Importance of Open Communication

Open communication should always be prioritized in both good times and bad times if there's any hope of a relationship lasting. It allows your thoughts, feelings and needs to be expressed and listened to so that conflicts can be resolved quicker and relationships strengthened.

Being physically present is just as important as opening up to others. With our lives being so hectic, it's easy to go weeks or even months without seeing someone we love. This kind of distance doesn't help develop relationships at all. Set aside some time for those who matter most in your life and engage in activities that will make lasting memories.

Shared experiences are also powerful in cultivating fulfilling relationships. Engaging in activities together, such as traveling, attending events, or even cooking a meal, can provide opportunities for bonding and creating shared memories. These experiences create a sense of connection, as you navigate new and exciting adventures together.

Remember, simplifying your life is not just about decluttering your physical space but also about fostering meaningful connections. Surround yourself with people who bring positivity and support into your life, and let go of relationships that no longer serve your well-being. By investing in cultivating fulfilling relationships through open communication, quality time, and shared experiences, you can experience a richer, more rewarding, and simplified life.

Continuous Learning and Personal Growth

Embracing a back to basics lifestyle in your 30's involves a commitment to continuous learning and personal growth. By seeking opportunities to expand your knowledge, develop new skills, and explore your interests, you can enhance both your personal and professional development. The journey of continuous learning not only keeps your mind engaged and active but also brings a sense of fulfillment and satisfaction to your life.

Embracing the Power of Saying "No"

When it comes to simplifying your life one of the most powerful tools you have is the ability to say "no" and set healthy boundaries. It's easy to get caught up in the desire to please others or take on more than you can handle. However learning to prioritize your own well-being decline commitments or activities that do not align with values or serve higher purpose is essential.

Saying "no" doesn't make you selfish; it allows you to create space for what truly matters to you. By setting boundaries saying "no" when necessary ,you can avoid overwhelm reduce stress focus your time energy on what brings you fulfillment joy.

Setting boundaries starts with knowing limits being honest with yourself about what realistically handle. It also means being assertive communicating boundaries clearly with others. Remember, you have the right to prioritize your own well-being and make choices that align with values goals.

By embracing the power of saying "no" and setting healthy boundaries, you can simplify your life, create more balance, and cultivate a greater sense of peace and contentment. So, don't be afraid to say "no" when necessary and make room for what truly matters.

Cultivating Mindful Technology Use

In today's fast-paced digital age it's essential to be mindful of our technology use. While technology offers numerous benefits and conveniences, it's important to create a healthy balance that allows for real-life interactions experiences. Mindful technology use encourages us to intentionally aware how we engage with our devices and to set boundaries that prioritize well-being connection in physical world.

One effective way to cultivate mindful technology use is by implementing regular digital detoxes. During these detoxes individuals intentionally disconnect from screens and prioritize face-to-face interactions, outdoor activities, and hobbies that nourish mind, body, and soul. By temporarily stepping away from digital realm ,we can reconnect with ourselves others, fostering deeper connections a sense of presence in present moment.

Creating boundaries around our technology use is another vital part of being mindful. Picking specific times or areas in our homes to be screen-free can give room for uninterrupted, quality time with loved ones, self-reflection and relaxation. With boundaries set, we can detach ourselves from distractions and devote all our attention to experiences that bring us joy.

Remember to not eliminate technology completely from your life; mindfulness isn't about that. It's about making a conscious effort to only engage with technology when it supports you and aligns with your values. By practicing mindfulness and setting limits, we can create a healthier relationship between tech, and ensure it enhances our lives rather than causes stress or disconnection.

Embrace Change, Let Go of Perfection

When simplifying your life you have to embrace change and let go of perfectionism. Understand that life is always changing so instead of fighting against it just take it as an opportunity for growth. On the path to simplicity, striving for perfection will only cause unnecessary stress and dissatisfaction which doesn't help at all.

No one is perfect so don't aim for something that's unattainable. Embrace imperfections because they show a willingness to learn from mistakes — which are invaluable lessons when it comes down to personal growth.

Once the need for absolute perfection is gone there's room for acceptance and self-compassion in your life. So remember this: Being kind to yourself is key while adapting to change and embracing imperfections will lead you towards a simplified existence that's more meaningful.

Emphasizing Self-Care and Well-being

Prioritizing self-care and well-being is vital when it comes to simplifying your life. It's easy to get wrapped up in the hustle and bustle of our everyday lives, but we mustn't forget about taking time for ourselves to recharge and rejuvenate. By focusing on self-care, you can nurture your physical, mental, and emotional well-being, leading to a more balanced and fulfilling life.

Self-care can show itself in many ways. From doing things that bring you joy and relaxation to practicing self-caring rituals that promote inner calmness and peace. This could be taking a long bath or walk in nature or even meditating or partaking in hobbies you love. Find what resonates with you most and dedicate some time each day to it.

The Importance of Self-Care Rituals

Self-care rituals provide structure and stability in your life which allows you cope better with daily stressors that come your way. By incorporating these into your routine, you make space for yourself to unwind, reflect, and recharge.

Think about simple practices such as starting the days with mindfulness or gratitude exercises, journaling thoughts and reflections or just enjoying a cup of tea by yourself before starting the day. These small yet meaningful rituals have a powerful impact on overall well-being.

Seeking Support When Needed

Remember self care goes beyond activities as it also encompasses seeking support when needed from professionals who know what they're talking about. Don't hesitate if you are struggling with anxiety, depression, stress, or any other challenge that's holding you back from simple living. Reach out because taking care of yourself isn't selfish; it's necessary step towards simplifying your life.

By emphasizing self-care and well-being as a priority in your life make space for a simplified one filled with meaning. Prioritize yourself first by listening to your needs then cultivate practices that nourish your mind body soul. The better you take care of yourself the more equipped you are to face the challenges of life efficiently and properly.

Engaging with a supportive community goes beyond simply receiving support—it's also about giving back. Share your own experiences, offer advice, and provide encouragement to others who are on a similar journey. By contributing to the community, you strengthen the connections and create a valuable space for everyone involved.

Remember that building a supportive community takes time and effort. Be patient and proactive in seeking out opportunities to connect with like-minded individuals. Embrace the connections you make and nurture them through active participation and genuine engagement. Creating a supportive community is an investment in your own personal growth and well-being. Surrounding yourself with like-minded individuals who share your values can provide the foundation you need to simplify your life and create a more meaningful and fulfilling existence.

Embracing the Journey of Simplification

Simplifying your life is a continuous journey, rather than a final destination. It involves embracing the process of simplification and allowing yourself to grow and evolve along the way. In this journey, it's important to stay open to new experiences, be flexible in your approach, and celebrate the progress you make.

As you simplify your life, you embark on a path of personal growth. By letting go of the unnecessary and focusing on what truly matters, you create space for joy, fulfillment, and peace. Embrace the opportunity to explore what brings you happiness and aligns with your values, as this is where true personal growth can be found.

Remember that each person's journey of simplification is unique. What works for one may not work for another, and that's perfectly okay. Find what resonates with you, whether it's minimalist living, setting boundaries, or nurturing relationships, and follow your own path. The key is to prioritize what brings you closer to a simplified, meaningful life

Chapter 25

Romantic Rendezvous:
Cultivating Love and Partnerships
******

To properly build me-aningful and satisfying romantic bonds, it is essential to start by recognizing your principle-s and goals within the relationship. Consider taking some- time for self-refle-ction on what qualities you truly seek in a companion and what you e-nvision your joint path looking like going forward. What characteristics are non-ne-gotiable? Which are flexible-? Envisioning your ideal relationship can help e-nsure you and your partner are pursuing the- same objectives. Communicating your re-lationship aims clearly and listening to understand your partne-r's hopes as well helps e-stablish a strong foundation for togetherness built on share-d understanding and trust. Continually checking in on one anothe-r's evolving desires ove-r time can further strengthe-n your unity and commitment to supporting each other's happine-ss.

As you consider moving forward in your dating life-, taking some time to refle-ct on relationships from your past can provide helpful le-ssons. Examine what succeede-d and what faced difficulties in your previous romantic e-xperiences. By analyzing both the- mistakes and successes, valuable- insights can be gained about your nee-ds and wants in a partnership. Look closely at where- communication broke down or mismatched expe-ctations caused issues. Similarly, recall inte-ractions that just felt easy and brought you both joy. This type of introspe-ction allows you to learn from history so you do not repeat past re-lationship patterns, but rather can identify the- qualities and behaviors you search for in a future- match.

When conte-mplating what you seek in a romantic partner, re-flect upon the qualities, value-s and characteristics most important for a meaningful relationship. Give- thought to shared perspective-s, priorities and life goals which align betwe-en you. Seek an e-motional bond where intere-sts align and compatibilities lay. Consider too the conne-ctions vital for fulfillment - interests share-d, values aligned and compatibilities pre-sent. This allows understanding what virtues and attribute-s nurture a relationship aligning with your own fulfilled life-style.

By clarifying your relationship goals, you will have a solid foundation for attracting and nurturing a partnership that aligns with your vision for the future. Remember that these goals may evolve and change over time, so it is important to regularly reassess and communicate your desires with your partnerDeveloping effective communication skills is essential for cultivating meaningful romantic partnerships. In order to express your needs, desires, and concerns effectively, it is important to practice open and honest communication with your partner. This means being transparent about your thoughts and feelings, as well as actively listening to your partner's perspective.

Cultivating emotional intimacy is additionally vital for a satisfying romantic re-lationship. This involves developing an e-nvironment where vulne-rability and compassion can flourish. Focused listening plays a pivotal part in nurturing emotional union, as it pe-rmits you to genuinely grasp and validate your partne-r's feelings. By sharing their e-xperiences through e-mpathetic ears, you can construct belie-f and intensify your closeness.

Cultivating caring and candid discussion is critical for sustaining a solid and wholesome- bond. It's imperative to foster a se-tting where both accomplices fe-el uninhibited communicating themse-lves without apprehension of asse-ssment or faultfinding. This expects proactive-ly urging your partner to impart their considerations and fe-elings, and reacting with compassion and comprehe-nsion. Listening thoughtfully and acknowledging another's point of vie-w, no matter how remote from your own, is basic. Make- an exertion to comprehe-nd where somebody e-lse is coming from before e-ndeavoring to be comprehe-nded.

Kee-p in mind that successful communication and emotional bonding nece-ssitate continuous effort and routine. It is e-ssential to organize consistent che-ck-ins and candid conversations with your partner to confirm that you kee-p cultivating and reinforcing your relationship. Maintaining balance through ope-n dialogue and quality time togethe-r can help resolve issue-s smoothly before they e-scalate. Try active listening to unde-rstand different perspe-ctives, then find solutions as a united te-am. Focus on each other's nee-ds and goals equally to strengthen trust and intimacy long-te-rm.

Striking the right e-quilibrium between autonomy and re-liance within a loving relationship is esse-ntial. Although preserving a fee-ling of uniqueness and chasing individual aims is significant, nurturing a powerful alliance- necessitates synchronizing the-se solitary drives. It is vital to pursue pe-rsonal interests and spend time- apart from your partner, but relationships thrive on quality time- together, shared e-xperiences, compromise- and mutual understanding. Maintaining some separate-ness while also making room for your partner is ke-y to ensuring both parties fee-l respected, supporte-d and that the connection remains strong ove-r the long term.

It is fundamentally important to acknowle-dge how vital self-improveme-nt is for both parties and aid each other's progre-ss. Motivate and applaud each individual's accomplishments, irre-spective of whethe-r they are caree-r or private triumphs. Craft a setting that permits both associate-s to flourish independently ye-t still nurtures the bond.

Regular discussion be-tween partners about pe-rsonal aims, dreams, and what each wants from the re-lationship is important for keeping the re-lationship balanced. Making time to talk through what matters most to e-ach individual can help make sure both partne-rs feel listene-d to and comprehended. It is fundame-ntal to attentively listen to what e-ach hopes for and worries about without criticism or an urge to de-fend oneself. By re-cognizing what each needs and wants, you can discove-r approaches to encourage one- another as you each chase your own ambitions. the- relationship. Frequent ope-n communication regarding objectives, visions, and the- expectations each has of the- other assists in sustaining equilibrium in the conne-ction. Constructively discussing private desire-s, concerns, and what is significant to every pe-rson permits both accomplices to fee-l heard and understood. It is vital to listen active-ly to every other's ye-arnings and issues without assessment or de-fensiveness. By acknowle-dging what every individual nee-ds and wants, you can discover ways of supporting one another while- seeking after singular obje-ctives.

Furthermore-, routinely re-examining how tasks and dutie-s are shared betwe-en both individuals within the relationship can he-lp retain equilibrium. It is crucial to confirm that each partne-r experience-s the same leve-l of contribution and satisfaction. Frankly conversing about anticipations, responsibilities, and positions can he-lp circumvent emotions of bitterne-ss or disproportion.

While e-mbracing compromise is important for maintaining balance in a relationship, it is also e-ssential that both partners fee-l heard and respecte-d. When conflicts arise, each individual should ope-nly discuss their perspective- and needs with the aim of re-aching an understanding, rather than a winner. Small conce-ssions made with care and willingness to se-e another's viewpoint can le-ad to creative solutions where- previously there se-emed none. With compassion and fle-xibility, many apparent difference-s dissolve into shared priorities, allowing the- relationship to strengthen through unity rathe-r than divide because of pe-rceived opposition. Open and hone-st dialogue is key, so that mutual understanding and accommodation le-ave both feeling value-d.

Lastly, kee-p in mind that change is unavoidable for both people- and relationships. Realize that individual e-volution may result in shifting aims and dreams as time passe-s. Welcome these- adjustments together, modifying and cultivating as a pair.

By balancing indepe-ndence with interde-pendence while- also managing individual objectives that compleme-nt a robust union, and endorsing each other's pe-rsonal evolution, couples can prese-rve a sound and rewarding bond. Recall that re-taining relationship equilibrium is a continuous method that ne-cessitates work, interaction, and compre-hension from both accomplices. Conflict Resolution and Proble-m-Solving require establishing common ground, active- listening without judgement, and e-xpressing how you genuinely fe-el in a respectful manne-r. By addressing problems respe-ctfully and finding mutually agreeable solutions, a couple- can strengthen their unde-rstanding and connection.

Disputes and diffe-rences of opinion are ine-scapable in any caring relationship. Yet, it is fundame-ntal to address them with a constructive attitude- and collectively evolve- approaches for addressing issues as companions. By acting in this manne-r, you can cultivate fortitude, intensify faith in one- another, and reinforce your unification.

When dispute-s emerge, it is absolute-ly essential to engage- in active listening. Give your companion your undivide-d attention and sincerely try to compre-hend their viewpoint. Re-frain from interrupting or crafting counterarguments while- they are communicating. Refle-ct on what they have expre-ssed to confirm you have understood prope-rly prior to reacting. By actively listening in this manne-r, you can better understand whe-re your partner is coming from and look for common ground or solutions that work for both parties. This approach facilitate-s more constructive discussion when disagre-ements arise.

Cultivating empathy is ke-y to seeing your partner's vie-wpoint and situation. Putting yourself in their shoes allows you to conside-r their emotions, expe-riences and nee-ds. This understanding fosters compassion and helps make- communication feel safe and hone-st. While perspective-s may differ, pausing to empathize can re-veal shared goals bene-ath surface conflicts. With care and effort, strong bonds may withstand life-'s complexities through open-minde-dness on both sides.

When disagre-ements arise in a re-lationship, it is important to consider whether an issue- truly warrants conflict or if it could be overlooked. Compromise- plays a vital role in any healthy relationship, so e-valuate how substantial a matter is before- deciding to engage in an argume-nt. For minor disagreements whe-re no severe- consequences will occur, atte-mpting to find middle ground or moving past the topic may be be-tter approaches than hostility. Make an e-ffort to thoughtfully resolve significant problems rathe-r than needlessly fighting ove-r trivial matters. The key is focusing your e-nergy on mending important differe-nces, while letting insignificant one-s fade without conflict causing damage. Working togethe-r cooperatively usually leads to stronge-r bonds than allowing every small disagree-ment to escalate into a full argume-nt.

While discussions involving strong e-motions can be challenging, taking brief bre-aks to allow heightened fe-elings to subside can help addre-ss issues more constructively. If an argume-nt begins to escalate, agre-eing to separate for a short time- demonstrates respe-ct for each other's perspe-ctives and mental state. The- separation permits each pe-rson's rational thinking abilities to regain control, improving the capacity for unde-rstanding different viewpoints whe-n discussions resume. Returning to topics afte-r short timeouts often allows for calmer, more-productive conversations.

While both partie-s may have differing viewpoints, it is important to find common ground and focus on share-d goals. Look for any areas of agreeme-nt or overlapping objectives that can be- built upon to help move the discussion forward in a positive- manner. Given that you both likely want what is be-st overall, searching for mutual intere-sts or aims can help redirect e-nergies towards discovering solutions that be-nefit all involved. This cooperative- spirit of finding shared ground is more conducive to productive- conflict resolution than stubbornly insisting on polarized positions alone.

When issue-s arise betwee-n partners, the most constructive path is to se-ek understanding rather than assign fault. Come- together with open and fle-xible minds, willing to see e-ach other's perspective-s. Brainstorm respectfully for answers that accommodate- both parties' needs and e-ase tensions. Explore multiple- potential solutions to address the conce-rns at hand. With patience and goodwill, resolution can be- found through cooperation instead of criticism. When communicating how a situation make-s you feel, it is best to use- "I" statements rather than accusatory "you" state-ments. Saying something like "I fe-el hurt when this occurs" is more constructive- than claiming "You always do this." "I" statements avoid placing blame while- still expressing your genuine- emotions. They encourage- taking ownership of personal fee-lings instead of attacking the other pe-rson. Describing how your own feelings have- been affecte-d in a situation prevents defe-nsiveness from the othe-r party. This approach facilitates more understanding be-tween both sides during challe-nging discussions. It allows difficult topics to be discussed openly while- maintaining respect and limiting tension be-tween those involve-d.

While compromise- is essential for healthy re-lationships, it's also important to find balance. Consider each partne-r's perspective to ide-ntify common ground and mutually agreeable solutions. Small conce-ssions, when made willingly, can strengthe-n bonds of trust and respect betwe-en two people committe-d to understanding one another. Not e-very decision will satisfy eve-ry preference-, yet prioritizing cooperation over individual wants allows ne-eds to be met without e-ither feeling unhe-ard. With open and honest discussion, a balance can form whe-re fairness is found through blending positions, not be-nding one completely. In re-lationships requiring teamwork, compromise is the- key to progress.

While mistake-s can happen in any relationship, it is important to acknowledge- errors respectfully and work towards re-solution. If one has unwittingly caused hurt or disappointed the-ir partner, sincerely apologizing and acce-pting accountability can help remedy the- situation. Similarly, being willing to forgive shortcomings and prioritize continuing as a unite-d front allows for growth together going forward. Open communication and mutual unde-rstanding can help smooth over unintende-d issues, strengthening the- bond for the future. While most re-lationship issues can be worked through with ope-n communication between partne-rs, some conflicts may require additional assistance- if they continue causing significant distress. Se-eking help from a license-d therapist can give anxious or overwhe-lmed couples useful strate-gies for addressing dee-per problems in a healthy, constructive- way. A counselor provides an impartial perspe-ctive and proven technique-s that partners may struggle to impleme-nt alone in the thick of disputes. The-ir guidance helps identify unde-rlying needs, desire-s, or unresolved past wounds fueling pre-sent tensions. With a counselor's me-diation, couples gain insight into each other's pe-rspectives while le-arning to express themse-lves calmly and listen actively. Re-solving conflicts takes time and effort, so be- willing to accept help from an objective- professional if frustrations persist longer than de-sired. With hard work and outside support tailored to individual

When disagre-ements arise be-tween two people- in a relationship, keeping in mind that re-solving conflicts takes continued effort can he-lp navigate issues calmly and reinforce- the connection. By listening with unde-rstanding, exploring each person's pe-rspective, and finding compromise through ope-n cooperation, disagreeme-nts need not damage the- relationship and may even stre-ngthen mutual understanding and trust with time and care-. No bond is perfect, but facing difficulties toge-ther respectfully can de-epen intimacy where- willingness exists to understand inste-ad of demand to be understood.

Keeping Romance Alive

To cultivate and maintain a meaningful romantic partnership, it's essential to prioritize and nurture the romance in your relationship. While the passion and excitement may naturally ebb and flow over time, there are proactive steps you can take to keep the romance alive. This section explores various strategies for reigniting the spark and continuously improving the quality of your relationship.

1. Date Nights: Carving Out Quality Time

- Schedule regular date nights to reconnect and spend quality time together.
- Explore new activities or revisit old favorites to keep things fresh.

- Make an effort to dress up and create a sense of occasion for your date nights.

2. Surprises and Small Gestures: Keeping the Spark Alive
- Surprise your partner with thoughtful gestures, such as leaving love notes or planning a surprise outing.
- Show appreciation for your partner through small acts of kindness and affection.
- Celebrate special occasions and milestones to commemorate your journey together.

3. Emotional Intimacy: Deepening Your Connection
- Prioritize open and honest communication to foster emotional intimacy.
- Share your dreams, fears, and aspirations with each other.
- Practice active listening and empathy to create a safe space for vulnerability.

4. Shared Experiences: Creating Lasting Memories
- Plan and participate in experiences that create lasting memories.
- Travel together, try new hobbies, or embark on shared adventures.
- Create traditions or rituals that strengthen your bond as a couple.

5. Shared Goals: Growing Together
- Set goals as a couple and work towards them collaboratively.
- Align your visions for the future and support each other's individual ambitions.
- Celebrate milestones and achievements together.

6. Physical Intimacy: Reigniting Passion
- Prioritize physical intimacy by making time for intimacy and exploring new ways to connect physically.
- Communicate openly about desires, fantasies, and boundaries.
- Invest in your sexual relationship by prioritizing pleasure and exploring new experiences.

7. Quality Communication: Building Trust and Understanding
- Establish a foundation of trust through open and honest communication.
- Practice active listening, empathy, and non-judgment to foster understanding.
- Address any unresolved conflicts or issues to maintain a healthy emotional connection.

Remember that keeping romance alive requires ongoing effort and intentional actions. It's important to adapt these strategies to suit your unique relationship dynamic and individual preferences. By prioritizing romance, nurturing emotional and physical intimacy, and engaging in shared experiences, you can keep the spark alive and continuously improve the quality of your romantic partnership.

Chapter 26

The Parenting Prospect: Considering Parenthood

****

Is Parenthood Right for You? Sometimes there are a lot of questions that come to mind when you're in your thirties. One major question is whether or not you should have kids. It's a deeply personal decision and can't be easily answered. It depends on what you want, what you value, and if you think it's the right time to take on the challenge of raising children. Reflect on your goals and desires when making this life-altering decision. Consider what you want your future to look like and if having children fits into that picture. Think about how having a family would affect your overall fulfillment.

Evaluate if you're ready to be responsible for someone other than yourself. Parenting is hard work and requires a lot of time, energy, and effort. Ask yourself if you could provide all the love, care, and support they need and deserve.

Another thing to consider is how becoming a parent will change things in your life personally and professionally. Being responsible for another human comes with sacrifices that may come at the expense of other areas in your life like career advancements or personal goals.

Remember this is not an easy question to answer as everyone has different values but there are no wrong answers.

Every situation is unique so take as much time as possible when deciding whether or not parenthood is right for you

Preparing for Challenges While also Embracing Joy

Becoming a parent can be one of the most fulfilling experiences anyone can have but it does bring forth challenges along with joy. Before diving into something new make sure that both parents are well prepared physically, emotionally, mentally, & financially so they don't feel overwhelmed later down the road.

Physical Demands

Taking care of children requires physical energy which some people might not have an excess amount of after work but it's necessary if they want happy healthy children running around their homes. To prepare themselves physically try putting together workout routines during pregnancy because it'll help with the stamina. It'll make it easier to deal with sleepless nights of tending to a newborn and chasing after toddlers.

Embracing Emotions

Children are never a one emotion thing. There will be good days but sometimes there will also be bad ones, and even harder days as they grow older. Take time and find ways to manage these emotions because it's not easy for the parents, especially if they're new at this.

Financial Responsibilities

If you're thinking about becoming parents, there's no doubt that preparing for that journey mentally, emotionally and even physically is important. There are a few things to consider if you want to be better prepared.

Financial Planning

It's no secret that having kids comes with a lot of financial challenges. From healthcare to education and more, it all adds up quickly. This is why creating a budget, saving for future expenses & emergencies and considering insurance options should be at the top of your list. Talking openly about shared financial goals and responsibilities with your partner will also be helpful.

Realistic Expectations: The Joys & Difficulties

Of course we know how amazing having kids can be. Witnessing their every milestone, experiencing unconditional love and forming deep bonds sounds like the greatest thing in the world; because it is! However, sleepless nights, tantrums and constant need for attention might sound familiar too. It's important to acknowledge these difficulties as well so they don't catch you off guard.

Creating a Supportive Environment

Before anything else, making sure you create an environment where both parents can thrive is crucial. Foster open communication with each other first & foremost but also in your home in general. Establish routines that will make everyone's life easier (especially yours). Lastly, build strong relationships with family & friends as they'll be able to give you support when needed.

Navigating Family Dynamics

The way our families raised us greatly shapes our beliefs and values on parenting today. That being said, it's important to identify which strengths & weaknesses we've kept from them by examining those dynamics further.

Unresolved issues could affect parenting decisions later down the line so try your best to resolve any conflicts or emotional burdens now instead of later when it gets worse. Doing this not only creates a healthier environment but one where children learn how to handle their emotions better early on too.

Establishing boundaries with extended family members is equally crucial. Openly talking about these boundaries can help prevent conflict and protect the overall well-being of both parents and children.

Effective communication strategies also help immensely in managing family dynamics. Being open & honest is key as it fosters understanding, reduces misunderstandings and strengthens relationships. Skills like active listening, expressing emotions constructively and resolving conflicts peacefully are always something to build on.

By addressing family dynamics head on we can break unhealthy patterns for future generations. With that said, a supportive network that promotes growth, love & connection will be built instead.

Building a strong and supportive family environment is crucial for fostering healthy relationships and ensuring the well-being of all family members. This section focuses on specific strategies to promote open communication, implement consistent discipline, and nurture a sense of mutual support and cooperation within the family.

Open Communication:

Effective communication is the foundation of a positive family environment. It allows family members to express their thoughts, feelings, and needs openly and honestly. Here are some ways to promote open communication within your family:

1. Create a Safe Space: Foster an atmosphere of trust and respect where everyone feels comfortable expressing themselves without fear of judgment or criticism.
2. Listen with Empathy: Practice active listening by giving your full attention and validating the emotions and experiences shared by each family member.
3. Encourage Dialogue: Regularly initiate conversations about various topics, encouraging each family member to contribute their thoughts and opinions.
4. Resolve Conflict Constructively: Teach family members how to resolve conflicts in a respectful and constructive manner, focusing on finding common ground and understanding.

Consistent Discipline:

Consistency in discipline helps establish clear boundaries and expectations within the family. Here are some principles to guide your approach to discipline:

1. Set Clear Rules and Expectations: Establish age-appropriate rules that reflect your family values and communicate them clearly to all family members.

2. Be Consistent: Enforce rules consistently without favoritism or exceptions. Consistency promotes fairness and ensures that everyone understands the consequences of their actions
3. Use Positive Reinforcement: Acknowledge and reward good behavior to encourage positive habits and attitudes within the family
4. Teach Responsibility: Help children develop a sense of responsibility by assigning age-appropriate chores and encouraging them to take ownership of their actions

Mutual Support Cooperation:

Nurturing a sense of mutual support and cooperation within the family strengthens bonds and creates a harmonious home environment consider implementing these strategies:

1. Foster Teamwork: Encourage family members to work together on tasks or projects, promoting a sense of unity and collaboration.
2. Practice Empathy and Compassion: Teach children to empathize with others' feelings and needs, fostering a supportive and caring environment.
3. Encourage Independence and interdependence: Balance promoting individual growth with cultivating interdependence and reliance on one another for support
4. Celebrate Achievements: Recognize and celebrate each family member's accomplishments, fostering a culture of encouragement and motivation

By creating a positive family environment through open communication, consistent discipline, and mutual support you lay the foundation for healthy relationships and happy thriving family dynamics these practices will strengthen your bond as a family unit and build the resilience needed to navigate any challenges that may arise.

Balancing Parenthood with Personal Growth and Development

Parenthood is full of joy but remember it doesn't define you by making sure not to lose yourself in being a parent You have your own life too It's crucial to maintain a sense of self and pursue personal growth outside of parenting By identifying what you want out of life prioritizing your needs establishing care routines it'll help create that balance between parenthood and personal development

Creating strong relationships can be a challenge, but it's all about how you approach and resolve conflicts. By using various communication methods, you'll have an easier time understanding others.

Every person has a different perspective on things. It's important to understand this because we're all molded by our distinct experiences. One disagreement isn't the end of the world, so value your partner's views as much as yours.

Often times conflict can occur just because partners aren't aware of each other's boundaries. It might sound obvious to ask what someone is comfortable with and what they are not; but many people still make these assumptions. So take the time to get to know how your partner interacts with arguments and see if it aligns with your approach.

There's no such thing as a perfect communicator, but that doesn't mean there isn't room for improvement. Everyone has their own unique style of arguing, some might be passive aggressive while others may be quite assertive; regardless though try critiquing yourself and grow from those reflections.

In "Fortify and Empower Yourself at Thirty: Rewriting the Life Success Script," readers will gain valuable insights and strategies for navigating conflicts in their relationships. The goal is to empower individuals to approach conflicts with compassion, active listening skills, and a willingness to find solutions that meet the needs of all parties involved

Effective communication is key in any relationship. To establish genuine and strong relationships with people, it is important to remember three things: empathy, active listening and non-verbal cues. In this chapter of the book we will be examining these topics.

Active listening allows us to truly connect with each other on a higher level. You know the feeling of being ignored vs someone genuinely understanding what you're saying — a whole different experience. It includes giving our full attention to the speaker, making eye contact and being present. When actively listening, we demonstrate respect for that persons thoughts and feelings which helps them feel comfortable enough to open up more.

After active listening comes empathy. This helps put ourselves in their shoes allowing us to understand their emotions and experiences from a deeper level. Before forming your own opinion, suspend judgment! Rather offer support and validation while they share their side because doing so strengthens relationships by creating space for vulnerability and open dialogue.

Lastly is non-verbal cues and body language. Sometimes the way words are said contradicts what is actually being said which makes reading these clues very important! A smile could mean happiness or evilness — without noticing how it was done gives off hints about what mood someone might be in without them even saying it directly.

To improve your communication skills, you must first practice self-awareness. Which means reflecting on your own communication patterns as well as finding areas where growth can take place. Are you always interrupting others? Dominating conversations? These questions can help you become better at communicating which will bring stronger relationships.

With all of this information it's clear that effective communication brings out resolutions that benefit both parties! Now let's get into conflict resolution strategies that can also help boost your skills in communicating effectively:

1) Compromising

2) Negotiating

It's natural to feel anger when you're in a disagreement. Being able to manage it properly is key. Remember to take deep breaths and practice self-awareness so that you know when you're getting angry.

Finding healthy ways to express your emotions can be really helpful. Try journaling or talking with someone you trust about how you feel. You don't want anything you say or do out of anger to make the situation worse or escalate it.

3. Finding win-win solutions that address the needs of all parties involved:

Start by finding out what everyone wants and needs from the situation. Try your best to truly understand what is important for everyone.

Try coming up with ideas that will benefit everyone without making anyone compromise their own values. Be open and accepting of new ideas while brainstorming with each other.

Using these strategies will improve communication between people, leading to better results through a conflict resolution. Always keep in mind that effective conflict resolution takes time and practice, so always be patient with yourself as well as others as conflicts arise.

Overcoming Communication Barriers:

One of the main things needed for understanding and resolving conflicts effectively is identifying problems that get in the way of good communication then overcoming them of course. By doing this, people are able to talk more openly which usually leads to better understanding and problem-solving.

Being defensive is one big barrier for sure though. When individuals feel attacked or criticized they'll immediately become defensive and close themselves off from any other possible perspective except their own.. If we really want to solve issues together then we should approach every argument with an open mind ready for whatever point it may be.

Misunderstandings are also a very common thing people tend not realize can cause fights when left unaddressed. More often than not misunderstandings happen because we just aren't listening.. There's a lot more but I'm going on too long here so you've got it!

Developing strategies for overcoming communication barriers can greatly enhance the effectiveness of conflict resolution. One helpful strategy is to practice active listening, which involves fully focusing on what the other person is saying without interrupting or formulating responses in your mind. This demonstrates respect for the speaker and allows for a more meaningful exchange of ideas.

Furthermore, cultivating assertiveness and respectful communication in difficult conversations can also break down barriers. Being assertive means expressing your needs, thoughts, and feelings in a direct yet respectful manner. It involves using "I" statements to express how you are personally impacted by a situation rather than blaming or attacking the other person. By taking ownership of your emotions and communicating them assertively, you create a safe space for open dialogue and problem-solving.

In conclusion, overcoming communication barriers such as defensiveness and misunderstandings is crucial for effective conflict resolution and healthy relationships. By actively listening, clarifying misunderstandings, and practicing assertiveness, individuals can foster an environment of understanding and respect where conflicts can be resolved constructively.

Nurturing Healthy Relationships:

In this section, we will explore the importance of trust, respect, and open communication in cultivating healthy relationships. These foundational elements are crucial for building strong, meaningful connections with others.

Trust is the cornerstone of any successful relationship. It is the confidence and reliance we have in another person's reliability, honesty, and integrity. Building trust takes time and consistency. It involves being transparent, keeping promises, and maintaining confidentiality. By demonstrating trustworthiness in our words and actions, we create a safe space for open communication and vulnerability.

Respect is another vital component of nurturing healthy relationships. It involves valuing the opinions, boundaries, and autonomy of others. Respecting someone means treating them with kindness, empathy, and consideration. It also means actively listening to their perspectives without judgment and validating their experiences. When both parties feel respected, they are more likely to engage in constructive communication and resolve conflicts effectively.

Open communication is the lifeblood of any relationship. It entails expressing thoughts, feelings, and needs honestly and respectfully. By communicating openly, we can address issues before they become major conflicts or sources of resentment. It allows for the sharing of ideas, aspirations, and concerns. Open communication fosters understanding, empathy, and compromise, deepening the connection between individuals.

Setting boundaries is an essential aspect of nurturing healthy relationships. Boundaries define what is acceptable and unacceptable in terms of behavior, personal space, and emotional well-being. Each individual has different needs and limits, so it is important to communicate and respect those boundaries. Setting clear boundaries helps prevent misunderstandings, promotes mutual respect, and ensures that both parties feel safe within the relationship.

Addressing issues proactively is crucial for maintaining healthy relationships. When conflicts or concerns arise, it is important to address them promptly and constructively. Ignoring or avoiding problems can lead to resentment and further damage the relationship. By approaching issues in a calm and respectful manner, both parties can work towards finding mutually beneficial solutions and strengthening the relationship.

Cultivating positive relationship habits is essential for long-term relationship success. This includes engaging in activities that foster connection, such as spending quality time together, expressing appreciation and gratitude, and showing support for each other's goals and dreams. Small gestures of kindness and affection go a long way in nurturing healthy relationships.

Ultimately, fostering a supportive environment is crucial for maintaining healthy relationships. Supporting each other's personal growth, offering encouragement during challenging times, and being a source of comfort and understanding all contribute to creating a safe and loving space. By intentionally fostering positivity, trust, respect, open communication, and support, we can nurture the health and longevity of our relationships.

Chapter 27

Solo Flight: The Value
of Independence
****

The Value of Independence in Your 30's

"The capacity to be alone is the capacity to love. It may look paradoxical to you, but it's not. It is an existential truth."

Osho

In your 30s, embracing independence becomes essential for personal growth and a fulfilling life. It is a time of self-discovery and exploration, where enjoying your own company allows you to dive deep into the depths of your soul, understand your true identity, and nurture a love for oneself. As you navigate the challenges and joys of this dynamic decade, discover the joys of solitude, the importance of self-sufficiency, and the power of embracing your independence.

Why Independence Matters

Embracing independence is a pivotal aspect of personal growth and empowerment in your 30s. It allows you to define your identity authentically, make decisions on your own terms, and foster self-confidence.

By embracing independence, you break free from societal expectations and discover your true passions and aspirations. You become the author of your own story, making choices that align with your values and desires.

Furthermore, independence encourages you to step outside of your comfort zone, take risks, and learn from both successes and failures. It instills a sense of resilience and adaptability, essential qualities for navigating the ups and downs of life.

Embracing independence also strengthens your self-worth and self-esteem. When you rely on yourself and believe in your abilities, you develop a deeper sense of confidence that radiates through all aspects of your life.

Building independence in your 30s is key to a satisfying and worthwhile life. It lets you pave your own way, welcome fresh experiences, and totally enjoy the ups and downs of adulthood.

Exploring Yourself and Growing Personally

Once you start enjoying being alone in your 30s, the doors to self-exploration and personal growth open. This journey lends a deeper understanding, creating an enjoyable and rewarding life.

Spending time alone for self-reflection gives insights into your passions, standards, and dreams. This introspection is a strong instrument for personal development, leading your life choices to coincide with your true identity. Self-learning can be through writing, meditation, or creative activities, making it meaningful.

Self-exploration may reveal hidden abilities or likes, adding personal development options. Knowing what really gives you happiness and gratification lets you organize your aims and follow a route that matches your genuine identity. This self-consciousness is vital for personal development and molding the life you wish for.

In addition to that, enjoying solitude helps grow self-assurance and tenacity. Depending solely on yourself for friendship and help transforms you into your cheerleader and motivator. Each step towards personal growth boosts your confidence in your abilities, building a solid sense of power.

As you embark on the journey of self-discovery and personal growth, remember that it is not a linear process. It is a continuous and evolving exploration of your desires, interests, and evolving sense of self. Embrace the adventure and open yourself up to the transformative power of enjoying your own company.

Cultivating Self-Reliance

One of the key aspects of embracing independence in your 30s is cultivating self-reliance. Self-reliance empowers you to confidently tackle challenges and make independent choices, leading to personal growth and a sense of fulfillment.

Developing self-reliance involves building skills and traits that allow you to rely on yourself and trust your abilities. It is about gaining the confidence to handle various situations and navigate through life with resilience.

An essential component of cultivating self-reliance is developing a growth mindset. Embracing a growth mindset means believing in your ability to learn, adapt, and improve. This mindset encourages you to seek out new experiences, step out of your comfort zone, and actively pursue personal growth.

Another important aspect of self-reliance is taking responsibility for your own actions and decisions. By becoming self-reliant, you become accountable for your choices and their consequences. This fosters a sense of ownership and control over your life, enabling you to shape your future according to your own values and aspirations.

Cultivating self-reliance also involves nurturing a strong sense of self-trust. Trusting yourself means having confidence in your judgment, intuition, and abilities. It allows you to rely on your own strengths and make decisions that align with your values and goals.

Building up self-reliance helps you stop relying on others for approval or guidance. You gain the ability to tackle life's hurdles with guts and persistence. This self-reliance boosts your overall wellness and triumphs.

We'll delve into ways to foster self-reliance and learn to love solitude in this portion. Self-reliance, starting from personal development to strengthening relationships, is key to a satisfying, independent life in your thirties.

Creating Strong Bonds

Relationships need a sturdy base. Interestingly, cherishing solitude can lead to deeper, healthier relationships.

Being independent clarifies and strengthen bonds. If you're okay with solitude and exert your independence. You bring calm confidence into your relationships allowing deeper connections, minus the need for constant approval or company.

Establishing bonds isn't only about having someone around, but also respecting each other's individuality. Having a good relationship with yourself makes you more tolerant of others. You start celebrating their rare traits and success rather than contrasting or competing with them.

Valuing Alone Time

Cherishing time with yourself is about spending precious moments in introspective thought and personal progression. This enhances your interactions as you are able to be fully engaged and understand your own needs better. Consequently, you are confident expressing these needs within your connections with others.

Putting self-care first and creating space for your hobbies and passions makes you a more complete person. This personal happiness reflects positively in your connections. You are more able to show understanding, empathize, and provide comfort to your loved ones.

A strong bond with oneself is the basis for making deeper connections with others. If both parties in a bond are self-sufficient and find joy within themselves, they can build a supportive and satisfying relationship.

Improving your self-sufficiency and dedicating time for your personal progression benefits not only you, but also strengthens the bonds with your social circle and significant others. This cultivates balance, reliance, and autonomy in your connections, nurturing greater closeness and insight.

So, appreciate your autonomy and enjoy being with yourself. Creating deeper connections starts with establishing a firm bond with yourself.

Discovering Satisfaction in Seclusion

Being alone can lead to joy in your life. When alone, you get a chance to really think about who you are. You can stop, link up with your inner feelings, and understand what's going on inside you.

Alone time lets creativity thrive. In the quiet, your thoughts can roam. This leads to fresh thoughts and views. Even simple things can spark your imagination, pushing your creative sides and unlocking new paths.

Also, alone time can restore you. Today's world is loud and busy, but setting aside personal time can restore your stamina and equilibrium. It lets you break from outside interruptions and refocus on what you want, need, and love.

Finding joy in solitude isn't only about being on your own or being lonely. It's about knowing being alone can be powerful and beautiful. It's about realizing your own company is precious and you can enjoy being by yourself.

In these times, you can do what you love, like reading, writing, reflecting, or doing hobbies that make you happy. This is a chance to care for yourself and take part in things that feed your spirit.

Enjoying solitude benefits are more than just for you. When you are satisfied in your own company, you bring honesty and contentment to your relationships. From a fulfilled place, you can love and be loved, without depending on others for approval or happiness.

So, embrace solitude. Allow yourself to revel in its gifts of self-reflection, creativity, and rejuvenation. Find fulfillment in the moments when you are alone, and let them ignite a sense of purpose and inner peace within you.

Pursuing Personal Passions

When you enjoy your own company, you have the freedom and focus to pursue your passions wholeheartedly. Dedicating time to your personal interests and hobbies not only brings you joy, but it also allows you to explore your creativity, cultivate new skills, and nurture your personal growth. Whether it's painting, writing, playing an instrument, or engaging in sports, pursuing your passions can provide a sense of fulfillment and purpose in your life.

By immersing yourself in activities that genuinely ignite your passion, you can tap into a state of flow and lose yourself in the process. This deep engagement often leads to a sense of accomplishment, self-discovery, and even personal breakthroughs. It's during these moments, when you are pursuing your passions, that you truly come alive and find a sense of meaning in what you do.

Moreover, pursuing personal passions can also have a positive impact on other areas of your life. It can boost your self-esteem, increase your resilience in the face of challenges, and enhance your overall well-being. It allows you to develop a deeper understanding of yourself and what truly brings you happiness and fulfillment.

So, don't hesitate to set aside time to explore and pursue your passions. Embrace the joy and fulfillment that comes with dedicating yourself to activities that truly resonate with your soul. By pursuing your passions, you not only enrich your own life but also inspire others to follow their own dreams and passions.

Self-Care and Well-Being Promotion

It's key to put your self-care and well-being first for a joyous, complete life. Relish being on your own. It makes looking after yourself simpler and nicer. See how this approach boosts your health and mindset:

1. Space for Quiet Thoughts and Rest

Alone time fosters quiet thoughts and rest. You recharge, rejuvenate, stress less, and heighten overall health.

2. Attuning to Your Wants

Self-care brings clarity on your needs. That insight helps you make good choices, achieving balance and a fulfilling life.

3. Awareness Here and Now

Being by yourself enhances awareness of the here and now. It lets you savour the present, enjoy life's simple pleasures, and find peace.

4. Pursuing What You Love

Self-care means doing what you love. Hobbies, nature walks, or pamper sessions are some examples. Doing things you love uplifts your welfare.

5. Drawing Lines and Saying No

Being independent allows you to say no, protecting your welfare. Putting yourself first promotes a healthier, balanced routine.

6. Building Resilience and Managing Stress

When you take time for self-care, you build resilience and enhance your ability to cope with stress. This allows you to navigate life's challenges with more ease and maintain a positive mindset.

By nurturing self-care and well-being, you can lead a more fulfilling life that is aligned with your own needs and desires. Embracing your independence and enjoying your own company are essential steps on this journey of self-care and personal growth.

Overcoming Fear of Missing Out (FOMO)

Fear of Missing out (FOMO) can be a powerful force that prevents us from fully embracing our independence and enjoying our own company. It is the fear that if we choose one thing, we will miss out on something better. This fear can lead to a constant need for validation, comparison, and anxiety about not being included in every social event or opportunity.

To overcome the fear of missing out, it is important to shift our mindset and embrace the present moment. Here are some strategies to help you overcome FOMO and fully embrace your independence:

1. **Mindful Awareness:** Practice mindfulness and be present in the moment. Instead of worrying about what you might be missing out on, focus on what you are currently experiencing and find gratitude in the present.
2. **Set Priorities:** Identify your values and priorities. By aligning your actions with what truly matters to you, you can make conscious choices and let go of the fear of missing out on things that do not align with your values.

Lay off social media: Platforms like these can enhance your fear of missing out. Be sure to take breaks or cut down the time you spend there. This will lower the unneeded stress that comes from constantly comparing your life to others'.

Try JOMO: Don't stress about missing out, instead, enjoy the Joy of Missing Out (JOMO). Cherish solitude and the unrestricted freedom it gives for personal improvement and wellness. Show kindness to yourself: Employ self-compassion. It's okay to put your needs first. Remember, not being a part of some events or chances does not determine your value or success.

Express gratitude: Change your view from what you might be missing to what you already possess. Develop a thankful disposition for the blessings, friendships, and openings that are already a part of your life.

Using these methods can defeat your fear of missing out, while reveling in your independence. Enjoying your solitary time and living in the moment are vital for personal progress, self-realization, and happiness in your journey.

Drawing Lines and Setting Priorities

Independence lets you set boundaries and prioritize vital matters in your life. When you prioritize, you use your time, energy, and resources wisely, focusing on actions and relationships that match your principles and ambitions. Drawing lines helps protect your well-being and ensures your needs are met.

Getting your life in order starts with knowing yourself. Reflect on what you cherish, long for, and what you can handle. Acknowledge your aspirations and what you can put up with. This understanding makes it easier for you to create boundaries that respect your values and guard your peace.

After you know your boundaries, share them. Be straightforward and voice your needs and limitations politely. It's important to remember; it's not about controlling others, it's about managing your experiences and creating a balance in your relationships.

Saying "no" is an essential part of defining boundaries. Organize your schedule and assignments considering your objectives and values. When an offer or request doesn't align with your values, it's okay to reject it or find a middle ground. Remember, declining one offer means welcoming something else of greater value.

As you journey towards self-reliance, remain open to changing your boundaries. Adjusting to changes is important, as your needs might vary. Constantly check-in with yourself to ensure that your boundaries still line up with your development and peace.

Enjoying Solo Journeys

Ever journeyed alone? It's like freeing yourself, exploring unknown territories at your pace. Traveling solo molds toughness, launches self-belief, and makes lasting impressions.

Unlock limitless possibilities by journeying alone. Be it hiking snow-topped mountains, exploring bustling cities, or relishing the serenity of nature; each outing can reveal your true self.

Why Solo Adventures Rock?

Solo adventures are beneficial in many ways. One, they dare you into the unknown, fortifying self-belief. You are solely accountable, facing all challenges on your own, developing a thick skin and faith in your abilities.

Moreover, these experiences enhance self-observation and revelation. There are no hindrances; you dive in, understanding your cravings, aspirations, and potential.

Finally, solo adventures promote self-reliance. You become your guide, problem-solver, and decider, which nurtures self-sustaining attitudes impacting diverse life areas positively.

Making Lasting Impressions

Among the delights of solo adventures is making exceptional memories. Viewing a stunning sunset in an exotic place, experiencing a different culture, or meeting fellow explorers, such experiences becomes lifelong treasures.

Going on solo adventures is super fun. You get to do what you want, when you want. The best part? Unexpected friends and cool stories to tell. Don't wait. Jump in! The world is ready for your adventure.

Your 30s is a great time to be happy with yourself. Make peace within. There is nothing like some alone time to reflect on your life, your dreams. Say hello to inner peace!

How to start? Easy. Be kind to yourself. Set personal boundaries. Do what makes you happy! Listen to your heart.

Care for your soul with activities you love. Read a book. Meditate. Follow a hobby. By doing this, you invest in your own happiness. Sounds good, doesn't it? So, start now.

The Power of Solitude and Self-Reflection

One of the keys to finding contentment in your own company is embracing solitude and self-reflection. Solitude allows you to disconnect from external distractions and turn inward. It provides a sacred space for introspection, self-discovery, and personal growth.

When you are alone, you have the freedom to explore your thoughts, emotions, and desires. You can uncover your true values, identify areas for personal improvement, and gain clarity on your life's purpose. This process of self-reflection is crucial for finding contentment and living a life aligned with your authentic self.

Moreover, solitude grants you the opportunity to recharge and rejuvenate. It allows you to disconnect from the busyness of daily life and allocate time for self-care and self-nurturing. By prioritizing moments of solitude, you can replenish your energy and cultivate a deep sense of well-being.

Finding contentment in your own company is a journey that requires patience, self-compassion, and a willingness to embrace solitude. Through self-reflection, self-care, and embracing the power of solitude, you can cultivate a lasting sense of inner peace and contentment that will positively impact every aspect of your life.

Independence as a Lifelong Journey

Embracing independence in your 30s is just the beginning of a transformative and empowering lifelong journey. It sets the foundation for personal growth, self-discovery, and a fulfilling life. By embracing independence, you open yourself up to new experiences, challenges, and opportunities that will shape the person you become.

Nourishing and sustaining your independence throughout life requires constant self-reflection, adaptability, and a commitment to embracing change. It's a lifelong process of learning, evolving, and continually expanding your boundaries.

Throughout this lifelong journey, you'll explore different aspects of independence, from enjoying your own company and pursuing your passions, to setting boundaries and prioritizing your well-being. Each step along the way contributes to your personal growth and allows you to become a more self-reliant and resilient individual.

Embracing independence is not about completely disconnecting from others or distancing yourself from meaningful relationships. Instead, it's a journey of finding the right balance between interdependence and self-sufficiency. It's about nurturing your independence while still fostering deep connections with loved ones and building a strong support system.

As you embark on this lifelong journey of embracing independence, remember that it's a process that takes time and patience. Be kind to yourself, celebrate your achievements, and be open to learning from both successes and setbacks. By embracing independence as a lifelong journey, you pave the way for personal growth, empowerment, and a life filled with purpose and fulfillment.

The Impact of Self-Sufficiency on Relationships

When it comes to relationships, developing self-sufficiency can have a profound impact. Rather than relying on others for our happiness or well-being, self-sufficiency allows us to cultivate healthier, more balanced connections based on interdependence rather than dependency.

By fostering a sense of self-sufficiency, we become more confident in our own abilities and less likely to seek validation or fulfillment solely from our relationships. This newfound independence enables us to bring our whole selves to the table, enhancing the quality of our interactions and fostering a deeper level of connection.

When both partners in a relationship have a strong sense of self-sufficiency, they are better able to support and uplift each other, rather than relying on one another to meet all of their emotional, physical, or intellectual needs. This shared self-sufficiency creates a dynamic where both individuals can thrive together while still maintaining their individuality.

Moreover, self-sufficiency encourages personal growth and development, which in turn benefits the relationship. As each partner continues to pursue their own interests, passions, and goals, they bring unique experiences and perspectives to the table, enriching the relationship and fostering a sense of constant growth and exploration.

In addition, self-sufficiency helps establish healthier boundaries and communication patterns within a relationship. When both partners have a strong sense of self and are comfortable with their own autonomy, they can effectively communicate their needs, desires, and boundaries, resulting in a greater sense of mutual respect and understanding.

Overall, self-sufficiency has a transformative effect on relationships, leading to greater mutual support, growth, and fulfillment. Embracing self-sufficiency allows individuals to bring their best selves to their relationships, fostering healthier connections built on interdependence and mutual respect.

Embracing Change and Adaptation

Independence empowers individuals to embrace change and navigate the uncertainties of life with resilience and confidence. When you enjoy your own company and embrace your independence, you develop valuable skills that help you adapt to any situation that comes your way.

Change is a constant in life, and being able to embrace it is crucial for personal growth and success. By cultivating independence and self-sufficiency, you become more adaptable and open to new experiences. You learn to let go of the fear of the unknown and approach change as an opportunity for growth.

Adaptation is the key to thriving in a fast-paced and ever-changing world. When you are comfortable with enjoying your own company and being self-reliant, you become better equipped to face unexpected challenges and adapt to new circumstances. Embracing independence allows you to tap into your inner strength and resourcefulness, enabling you to find creative and innovative solutions to any problems that arise.

Moreover, by embracing change and adaptation, you become more resilient and flexible. You learn to let go of rigid expectations and embrace the uncertainties that life brings. This mindset shift allows you to navigate transitions with grace and confidence, maintaining a sense of stability even in challenging times.

In conclusion, embracing change and adaptation is a natural progression of embracing independence. By enjoying your own company and fostering self-sufficiency, you develop the skills and mindset needed to thrive in an ever-changing world. Embrace the opportunities for growth and learning that come with change, and see how it transforms your life in remarkable ways.

The Wrap-Up

Your 30s is a great time to become more independent. This adventure enhances life in incredible ways. We've talked about how important it is to be happy with just you. And, the good things that come with it.

When you're fine being alone and can rely on yourself, cool stuff happens. You learn more about you. You grow as a person. You can chase after your dreams without holding back. You're able to have stronger bonds and enjoy your own space. This helps your well-being and boosts your ties with others.

Plus, being independent gets you ready for challenges. You worry less about missing out. You can roll with life's punches. You start setting healthy limits and focusing on what's really important. This leads to happiness and tranquility.

Always remember, independence is not an end goal. It's an ongoing journey. By learning to stand on your own two feet, you're setting up for a happier, direction-filled life. So, why wait? Find joy in your own space. Welcome the liberties of independence. This empowering step is perfect in your 30s.

Chapter 28

Global Mindset: The World as Your Oyster

****

Did you know that having a global mindset can open you up to unprecedented personal growth? In our rapidly evolving world, a global mindset is more important than ever before. Whether it's going on vacation to different places or immersing yourself in other cultures, the benefits are endless. Expand your horizons and reach your potential as we dive into the ways embracing a global mindset can help you grow personally from developing cultural intelligence to encouraging innovation. Get ready to embark on a journey of self-discovery as we explore the incredible ways a global mindset can transform your life.

The Benefits of Thinking Globally

Having an international mindset can work wonders for personal development by helping us expand our horizons, in turn improving our cultural intelligence and ability to navigate this interconnected world.

When we think globally, our viewpoints and grasp on reality widen. We gain interest in different cultures, traditions, and ways of life which helps us become more round individuals. This newfound knowledge helps us appreciate diversity and promotes open-mindedness that plays a role in personal growth.

Cultural intelligence is also acquired through having a global mindset and helps one navigate diverse environments along with being able to communicate effectively with people from various backgrounds. Its understanding allows for strong connections between people across the globe which ultimately strengthens relationships which are key in reaching personal growth.

Expanding boundaries is another way personal growth thrives because it challenges everything we thought we knew about how things were done but now questions why they must be that way at all. A global mentality not only exposes us new ideas but it pushes us outside of our comfort zones so that change becomes second naturea crucial skill in order to adapt quicklyin order to thrive within these conditions.

In conclusion thinking globally is the push many need to overcome barriers break down stereotypes and set foot onto the path where lives' are transformed through their own selves.. It's How you discover yourself learn continuously while transforming yourself throughout it all.

Expand Your Perspectives through Travel

Going on vacation isn't just a destination it's an experience that can impact personal growth the most. As we step out of our typical routines and embark on new things doors open and endless possibilities begin to appear. Traveling allows us to gain new insights, expand our thought process, and embrace open-mindedness that can lead to tremendous personal growth.

When traveling we have the opportunity to interact with cultures, traditions, and ways of life that are foreign to us. This helps us grow as human beings by challenging everything we know about the world. It encourages us to question ourselves break free from comfort zones all in hopes of thinking different perspectives. The more we're out there experiencing these types of things the better chance we have at becoming adaptable resilient and open-minded individuals.

The Power of New Experiences

Traveling helps us break through our normal routine and puts us in a position where were always trying new things. Whether it be trying new foods or interacting with locals each provides valuable lessons while helping us grasp how diverse our world really is

By embracing the new, we gain awe, curiosity and wonder. This allows us to be receptive to the unexpected and adaptable to change. Being a person who is open minded is essential for growth as it helps you develop a wider mindset and also let's you navigate through unknown situations with grace and confidence.

Traveling also challenges our comfort zones, allowing us to face fears that we might have never thought about before. Whether that be overcoming language barriers or just trying out an extreme sport, each one of these obstacles makes us stronger. These experiences allow us to embrace uncertainty which is a key factor in living life with a growth mindset.

In the end, travel gives so many opportunities for personal growth. And once we step outside of our own perspectives, we are able to see how diverse the world really is. Through this adventure of ours, new experiences will come our way and we must always keep an open mind in order to learn from them.

Effective Communication on a Global Scale

Mastering effective communication on a global scale is an essential skill that helps us navigate the complexities of our interconnected world. It enables us to connect with people from diverse backgrounds, build strong relationships, and foster collaboration.

As we engage in meaningful conversations with individuals from different cultures and backgrounds, we gain new insights, learn from their experiences, and broaden our perspectives. Effective communication breaks down barriers and creates an inclusive environment where everyone feels heard and understood.

However, communicating effectively across cultures can be challenging. Different cultures have unique approaches to verbal and non-verbal communication. For example, while Americans are generally direct when they communicate, Asian cultures tend to be more indirect and rely heavily on context.

When interacting with individuals from different cultures who speak different languages than ours or use different methods of communication, we must exercise patience and empathy. We need to be flexible in our approach and willing to adapt to the other person's style of communication.

By doing so, we prevent misunderstandings, cultivate trust-based relationships built on mutual respect, increase productivity within teams that span across borders, and drive innovation through collaboration.

To master effective communication on a global scale takes time as it requires self-awareness about our own cultural biases, active listening skills, openness to feedback from others about how we can improve our communication styles even further.

Lastly but most importantly it requires us to always have kindness at the forefront of our communications. These skills need practice but once mastered they will take you far in both your professional life as well as your personal life.

Effective communication is key to personal growth, especially in a world that is more connected than ever. The more we communicate with others from different cultures and backgrounds, the more we learn about them which helps us develop our understanding of cultural values and norms.

Connecting people from all over the globe bridges gaps we'll naturally have due to distance. Because of this, we're able to expand our perspectives, challenge assumptions and see things from another person's point of view.

Understanding other cultures comes from actively listening, being empathetic and respecting another's views. The more conversations are had the better you will become at adapting to any culture thrown your way, allowing growth in multiple aspects.

Building relationships is an underrated benefit for global communication. If you're friends with someone from a different country or background that could open up many opportunities such as collaborations on projects or even job opportunities.

Not only that but it's been proven time and time again that when you have a diverse team it often leads to innovative ideas since everyone will be bringing their own unique thought process to the table.

It's safe to say effective global communication is crucial for personal growth as it allows us to understand different cultures, form meaningful relationships and bring everyone together through ideas or projects.

Creating Opportunities for Abroad Work

If you're looking for personal growth then look no further than working abroad. Going anywhere outside of your comfort zone has the ability to shift everything around including your career development.

Working abroad allows professionals like yourself an opportunity of a lifetime by immersing yourself in new languages, cultures and perspectives. Not only does this give you an idea of how different countries operate but also puts things into perspective with where you stand on a global level within your profession.

Being able to work abroad also improves adaptability since there will be many times where things won't go according to plan. But finding solutions that work for everyone involved shows incredible strength between both parties which can lead down many paths.

Even people from different countries will be able to resonate with your experience and who knows, you might even find yourself working on a global project.

Through working abroad, individuals are given insights into global markets and industries. They are exposed to new approaches, trends, and innovations. It teaches them how to navigate diverse business environments while improving their problem-solving and decision-making skills. This experience strengthens a person's skill set as well as gives them a deeper understanding of cultural differences.

Work abroad experiences also lead to personal growth in many ways. People are challenged to step out of their comfort zones when they have to live and work in a foreign country. This helps foster self-confidence, independence, and self-discovery all at the same time. Another benefit is that it broadens a person's worldview and encourages open-mindedness.

Many well-known companies see the value in these types of experiences for employees. In fact, many actively provide or help facilitate work abroad opportunities for employees. Workers who have gained international exposure offer more value than colleagues who haven't. This type of employee has unique perspectives due to cultural sensitivity and adaptability.

Whether it is only for a short-term or long-term basis, working abroad can be an unforgettable experience that grows careers exponentially. Opening up new possibilities by helping professionals broaden horizons makes today's world thrive with this type of interconnectedness.

Technology and Opportunities Going Global

Technology has completely changed our lifestyle on all fronts over the years since its creation. On top of that it continues to be a driving force behind personal development by giving individuals access to global opportunities so they can chase entrepreneurial dreams.

Personal connections have never been easier thanks to technology's ability to connect us globally in seconds or less even at times. With that it brings endless benefits such as growing personally for both professional reasons then entrepreneurship.

We now have the ability through tech advancements where we can collaborate with others around the world seamlessly. Exchanging ideas and knowledge leading hopefully to valuable partnerships down the line will continue expanding networks daily.

With social media platforms playing huge roles in everyone's lives connecting with diverse cultures comes naturally now. This will lead to a global perspective and allow for markets to be tapped into that may have seemed impossible just 10 years ago.

Digital Nomadism Expanding the Mind

The rise of digital nomadism has been made possible only thanks to tech advancements. With the freedom that remote work provides young professionals are now able to explore the world all while pursuing career goals.

This path in life leads directly to not only working in different countries but also opens eyes on various cultures. It's a journey that anyone who wishes can take where personal growth is limitless.

Supporting Entrepreneurship with Tech

In order for something new to grow, it needs someone who believes in it and will support its every need. The same can be said when it comes to innovation and entrepreneurship which technology plays a vital role in supporting.

Different platforms online empower aspiring entrepreneurs around the globe allowing them to reach audiences they never thought were possible before the internet boom. On top of that accessing resources from experts worldwide makes learning about your own business easier than ever.

By combining e-commerce, crowdfunding, and digital marketing you've got yourself a recipe for success if used right. All great businesses start with an idea so once you've found yours don't hesitate on putting all your focus into making it happen because at this point technology allows us endless possibilities.

Once we've embraced what technology brings us our lives become easier when navigating today's fast-paced lifestyle. Adapting, innovating, then seizing opportunities before others do are all benefits of staying ahead with tech trends.

The journey to personal growth in a global context is built on a foundation of two things: resilience and adaptability. These two core skills act as stepping stones that will allow you to get through any setbacks you face when trying to progress. The journey you're about to embark on won't be easy, but it'll be worth it. One of the most important things for your success is perseverance, and with these two qualities, you will definitely have that.

Building Resilience

When going through something like this, there's likely going to be a lot of uncertainty. You need to have resilience so when you come across this type of stuff, it doesn't bother you much. You should want to keep pushing forward against all odds and not let anything stop you from progressing. If you develop this skill, it'll make your path to personal growth much smoother.

Fostering Adaptability

Another very important thing in this process is being open to change and embracing diversity. As we know, no two cultures are alike so if we don't learn how to adapt quickly then it could become very difficult for us when dealing with different market frameworks or diverse teams. Honing in on this skill will also allow us to seize countless opportunities that we otherwise wouldn't even notice. If we can do that then there's no doubt about it - success is ours.

With these two qualities at our disposal, nothing feels impossible anymore. Instead of treating obstacles like they're roadblocks, we can flip the script and use them as stepping stones. used correctly though, they aren't just gonna help us overcome obstacles - they'll help us seize opportunities too.

How Collaboration Can Help Us Grow

It's 2021...we all know how powerful collaboration can be by now right? It can drive personal growth for one...but its impact isn't just limited there though -

Whenever people come together from different backgrounds and work towards a common goal, we see new and innovative ideas arise to the surface. The exchange of ideas and experiences is what sparks creativity.

On top of that, collaborating on a global scale will give us a much better understanding of the world. Even in today's interconnected world every culture still has its own customs and traditions. So being able to collaborate with people from different cultures will allow us to challenge our assumptions and gain insights from different perspectives.

Diversity also leads to personal growth. When you're around people that have very different ideas, beliefs, or experiences than yourself it'll force you to become more open-minded and empathetic. By doing this we can step out of our comfort zones which ultimately leads to growth.

In today's era, collaboration isn't just something that benefits individuals either - it helps organizations too! If multiple communities come together then there's nothing they can't overcome. Tackling complex problems is made 100x easier when done as a collective

By embracing diversity through global collaboration we can start contributing towards a more interconnected world that's prosperous for all

Furthermore, interacting with people who come from various cultural backgrounds is crucial for team collaboration and the sharing of ideas. Learning lessons from what makes their unique approach to life different than others can also bring a fresh perspective on our own way of thinking.

Personal Growth Benefits of Cultural Exchange:

1. Inspiration: When you experience different cultures it ignites an unconscious inspiration that causes you to create innovative, boundary-pushing work.
2. Open-mindedness: When we do exchanges like this, it stimulates open-mindedness — making us open to new perspectives and challenges any bias we may have held onto.
3. Adaptability: By immersing ourselves in foreign cultures, we force ourselves to be adaptable. This skill is essential when trying to navigate through unfamiliar environments.
4. Cultural sensitivity: The more engaged you are with other cultures, the more empathy and sensitivity you will develop towards them. This allows us to connect better with different types of people and establish bonds that wouldn't be possible without this knowledge.

In today's world where creativity reigns supreme, using cultural exchange as a tool for personal growth and development is only logical. It opens up doors for inspiration that remain locked when closed off from other cultures; allowing us to broaden our creative horizons while deepening our understanding of ourselves and everything around us.

Using Global Networks to Personal Development

Creating connections all over the world can significantly benefit anyone looking for personal growth and development. These networks give access to so many new experiences and views that would never have been available before.

With all the connections comes professionals from every type of field imaginable — which gives even more opportunities for personal growth because they can act as mentors or guides in your journey. They are already at the point where you want to be so why wouldn't you take advantage?

Networking also creates this sense of community and collaboration that's needed when growing personally because if everyone has a common goal then there will never be a shortage of learning and inspiration. By surrounding yourself with like-minded individuals you increase your odds of stepping out of your comfort zone which will bring on new challenges that aid in self-improvement.

Long story short, the method of using global networks for personal growth and development is no secret; if you participate fully then knowledge will come from every angle, new perspectives will be gained, and mentorship is guaranteed.

In our "global village," where we're more connected than ever before, having an open mind and being curious is invaluable. It lets us embrace a world of different perspectives, cultures, and ideas. This leads to personal growth on a global scale.

As we continue to nurture these values in ourselves we also contribute to a more connected world that fosters diverse ideas and ways of seeing the world.

So let's keep our minds open, stay curious, and make learning a lifelong journey that never ends.

The Future of Personal Growth in a Globalized World

In today's rapidly evolving global landscape, personal growth has become intertwined with embracing a global mindset, adapting to future trends, and committing to lifelong learning. As we navigate an increasingly interconnected world, the potential for personal growth expands exponentially.

A global mindset is a critical foundation for personal growth in a globalized world. It encompasses an open-mindedness, cultural intelligence, and a willingness to embrace diversity. By adopting a global mindset, individuals can broaden their horizons, gain a deeper understanding of different cultures, and develop the adaptability necessary to thrive in an ever-changing environment.

Looking ahead, future trends will play a pivotal role in shaping personal growth. Rapid advancements in technology, artificial intelligence (AI), and automation will create new opportunities and challenges. To remain ahead of the curve, individuals must cultivate a habit of lifelong learning—constantly acquiring new skills and knowledge to adapt and thrive in the face of these emerging trends.

Embracing lifelong learning is not limited by formal education systems; rather it goes beyond traditional boundaries by encompassing curiosity-driven pursuit of knowledge and self-growth. Whether it's through online courses or workshops—or simply self-directed learning—individuals must continuously upskill themselves through reskilling programs made available by institutions like Udemy or Coursera as well as independent study techniques so they maintain relevance both personally as well as professionally.

Chapter 29

Intelligence: Strengthening Your Inner Compass

*****

Emotional intelligence significantly influences our interpersonal dynamics, empowering us to adeptly handle complex emotional landscapes and cultivate deeper bonds with those around us. Throughout this section, we will delve into the essence of emotional intelligence and its pivotal role in forging and sustaining robust relationships.

The essence of emotional intelligence is encapsulated in its capacity to discern, comprehend, and modulate not only our own emotions but also those of others. It is structured around five core elements: self-awareness, self-regulation, motivation, empathy, and social proficiency.

The bedrock of emotional intelligence is self-awareness, which entails an acute consciousness of our own emotional states, strengths, vulnerabilities, and stimuli that trigger various responses. This heightened self-awareness enables us to perceive the influence of our emotions on our actions and their subsequent impact on our interactions with others.

Self-regulation is about mastering control over our emotions. This competency involves maintaining composure in challenging scenarios, effectively managing stress, and reacting in a deliberate, constructive manner. Through self-regulation, we can avert knee-jerk reactions that might jeopardize our relational dynamics.

An integral component of emotional intelligence is motivation, the inner zeal that drives us towards achieving our aspirations and overcoming obstacles. Motivated individuals exude positivity, resilience, and a spirit of initiative. Their enthusiastic and determined demeanor serves as inspiration, encouraging those around them.

Empathy represents the capacity to resonate with and appreciate the feelings of others. It transcends mere sympathy or compassion, inviting us to genuinely immerse ourselves in another's experience. Empathetic individuals engage in attentive listening, acknowledge and validate the emotions of others, and demonstrate sincere care and comprehension, thereby fostering deeper relational ties.

Social skills are a diverse set of competencies essential for adeptly navigating social contexts. These include proficient listening, articulate communication, effective conflict resolution, and collaborative cooperation. Individuals equipped with robust social skills excel in creating rapport, amicably resolving disputes, and promoting positive interactions.

Acknowledging the significance of emotional intelligence in relational contexts is essential for nurturing healthy, rewarding connections. By honing self-awareness, self-regulation, motivation, empathy, and social skills, we are better equipped to manage complex emotions, communicate effectively, and establish strong emotional connections with others.

Subsequent sections of this chapter will offer a deeper examination of each emotional intelligence component and present actionable strategies for augmenting our emotional intelligence within the sphere of relationships. By leveraging emotional intelligence, we can forge more resilient bonds, amicably resolve conflicts, and nurture meaningful, enduring relationships.

Elevating self-awareness is pivotal for tapping into the benefits of emotional intelligence in relationships. Reflecting on our emotions, triggers, and conversational tendencies enables us to gain a more profound understanding of ourselves and our relational interactions.

Consider your emotional responses in various relational contexts. Are there particular scenarios or subjects that provoke intense emotional reactions in you? What are your default communicative strategies during conflicts or challenging discussions? Identifying these patterns aids in becoming more aware of your emotional reactions and mastering them more effectively.

Mindfulness is an invaluable practice for boosting self-awareness and managing emotions. It entails being fully present in the moment and observing our thoughts, emotions, and physical sensations without judgment. This practice fosters an enhanced awareness of our emotional states, offering a moment to pause before reacting impulsively.

Incorporate mindfulness practices into your daily routine, such as meditation, deep breathing exercises, or simply pausing throughout the day to introspect and observe your emotions without judgment. This cultivation of self-awareness facilitates a better understanding of the impact of our emotions on our relationships and empowers us to make more conscious choices in our responses.

Remember, the journey to developing self-awareness is continuous, necessitating ongoing reflection and practice. By committing time and effort to deepening your understanding of yourself, you can amplify your emotional intelligence and foster healthier, more fulfilling relationships.

Fostering Empathy and Comprehension

To enhance the quality and depth of our relationships, it is crucial to nurture empathy and comprehension. This requires adopting others' perspectives and viewing situations through their lens. By actively practicing empathy, we can gain a richer understanding of the emotional experiences and states of others, leading to stronger connections and more harmonious relationships.

Active listening is a key strategy for developing empathy. Make a concerted effort to genuinely listen and grasp the viewpoint of others without interruption or pre-empting your response. By acknowledging and validating their emotions, you affirm their experiences and convey genuine concern for their well-being.

Another essential aspect of fostering empathy is the ability to place ourselves in the shoes of others. Endeavor to envisage their feelings and circumstances in specific situations. This empathetic stance fosters a more compassionate and understanding attitude towards others, which can solidify our relationships and build a foundation of trust.

Empathy cultivation demands practice and dedication. It requires setting aside personal biases and judgments, approaching each interaction with openness and a compassionate heart. By actively enhancing our capacity for emotional connection and empathy, we lay the groundwork for deeper, more meaningful relationships.

By nurturing empathy and comprehension, we pave the way for

Healthier and more satisfying relationships. This section introduces strategies and techniques for honing these skills, including active listening, emotional validation, and adopting others' perspectives. Integrating these practices into our interactions fosters a more empathetic and harmonious environment, conducive to the growth and enrichment of our relationships.

Boosting communication is fundamental to leveraging emotional intelligence in relationships. Proficient communication enables individuals to articulate their emotions constructively and assertively, facilitating better understanding, connection, and resolution of conflicts. This segment will explore methods and tactics to refine communication skills, enhancing emotional intelligence.

Articulating Emotions Effectively and Assertively:

A facet of emotional intelligence is the accurate identification and expression of emotions. It's vital to convey your feelings openly and truthfully, without repression or exaggeration. Effective emotional expression involves utilizing "I" statements to claim ownership of your emotions while refraining from blaming or criticizing the other party. For instance, rather than saying, "You always make me angry," opt for, "I feel upset when this occurs."

Communicating Needs, Boundaries, and Expectations Clearly:

Transparent communication of needs, boundaries, and expectations is key to sustaining healthy relationships. It's crucial to express your needs candidly and directly, enabling your partner or loved ones to grasp what you require for emotional well-being. Likewise, establishing and communicating boundaries fosters mutual respect in relationships, delineating acceptable behaviors and clearly conveying them.

Formulating Conflict Resolution Strategies:

Conflict is an inevitable component of any relationship. Emotional intelligence equips individuals to address conflicts with empathy and understanding, seeking resolutions that consider the welfare of all involved. Rather than aiming to win or prove a point, emotional intelligence advocates for active listening and seeking common ground through compromise. Acknowledging the emotions and viewpoints of all parties enables the identification of solutions that satisfy both personal and collective needs.

By enhancing communication skills in the realm of emotional intelligence, individuals can foster an atmosphere of open dialogue and comprehension within their relationships. These capabilities encourage healthy connections, effective conflict resolution, and overall relationship satisfaction. Through continuous practice and self-reflection, individuals can bolster their communication prowess, contributing to more harmonious and rewarding relationships.

Strengthening Emotional Ties

Cultivating an emotional connection is vital for the development and maintenance of healthy relationships. By dedicating quality time, sharing experiences, and embracing vulnerability, you can intensify the emotional bond with your partner, family, friends, or romantic interests.

1. Quality Time:

Prioritize spending significant time with your loved ones. This involves eliminating distractions and genuinely engaging with them. Participate in mutually enjoyable activities and foster opportunities for candid conversations. Whether through regular date nights, family excursions, or simply sharing meals, quality time nurtures emotional connections.

2. Shared Experiences:

Creating shared memories through collective experiences strengthens bonds. Participate in activities that promote teamwork, cooperation, and personal development. This could involve traveling together, exploring new hobbies as a couple or group, or engaging in community events. Experiencing novel situations together lays a foundation of common narratives and deepens emotional ties.

3. Vulnerability:

Vulnerability means openly sharing your true thoughts and feelings, embracing authenticity, and allowing yourself to be genuinely seen. It takes trust and bravery to be vulnerable, inviting others to do the same and thus deepening relational understanding and connection.

4. Emotional Availability:

Being emotionally available entails attentive listening, demonstrating empathy, and offering support when necessary. It means being present and engaged in conversations, providing a safe space for others to share their emotions without judgment. Strive to be attentive and responsive to the emotional needs of your loved ones, reinforcing the emotional connection between you.

5. Emotional Safety:

Establishing emotional safety in your relationships is critical for open communication and mutual support. Create an environment where individuals feel free to express their thoughts, concerns, and emotions without fear of rejection or criticism. Cultivate trust, respect, and understanding by valuing each other's emotions and maintaining confidentiality.

Fostering emotional connections through quality time, shared experiences, vulnerability, emotional availability, and emotional safety fortifies relational bonds. These practices lay a robust foundation of trust and intimacy, promoting deeper connections and more satisfying relationships.

Chapter 30

The Spiritual Quest:
Exploring Your Inner Self
*****

Let's Learn About Spirituality:

We'll start on a journey. This journey is about spirituality and how it helps us grow. Spirituality isn't just a word. It works like a guide in our lives.

Spirituality isn't just about religion. It's broad. It helps us find life goals, feel connected to big ideas, and understand ourselves better. Think of spirituality as an adventure into our minds and human existence.

We journey through spiritual rites and faiths, growing as we go. There are lots of spiritual techniques to choose from. Meditation, prayer, paying attention, and rituals are but a few. Each has lessons about us and the world.

Being spiritual lets us find joy and purpose. It wakes us up to life's awe-inspiring secrets. It insists on questioning our ideas, values, and wants. It makes us think about what matters to us. Spirituality offers a fresh outlook on life and spurs conversations about our purpose.

In this chapter, we're going to study spirituality. We'll look at it from different angles. From strange theories to practical parts, be ready to learn about it all. We hope you'll start your own spiritual adventure. You'll be amazed by the power inside you. Now, let's explore spirituality and personal growth together. Understanding and considering your beliefs and values is helpful. It gives you a better idea of who you are and where you fit in the world.

Start by blocking out time for personal thinking. Do this by writing in a diary, meditating, or quietly pondering in a peaceful place. Think about these key questions: What are my beliefs? What principles hold value for me? How do they influence who I am?

During your personal thinking period, look at how spirituality and your identity link. How does spirituality influence who you are? Do you think there are parts of your identity tied to your spiritual beliefs? Looking at this link can offer a better understanding of how spirituality alters your personal wellness and growth.

Spotting where you need to grow spiritually and where you have potential for this growth is key in personal thinking. See where you want to grow in your spiritual life. This could mean understanding a belief system more fully, trying new spiritual customs, or bonding more with a higher force or universal energy.

In doing this, it's key to think personally with an open mind and no preconceived notions. Allow yourself to explore different beliefs and viewpoints, even if they're different from yours. Be eager to learn and curious as you start this journey of self-understanding and spiritual investigation.

Remember, personal thinking and connecting are ongoing. As you keep exploring personal and spiritual growth, keep revisiting these questions and think about any changes in your beliefs and values. By staying connected to yourself and thinking personally, you can better understand spirituality and encourage personal growth. Various routes to spiritual growth:

Ready to grow spiritually? Let's dive into various spiritual teachings. Every path teaches unique ideas. You can find practices that match your beliefs.

Eastern Philosophies:

- Take a look at Buddhism, Hinduism, Taoism, etc.
- Understand meditation, mindfulness, inner peace techniques.
- Know about non-attachment, compassion, self-awareness.

Western Religions:

- Dig into Christianity, Islam, Judaism teachings.
- See how prayer, rituals help in spiritual growth.

- Understand personal development through moral principles.

New Age Spirituality:
- Learn New Age spirituality for personal growth, wellness.
- Understand crystal healing, energy work, astrology, tarot.
- Connect with a higher consciousness or universal energy.

Mindfulness and Meditation:
- Benefit from mindfulness and living in the moment.
- Explore different meditation techniques, including breath-focused meditation and loving-kindness meditation.
- Discover how mindfulness and meditation can enhance your overall well-being and promote spiritual growth.

5. Nature-Based Spirituality:
- Connect with the natural world through practices such as eco-spirituality or earth-based religions.
- Explore the concept of sacred spaces and rituals in nature.
- Cultivate a deeper appreciation for the interconnectedness of all living beings.

6. Mystical Traditions:
- Dive into mystical traditions such as Sufism, Kabbalah, or Christian mysticism.
- Explore the practices of contemplation, ecstatic experiences, and connecting with the divine.
- Gain insight into the transcendent aspects of spirituality and its potential for personal transformation.

7. Personalized Spiritual Practices:
Understand the importance of creating a personalized spiritual practice that resonates with your beliefs and values.

Combine elements from different traditions or develop your own unique rituals.

Embrace spirituality as a journey of self-discovery and continual growth.

Remember, there is no one-size-fits-all approach to spirituality. It is up to you to explore and discover the paths that resonate with your heart and soul. By incorporating spiritual rituals or practices into your daily life, you can deepen your connection to yourself, others, and the world around you Nurturing Inner Peace and Joy:

We'll dive into finding peace from within using various spiritual methods. Note that spirituality is a personal journey, it can take many shapes, and it's okay if your approach aligns with your own values and beliefs.

1. Growing Inner Peace:
Meditation: Implement frequent meditation into your routine. This will quiet your mind, decrease stress, and increase self-realization. There are many types of meditation, like mindfulness, transcendental, or loving-kindness. Find one you connect with.

Breathwork: Look into breathwork methods that refocus and de-stress your mind. Techniques such as alternate nostril breathing, deep breathing, or breath awareness can be fruitful in finding tranquility.

Yoga or Tai Chi: Participating in soothing movement-based activities like yoga or tai chi will not just improve your physical health, but also promote a peaceful state of mind.

2. Tackling Stress and Maintaining Equilibrium:
Mindful Stress Management: Utilize mindfulness practices to capably manage stress. Monitor your thoughts and feelings without judgment, engage in mindful movements or tasks, or utilize relaxation techniques.

Setting Boundaries: Create definitive boundaries in your personal and professional life. This will prevent overwhelming stress and burnout. Prioritize tasks according to your needs and ensure self-care.

Self-Care Comes First: Enjoy things that make you happy and refreshed. Take care of yourself with fun baths, favorite hobbies, outdoor times, or artistic pursuits. Self-care helps you stay well.

3. Find Your Happy and Grateful Spots:

A Daily "Thank You" Routine: Grow a grateful heart by enjoying positive parts of your life. Use a "thank you" journal and write a few thankful points every day. Doing this can help you focus on happiness and plenty.

Do Things You Love: Pick activities or hobbies you love and do them often. From painting or dancing to playing music or sports, make these your priority for a joyful life.

Choose Happy People: Stick with positive and supportive folks who lift you up. Share fun times and build happy memories with friends and family who make you laugh.

Don't forget that finding peace and happiness is individual. You may need time to find what works for you, so stay open and patient as you explore different spiritual paths. Grab the chance to figure out what brings you joy and peace and make these a part of your everyday life for a well-rounded life. Daily Life Integration:

Applying spiritual principles to relationships, work, and daily routines can help create a sense of harmony and fulfillment in one's life. It's important to find ways to balance spiritual growth with other life priorities while remaining true to personal values and goals. Here are some practical strategies for integrating spirituality into daily life:

1. Relationships:

Practice compassion and empathy towards others, fostering positive and supportive connections.

Communicate openly and honestly, maintaining respectful and loving relationships.

Foster a sense of unity and interconnectedness, recognizing the divine presence in all beings.

2. Work:

Infuse your work with a sense of purpose by aligning it with your core values and beliefs.

Cultivate gratitude for the opportunity to contribute and make a difference through your work.

Create a harmonious work environment by promoting kindness, collaboration, and mindfulness.

3. Daily Routines:

Start and end each day with a moment of reflection or prayer, setting positive intentions for the day.

Incorporate mindful practices such as meditation, yoga, or breathwork into your daily routine. Find moments throughout the day to pause, reconnect with your inner self, and cultivate gratitude.

4. Balancing Priorities:

Prioritize self-care and allocate time for spiritual practices amidst other commitments.

Set boundaries to protect your spiritual practice and avoid overextending yourself.

Evaluate your priorities regularly, ensuring that spiritual growth remains a central focus in your life.

5. Creating a Sustainable Spiritual Practice:

Experiment with different spiritual practices to find what resonates with you personally.

Start small and gradually increase the time dedicated to your spiritual practice to ensure consistency.

Seek guidance from spiritual teachers, mentors, or community groups for support and inspiration.

Remember that spirituality is a deeply personal journey, and there is no one-size-fits-all approach. Adapt these strategies to your own needs and preferences, allowing spirituality to become an integral part of your everyday life. By consciously integrating spiritual principles into your relationships, work, and daily routines, you can cultivate a sense of inner peace, joy, and purpose that permeates all aspects of your life

Chapter 32

Art of Adaptability: Navigating Change

***

Recognizing the Need for Change:

Change is an inevitable and crucial part of life. It is through change that we grow, learn, and evolve as individuals. Recognizing the need for change is the first step towards embracing it and reinventing ourselves for a better future.

There are several signs that indicate a need for change in our lives. These signs may manifest in various aspects, such as dissatisfaction with our current situation, feeling stuck or stagnant, or longing for something more fulfilling. It's important to pay attention to these signs and acknowledge that they serve as a catalyst for personal growth.

Making room for transformation is key in personal growth, helping us reach our abilities' peak. Change let's us challenge our restrictions, probes new potential, and unearths hidden skills. Accepting change opens doorways to thrilling escapades and experiences, directing us on a path to a purposeful, enriching life.

It's natural to be scared or even fight change. The leap from our comfort zone is nerve-wracking. But, by daring and stretching past our boundaries, we unlock access to unprecedented success and joy.

Grasping the importance of transformation becomes vital to our growth. Changes offer us the chance to adapt and evolve. Resistance to change shrinks our potential, robbing us of our real satisfaction.

True acceptance of change, and remaking ourselves, requires an open mind and a readiness to release outdated patterns and convictions. Identifying the necessity for change and its relevance in our lives lets us step onto a journey of self-exploration, transformation leading us to a more satisfying future. Assessing Your Current Reality:

Prior to launching into a fruitful path of remaking oneself, it's key to evaluate your present condition. This involves a deep self-evaluation to identify areas of your life where a transformation could be beneficial and reflection on your ambitions, principles, and expectations.

Begin by taking a step back and examining various aspects of your life, including your career, relationships, health, and personal growth. Ask yourself honest and introspective questions such as:

1. **Career:** Am I satisfied and fulfilled in my current job or profession? Does it align with my passions and long-term goals? Are there new skills or industries I want to explore?
2. **Relationships:** Are my relationships supportive and healthy? Do they contribute positively to my overall well-being? Are there any toxic or draining relationships that need to be addressed or let go?
3. **Health:** How am I prioritizing my physical and mental well-being? Are there any changes I can make to improve my overall health? Do I need to establish healthier habits or seek professional help?
4. **Personal Growth:** Am I continuously learning and expanding my knowledge and skills? What areas of personal development do I want to focus on? Are there any hobbies or passions I want to pursue further?

During this assessment, take the time to listen to your inner voice and trust your instincts. Reflect on what truly matters to you and the kind of life you envision for yourself in the future. Consider what brings you joy, fulfillment, and a sense of purpose.

As you assess your current situation, remember that this process is meant to be an opportunity for self-discovery and growth. Avoid judgment or criticism towards yourself. Instead, approach it with curiosity and openness.

After identifying what needs to change in your life, you can start to make a plan. This roadmap helps guide you. You'll be on your way to changing yourself and building a life that matches your deepest wishes and dreams.

Navigating Change in Your 30's: A Step-by-Step Guide

Change is an inevitable part of life, and as you enter your 30's, you may find yourself facing significant transitions in various aspects of your life. Whether it's related to your career, relationships, or personal growth, navigating change in your 30's can be both exciting and challenging. This step-by-step guide aims to provide practical advice to help you embrace and navigate change effectively during this transformative period of your life.

Step 1: Embracing Change

Acknowledge the Inevitability of Change

Understand that change is a natural part of life and that embracing it is essential for personal growth and development.

Reflect on past experiences of change and how they have contributed to your personal and professional development.

Cultivate a Growth Mindset

Adopt a growth mindset that enables you to view challenges as opportunities for learning and self-improvement.

Embrace the belief that your abilities and intelligence can be developed through dedication and hard work.

Step 2: Self-Reflection and Goal Setting

Reflect on Your Values and Priorities

Take time to reflect on your core values and what truly matters to you in life.

Identify your priorities and assess whether your current lifestyle aligns with them.

Set Clear and Attainable Goals

Define short-term and long-term goals that reflect your aspirations and ambitions.

Ensure that your goals are specific, measurable, achievable, relevant, and time-bound (SMART).

Step 3: Career Transitions

Assess Your Career Trajectory

Evaluate your current job satisfaction and career trajectory.

Consider whether your skills and interests are aligned with your current career path.

Explore New Opportunities

Research potential career paths or job opportunities that align with your skills and interests.

Network with professionals in your desired field and seek mentorship or advice from those who have successfully navigated similar career transitions.

Upgrade Your Skills

Identify any skill gaps that may hinder your transition to a new career path.

Enroll in relevant courses, workshops, or certification programs to enhance your skill set and increase your marketability.

Step 4: Personal Development

Nurture Meaningful Relationships

Evaluate your personal relationships and determine which ones contribute positively to your life.

Invest time and effort in nurturing meaningful connections with friends, family, and potential mentors.

Prioritize Self-Care

Develop a self-care routine that encompasses physical, emotional, and mental well-being.

Engage in activities that promote relaxation, such as meditation, exercise, or hobbies that bring you joy.

Seek Personal Growth Opportunities

Embrace new experiences and challenges that foster personal growth and self-discovery.

Consider volunteering, traveling, or participating in community initiatives that align with your values and interests.

Step 5: Financial Planning

Review Your Financial Situation

Assess your current financial status, including income, expenses, savings, and investments.

Identify areas where you can optimize your financial management and make necessary adjustments.

Set Financial Goals

Establish clear financial goals, such as saving for a major purchase, investing for retirement, or paying off debt.

Create a realistic budget that aligns with your financial goals and helps you track your progress.

Seek Professional Advice

Consider consulting a financial advisor to receive personalized guidance on investment strategies, retirement planning, and wealth management.

Step 6: Embracing Change and Adaptability

Embrace Flexibility and Adaptability

Recognize that change often requires flexibility and adaptability in your thinking and actions.

Cultivate the ability to adjust to new circumstances and embrace uncertainty with confidence.

Learn from Setbacks

Understand that setbacks are a natural part of the change process.

Reflect on setbacks as opportunities for learning and resilience-building rather than reasons for discouragement.

Celebrate Milestones

Acknowledge and celebrate your achievements and milestones, no matter how small.

Recognize the progress you've made and use it as motivation to continue navigating change with confidence.

Navigating change in your 30's can be a transformative and empowering experience when approached with the right mindset and strategies. By embracing change, setting clear goals, prioritizing personal and professional development, and maintaining adaptability, you can navigate this period of transition with confidence and resilience. Remember that change is an opportunity for growth, and by following this step-by-step guide, you can effectively navigate the changes that come your way in your 30's.

This comprehensive guide aims to equip you with the tools and mindset needed to navigate change effectively in your 30's, allowing you to embrace new opportunities and achieve personal and professional fulfillment.

Chapter 33

Fearlessness: Taking Calculated Risks for Change

****

Breaking Free from Comfort Zones: Overcoming fear and resistance to change can be a daunting task, but it is an essential aspect of embracing change and reinventing yourself. Often, we become comfortable with our routines and familiar surroundings, even if they no longer serve us. However, true growth and transformation can only occur when we step outside of our comfort zones and explore new opportunities and possibilities.

One of the primary reasons people resist change is fear. Fear of the unknown, fear of failure, and fear of stepping into the unfamiliar territory can hold us back from making necessary changes in our lives. It's important to acknowledge these fears and understand that they are normal. However, it's also crucial to recognize that staying within our comfort zones prevents us from experiencing personal growth and discovering our true potential.

To embrace change and break free from comfort zones, it's helpful to challenge the negative thoughts and beliefs that fuel our resistance. Start by questioning the validity of your fears and reframing them as opportunities for growth. Instead of focusing on what could go wrong, shift your mindset to what you stand to gain by venturing outside of your comfort zone.

Exploring new opportunities requires a willingness to try new things and take risks. This may involve pursuing a new career path, developing a new skill, or engaging in activities outside of your usual routine. Step out of your familiar surroundings and seek out experiences that challenge you intellectually, emotionally, or physically.

Surround yourself with supportive individuals who encourage you to step outside of your comfort zone. Seek guidance from mentors or friends who have successfully embraced change in their own lives. By surrounding yourself with positive influences, you will find the motivation and support necessary to overcome your resistance to change.

Remember that embracing change is a journey, not a destination. It takes time and effort to break free from comfort zones and explore new possibilities. Be patient with yourself and celebrate small victories along the way. Each step outside of your comfort zone is a valuable opportunity for growth and self-discovery.

In summary, breaking free from comfort zones is an essential part of embracing change and reinventing yourself. Overcoming fear and resistance to change allows you to explore new opportunities and possibilities outside of your comfort zone. Challenge your negative thoughts and beliefs, surround yourself with positive influences, and celebrate each small step towards personal growth. Embrace the journey of change and discover the incredible potential that lies beyond your comfort zoneDeveloping a Reinvention Plan:

Setting clear goals and intentions for your reinvention is a crucial step in the process of embracing change and reinventing yourself. By defining what you want to achieve and the outcomes you desire, you can create a roadmap that will guide your journey towards transformation.

To start, take some time for self-reflection and exploration. Ask yourself questions such as: What areas of my life do I want to change or improve? What aspects of myself do I want to develop or enhance? What new experiences or opportunities do I want to pursue?

Once you have a clearer understanding of what you want, it's time to set SMART goals - Specific, Measurable, Achievable, Relevant, and Time-bound. Break down your desired outcomes into smaller, actionable steps that are realistic and attainable. This will help you stay focused and motivated throughout the process.

Consider seeking support from trusted friends, mentors, or professionals who can provide guidance and accountability as you work towards your goals. They can offer valuable insights and help you stay on track even when faced with challenges or setbacks.

Remember that your reinvention plan is not set in stone; it can and should evolve as you progress. Be open to tweaking or adjusting your goals as needed. Stay flexible and adaptable, allowing room for unexpected opportunities or changes to emerge along the way.

Furthermore, celebrate your achievements and milestones along your reinvention journey. Acknowledge the progress you make, no matter how small, and use it as fuel to propel you forward.

By developing a clear reinvention plan and committing to taking action towards your goals, you lay a solid foundation for embracing change and reinventing yourself. Your plan will serve as a compass during times of uncertainty and a reminder of the growth and transformation that lies ahead Embracing Flexibility and Adaptability:

In this chapter, we have explored the importance of embracing change and reinventing yourself. Now, let's delve into another crucial aspect of this journey: the significance of adaptability and flexibility.

As you embark on the path of reinvention, it is crucial to develop a mindset that is open to change. Embracing flexibility allows you to navigate the twists and turns that come with reinventing yourself, enabling you to adapt to new circumstances and opportunities that arise along the way.

One key aspect of cultivating adaptability is being open to different perspectives and ideas. Recognize that there are multiple paths to success and that your reinvention journey may take unexpected turns. By embracing new possibilities and being willing to revise your plans, you create space for growth and innovation.

Additionally, learning from setbacks is an integral part of developing resilience during the process of reinventing yourself. Setbacks are inevitable, but they also offer valuable lessons to propel you forward. When faced with challenges, take the time to reflect on what went wrong and how you can improve. By adopting a growth mindset, you can view setbacks as opportunities for learning and personal development.

It's also important to remain adaptable in the face of changing circumstances. The world around us is constantly evolving, and being able to adjust your course of action is crucial for success. Stay attuned to market trends, technological advancements, and societal shifts that may impact your reinvention journey. By staying flexible and adaptable, you can seize new opportunities that align with your goals and values.

Remember, your reinvention journey is not a linear path. It may involve detours, unexpected challenges, and moments of doubt. However, by embracing flexibility and adaptability, you can navigate these hurdles with resilience and grace. Remain open-minded, willing to learn from setbacks, and ready to pivot when necessary. These qualities will empower you to successfully reinvent yourself and create a life that aligns with your true passions and aspirations Understanding Imposter Syndrome

Imposter syndrome is a phenomenon that affects many individuals, regardless of their accomplishments or qualifications. It is characterized by persistent feelings of self-doubt and a fear of being exposed as a fraud, despite evidence to the contrary. Understanding imposter syndrome is crucial for overcoming its negative impact on self-confidence.

First and foremost, it is important to define imposter syndrome and recognize its influence on self-confidence. Imposter syndrome refers to the belief that one's achievements are the result of luck or deception rather than genuine ability. This mindset can lead to feelings of inadequacy, anxiety, and a constant fear of being discovered as a fraud.

Identifying the signs and symptoms of imposter syndrome is key to addressing this issue. Some common indicators include an inability to internalize success, attributing achievements to external factors rather than personal abilities, feeling undeserving of praise or recognition, and constantly comparing oneself to others. By recognizing these signs, individuals can begin to understand how imposter syndrome may be affecting their self-confidence.

Moreover, it is important to acknowledge the ways in which imposter syndrome can hold individuals back both personally and professionally. The fear of being exposed as a fraud can prevent individuals from taking on new challenges or pursuing opportunities that would enhance their personal or professional growth. It can lead to self-sabotaging behaviors such as procrastination or perfectionism, hindering progress and success.

By understanding imposter syndrome and its impact on self-confidence, individuals can begin to take steps towards overcoming it. Through self-reflection and self-awareness, one can start challenging negative thoughts and beliefs that contribute to imposter syndrome. It involves questioning the validity of self-doubts and reframing them in a more positive light.

In the upcoming sections of this chapter, we will explore various strategies and techniques for overcoming imposter syndrome and boosting self-confidence. By developing a better understanding of imposter syndrome and its effects, individuals can take proactive steps towards regaining confidence in their abilities and accomplishments Challenging Negative Self-Talk

Negative self-talk is a common contributing factor to imposter syndrome, a phenomenon in which individuals doubt their accomplishments and fear being exposed as a fraud. Recognizing and challenging these negative thoughts is essential to overcoming imposter syndrome and building self-confidence. In this section, we will explore techniques to challenge and reframe negative thoughts, as well as the practice of positive affirmations and self-compassion.

Identifying Negative Self-Talk Patterns

One of the first steps in challenging negative self-talk is becoming aware of the patterns and beliefs that fuel it. Take some time to reflect on your inner dialogue and identify the recurring negative thoughts that you often experience. These may include thoughts like "I'm not qualified enough," "I don't deserve my success," or "I'm just lucky." By pinpointing these patterns, you can begin to address them directly.

Learning Techniques to Challenge and Reframe Negative Thoughts

Once you have identified your negative self-talk patterns, it's time to challenge them with rational and constructive thinking. When negative thoughts arise, ask yourself:

1. Is there any evidence to support this thought?
2. What are alternative explanations or perspectives?
3. How would I respond if a friend expressed this same thought?

These questions help you challenge the validity of your negative thoughts and introduce alternative perspectives that are more grounded in reality. Remember, imposter syndrome often distorts your perception of your abilities and achievements, so it's crucial to question the accuracy of your negative thoughts.

Practicing Positive Affirmations and Self-Compassion

Positive affirmations are powerful tools for building self-confidence and combating imposter syndrome. Choose affirmations that resonate with you personally, such as "I am competent and capable," "I deserve success," or "I am worthy of recognition." Repeat these affirmations daily, especially when you notice negative self-talk creeping in.

In addition to positive affirmations, practicing self-compassion is vital. Be gentle and understanding with yourself when imposter syndrome strikes. Treat yourself with the same kindness and empathy you would extend to a friend facing similar doubts. Remind yourself that everyone experiences self-doubt at times, and it does not diminish your worth or abilities. By challenging negative self-talk, reframing thoughts, practicing positive affirmations, and embracing self-compassion, you can break free from the grip of imposter syndrome and cultivate a strong sense of self-confidence. Remember that building self-confidence is an ongoing process, so be patient and celebrate even the smallest victories along the way Embracing Your Achievements and Abilities:

In this section, we will focus on reflecting on your past accomplishments and recognizing your strengths. This is an important step in boosting self-confidence and overcoming imposter syndrome. Too often, we downplay our achievements or attribute them to luck or external factors. It's time to change that mindset and give yourself credit where it's due.

To begin, take some time to reflect on your past accomplishments. Think about the challenges you have overcome, the goals you have achieved, and the skills you have developed. Write them down and allow yourself to acknowledge the hard work and effort you put into each accomplishment.

Next, it's important to apply the concept of "internal validation" when acknowledging your achievements. Internal validation means recognizing your worth and accepting your accomplishments without seeking external validation or approval. Instead of relying on others' opinions to determine your self-worth, trust in your own judgment and recognition of your abilities.

Cultivating a healthy sense of self-worth and confidence in your abilities is essential for overcoming imposter syndrome. Make a conscious effort to remind yourself of your strengths and successes regularly. Challenge any negative thoughts or self-doubt by reminding yourself of past achievements and the capabilities that led you to accomplish them.

Additionally, surround yourself with positive influences and supportive individuals who appreciate and recognize your talents. Seek out mentors or trusted friends who can offer constructive feedback and encouragement. By building a support network of people who believe in you, you'll find it easier to cultivate self-confidence.

Remember, confidence comes from within. It's about recognizing your own abilities, appreciating your unique talents, and embracing your achievements. By reflecting on your past accomplishments and finding validation internally, you can develop a healthy sense of self-worth that will help you overcome imposter syndrome and boost your overall confidence. Believe in yourself, because you are capable of great thingsSeeking Support and Sharing Experiences

We all have moments of self-doubt and fear that we're not good enough, especially when facing new challenges or pursuing our goals. One powerful way to overcome imposter syndrome and boost self-confidence is by seeking support and sharing experiences with others who have experienced similar feelings.

Connecting with others who have gone through or are currently going through imposter syndrome can be incredibly validating and reassuring. It helps you realize that you're not alone in your struggles and that these feelings are a common part of the human experience. By hearing about their journeys and how they overcame imposter syndrome, you can gain valuable insights and strategies to apply to your own life.

Sharing your own experiences with imposter syndrome can also be therapeutic and empowering. Opening up about your fears and insecurities not only helps you process those emotions but also allows others to support you and cheer you on. When you share your vulnerabilities, you create an atmosphere of trust and authenticity, which encourages others to do the same.

Building a support network is essential for combatting imposter syndrome. Surrounding yourself with people who believe in you and your abilities can help counteract the negative thoughts and self-doubt. Seek out mentors, colleagues, friends, or family members who uplift and empower you. These individuals can provide encouragement, guidance, and feedback as you navigate through challenging situations.

Consider joining professional or social groups where you can connect with like-minded individuals who understand the unique challenges of your field or stage of life. Attend networking events, workshops, or conferences related to your interests or career. Engage in online communities or forums where you can exchange ideas, ask questions, and find support from people who have faced similar struggles.

Remember, seeking support and sharing experiences doesn't mean comparing yourself to others or seeking validation externally. Instead, it's about finding a community of individuals who can relate to your experiences, offer guidance, and provide a safe space for you to grow and learn. Building a support network will remind you that everyone has their own journey, and success looks different for each person.

By connecting with others who have experienced imposter syndrome, sharing your own stories, and building a support network, you can gain the encouragement, empathy, and feedback needed to overcome imposter syndrome and boost your self-confidence. Together, we can break through the barriers that hold us back and embrace our true potentialsTaking Action Steps Towards Self-Confidence:

To overcome imposter syndrome and boost your self-confidence, it's important to take proactive steps towards personal growth. In this section, we will explore practical strategies and techniques that can help you build self-assurance and overcome self-doubt.

1. Setting Achievable Goals:

One effective way to combat imposter syndrome is to set achievable goals for yourself. Start by breaking down larger objectives into smaller, more manageable tasks. By doing so, you can create a roadmap that allows you to track your progress and celebrate each milestone along the way. Remember to set realistic expectations for yourself and focus on continuous improvement rather than perfection.

2. Implementing Strategies for Self-Care:

Self-care plays a vital role in boosting self-confidence. Taking care of your physical, mental, and emotional well-being is essential for maintaining a positive mindset and building resilience. Incorporate practices such as exercise, meditation, journaling, or engaging in hobbies that bring you joy and relaxation. Prioritize self-care activities regularly and make them non-negotiable parts of your routine.

3. Mindfulness and Stress Management:

Practicing mindfulness can help you become more aware of negative self-talk and break free from the cycle of imposter syndrome. Mindfulness exercises, such as deep breathing or mindful meditation, can help you stay present and grounded, reducing anxiety and promoting a sense of calmness. Additionally, learning effective stress management techniques can help you navigate challenging situations with confidence and composure.

4. Celebrating Small Victories:

Often, imposter syndrome causes individuals to overlook their achievements and downplay their successes. To counteract this tendency, make it a habit to celebrate even the smallest victories along your journey. Whether it's completing a challenging task at work or overcoming a personal obstacle, acknowledging and celebrating these accomplishments reinforces your belief in your abilities and boosts your self-confidence.

By implementing these action steps towards self-confidence, you are actively taking control of your mindset and empowering yourself to overcome imposter syndrome. Remember that building self-assurance is a continuous process, and it's okay to have setbacks along the way. Stay committed to your personal growth journey, and celebrate your progress as you rewrite your own success script Recognizing the Importance of a Supportive Community

Surrounding yourself with like-minded individuals is a crucial aspect of personal growth and development. When you find a supportive community of people who share your values and interests, it can have a profound impact on your journey towards success.

One of the key benefits of being part of a supportive community is the opportunity for mutual inspiration and motivation. When you're surrounded by individuals who are driven and passionate about similar things, their energy and enthusiasm can fuel your own aspirations. They serve as reminders that you're not alone in your pursuits and provide encouragement during challenging times.

A supportive community also offers a safe space for personal growth and self-expression. Being able to share your goals, dreams, and struggles with like-minded individuals allows you to be vulnerable and receive valuable feedback and guidance. It's within this community that you can openly explore new ideas, experiment with different approaches, and challenge yourself to reach new heights.

Additionally, a supportive community provides access to a wealth of knowledge and resources. By connecting with like-minded individuals, you gain access to their expertise, experiences, and insights. This collective wisdom can help you navigate obstacles more effectively, make informed decisions, and accelerate your progress towards your goals.

Furthermore, being part of a supportive community fosters a sense of belonging and camaraderie. Human beings are social creatures, and having a group of individuals who "get" you on a deeper level creates a sense of camaraderie and understanding. It allows you to connect with others who share your passions, quirks, and ambitions, cultivating authentic relationships that enrich both your personal and professional life.

In summary, surrounding yourself with like-minded individuals in a supportive community has numerous advantages that contribute to personal growth and motivation. It provides inspiration, opportunities for growth, access to knowledge, and a sense of belonging. As you embark on your journey towards rewriting the life success script in your thirties, remember the power of a supportive community and seek out those who will uplift and empower you along the way Identifying Your Values and Interests

In order to build a supportive community of like-minded individuals, it's essential to first reflect on your own values and interests. Understanding what matters most to you and the type of community you seek will guide your search for potential members who align with your beliefs and goals.

Take some time for self-reflection and consider what truly matters to you in life. What are your core values? These may include concepts like honesty, compassion, growth, or adventure. Identifying your values will help you attract individuals who share similar beliefs and can contribute positively to your journey.

Next, think about your interests and passions. What activities do you enjoy doing in your free time? What hobbies or subjects fascinate you? Identifying these interests will not only help you find communities centered around those topics but also provide common ground for connecting with others who share your enthusiasm.

Once you have a clear understanding of your values and interests, it's important to evaluate which qualities and characteristics are important in potential community members. Consider the following aspects:

1. Authenticity: Look for individuals who are genuine and true to themselves. Building relationships with people who share their true selves creates an environment of trust and support.

2. Positivity: Seek out individuals who radiate positivity and optimism. Surrounding yourself with positive influences will uplift and motivate you on your own journey.

3. Open-mindedness: Find people who are open to different perspectives and willing to listen. Engaging with individuals who are open-minded fosters intellectual growth and encourages healthy discussions.

4. Supportiveness: Look for individuals who genuinely support and uplift others. A supportive community is crucial for personal growth, as it provides encouragement during challenging times and celebrates successes.

5. Shared Goals: Connect with individuals who have similar aspirations and goals. Being part of a community that shares common objectives allows you to collaborate, exchange ideas, and inspire one another.

Remember, building a supportive community is about finding individuals who align with your values and interests while also being open to diversity. Embrace the opportunity to connect with people from different backgrounds, as they can offer unique perspectives and experiences that enrich your own personal journey.

By identifying your values, interests, and the qualities you seek in potential community members, you'll be well-equipped to actively seek out and engage with like-minded individuals who will contribute positively to your personal growth and provide the support you need on your journey Connecting with Like-minded Individuals

In order to build a supportive community of like-minded individuals, it's important to explore various avenues for connecting with people who share similar passions and interests. This can be done through social clubs, networking events, and online communities.

Social clubs and organizations dedicated to specific hobbies or interests are great places to meet people who share your passions. Whether it's a book club, a sports team, or a gardening group, these clubs offer opportunities to connect with individuals who have similar interests and values.

Networking events, whether in-person or virtual, provide a space to meet professionals who are in similar industries or fields. Attending conferences, seminars, or industry-specific gatherings can help you connect with like-minded individuals who share similar career goals and aspirations.

Utilizing social media platforms and specialized websites can also be an effective way to find individuals with similar passions and interests. Joining online communities, such as Facebook groups or forums dedicated to specific topics, allows you to engage in discussions and connect with individuals who have similar hobbies or goals.

When seeking out like-minded individuals, it's important to be open-minded and approachable. Be willing to participate in conversations and activities related to your interests, ask questions, and show genuine interest in others' experiences. By actively engaging in these communities, you increase your chances of forming meaningful connections with like-minded individuals.

Remember to tailor your approach based on your own values and interests, and always prioritize building genuine connections. Building a supportive community takes time and effort, but the benefits of surrounding yourself with like-minded individuals are invaluable for personal growth and motivation Nurturing Relationships and Building Trust

In this section, we will delve deeper into the importance of developing genuine connections within your community. Nurturing these relationships is essential for building a strong support system and fostering mutual trust and support.

One of the key aspects of nurturing relationships within a community is active listening. When engaging in conversations with fellow community members, make a conscious effort to truly listen and understand their perspectives. This means being fully present in the moment and giving them your undivided attention. By actively listening, you demonstrate respect for others' opinions and experiences, leading to deeper connections and stronger bonds.

Another vital component of nurturing relationships is empathy. Show genuine concern for others' well-being and seek to understand their emotions and experiences. Empathy helps create a safe space within the community, where individuals feel supported and understood. Through empathy, you can offer comfort, perspective, and guidance to your fellow community members, establishing yourself as a valuable source of support.

Sharing experiences is another powerful way to nurture relationships within your community. By opening up about your own challenges, successes, and personal growth journey, you create opportunities for connection and vulnerability. This authenticity encourages others to do the same, fostering an environment of trust and mutual understanding. Through shared experiences, you can find common ground with like-minded individuals and build deeper connections based on shared values and aspirations.

It's important to note that building trust takes time and consistency. Be reliable and dependable within your community, showing up consistently and following through on commitments. Transparency and open communication also play a crucial role in fostering trust. Be honest about your intentions and communicate openly with fellow community members about any concerns or issues that may arise.

Vulnerability is another key element in building trust within your community. Share your fears, insecurities, and failures with others, allowing them to see your authentic self. By demonstrating vulnerability, you show that it is safe for others to do the same and create an environment where individuals can openly share their thoughts, feelings, and experiences.

By nurturing relationships and building trust within your community, you create a supportive network of like-minded individuals who are invested in your personal growth journey. These connections provide encouragement, accountability, and inspiration as you navigate the challenges and opportunities of your thirties.

Remember, genuine connections are built on active listening, empathy, shared experiences, transparency, and vulnerability. By cultivating these qualities within your community, you can foster an environment of trust, support, and growth for everyone involvedContributing and Benefiting from the Community

A key aspect of building a supportive community is not only receiving support but also actively contributing to the growth and well-being of others. By sharing your knowledge, resources, and support, you not only uplift others but also enhance your own personal growth.

One way to contribute to the community is by sharing your expertise and knowledge. Identify areas where you excel or possess valuable insights, and offer guidance or advice to others who may benefit from your expertise. This could involve participating in discussion forums, hosting workshops or webinars, or even writing blogs or articles on topics that align with your passions and interests. By sharing your knowledge, you become a valuable resource within the community and establish yourself as a trusted authority.

Another way to contribute is by offering support and encouragement to fellow community members. Show empathy and understanding when others are facing challenges or setbacks. Celebrate their successes and provide a listening ear when they need someone to talk to. By offering genuine support, you create a safe space for open communication and vulnerability within the community.

Additionally, consider sharing resources that you find helpful or relevant. This could include recommending books, podcasts, websites, or tools that have enriched your own personal growth journey. By sharing these resources, you help others access information and tools that can positively impact their lives.

While contributing to the community is important, it's equally vital to benefit from the collective wisdom of the community. Take advantage of the diverse perspectives and experiences of other like-minded individuals to gain insights, advice, and inspiration for your own personal growth and development. Engage in discussions, ask thought-provoking questions, and seek guidance from those who have overcome similar challenges. The community becomes a treasure trove of wisdom that can propel your own journey towards success.

Remember, building a supportive community is a reciprocal process. As you contribute to the growth of others, you simultaneously create an environment where others contribute to your growth. By harnessing the collective wisdom and support of the community, you create a powerful network that uplifts everyone involved. Embrace the opportunities to contribute and benefit from your like-minded community, recognizing that together, you can achieve far more than you ever could alone.

Chapter 34

A Creative Spark:
Pursuing Passions and Hobbies
****

Identifying and prioritizing your passions is an essential step towards pursuing passion projects outside of work. It allows you to engage in activities that bring you joy and fulfillment, aligning them with your values and long-term goals. Here are some key points to consider:

1. Reflect on activities or hobbies that bring you joy and fulfillment: Take the time to introspect and think about the things that genuinely make you happy. Consider the activities or hobbies you currently enjoy or have enjoyed in the past. Reflect on the moments when you have felt most alive and engaged.

2. Determine which passions align with your values and long-term goals: Once you have identified potential areas of interest, evaluate how they align with your values and long-term aspirations. Consider whether your passion projects can contribute to personal growth, career advancement, or any other meaningful objectives you have set for yourself.

By taking the time to identify and prioritize your passions, you can ensure that your passion projects outside of work are aligned with your authentic self and contribute positively to your overall   well-being

Time management strategies are crucial for pursuing passion projects outside of work. To effectively make time for your passions, start by evaluating your current commitments and responsibilities. Consider which activities or obligations you can reduce or eliminate to create space for your passion projects.

Once you have identified areas where you can free up time, set aside dedicated blocks each week or month to work on your passion projects. Treat this time as sacred and non-negotiable, just like any other important commitment in your schedule. By prioritizing these dedicated periods, you ensure that progress is consistently made on your passion projects.

Balancing work, personal life, and passion projects can be challenging, but it is possible with proper planning and organization. Explore efficient ways to structure your schedule and find a rhythm that allows you to manage all aspects of your life effectively. This may involve setting boundaries, delegating tasks, or finding creative solutions that optimize your time.

Remember, effective time management is not about squeezing every minute out of the day but rather making intentional choices about how you allocate your time. By consciously prioritizing your passion projects and creating dedicated time slots for them, you can make significant progress while still maintaining a healthy work-life balance.

Ultimately, it's essential to find a time management system that works best for you. Experiment with different approaches and strategies until you discover what allows you to maximize productivity and enjoyment in pursuing your passion projects outside of work

Creating a plan and setting goals for your passion projects is crucial to their success. By defining clear goals, you give yourself a sense of direction and purpose. Whether your goal is to complete a specific project or learn a new skill, having clarity about what you want to achieve will help keep you motivated and focused.

Break down your goals into actionable steps to make them more manageable. This allows you to tackle one task at a time and move forward progressively. For example, if your passion project is writing a book, your actionable steps could include outlining the chapters, conducting research, writing a certain number of pages each week, and editing the completed manuscript.

Creating a timeline for achieving your goals adds structure and accountability to your plan. Determine realistic deadlines for each step of the process and set aside dedicated time to work on your passion projects. Consider using a planner or digital tools to help you stay organized and track your progress.

It's important to keep in mind that your plan should be flexible to accommodate unexpected changes or delays. Life can often throw curveballs, and it's essential to adapt and adjust your plan accordingly. Give yourself permission to modify timelines and make necessary revisions, all while keeping your end goal in sight.

Remember, the journey towards pursuing your passion projects is just as important as reaching the final destination. Embrace the process, enjoy the learning experiences along the way, and celebrate small wins as you progress towards accomplishing your goals. With a well-defined plan and clear goals, you'll be well-equipped to pursue your passion projects outside of work successfully.

Overcoming obstacles and staying motivated are essential components when pursuing passion projects outside of work. It is crucial to anticipate potential challenges that may arise along the way and develop strategies to overcome them.

One common obstacle is facing creative blocks or periods of low motivation. To tackle this, consider scheduling creative blocks in your routine. Set aside specific times where you can focus solely on your passion projects, allowing yourself to explore new ideas and brainstorm creative solutions. Additionally, seek support from like-minded individuals who can provide encouragement and inspiration. Surrounding yourself with a supportive network can help reignite your motivation and provide fresh perspectives when faced with challenges.

It's also important to celebrate small victories along the way. Recognize and acknowledge your progress, no matter how small it may seem. By celebrating milestones, you create a positive feedback loop that fuels your motivation and keeps you engaged in your passion projects. Consider keeping track of your accomplishments by documenting them in a journal or creating a visual representation of your progress.

Regularly reminding yourself of the importance of your passion projects can help maintain motivation even during difficult times. Reflect on why these projects matter to you and how they align with your values and long-term goals. Visualize the impact or fulfillment they will bring into your life, which can serve as a powerful reminder during challenging moments.

By anticipating obstacles, developing strategies to overcome them, celebrating small victories, and staying connected to the importance of your passion projects, you can navigate through any setbacks and stay motivated on your journey towards realizing your passions outside of work

Building a supportive network is an essential aspect of pursuing passion projects outside of work. By connecting with others who share similar interests and passions, you can gain valuable insights, support, and inspiration to fuel your own creativity and motivation.

One way to build a supportive network is by joining online communities centered around your specific passion projects. These communities provide a space for like-minded individuals to connect, share ideas, ask questions, and offer support. Engaging in online discussions, participating in forums or groups, and even collaborating on projects with other community members can greatly enhance your experience and progress in pursuing your passion projects.

In addition to virtual communities, attending workshops or events related to your passion projects can also be a great opportunity to connect with others who share similar interests. These events often bring together individuals with a common passion, offering the chance to learn from experts in the field, gain new perspectives, and establish meaningful connections that can potentially lead to collaborations or mentorship opportunities.

Seeking mentorship or collaborating with others who have expertise or experience in your chosen area can provide invaluable guidance and support as you pursue your passion projects. Mentors can offer valuable insights, advice, and encouragement based on their own experiences. Collaborating with other passionate individuals allows for the sharing of ideas, resources, and skills, fostering a sense of camaraderie and providing mutual support throughout the journey.

Remember, building a supportive network is not only about what you can gain from others but also what you can contribute. Show genuine interest in others' projects, offer assistance when needed, and be open to sharing your own knowledge and experiences. Cultivating positive relationships within your network will not only benefit your personal growth but also create a community of support and encouragement for everyone involved.

By actively seeking out and nurturing connections within a supportive network, you can enhance your passion projects outside of work, gain new perspectives, and foster meaningful collaborations. Building a supportive network is an integral part of pursuing your passion projects and can greatly contribute to your overall success and fulfillment in these endeavors

Chapter **35**

Mindfulness and
Presence: Living in the Now

Understanding Mindfulness:
Before we can get into the specific techniques and practices, let's try to understand what mindfulness really is and debunk some of the misconceptions around it. The definition of mindfulness is the practice of bringing one's attention and awareness to the present moment without judgment. Being fully engaged in the here and now, observing thoughts and sensations as they arise, and accepting them without attachment or aversion.

Contrary to popular belief, mindfulness doesn't mean emptying your mind or achieving complete calmness. It means simply acknowledging and accepting what comes up in that moment whether it is good or bad without being overtaken by it.

Scientific research has shown that practicing mindfulness regularly can have a positive impact on mental health. Studies have found correlations between mindfulness and reduced stress, improved focus/attention span, increased emotional regulation, enhanced immune function, and even changes in brain structure.

By being mindful individuals can develop a greater sense of self-awareness resulting in better understanding their thoughts/emotions/behaviors. This heightened awareness allows for more intentional decision making as well as better management of stress throughout life.

In this section we will explore various breathing techniques such as focused breathing which promotes deep/intentional breaths allowing readers to incorporate mindful breathing into their daily lives.

Technique 1: Diaphragmatic Breathing
Diaphragmatic breathing is also known as belly/deep breathing which is an essential technique for cultivating mindfulness. It involves engaging the diaphragm (muscle located below lungs) taking deep breaths expanding your belly to its fullest capacity.

To practice diaphragmatic breathing you must:
1. Get comfortable either by sitting down or lying on your back.
2. Place one hand on your chest another on your abdomen.
3. Slowly inhale through your nose letting your belly rise as you fill lungs with air.
4. Gently exhale through mouth feeling gentle contraction in stomach.
5. Repeat process for several breaths and focus on feeling your abdomen rise/fall with each breath.

This technique helps activate body's relaxation response reducing stress and promoting a greater sense of calm.

Technique 2: Box Breathing
Box breathing is a simple yet effective technique that can be practiced anywhere at anytime. It involves inhaling, holding breath, exhaling, then holding again in a rhythmic pattern resembling the sides of a box.

To practice box breathing you must:
1. Sit down in comfortable position and bring attention to your breath.
2. Take slow deep inhale through nose for count of four, visualize tracing first side of box.
3. Hold breath for another count of four imagining tracing second side.
4. Exhale slowly through nose/mouth for another count of four (while tracing third side).
5. Repeat this pattern for several rounds, focusing on the breath and visualization.

Box breathing helps regulate the nervous system, promoting balance and stability when things get tough. A handy tool to use during moments of stress or anxiety.

Technique 3: Visualization Breathing

Visualization breathing combines focused breathing with imagery. By using your breath to guide your attention through visualizations that promote relaxation and stress reduction.

To practice visualization breathing:

1. Find a quiet space where you can sit comfortably.
2. Close your eyes and take a few deep breaths to center yourself.
3. Envision a serene place in your mind, such as a tranquil beach or a peaceful forest.
4. Inhale while imagining you're absorbing the calmness and beauty of that place into you body.
5. Exhale while visualizing all your tension and stress leaving your body

Continue this practice until you feel it's enough. Once again, shifting focus from mental chatter into peace of mind.

By incorporating these mindful breathing techniques into daily life, readers can cultivate a greater sense of awareness and calmness. These techniques can be integrated during various activities, such as before important meetings or during moments of stress. Regular practice will reinforce the habit of mindful breathing, allowing individuals to tap into its benefits whenever needed

Cultivating a Meditation Practice:

In this section, we will discuss different types of meditation practices and provide guidance on finding a suitable meditation style. Additionally, we will offer tips for establishing a consistent meditation routine.

Meditation is an essential tool in developing mindfulness for well being . There are many different ways to meditate each offering unique benefits . By exploring these different techniques , users can find one that resonates with them .

Focused attention meditation: This type is also known as concentrative meditation.The goal is to focus the users attention on something like their breath , repeating words , or visualizing images . This way they can develop present-moment awareness .

Loving-kindness meditation : Also referred to as metta meditation . This type focuses on self love , compassion and goodwill, towards oneself and others. Allowing you to feel more connected with the world

Body scan meditation: The goal here is to get users to mentally scan their body from head to toe , checking for any physical tension .

Walking meditation: This type of mindful motion involves taking a walk but being aware of every step you take.

Find what works for you and practice it regularly!

For those who are new to it, meditating can seem like a daunting task. For others, they find themselves bored when doing it but continue because of the benefits it brings them. There's no 'one size fits all' method or routine. It will take time, exploring different types and techniques to find what works for you best.

The environment also plays a role in how well your meditation sessions go. Find yourself a quiet, peaceful space where you can avoid any distractions or interruptions that may throw off your focus. Even if you can only spare 5 minutes a day, prioritize a set time each day solely for meditating.

Your concentration levels and comfort for long sessions will increase gradually with practice. So don't be too hard on yourself if you find yourself getting distracted easily during these sessions at first. At the end of the day, consistency matters more than anything else in this case. While experimenting with different times throughout the day to see when you personally have the clearest mind is important as well. Morning? Evening? Mid-day after lunch? Whichever one gives you the greatest focus should be what you aim for everyday moving forward.

Other tips involve incorporating meditation into your existing daily routine. Such as before or after exercise, while taking breaks away from work or even during your lunch break. This way, it won't be something that feels like an extra task needing completion but rather something already apart of your normal daily activities.

Keep in mind that practicing meditation will require patience and consistency above all else. Nobody has been able to master meditation overnight so expecting to would just be unrealistic and unfair towards yourself. By committing to this however and being patient with yourself overtime will give your future self great experience in this field!

Incorporating Mindfulness into Everyday Activities:

Whether we notice it or not — there's always an activity we do everyday that takes up most of our thoughts and attention throughout our days! By engaging in this activity with full awareness and in the present moment, we can find that sense of fulfillment even in the simplest tasks. Here are some practical tips for incorporating mindfulness into various aspects of your daily life:

1. Mindful Eating:

- Instead of just digging in after sitting down — take a moment to appreciate the appearance, aroma and texture of your food.
- Take your time chewing each bite slowly and savoring them, paying attention to the flavors and sensations in your mouth.
- Pay attention to any thoughts or judgments you may have while eating and redirect them back to the present moment.
- Avoid any distractions such as being on your phone or watching TV during these meals as well!

2. Mindful Walking:

- Slow down your walking pace and pay attention to the physical sensations you feel with each step taken — leg movement, feet onto ground contact etc.
- Notice other senses as well like air on skin, sounds around you or sights across from you
- Keep yourself present by focusing on your breaths throughout this walk too

3. Mindful Working:

- Before you start a task, set an intention. It may sound silly, but it can change how you perform.
- Focus on one thing at a time, putting all your focus into each individual task.
- Keep an eye out for thoughts and emotions that pop up while working. Don't think too much about them, just observe them without any judgement.
- Take small breaks throughout the day to stretch or do some deep breathing exercises.
- This helps you recharge and refocus your energy.

4. Mindful Listening and Communication:

- When talking to someone, really listen to what they have to say. Give them your full attention in order to better understand their point of view.
- You'll start noticing when it's tempting to interrupt someone just so you can speak your own mind. Catch yourself doing this and try understanding the other person before replying.
- Little things like body language or tone of voice can convey a lot more than words alone. Keep these in mind as well.

- Respond with care in order to make sure your message is delivered exactly how you want it to be.

5. Staying Present and Engaged:

- Check yourself throughout the day by focusing on your breath and body. Reconnect with yourself by doing this whenever you feel overwhelmed or stressed.
- Pay attention to everything around you like sounds or sensations within your own body. This way you stay grounded instead of being too much "in your head".

- Redirect any thoughts about the past or future back into the present moment whenever they arise
- Finally, embrace moments of stillness throughout the day so that you calm down and clear your head
- Doing these everyday things will bring more presence, meaning, and appreciation into your life if done right! Just keep practicing; don't worry because mindfulness is something we learn with time after all!

Overcoming Challenges and Sustaining Mindfulness:

Of course there are challenges when trying out new things! Mindfulness especially has its own set of obstacles that many people aren't prepared for. However, knowing about them and having strategies ready will make everything easier.

The first issue is finding time in a busy life schedule. It's hard to be mindful when you have 100 things to do! But don't worry because not everything has to take up so much time. Even just taking a second to breathe or look at your surroundings count as mindfulness.

Next is staying motivated and consistent with mindfulness techniques. Remember that like anything else, it requires practice to see real benefits from it. Set goals if you need help being consistent; start off small and slowly increase the duration of your sessions as you get better.

Finally, find what works best for yourself! There are a ton of different styles and techniques that can be used for meditation, so try them all out to find what resonates most with you.

Lastly, be kind to yourself and don't judge yourself. Some days your mind will be so restless it feels like a caged lion, and sometimes it'll be tough to stay present. This is normal! That's what I'm trying to get at. Instead of beating yourself up about it all, just remember that this is a learning process. Be kind to yourself and know that you're learning something new here.

It's time to treat your mindfulness practice as an opportunity for growth. The only way you're going to grow is if you come face-to-face with challenges, so next time one comes around take it in stride because it's an opportunity for self-discovery. Not a task that makes you pull your hair out.

Just keep these three things in mind and you'll see the full benefits of mindfulness: Consistency Adaptability   Self-compassion

Chapter 36

The Harmony of Health and Hustle: Finding Balance

****

In today's fast-paced, overwork culture, it's easy to become a workaholic, constantly striving for success and losing sight of our well-being. However, the detrimental effects of this lifestyle can lead to burnout and negatively impact our health.

In this section, we will explore the realities of overwork culture and its toll on our physical and mental well-being. We will delve into the concept of workaholism and its underlying causes, helping us understand why we fall into this trap.

But fear not! There are strategies and techniques that can help us avoid burnout and find a healthier balance between work and life. We will share practical tips and insights on how to prevent burnout, prioritize self-care, and create boundaries to achieve a more sustainable work-life routine.

Join us as we embark on a journey to discover the harmony between health and hustle, finding a balance that allows us to thrive professionally while taking care of our well-being and preventing burnout.

Establishing a Work-Life Equilibrium

a healthy work-life equilibrium is crucial for overall well-being and productivity. In today's fast-paced and interconnected world, it's all too easy for work to spill over into personal life, blurring the boundaries and causing stress and burnout. However, by setting clear boundaries and integrating work and personal responsibilities, you can achieve a harmonious balance that promotes both professional success and personal fulfillment.

Setting Boundaries: The Key to Work-Life Equilibrium

One of the first steps in establishing a work-life equilibrium is setting clear boundaries between work and personal life. By defining specific hours for work and leisure activities, you can avoid the tendency to constantly be "on" and give yourself dedicated time for relaxation and self-care. Communicate these boundaries with your colleagues and loved ones to ensure they are respected and supported.

Additionally, establish physical boundaries by creating a separate workspace at home, if possible. This physical separation can help you mentally switch between work and personal life, allowing you to fully engage in each domain without distractions or interruptions.

Work-Life Integration: Finding the Sweet Spot

While boundaries are important, work-life equilibrium is not about completely separating work and personal life. It's about integrating these two aspects in a way that allows you to fulfill your professional obligations and still enjoy a fulfilling personal life. Seek opportunities to blend work and personal activities. For instance, consider using your lunch breaks to engage in hobbies or spend quality time with loved ones.

Another way to integrate work and personal life is to prioritize tasks based on their importance and urgency. By effectively managing your time and energy, you can allocate dedicated periods for both work-related tasks and personal activities, ensuring that neither takes precedence over the other.

Remember, achieving work-life equilibrium is an ongoing process that requires constant evaluation and adjustment. Regularly assess your boundaries and integration strategies to ensure they align with your changing needs and priorities.

Prioritizing Self-Care

When it comes to maintaining optimal performance in both professional and personal endeavors, prioritizing self-care is absolutely crucial. Taking care of your mental, emotional, and physical well-being is not only beneficial for your overall health, but it can also have a positive impact on your productivity and success.

Self-care is about intentionally setting aside time to nurture yourself and engage in activities that promote your well-being. It involves being mindful of your needs and making choices that prioritize your mental health and balance in life. Self-care is not selfish; it is a necessary investment in yourself that allows you to show up fully in all aspects of your life.

Various Self-Care Practices

Self-care practices can take many forms and can be tailored to suit your individual needs and preferences. Here are a few examples:

Meditation and Mindfulness: Taking a few minutes each day to meditate or practice mindfulness can help reduce stress, increase focus, and improve overall well-being.

Exercise: Engaging in regular physical activity boosts energy levels, improves mood, and helps manage stress. Find activities you enjoy, whether it's going for a walk, practicing yoga, or participating in team sports.

Healthy Eating: Nourishing your body with nutritious foods supports your overall well-being. Focus on incorporating whole foods, fruits, vegetables, lean proteins, and healthy fats into your diet.

Rest and Relaxation: Prioritize getting enough sleep, as it plays a vital role in your mental and physical health. Allow yourself to unwind and recharge by engaging in activities that help you relax, such as reading, taking a bath, or practicing a hobby.

Setting Boundaries: Learn to say no and establish boundaries that protect your time and energy. This means allocating time for activities you enjoy and not overcommitting yourself.

By incorporating self-care practices into your daily routine, you can enhance your overall well-being and cultivate a healthier, more balanced lifestyle. Remember, self-care is not a luxury—it is an essential component of living a fulfilling and productive life.

Nourishing the Body

In this section, we will delve into the vital link between nutrition and productivity. A healthy eating regimen is not only crucial for physical well-being but also plays a significant role in sustaining energy levels and enhancing focus throughout the day.

When it comes to nutrition, making mindful choices can make all the difference. Incorporating a variety of nutrient-dense foods into your diet, such as fruits, vegetables, whole grains, lean proteins, and healthy fats, can provide the essential nutrients your body needs to function optimally.

Additionally, prioritizing regular meals and snacks can help stabilize blood sugar levels, preventing energy crashes and promoting sustained productivity. Fueling your body with balanced meals throughout the day ensures a steady supply of nutrients and energy to keep you on top of your game.

Eating a well-rounded diet not only supports physical health but also positively impacts mental well-being. Research shows that certain nutrients, like omega-3 fatty acids found in fatty fish, nuts, and seeds, can boost brain health and cognitive function. Proper nourishment not only enhances focus but also contributes to improved mood and overall mental clarity.

Furthermore, hydration is a crucial aspect of nurturing the body. Staying adequately hydrated throughout the day helps maintain energy levels and supports brain function. Be sure to drink enough water or other hydrating fluids to stay refreshed and focused.

By prioritizing nutrition and making healthy eating choices, you can optimize your energy levels and promote sustained productivity. In the following sections, we will explore additional strategies to enhance well-being and achieve a harmonious balance between work and personal life.

Moving for Momentum

Physical activity and regular exercise have been shown to have a substantial impact on productivity and stress reduction. Incorporating movement into your daily routine can provide the momentum you need to excel in both your personal and professional life.

Engaging in physical activity releases endorphins, chemicals in the brain that act as natural mood lifters. This, in turn, enhances focus and boosts overall well-being, leading to increased productivity. Exercise also helps reduce feelings of stress and anxiety, improving mental clarity and promoting a positive mindset.

Here are some tips for fitting physical activity into a busy schedule:

Set aside specific times for exercise: Schedule regular workout sessions or breaks for physical activity throughout your day. Treat these times as non-negotiable appointments with yourself.

Choose activities you enjoy: Find activities that you genuinely enjoy and are more likely to stick with. Whether it's walking, running, dancing, or playing a sport, make it a fun and enjoyable experience.

Make it a social activity: Invite a friend or colleague to join you for a workout or engage in physical activities together. This not only adds a social component but also helps hold you accountable.

Make use of small pockets of time: If you have limited time, break your exercise routine into shorter bursts throughout the day. Take the stairs instead of the elevator, go for a brisk walk during your lunch break, or do some stretching exercises at your desk.

Be flexible with your routine: On busy days, adjust your workout routine to fit your schedule. It's better to do a shorter workout than skip it altogether.

By prioritizing physical activity and incorporating it into your daily life, you can experience increased energy levels, improved focus, and enhanced productivity. Remember, even small amounts of movement can make a significant difference in your overall well-being and work performance.

Cultivating Focus and Resilience

Enhancing focus and productivity requires more than just time management techniques. It demands a deep understanding of oneself and the ability to navigate challenges with resilience. Cultivating focus and resilience through mindfulness and a positive mindset can help individuals thrive in the face of adversity.

The Power of Mindfulness

Mindfulness is the practice of being fully present and aware of the present moment without judgment. It involves paying attention to thoughts, emotions, and physical sensations, allowing one to develop a deeper understanding of their inner world. By training the mind to focus on the present, individuals can improve concentration and reduce the impact of distractions. Mindfulness also promotes emotional regulation and stress reduction, enhancing overall well-being.

Cultivating a Resilient Mindset

A resilient mindset is crucial for maintaining focus and productivity in the face of challenges. It involves developing a positive outlook and adapting to setbacks with flexibility. Cultivating resilience requires recognizing and challenging negative thought patterns, reframing obstacles as learning opportunities, and building a support network. By embracing resilience, individuals develop the capacity to bounce back from setbacks and forge ahead with determination.

Practicing Mindfulness Techniques

There are various techniques that individuals can incorporate into their daily lives to cultivate mindfulness and enhance focus. These include:

Meditation: Set aside a few minutes each day to sit quietly and focus on your breath or a specific object of attention. This practice trains the mind to stay present and enhances overall mindfulness.

Body Scan: Take a few moments to scan your body from head to toe, observing any sensations or tension. This technique increases body awareness and promotes relaxation.

Journaling: Write down your thoughts and emotions, allowing yourself to explore them without judgment. This practice encourages self-reflection and helps uncover patterns and triggers.

Cultivating a Positive Outlook

Developing a positive mindset is essential for maintaining focus and resilience. It involves reframing negative thoughts into positive ones and practicing gratitude. By consciously focusing on the good in life, individuals can train their minds to seek solutions rather than dwell on problems, leading to increased productivity and a more fulfilling work-life balance.

Ultimately, by incorporating mindfulness practices and cultivating a resilient mindset, individuals can enhance their focus and productivity. Mindfulness and a positive outlook can serve as powerful tools for navigating challenges, reducing stress, and achieving long-term success.

Rest and Recovery

Rest and recovery are essential elements for maintaining long-term success and overall well-being. In our fast-paced society, where hustle and productivity are highly valued, it's easy to overlook the importance of giving our bodies and minds the rest they need.

Sleep plays a critical role in our rejuvenation process. Quality sleep allows our bodies to repair and regenerate cells, strengthens the immune system, and enhances cognitive function. Without sufficient sleep, we may experience fatigue, reduced focus, and impaired decision-making abilities.

The Benefits of Quality Sleep

Quality sleep offers numerous benefits that contribute to our overall health and success. It improves memory consolidation, enhances creativity, and reduces stress levels. When we prioritize sleep, we wake up feeling refreshed and energized, ready to take on the day.

Developing healthy sleep habits can greatly enhance our well-being and productivity. It's important to establish a consistent sleep schedule by going to bed and waking up at the same time each day. Creating a relaxing bedtime routine, avoiding electronic devices before sleep, and ensuring a comfortable sleep environment can all contribute to better sleep quality.

Strategies for Rest and Recovery

In addition to quality sleep, incorporating rest and recovery activities into our daily lives is equally important. Rest and recovery allow our bodies to repair, rebuild, and replenish. They help prevent burnout and enhance our ability to perform at our best.

Some effective strategies for rest and recovery include:

Taking short breaks throughout the day to stretch and relax your mind. Engaging in activities that bring you joy and relaxation, such as reading a book, taking a walk in nature, or practicing mindfulness. Scheduling regular massages or indulging in self-care practices, like taking a warm bath or practicing yoga.

Carving out dedicated downtime in your schedule to do nothing and simply recharge.By incorporating these rest and recovery strategies into our routine, we can restore our energy, improve our focus, and enhance our overall well-being. Remember, rest is not a luxury but a necessity for sustained success in all aspects of our lives.

Lifestyle Habits for Long-Term Success

When it comes to maintaining a healthy work-life balance and achieving long-term success, sustainable habits are key. These habits not only support your overall well-being but also help you stay focused, productive, and resilient in the face of challenges.

One important sustainable habit to cultivate is prioritizing self-care. Taking time for yourself and engaging in activities that promote relaxation and rejuvenation is crucial for maintaining a healthy work-life balance. Whether it's practicing mindfulness, indulging in a hobby, or simply spending quality time with loved ones, make self-care a non-negotiable part of your routine.

In addition to self-care, nourishing your body with wholesome nutrition is essential for sustaining energy levels and enhancing focus. Incorporate healthy eating habits into your lifestyle, such as consuming a balanced diet rich in fruits, vegetables, lean proteins, and whole grains. Remember, fueling your body with the right nutrients not only enhances your physical health but also boosts cognitive function and productivity.

Lastly, don't forget the importance of regular physical activity. Incorporating exercise into your daily routine not only improves your physical fitness but also has a positive impact on your mental well-being. Whether you prefer a vigorous workout or a leisurely stroll outdoors, find an activity that brings you joy and commit to making it a regular part of your life.

Chapter 37

Community and Connection: Building Your Tribe

******

Do you ever feel like you're navigating the digital world alone, longing for deep connections and a strong support system? In today's fast-paced, ever-evolving age, building a support network has never been more important. It is the key to nurturing authentic relationships, fostering personal growth, and finding your tribe of like-minded individuals who share your values and goals.

But how do you build a support network that goes beyond superficial connections? How do you create a tribe that uplifts and empowers you in an increasingly digital age?

In this section, we will explore the significance of building a support network and the importance of having a strong support system in your life. We will delve into strategies for fostering deep connections, cultivating authentic relationships, and leveraging technology to enhance your network. Join us as we uncover the secrets to building a tribe that will enrich every aspect of your life.

Understanding the Power of Connection

In today's fast-paced and digitally connected world, building a support network is essential for personal growth and success. Having a strong support system can provide a sense of belonging, validation, and encouragement, giving you the confidence to overcome challenges and pursue your goals.

When you surround yourself with like-minded individuals who understand your aspirations and share similar values, you create an environment that fosters growth and mutual support. Your support network becomes a safe space where you can seek advice, share accomplishments, and find solace during difficult times.

Building a support network takes time and effort. It's important to cultivate genuine connections with individuals who genuinely care about your well-being and personal growth. These connections should be based on shared interests, values, and a genuine desire to support one another.

Not only does a support system provide emotional support, but it can also open doors to new opportunities and experiences. Through networking within your support network, you can access valuable resources, gain insights from others' experiences, and collaborate on projects or personal endeavors.

Finding Your Tribe

Identifying like-minded individuals is crucial in building a support network. Your tribe consists of people who understand your journey, provide guidance, and empower you to reach your full potential. Look for individuals who share your passions, hobbies, and career aspirations. Engage in activities and communities where these individuals gather, whether it's attending meetings, joining online forums, or participating in networking events.

Remember, building a support network requires reciprocity. Be willing to offer support and encouragement to others in your network. In turn, you'll reap the rewards of having a community that celebrates your victories and uplifts you during challenging times.

Nurturing Authentic Relationships

In today's digital age, fostering deep connections and building a support network is more important than ever. The virtual world offers numerous opportunities to connect with others, but it can also create a sense of disconnection and superficiality. In this section, we will explore strategies for building genuine and authentic relationships.

Effective Communication

Communication is the foundation of any relationship, and it plays a crucial role in nurturing deep connections. When interacting with others, it's important to be present, actively listen, and respond with empathy. Open and honest communication promotes understanding, trust, and mutual respect.

Whether you're engaging in face-to-face conversations or connecting through digital platforms, strive for clarity and sincerity in your communication. Avoid making assumptions and actively engage in dialogues that encourage both parties to express their thoughts and feelings.

Vulnerability and Trust

Vulnerability is the key to establishing authentic connections. Sharing your experiences, fears, and aspirations with others can create a strong foundation of trust. When you open up and allow others to see your authentic self, it encourages them to do the same.

However, it's important to exercise caution when sharing personal information online. Use discretion and only share what you're comfortable with. Building trust takes time, and it requires both parties to consistently support and respect each other's boundaries.

Shared Activities and Interests

Shared activities and interests provide a strong bond for building deep connections. Engaging in activities together allows you to learn more about each other and find common ground. It could be joining a club or organization, participating in group hobbies, or attending events related to your shared interests.

Explore different communities and online platforms that align with your passions. Connect with like-minded individuals who share your enthusiasm and seek meaningful connections within these communities.

Support and Empathy

A support network thrives on support and empathy. Be there for others when they need you, offering a listening ear and kind words of encouragement. Show empathy by validating their experiences and emotions, helping them feel understood and supported.

Building authentic relationships is a reciprocal process. It's important to remember that you are also deserving of support and empathy. Surround yourself with individuals who genuinely care about your well-being and prioritize your needs.

Fostering deep connections in a digital age requires intentionality, patience, and genuine effort. By implementing these strategies, you can build a support network filled with authentic relationships that enrich your life and provide a strong foundation for personal growth and happiness.

Finding Your Tribe: Identifying Like-Minded Individuals

In today's interconnected world, building a support network has become more important than ever. Finding your tribe – a group of like-minded individuals who share your values, interests, and goals – can provide a strong foundation for personal growth and well-being. The importance of a support system cannot be overstated, as it offers a sense of belonging, understanding, and encouragement.

So, how can you identify potential tribe members and create meaningful connections? Here are some tips to help you on your journey:

1. Explore Your Interests:

Start by exploring your own interests and passions. Look for communities, clubs, or organizations that align with your values and offer opportunities for connection. Whether it's a hobby, a cause, or a professional interest, finding like-minded individuals begins with immersing yourself in spaces where your passions are shared.

2. Attend Events and Workshops:

Attend events, workshops, and conferences related to your interests. These gatherings provide excellent opportunities to meet people who share your enthusiasm and can potentially become part of your support system. Take the time to engage in conversations, exchange contact information, and follow up with individuals who resonate with you.

3. Utilize Online Platforms:

Thanks to the digital age, connecting with like-minded individuals has become easier than ever. Utilize online platforms such as social media, dedicated forums, and professional networking

166

sites to expand your reach and find communities that align with your values. Engage in conversations, share your thoughts, and actively participate in online communities to establish genuine connections.

4. Seek Shared Experiences:

Consider engaging in activities and experiences that naturally attract like-minded individuals. Whether it's joining a sports team, volunteering for a cause you care about, or taking a class on a subject that interests you, shared experiences can provide fertile ground for building connections and finding your tribe.

5. Network Through Existing Connections:

Don't overlook the power of your existing connections. Reach out to friends, family, and colleagues who may know people with similar interests. Networking through trusted individuals can help you discover like-minded individuals who are already part of their own support networks.

Building a support network takes time and effort, but the rewards are immeasurable. By identifying like-minded individuals who share your values, interests, and goals, you can create a community that nurtures your personal growth and wellbeing. Remember, your tribe is out there – go out and find them!

Cultivating Supportive Friendships

To build a strong support network, it is crucial to cultivate supportive friendships. These friendships provide a foundation of trust, understanding, and encouragement, enabling you to navigate the challenges of life with ease.

To be a supportive friend, it is important to show empathy and actively listen to your friends' needs and concerns. By offering a shoulder to lean on and being there during difficult times, you create a safe space that fosters deep connections.

Setting boundaries is also essential in cultivating supportive friendships. Clearly communicating your needs and limitations ensures that both parties feel respected and understood. It allows for a balanced give-and-take, where each person's well-being is prioritized.

Fostering trust is another key aspect of building supportive friendships. Being reliable, honest, and loyal helps establish a solid foundation of trust. It means being there for your friends when they need you, maintaining confidentiality, and championing their successes.

Remember, cultivating supportive friendships is a journey that requires time and effort. Nurturing these relationships will not only enrich your life but also contribute to building a strong and reliable support network.

Leveraging Technology for Connection

In today's digital age, technology has become an integral part of our lives, shaping the way we connect and interact with others. It offers countless opportunities for building connections and maintaining relationships, making it an invaluable tool for fostering deep connections in a digital age and building a support network.

Social media platforms have provided us with a means to connect with people across the globe, allowing us to explore shared interests, engage in meaningful conversations, and find like-minded individuals. By leveraging these platforms, we can expand our support network beyond geographical constraints, connecting with individuals who can offer valuable insights and support.

Online communities are another powerful tool for building connections. Whether it's joining forums, participating in online groups, or engaging in discussions on platforms like Reddit or Quora, these communities provide a space to connect with individuals who share similar passions, interests, or goals. Participating actively in these communities not only allows us to receive support but also provides an opportunity to offer support to others, fostering deeper connections.

Additionally, digital platforms such as video conferencing apps have revolutionized the way we communicate, making it easier to connect face-to-face with individuals who may be geographically distant. These platforms enable us to have meaningful conversations, maintain personal connections, and even organize virtual events or support groups.

By leveraging technology, we can overcome barriers of distance and time, ensuring that building and maintaining connections is a seamless process. However, it's important to remember that technology should be used mindfully. While it offers immense benefits, it's essential to strike a balance between digital and face-to-face interactions, fostering a holistic support network that includes both virtual and physical connections.

Building a Diverse and Inclusive Support Network

Building a support network is about more than just finding people who share similar interests and goals. It's also important to create a network that embraces diversity and inclusivity. By doing so, you can foster personal growth, expand your horizons, and gain valuable insights from people with different perspectives and experiences.

When you surround yourself with a diverse group of individuals, you open yourself up to new ideas, challenges, and opportunities. Each person brings their unique background and knowledge, which can enrich your own understanding of the world. This diverse network becomes a source of inspiration, support, and encouragement as you navigate through life's ups and downs.

One of the key strategies for building a diverse and inclusive support network is to actively seek out individuals from different backgrounds. Attend networking events, join professional organizations, and engage in online communities that celebrate diversity. By intentionally seeking out connections with people who have different ethnicities, cultures, genders, abilities, and perspectives, you create a vibrant and inclusive network.

Moreover, it's essential to create a safe and welcoming space for everyone in your support network. Foster an environment where everyone feels heard, respected, and valued. Actively listen to different opinions and encourage open and honest discussions. Embrace opportunities for learning and growth as you gain a deeper understanding of the world through the perspectives of others.

By building a diverse and inclusive support network, you not only enhance your personal development, but you also contribute to a more inclusive society. Your network becomes a microcosm of the diverse world we live in, demonstrating the power of unity in the face of adversity.

Giving and Receiving Support

Fostering deep connections in a digital age and building a support network is not just about receiving support, but also about giving it back. Support networks thrive on reciprocity, creating a mutually beneficial environment where everyone can lean on each other.

Being a Valuable Source of Support

To be a valuable source of support within your network, it is important to actively listen and empathize with others. Show genuine concern and offer your help when someone is going through a challenging time. Whether it's lending a listening ear, providing advice, or offering practical assistance, your support can make a significant difference in someone's life.

Additionally, seeking ways to uplift and celebrate others' achievements is vital. By acknowledging and applauding their successes, you help foster a positive and encouraging atmosphere within your support network.

Learning to Accept Help from Others

Building a support network also means learning to accept help from others when you need it. Recognize that asking for assistance is not a sign of weakness, but a demonstration of trust and vulnerability. Being open to receiving support allows others to contribute and strengthens the bonds within your network.

When accepting help, express your gratitude and acknowledge the impact it has on you. By receiving support graciously, you further nurture the connections within your network and create an environment where everyone feels valued and appreciated.

In conclusion, fostering deep connections in a digital age and building a support network involves both giving and receiving support. Being a valuable source of support for others and learning to accept help leads to a stronger and more harmonious network.

Maintaining and Growing Your Network

Building a support network is not a one-time task; it requires ongoing effort and nurturing. As you navigate different stages of life, it's important to maintain and grow your network to ensure continued support and connection. Here are some strategies to consider:

- Regular Check-ins: Take the time to check in with your network regularly. Whether it's through phone calls, video chats, or face-to-face meetings, staying connected on a consistent basis helps to strengthen relationships and ensure that you are there for one another when needed.

- Networking Events: Attend networking events and industry conferences to expand your network. These events provide an opportunity to meet new people who share your interests or professional goals. Be open to initiating conversations, exchanging contact information, and following up with potential connections afterward.

- Embrace Opportunities for Growth: Seek out opportunities for personal and professional growth that align with your interests and passions. Join clubs, organizations, or online communities that focus on your areas of interest. This not only allows you to learn and develop new skills but also provides a platform for meeting like-minded individuals and expanding your support network.

Summary:

Building a support network is an ongoing process that requires effort, but the rewards are immeasurable. By maintaining regular check-ins, attending networking events, and embracing growth opportunities, you can foster deep connections and ensure that your support network continues to thrive in the digital age.

Chapter 38

Defining Success on Your Terms:
What Does Success Really Mean?
*****

What does success look like to you? Is it a big house, a fancy car, and a high-paying job? Or is it something deeper, more meaningful? In a world that often equates success with material wealth and external achievements, it's easy to lose sight of our own personal definitions of success. But here's the question: What if success isn't about the things we acquire, but about the person we become?

In this thought-provoking section, we delve into the essence of success in life, exploring personal definitions that go beyond the conventional measures. We'll guide you on a journey of self-reflection, challenge societal norms, and share practical strategies to help you measure your success non-materialistically. It's time to redefine success on your own terms and unlock the true meaning of personal triumph.

The Journey to Discovering Your Personal Definition of Success

Embark on a transformative journey of self-reflection to uncover the true meaning of success in your life. Success is not defined solely by society's standards or materialistic gains, but rather by your own personal definitions and aspirations. It is a journey that requires exploration of your values, passions, and dreams, allowing you to create a unique and authentic definition of success.

To begin this journey, take the time to reflect on what truly matters to you. Ask yourself: What brings fulfillment and joy into your life? What are your core values and beliefs? What do you aspire to achieve and contribute to the world? By understanding your intrinsic motivations and desires, you can start to craft a personal definition of success that resonates with your authentic self.

Consider the aspects of your life that are most significant to you. It could be your relationships, personal growth, health and well-being, or making a positive impact on others. Success is not a one-size-fits-all concept, and by exploring what matters most to you, you can define success on your own terms.

Explore Your Values:

Clarifying your values is an essential step in discovering your personal definition of success. Consider what principles you hold dear and how they guide your choices and actions. Whether it's integrity, creativity, compassion, or something else, your values reflect what is truly important to you. Aligning your definition of success with these core values will help you create a meaningful and fulfilling life.

Pursue Your Passions:

Success is intimately connected to your passions and interests. Take a moment to identify the activities, hobbies, or causes that ignite your soul. When you align your goals and definition of success with your passions, you are more likely to feel a sense of fulfillment and purpose in your daily life.

Realize Your Dreams:

What are your aspirations? What dreams have you dared to imagine for yourself? Success is not simply about achieving predetermined milestones; it is about actively pursuing your dreams and creating a life that encompasses your deepest desires. By identifying your dreams and setting goals that align with them, you can live a life that is true to your authentic self.

Keep in mind that personal definitions of success can change and evolve as you grow and experience new things. This journey is about constant self-reflection and being open to reassessing what success means to you. It is not about comparing yourself to others or striving for unattainable ideals, but rather about embracing your unique path and crafting a definition of success that resonates with your heart and soul.

Redefining Success: Moving Beyond Material Measures

When it comes to measuring success, society often places undue emphasis on material possessions and external achievements. However, true success goes far beyond these superficial markers. It is a deeply personal journey that is unique to each individual. So, how can you measure your success in life in a non-materialistic way?

One crucial step is to challenge societal norms and traditional measures of success. Instead of solely focusing on wealth or status, consider alternative ways to assess your accomplishments. Look inward and prioritize personal growth, happiness, and fulfillment as the yardstick of success.

By shifting your perspective, you can redefine success based on your own values and aspirations. It may be about making a positive impact on others, cultivating deep relationships, or finding joy and contentment in everyday life. The key is to align your definition of success with what truly matters to you.

This shift in mindset allows you to break free from the constant comparison trap and societal expectations. It empowers you to live life on your own terms and find fulfillment in your unique journey, rather than chasing after external validation.

Remember, success should not be measured by the size of your bank account or the number of accolades you possess. It's about finding meaning, growth, and inner satisfaction. So, embrace your personal definitions of success and uncover what truly matters to you.

The Importance of Setting Meaningful Goals

In order to achieve success in life, it is crucial to set goals that align with your personal definitions of success. These goals go beyond materialistic measures and reflect your values, interests, and long-term aspirations.

Setting meaningful goals provides clarity and direction, guiding your actions towards what truly matters to you. By defining your own path to success, you are empowered to make choices that align with your authentic self and bring a sense of fulfillment.

The Power of Effective Goal-Setting Strategies

To ensure your goals are meaningful and achievable, it is important to employ effective goal-setting strategies. One such strategy is to create SMART goals:

Specific: Clearly define what you want to achieve.

- **Measurable:** Establish criteria to track and measure your progress.
- **Achievable:** Set realistic and attainable goals that push you outside of your comfort zone.
- **Relevant:** Ensure your goals align with your personal values and aspirations.
- **Time-bound:** Set a timeframe to create a sense of urgency and accountability.
- By following the SMART framework, you can transform broad aspirations into actionable steps, increasing the likelihood of successfully attaining your goals.

Furthermore, remember to break down larger goals into smaller, manageable tasks. This allows you to track progress, celebrate milestones, and stay motivated along the way.

Aligning Goals with Personal Definitions of Success

When setting goals, it is essential to consider how they align with your personal definitions of success. Reflect on what truly matters to you in life and identify areas where you want to grow, improve, or make a positive impact.

Ask yourself, "What does success mean to me?" Is it cultivating deep relationships, making a difference in your community, or excelling in your chosen field? By aligning your goals with your own unique definition of success, you are more likely to experience a sense of fulfillment and purpose as you work towards achieving them.

Remember, success is not solely determined by external achievements or possessions. It is a deeply personal and subjective measure of how you live your life and the impact you have on yourself and others.

Cultivating a Growth Mindset for Lifelong Success

When it comes to achieving ongoing success in life, cultivating a growth mindset is key. A growth mindset is a belief that your abilities, intelligence, and talents can be developed through dedication, effort, and continuous learning. It is the understanding that failure and challenges are opportunities for growth, rather than setbacks. By adopting a growth mindset, you can unlock your full potential and overcome obstacles on your path to success.

One of the core principles of a growth mindset is the belief that your personal definition of success goes beyond materialistic measures. Instead of solely focusing on external achievements, a growth mindset encourages you to measure your success based on personal growth, resilience, and adaptability.

With a growth mindset, you embrace challenges as stepping stones towards personal growth. Failure becomes a learning opportunity, and setbacks are seen as temporary roadblocks rather than permanent obstacles. By cultivating a growth mindset, you develop the ability to adapt to change, learn from your experiences, and continuously improve.

Embracing Continuous Learning

A growth mindset is closely tied to the concept of continuous learning. By recognizing that intelligence and abilities can be developed, you become more open to acquiring new knowledge, skills, and perspectives.

Embracing lifelong learning allows you to constantly expand your horizons, stay curious, and adapt to new challenges. Whether it's through formal education, self-study, or seeking mentorship, the pursuit of knowledge becomes a fundamental part of your success journey.

With a growth mindset, you understand that success isn't just about reaching a specific destination; it's about the continuous pursuit of improvement and personal growth. Each day presents an opportunity to learn, grow, and become better than you were yesterday.

Building Resilience and Adaptability

Resilience and adaptability are essential qualities for long-term success. A growth mindset empowers you to bounce back from setbacks, overcome obstacles, and adapt to changing circumstances.

By reframing failures as learning experiences, you develop the resilience to persevere in the face of challenges. You view setbacks as temporary and understand that they provide valuable lessons for future success.

Furthermore, a growth mindset allows you to embrace change and adapt to new situations. You understand that personal growth requires stepping outside of your comfort zone, taking risks, and embracing new opportunities.

When faced with obstacles or setbacks, those with a growth mindset respond with determination, resilience, and adaptability. Instead of giving up, they persevere and find alternative paths to success.

Finding Balance: Nurturing Well-being Alongside Success

Success in life extends beyond material achievements and professional accomplishments. It encompasses a holistic approach that includes nurturing your overall well-being and maintaining a healthy work-life balance. While striving for success, it's important to prioritize self-care, manage stress effectively, and achieve harmony in various aspects of your life.

To achieve this balance, there are practical strategies that you can incorporate into your daily routine. Prioritize self-care by engaging in activities that promote physical and mental well-being. This could be taking regular exercise, practicing mindfulness or meditation, or engaging in hobbies that bring you joy and relaxation.

Manage Stress Effectively

Stress can be an inevitable part of life, particularly when striving for success. However, managing stress effectively is crucial to maintain overall well-being. Identify stress triggers and find healthy coping mechanisms such as deep breathing exercises, journaling, or seeking support from loved ones. Prioritizing stress management techniques will enable you to stay focused, productive, and resilient in the face of challenges.

Creating boundaries between work and personal life is essential for achieving a healthy work-life balance. Establish set working hours, take regular breaks, and be present in your personal life without the constant intrusion of work-related stress. Prioritize family time, engage in activities you love, and connect with loved ones to cultivate a sense of fulfillment beyond your professional aspirations.

Remember, success is not solely measured by external achievements, but by your personal satisfaction, overall well-being, and the positive impact you have on others. By nurturing your well-being alongside your pursuit of success, you can create a balanced and fulfilling life.

Embracing Failure as a Stepping Stone to Success

Failure often carries a negative connotation, but shifting your perspective on it can unlock immense growth and resilience on your journey towards personal success. Rather than viewing failure as an endpoint, embracing it as a stepping stone allows you to learn, adapt, and ultimately achieve your goals and aspirations.

Reframing failures as valuable learning experiences is crucial in measuring your success non-materialistically. It is a process that propels you forward, equipping you with valuable insights and enhancing your problem-solving skills. When you approach failure with a growth mindset, it becomes an opportunity for self-improvement and personal development.

One effective way to embrace failure is by analyzing your past setbacks and identifying key lessons learned. Reflect on what went wrong, what could be done differently, and how you can use this newfound knowledge to forge a more successful path. The ability to adapt and learn from failures ultimately leads to resilience and propels you closer to achieving your personal definition of success.

Furthermore, understanding that failure is not a reflection of your worth but rather a natural part of the success journey can help you perceive setbacks in a healthier light. By removing the fear of failure and embracing it as part of the process, you free yourself to take calculated risks, explore new opportunities, and step outside of your comfort zone.

Remember, success in life is not solely defined by materialistic achievements. It is about personal growth, learning, and constantly striving to become the best version of yourself. By reframing failures, you can overcome obstacles, adapt to challenges, and pave the way for your own unique path to success.

Building Strong Relationships: The Key to Sustainable Success

When it comes to achieving success in life, personal definitions of success vary from person to person. While some may equate success with material wealth or career accomplishments, others prioritize relationships, personal growth, and overall well-being. In order to measure your success non-materialistically, it is crucial to recognize the significance of building and nurturing strong relationships throughout your journey.

Strong connections, whether personal or professional, play a vital role in sustainable success. Building meaningful relationships allows you to tap into a network of support, guidance, and opportunities. By leveraging these networks, you can learn from others' experiences, gain valuable insights, and collaborate on projects that contribute to your personal and professional growth.

H3>Strategies for Building Strong Relationships

1. Authenticity: Be genuine in your interactions and cultivate a sense of trust. Show interest in others, listen actively, and be open to sharing your own experiences. Authenticity creates a foundation for meaningful connections.
2. Communication: Effective communication is the key to fostering strong relationships. Listen attentively, express yourself clearly, and be respectful of others' opinions. Regular and open communication nurtures understanding and strengthens connections.
3. Empathy: Understanding and empathizing with others' perspectives and experiences is crucial in building strong relationships. Put yourself in their shoes, practice active empathy, and show genuine care and support. Empathy fosters emotional connections and strengthens bonds.

4. Reciprocity: Build relationships based on mutual support and shared experiences. Be willing to offer help and support to others in their endeavors. A culture of reciprocity cultivates long-lasting connections.

5. Networking: Actively participate in networking events and communities related to your field of interest. Attend conferences, engage in industry-specific groups, and connect with like-minded individuals. Expanding your network can lead to valuable collaborations and new opportunities.

6. Gratitude: Show appreciation for the relationships you have cultivated. Expressing gratitude reinforces the bond and encourages continued support and collaboration.

By recognizing the importance of building strong relationships in your journey towards success, you open yourself up to a world of possibilities. Cultivating these connections not only contributes to personal and professional growth but also enriches your overall well-being. Remember, success goes beyond material gains, and building strong relationships is a key component in measuring your success non-materialistically.

The Role of Purpose: Finding Meaning in Your Success

Success in life is not solely determined by material achievements or external validation. It is also deeply connected to a sense of purpose and meaning. When you align your personal definition of success with a greater purpose, your accomplishments take on a whole new level of significance.

Many people find themselves striving for success without truly understanding the why behind their pursuit. However, by reflecting on your values, passions, and what truly matters to you, you can find a sense of purpose that guides your journey.

Living a purpose-driven life goes beyond measuring success based on material possessions or societal standards. It means finding fulfillment in the work you do, expressing your true self, and making a positive impact on the world.

When you have a clear sense of purpose, you can navigate the ups and downs of life with confidence and resilience. Challenges and setbacks become opportunities for growth rather than deterrents to success. Your purpose becomes a driving force that keeps you motivated and focused on your goals.

Discovering and embracing your purpose is a deeply personal and introspective process. It requires self-reflection, asking yourself important questions, and being open to exploring new paths. There is no one-size-fits-all approach to finding purpose, as it varies from individual to individual.

Some people find meaning in pursuing a career that aligns with their passion, while others find it through volunteering, creative endeavors, or nurturing relationships. The key is to identify what brings you a sense of fulfillment and align your personal definition of success with those pursuits.

When you infuse purpose into your success, you elevate your overall satisfaction and fulfillment. You feel a deeper sense of contentment knowing that your accomplishments are not just about personal gain, but also about making a positive impact in the world.

So take the time to reflect on your values, passions, and what truly matters to you. Ask yourself the tough questions, and explore different avenues that can bring meaning to your life. When you find your purpose and align it with your personal definition of success, you unlock a whole new level of fulfillment and achieve success that goes far beyond material achievements.

Celebrating Success: Recognizing and Appreciating Your Accomplishments

in life is not solely determined by material possessions or external achievements. It's essential to take the time to recognize and appreciate your accomplishments, big or small, along your journey. Celebrating success is not about boasting or seeking validation from others, but rather about cultivating a positive mindset and nurturing your personal growth.

One way to appreciate your accomplishments is by reflecting on the progress you have made and the obstacles you have overcome. Take pride in the effort and dedication you have put forth to achieve your goals, as every step forward is a testament to your resilience and determination. By acknowledging your accomplishments, you reinforce a sense of confidence and motivation, fueling further success.

Remember, success is a continuous process rather than a destination. It's important to celebrate not only the end results but also the small victories along the way. Recognize the lessons learned from both successes and failures and appreciate how they have shaped you into the person you are today. Taking time to appreciate your successes helps you maintain a positive mindset and fosters a sense of gratitude for the opportunities and growth that come your way. Ultimately, celebrating success is about recognizing your own worth and acknowledging the unique path you have taken. Embrace your achievements and let them serve as a reminder of your capabilities and potential. By appreciating your personal definition of success and the journey you have embarked upon, you cultivate resilience, motivation, and a mindset that propels you towards even greater accomplishments in the future.

Chapter 39

Fostering Creativity and
Innovation in Your Everyday Routine

******

Why Creativity Matters

Creativity is like a helpful tool. It helps us grow in many ways. In the fast-paced world we live in, being creative is important. It helps us think of fresh ideas that can be worth a lot. It helps us solve problems in new ways, find good things, and handle changes well.

In our personal life, creativity lets us be true to ourselves and explore what's not yet known. It helps us understand ourselves better and feels rewarding. Through activating our creative senses, we can discover things we are good at. This leads to a life rich with joy and success.

At work, being creative is often desired by bosses. It helps us answer hard questions with new ideas, which makes us work better and compete well. Creative ideas often result in big improvements that can push businesses to new heights.

Also, creativity makes us think differently. It challenges trending ideas. By thinking anew and presenting fresh thoughts, creative people can shake up old systems for the better. Whether it's art, tech, business, or other fields, creativity sparks new things and growth.

Knowing why creativity matters lets us see it as a useful asset. By growing our creativity and using it more, we can achieve our best and set the path for ongoing success. Overcoming Stopped Creativity

We often find creativity thrusting us ahead in our jobs and private lives. But sometimes, we hit a creativity roadblock. These snags can annoy and dishearten us. Unraveling usual creativity roadblocks and knowing how to jump them is vital to fostering an attitude of exploration and trial.

One usual creativity roadblock is fear of messing up. Overthinking about creating perfect work can freeze us, hindering novel ideas. Beating this fear means accepting errors and failures as part of the innovation journey. By looking at failure as a precious learning lesson, we can break free from perfectionism's shackles and embrace new opportunities.

Insecurity is another creativity roadblock. We may doubt our skills or get nervous about exposing our concepts to others. Internal cynics can persist, damaging our assurance and stopping us from daring. Accepting and quieting this critical voice is key to unlocking our creative ability. Using positive daily practices, like affirmations or positive self-talk, can build resilience against self-doubt.

External interruptions also play a prominent role in hampering creativity. Our always-on society pelts us with alerts and interruptions, making creative tasks hard. Making an undisturbed zone and time for creativity can reduce distractions and promote flow states. Disabling notifications, setting technology boundaries, and using mindfulness techniques can all help a more focused and productive creative process.

Trapped viewpoints can stifle creativity. Sticking to routine or drawing from the same sources can leave your ideas feeling tired. Breaking out of this means finding new experiences, looking at other cultures, or trying out different art styles. These things can expand our view and spark fresh thinking.

On the other hand, stress and burnout can suck us dry of creative juices. Our creativity tanks when we're swamped or too tired. Looking after ourselves, setting limits, and recharging are key to staying mentally fit for creativity. Breaks, relaxation, and doing things we love refuel us, helping beat burnout and boost creativity.

We can grow curiosity and a trial-and-error attitude by addressing creativity roadblocks. Accepting mistakes, quieting self-doubt, cutting out distractions, embracing new views, and looking after ourselves help break through creative blocks. These steps let us unlock our creative power and stir up innovation in our day-to-day lives. An environment that feeds creativity and innovation is crucial. With certain elements in your surrounding, you can create a place that nurtures ideas and boosts creative thinking.

Think about sunlight. It's been proven to brighten moods, boost work rate, and spark creativity. Try working close to a window for plenty of sunlight. If sunshine is scarce, full-spectrum lights can provide a sun-like glow.

Nature too brings a creative buzz. Add a plant or flowers to your workspace. They're not just pretty to look at, but they clean the air and carry a calm feel. Being around nature can chill you out and ignite creative thoughts.

You could also showcase keepsakes. Show off photos, art, or inspiring items. These personal details create a welcoming feel and remind you of your creative motive.

Keeping your place neat supports creativity too. A tidy, junk-free space removes distractions and clears the mind. Buy storage items to keep your workspace organized. This way, you can focus on being creative without feeling swamped in stuff.

Finally, think about where you put your furniture and stuff. Position them for easy reach and free movement. Try different setups until you find one that leaves you comfortable and fired-up.

Designing a creative environment means making a space that matches your individual likes and assists your personal creative process. Try out different elements, observe what gives you energy and sparks your creativity, and tweak as necessary. A place that encourages creativity will help you think differently, achieve innovative expressions, and boost creativity in all areas of your life - that's the power of nurturing creative habits.

For supporting creativity daily, it's important to make habits that boost ingenuity. Habits like regular journaling, meditation, and brainstorming can enhance creative skills and unlock potential.

1. Journaling: A potent way to nurture creativity is the habit of journaling. Allocating regular time daily to express your thoughts, ideas, and visions gives room for self-expression and self-reflection. This habit can unravel new viewpoints, trigger innovative concepts, and solutions.

2. Think about using various sorts of journals to meet your needs, like a gratitude journal for positivity or a dream journal for subconscious thoughts exploration. Allow yourself free reign to experiment with different writing methods, like spontaneous writing or continuous prose, to stimulate creativity and find hidden inspiration.

3. Meditation works wonders in fostering creativity. Set aside a bit of time every day for some quiet thinking. This can help clear your mind, making space for fresh ideas. Meditation boosts focus, reduces mental chaos, and improves mental health.

4. During medication, just watch your thoughts. Don't judge or attach. This will pave way for a calm mind, from where creative thoughts can effortlessly spring forth. Try blending in guided imagery or creative-focused affirmations in your meditation for a more fruitful experience.

5. Brainstorming instigates creative thinking. Assign a specific time every week for this activity. Brainstorm on things that matter to you or your work. Ensure the place you choose for this is calming, and inspires you think freely.

In your brainstorming sessions, allow every idea to come in without being critical about its practicality. Often, the most unique and 'crazy' ideas lead to the best solutions. Use visualization methods, mind-mapping, or team-up with others for brainstorming. This can result in a wide variety of ideas.

Making these creativity-boosting habits part of your daily life, you can generate a great environment for innovative ideas. Allow yourself to experiment and be daring. Try to always think differently. By doing this constantly, and with a dedication towards nurturing your creative abilities, you will be able to fully explore your capabilities. This can give you a fresh look on life and every challenge it tosses your way. So, here's to Bringing Creativity into Everyday Life!

Adding a dash of creativity to everyday activities is an excellent strategy for finding happiness and fulfillment. By injecting creativity into our daily tasks, we can discover fresh viewpoints, boost our ability to tackle problems, and feel more content. Here, we'll talk about simple methods to make different parts of your daily life more creative - from sprucing up your home to whipping up a storm in the kitchen and immersing in hobbies that let your creativity shine.

1. **Home Decor:** Your living space is a personal canvas reflecting your distinct persona and style. Play around with various color combinations, textures, and designs. Think about giving a second life to old furniture or taking on DIY tasks to add individuality to your home. Include elements that spark your passion, like art, pictures, or plants. Remember, when crafting a space that mirrors your creative side, it's okay to step outside conventional boundaries.

2. **Cooking and Baking:** Make your meals a visual treat by experimenting with taste, how it looks, and the ingredients used. Play around with new recipes or add your unique spin to traditional dishes. Use colorful herbs and spices to give your dishes a vibrant look and rich taste. Involve friends or family in this fun kitchen project. Cooking and baking can indeed nourish your physical and artistic self.

3. **Writing and Journaling:** Writing is a great avenue for expressing ourselves and exploring concepts. Keep a journal for jotting down your thoughts, feelings, and aspirations. Try different writing types, like poems or short tales. Pen down heartfelt letters to your loved ones or push your creativity boundaries through writing challenges. Writing can be a therapeutic process and an effective medium to unleash your creativity.

4. **Visual Arts:** Dabbling in painting, drawing or sketching is therapeutic and lets you express yourself. Carve out time for art and experiment with various tools, methods, and art forms. Try out an art lesson or get involved in a local art circle to gather insights and get motivated. Lack of skill isn't a setback - the journey of making art weighs more than the final piece, and everyone has their distinct artistic touch.

5. **Performing Arts:** Unleash your inner artist via music, dancing, or drama. Master a musical tool or be part of a local singing group. Get interested in dancing for fun or join in hometown theater shows. These pursuits not only let you manifest yourself artistically but also pave the way for self-improvement, teamwork, and bonding with like-minded folks.

Remember, creativity isn't confined to certain fields. It's found in every life facet, from dressing style to tackling problems at work. By encouraging your creative side, you'll reveal new opportunities, perceive the world with a new perspective, and bring happiness into even the most basic tasks. Welcome your inherent creativity and let it thrive in every part of your daily routine

Chapter 40

Expanding Your Cultural Awareness and Appreciation

****

In this chapter, we will delve into the importance of cultural awareness in personal growth and development. Understanding and appreciating different cultures can greatly enrich our lives and broaden our perspectives. Here, we will explore the significance of cultural awareness and recognize the benefits of being culturally sensitive in a diverse society.

Cultural awareness is essential because it allows us to understand and appreciate the values, customs, traditions, and beliefs of different cultures. By expanding our knowledge and understanding of other cultures, we become more empathetic and open-minded individuals. This awareness helps break down barriers and fosters greater respect and harmony within our communities.

One of the key benefits of cultural awareness is the ability to navigate multicultural environments with ease. When we are aware and sensitive to cultural differences, we can avoid misunderstandings and miscommunication. This leads to better relationships, both personally and professionally.

Moreover, cultural awareness opens doors to new experiences and opportunities. By embracing different cultures through travel, literature, art, or engaging with diverse communities, we gain a deeper understanding of the world around us. We learn to challenge our assumptions and broaden our perspectives. This exposure helps us develop a broader worldview and adaptability in an ever-changing global landscape.

By recognizing the importance of cultural awareness in personal growth, we are taking steps towards becoming more inclusive individuals. It is crucial to embrace diversity and foster an environment where everyone feels valued and respected. By celebrating different cultures, we contribute to a more harmonious society that thrives on mutual understanding and appreciation. Let's jump in and learn how to boost our understanding of diverse cultures, discuss diversity and inclusion, and enhance cross-cultural connections. Ready?

Growing Your Cultural Knowledge and Valuing Diversity

Dipping Your Toes into Various Cultures:

Unleashing the Explorer in You: Wander, Read, Appreciate Art. Being part of diverse cultures is a great strategy to increase your cultural understanding. Travel, books, and art are excellent avenues for this. Each gives you unique chances to understand and value diverse viewpoints.

Visiting new places lets you enjoy firsthand the varied traditions, customs, and lifestyles. It also helps alter your pre-existing views and enlarge your outlook. Engage directly with the place's culture. Try their food, join their festivals, talk to the locals. You'll see that embracing various cultural practices leads to connection and unity, despite our differences.

Books are potent resources to appreciate cultures. Works by a mix of authors grant us an inside look at the narrations, customs, and principles of different societies. With a variety of stories, you'll grasp a deeper feel for the intricacy and splendid aspects of diverse cultures. Choose books about movements, identities, societal matters, and historical events to enhance your view.

Travel, books, a remarkable path opens through art to explore different cultures. Visit art hubs like museums or galleries. They house art from across the globe. It's a chance to value the variety in artistic expression and stories that mirror diverse cultures. Try out various art forms-paintings, sculptures, music, dance, theater, film. Every art form gives a fresh perspective to understand where it roots from. How to Interact with Varied Communities to Expand Views and Question Assumptions

Travel, books, art, are good ways to explore cultures solo. But, trying to mingle with varied communities takes you to a fresh sea of cultural discovery. Always be on the lookout to interact with people of different roots, races, faiths, and outlooks. In doing so, you go deep into their culture and test your own thoughts and prejudices.

Go to events or festivals that honor the rituals and habits of different societies. These occasions often have music, dance, food, and other facets that give you a peek into the richness and variety of cultures. Talk to residents from these communities to know about their experiences, beliefs, principles. Be polite, open-minded and listen keenly to their tales and standpoints.

Contributing time to organizations that deal with multiethnic communities is one sturdy step to expand cultural knowledge. This helps you give your time and abilities and also see the hardships and wins faced by other cultures first hand. Through such acts, you form lasting bonds, foster understanding, and have a positive impact on others' lives.

Keep in mind, boosting cultural knowledge is a continuous path. It involves staying open-minded, empathetic, and eager to learn. When you explore different cultures through travels, books, artistic pursuits, or connecting with varied communities, you not only enrich your own viewpoint, but you also make the world more embracing and interlinked. To elevate your cultural knowledge and foster respect in a multi-ethnic society, it's key to grasp an understanding of cultural habits, celebrations, and customs.

Start growing cultural warmth and regard by embracing each culture without bias and an open heart. Understand that cultural standards differ immensely from what you're used to. A gesture considered respectful in one culture might not hold the same value in another. Devote time to educate yourself about different cultural habits and celebrations. You can do this by reading, viewing documentaries, or talking to people of different cultures.

Remember, powerful intercultural exchanges depend a lot on the way we communicate. When talking to people from different cultures, pay attention to your language, speech tone, and even non-spoken signals like your body movements and facial expressions. Refrain from assuming or generalizing. This can cause confusion and uphold stereotypes. Preferably, meet your interactions with an interest to learn and humility, asking questions to better comprehend their viewpoints and experiences.

Let's make every space welcoming for all in diverse settings. How? Listen to peoples' stories, recognize any biases you might have, and change your behavior if needed. This commitment to understanding and respect builds a place where people from all walks of life find success.

Building cultural sensitivity is a journey, not a destination. It means always learning, always welcoming new experiences, and challenging your own preconceptions. Seek out moments to embrace other cultures. Perhaps a local cultural festival or a workshop promoting diversity. This opens doors to deeper understanding and meaningful relationships with people from diverse backgrounds.

Wrapping up, being culturally sensitive and respectful means understanding varied norms, traditions, and ways of communication. It means showing respect in diverse settings. By getting to know different cultures, challenging stereotypes, and promoting equality, we can cultivate a harmonious and culturally aware society True change comes from meaningful conversations about different cultures and viewpoints. Actively search for opportunities to understand diversity and inclusion to overcome unconscious bias and stereotypes.

Beating bias and negative preconceptions means learning about ignored or disadvantaged groups. This could include reading works by writers from many backgrounds, watching films or documentaries about various cultures, or going to events discussing diversity and inclusion. Another key step is listening. Listen to people from different backgrounds – really listen. Doing this improves understanding of their unique views and hurdles. Open and respectful chats can help push past walls of misunderstanding.

We also need to evaluate our own preconceptions. We should be willing to look at ourselves, to question ingrained stereotypes. By exploring our own biases, we can begin to unlearn damaging stereotypes and open our minds.

Joining activities or projects that encourage connections between cultures can help beat biases too. We can go to cultural festivals, become members of multicultural groups, or give time to community events celebrating diversity. Interaction with different cultures can fight misunderstandings and promote the wonderful variety of humanity.

Dealing with hidden biases and breaking stereotypes demands constant self-checking, learning, and an open mindset. By consciously trying to know vaster cultures and communities, we can recognize our own biases and work to build a more accepting society. It's about enhancing cultural interaction and working together.

Supporting programs that boost cultural understanding is crucial to improve your knowledge and respect for different cultures. Taking part in community events or other initiatives promoting diversity would get you to have meaningful exchanges with individuals from diverse backgrounds. In turn, this creates mutual respect and empathy, and provides a richer view of diverse customs.

Try attending cultural festivals or exhibits. It's an excellent way to see a wide range of cultural experiences. Events like these typically exhibit traditional music, arts, and food. These are chances to learn the customs and traditions directly. Active participation can give you a deep understanding of different cultural perspectives.

Think about joining workshops or courses that work to fill cultural distances. Taking language lessons, cooking classes, or traditional crafting are great avenues to learn more than just new skills. It also helps to value the culture they are rooted in. Hands-on experiences provide the chance to interact with the people you're learning from, promoting collaboration and building bridges between cultures.

Joining groups focused on diversity can boost cross-cultural understanding. These groups often plan activities to teach about different cultures. Volunteering or participating directly supports a more inclusive society.

Also, consider online communities where you can talk about multiple cultures. You can discuss cultural differences, share personal stories, and challenge biases. These exchanges widen your outlook.

Open-mindedness is essential to understand diverse cultures. Looking for cultural exchange and collaboration opportunities enriches you. Plus, it helps foster an inclusive, peaceful society.

Chapter 41

The Legacy Project: What Will You Leave Behind?

*****

Have you ever stopped to ponder what kind of legacy you will leave behind? In a world where we are constantly striving for success and significance, it is important to reflect on the impact we want to make. Creating a personal legacy goes beyond individual accomplishments; it is about leaving a lasting mark that inspires change and influences future generations.

So, what will your legacy be? Will you be remembered for the lives you transformed, the communities you uplifted, or the ideas you championed? Will your legacy be a testament to your values and passions, or will it fade away without a trace?

In this section, we will explore the concept of creating a personal legacy and delve into why it is important. We will guide you through the process of defining and crafting your legacy, setting goals, taking action, and leaving a lasting impact. We will also discuss the power of sharing your story and wisdom to inspire change and explore how you can leave a legacy in different areas of your life.

But perhaps most importantly, we will challenge you to reflect on your legacy and ask yourself: What will you leave behind? Are you taking the necessary steps to create the impact you want to make? Join us on this journey of self-reflection and discover how you can build a personal legacy that truly reflects who you are and what you stand for.

Why Is Your Legacy Important?

Your legacy is not just about what you leave behind when you're gone, but also about the impact you make while you're here. It is a reflection of the difference you want to make in the world and the values you want to uphold. Creating a personal legacy is important because it gives your life a sense of purpose and fulfillment.

When you actively think about the legacy you want to leave, it shapes the way you live your life. It inspires you to make choices that align with your values and aspirations. By knowing the mark you want to leave on the world, you can strive to make a positive impact in everything you do.

Leaving a personal legacy is not just about individual achievements, but also about the larger impact you can have on others and future generations. It is about inspiring change, sharing your story and wisdom, and creating a ripple effect that continues to resonate long after you're gone.

Your legacy is a testament to who you are as a person and the values you hold dear. By actively creating a personal legacy, you can leave a lasting positive impact in different areas of life, such as your career, relationships, and community. Your legacy is your opportunity to contribute to a better world and inspire others to do the same.

So, why is your legacy important? It is an expression of who you are, what you stand for, and the impact you want to make. It gives your life meaning and ensures that your values continue to shape the world even after you're gone. Creating a personal legacy is a powerful way to leave your mark and inspire change.

Defining Your Legacy: Reflecting on Values and Passions

Creating a personal legacy begins with reflection - taking the time to understand your core values and passions. By examining what truly matters to you, you can shape the impact you want to make on the world.

Your legacy is more than just the things you leave behind; it's about the values and principles that guide your actions. To define your personal legacy, start by asking yourself what you want to be remembered for. What kind of mark do you want to leave on the world?

Consider your core values - the beliefs and principles that you hold dear. Reflect on what brings you joy, what ignites your passion, and what truly matters to you. This introspection will help you uncover the essence of your legacy.

When your actions align with your core values and passions, your impact becomes genuine and powerful. It's about finding that sweet spot where what you believe in intersects with what you love. By living authentically and pursuing what inspires you, you naturally create a personal legacy that is meaningful and lasting.

Defining your legacy is an ongoing process. As you grow and evolve, your values and passions may shift, and that is perfectly okay. Take the time to regularly reflect on your core values and ensure that your actions continue to align with them. By staying true to yourself and embracing the changes that life brings, you can continuously refine and strengthen your personal legacy.

Crafting Your Legacy: Setting Goals and Taking Action

Creating a personal legacy involves more than just having a vision. It requires setting meaningful goals and taking intentional action towards making a positive difference in the world. Your legacy is a reflection of the impact you want to make and the lasting mark you want to leave behind.

To craft your legacy, start by identifying the values and passions that drive you. What truly matters to you? What are you most passionate about? Reflecting on these questions will help you align your actions with your desired legacy, ensuring that every step you take is purposeful and in line with your values.

Once you have defined your values and passions, the next step is to set specific goals. These goals should be achievable, measurable, and time-bound. By setting clear objectives, you create a roadmap that guides your actions and keeps you focused on what truly matters in the pursuit of your legacy.

Remember, crafting your legacy doesn't require grand gestures or massive achievements. It's about the small, consistent actions that you take every day. These actions can be as simple as volunteering in your community, mentoring someone in need, or advocating for causes that align with your values.

By taking intentional action towards your goals, you not only create a positive impact in the world, but you also inspire those around you to do the same. Your legacy becomes a catalyst for change, encouraging others to join you in making a difference. It's through these collective efforts that lasting change is achieved.

So, as you navigate through life, remember that each decision you make and every action you take contributes to your personal legacy. Stay true to your values, set meaningful goals, and take intentional action to build a legacy that reflects the best version of yourself.

Leaving a Lasting Impact: Creating a Ripple Effect

When it comes to creating your personal legacy, it's not just about the impact you want to make during your lifetime. It's about leaving a lasting imprint that continues to resonate long after you're gone. By creating a ripple effect, you have the power to inspire and uplift others, ensuring that your legacy extends far beyond what you could have ever imagined.

Small acts of kindness have the ability to create a ripple effect that reaches far and wide. Whether it's lending a helping hand to a stranger or volunteering your time for a cause you believe in, these simple gestures can have a profound impact on those around you. By consistently choosing to spread positivity and compassion, you can leave a legacy of love that will continue to touch lives for generations to come.

The Power of Inspiration

Inspiring others is another powerful way to create a ripple effect. By sharing your story and wisdom, you have the ability to ignite a spark within others, motivating them to pursue their own passions and make a difference in the world. Whether it's through mentorship, public speaking, or writing, your words and actions can serve as a guiding light for future generations. Consider the individuals who have left a lasting impact on your own life. They may be historical figures, family members, or even friends who have inspired you to become the best version of yourself. Now, imagine the ripple effect they have created by simply following their own passions and leaving a positive mark on the world. By striving to do the same, you can continue this legacy of inspiration, making a significant impact on those who come after you. Your legacy is not limited to your own achievements. It's about the lives you touch, the hearts you inspire, and the positive change you initiate. By creating a ripple effect through acts of kindness and inspiring others, you can leave a legacy that will bring joy, hope, and inspiration to countless individuals for years to come. So, embrace the power of your legacy and make it a legacy that truly matters.

Inspiring Change: Sharing Your Story and Wisdom

When it comes to creating a personal legacy, one of the most powerful ways to inspire change is by sharing your story and wisdom with others. Your unique experiences, knowledge, and perspectives have the potential to make a lasting impact on future generations, ensuring that your legacy lives on.

Sharing your story allows you to connect with others on a deeper level, fostering empathy and understanding. By opening up about your triumphs, struggles, and lessons learned, you provide a valuable source of inspiration and guidance for those who may be facing similar challenges. Your story becomes a beacon of hope, showing others that they too can overcome obstacles and create a meaningful legacy.

Wisdom gained through a lifetime of learning is a treasure that deserves to be shared. Whether it's career advice, life lessons, or insights into navigating relationships, your knowledge can empower others to make positive changes in their own lives. By passing on your wisdom, you become a mentor and guide, helping others make informed decisions and avoid pitfalls.

Sharing your story and wisdom is not limited to in-person interactions. In today's digital age, there are countless platforms and mediums to reach a wider audience. You can write books, start a blog, create podcasts, or share your journey on social media. The possibilities are endless, and the impact can reach far and wide.

Remember, creating a personal legacy is not just about the impact you want to make in the present moment. It's about ensuring that your legacy lives on through others, inspiring change and shaping future generations. By sharing your story and wisdom, you have the power to make a lasting difference in the world.

Leaving a Legacy in Different Areas of Life

Creating a personal legacy goes beyond individual accomplishments. It is about making a lasting impact in various areas of life, including your career, relationships, and community. By understanding how you can contribute to a better world, you have the power to shape your legacy in meaningful ways.

Overcoming Obstacles: Embracing Resilience and Adaptability

In your journey of creating a personal legacy, one of the key elements to consider is the ability to overcome obstacles. These challenges can come in various forms, such as unexpected setbacks, failures, or even self-doubt.

Embracing resilience and adaptability is crucial when faced with these obstacles. Resilience allows you to bounce back from setbacks and grow stronger, while adaptability enables you to adjust your approach and find alternative solutions.

When you encounter obstacles along the way, remember that they are not roadblocks but opportunities for growth and learning. Each challenge presents a chance to refine your path, strengthen your character, and shape your legacy.

Resilience and adaptability can also enhance the impact of your legacy. By embracing these qualities, you demonstrate to others the power of perseverance and the ability to navigate through difficult times.

Moreover, when you face adversity with resilience and adaptability, you inspire others to do the same. Your ability to overcome obstacles becomes a guiding light, motivating others to confront their own challenges and strive for their own legacies.

The Power of Legacy: Inspiring Others and Future Generations

Creating a personal legacy is not only about the impact you want to make in your own lifetime, but also about inspiring others and future generations. Your actions and values can serve as a guide, showing others what is possible and encouraging them to follow in your footsteps.

When you take the time to reflect on the legacy you want to leave behind, you are not only shaping your own life, but also setting an example for those around you. By living a life aligned with your values and making a positive difference in the world, you can inspire others to do the same.

Imagine the ripple effect that can occur when your legacy influences others. Each person you inspire has the potential to inspire someone else, creating a chain reaction of positive change. Your legacy becomes a catalyst for transformation, shaping the lives of countless individuals who come after you.

Furthermore, your legacy can extend far beyond your own lifetime. When you create a personal legacy based on values that endure, you are passing down a legacy that can continue to inspire and guide future generations. Your impact becomes a part of a larger tapestry, contributing to a chain of positive influence that spans across time.

Whether it's through sharing your story, imparting wisdom, or simply living a life of purpose and compassion, your legacy has the power to touch the lives of others in ways you may never fully realize.

So, as you strive to create a personal legacy, remember that it's not just about the impact you want to make in your own life. It's also about the lasting influence you can have on others and the future generations to come. Your legacy has the power to inspire change, leaving behind a world that is better, brighter, and filled with hope.

Reflecting on Your Legacy: Reviewing and Adjusting

Creating a personal legacy is an ongoing journey of growth and self-reflection. To ensure that your legacy remains aligned with your values and aspirations, it's important to regularly take the time to reflect and make necessary adjustments along the way.

By periodically reviewing your legacy, you can assess the impact you have made and identify areas where you may want to course-correct or amplify your efforts. Reflecting on your legacy allows you to evaluate whether you are still on track to create the impact you want to make in the world.

During the reflective process, consider questions such as:

- How have my actions and choices contributed to my personal legacy?
- Am I living according to my core values and passions?
- What kind of impact am I making on others and the world around me?
- Are there areas where I can improve or make a bigger difference?
- This self-assessment is an opportunity for personal growth and improvement. It allows you to realign your actions and intentions with the legacy you want to leave behind, giving you the chance to make any necessary adjustments.

Remember, creating a personal legacy is a lifelong journey. As you reflect and adjust, be open to new insights and opportunities for growth. Embrace the chance to continuously improve and expand the impact you make on the world.

Building Your Legacy: Taking Action Today

Creating a personal legacy is not just a lofty goal, but a meaningful journey that begins with taking action today. Your legacy is not something that happens overnight; it is built through consistent effort and intentional choices. By making a difference in the lives of others and leaving a positive impact, you can create a personal legacy that reflects your truest self.

So, where do you start? Begin by identifying the values and passions that drive you. What causes ignite a fire within you? What are the issues you care deeply about? Once you have a clear understanding of your core values, you can align your actions with them.

Remember, your legacy is not limited to grand gestures. Small, everyday actions can have a ripple effect and leave a lasting impact. Practice kindness, empathy, and generosity in your interactions with others. Share your knowledge and experiences to inspire change. It is through these simple acts that your personal legacy takes shape.

Building your legacy requires resilience and adaptability. Along the way, you may encounter obstacles and setbacks. Embrace these challenges as opportunities for growth and learn from them. Adjust your approach, but never lose sight of your purpose. Stay committed to creating a legacy that reflects who you truly are.

Chapter 42

Reassess and Realign:
When Life Calls for a Pivot
*****

Have you ever felt stuck, unsure of where your life is headed? Maybe you find yourself longing for a change, but you're not quite sure how to make it happen. It's time to recognize when it's time to make a major change and embark on a new path. Welcome to the world of life pivots.

In this section, we will explore the concept of life pivots, those transformative moments when we reassess and realign our lives. By recognizing the signs and learning effective strategies, you can navigate these transitions successfully and move towards a more fulfilling future.

Join us as we dive into the insights from the book, "Fortify and Empower Yourself at Thirty: Rewriting the Life Success Script," and discover the key to recognizing when it's time for a major change, and the strategies for making a successful pivot.

Understanding Life Pivots

Life is a journey filled with twists and turns, and sometimes we come to a point where it becomes necessary to make a major change. These moments, known as life pivots, are pivotal junctures where we recognize that it's time to reassess and realign our lives. Understanding the meaning and significance of life pivots is essential in navigating these transitions successfully.

A life pivot can be defined as a significant shift in direction, purpose, or mindset that propels us towards a new path of growth and fulfillment. It is a conscious decision to break away from the familiar and embrace the unknown. Recognizing when it's time to make a major change is often a result of various signs and signals that manifest in our lives.

One of the key indicators that it's time for a life pivot is a deep sense of dissatisfaction or unfulfillment. When we constantly feel stuck or trapped in our current situation, it may be a sign that something needs to change. This dissatisfaction can manifest in various aspects of our lives, such as career, relationships, or personal growth.

Furthermore, encountering obstacles or challenges that seem insurmountable can be a clear indication that a major change is needed. These obstacles often serve as wake-up calls, urging us to reevaluate our current path and explore new possibilities.

H3: Signs to Watch Out for

In addition to dissatisfaction and obstacles, there are other signs to watch out for that indicate it's time to make a major change. These signs may manifest as a feeling of restlessness or a desire for something more meaningful in life. It could be a persistent feeling that there's a gap between where we are and where we want to be.

Another significant sign is when our values and priorities no longer align with our current circumstances. Our authentic selves are constantly evolving, and sometimes our current life choices may no longer reflect who we truly are or who we aspire to be.

Recognizing these signs requires self-awareness and a willingness to listen to our intuition. By paying attention to our emotions, thoughts, and desires, we can gain clarity on whether it's time for a major life change.

The Importance of Self-Reflection

Recognizing when it's time to make a major change in our lives can be a challenging task. This is where self-reflection comes into play. Taking the time to pause, evaluate, and understand our thoughts, emotions, and desires can provide valuable insights and clarity.

Self-reflection allows us to navigate the complexities of life pivots by helping us recognize when we're feeling stuck, unfulfilled, or longing for something different. It gives us the opportunity to examine our current circumstances and assess whether they align with our goals, values, and aspirations.

Through self-reflection, we gain a deeper understanding of ourselves and our needs. We can uncover hidden talents, passions, and interests that may have been neglected or overshadowed. This newfound knowledge empowers us to make informed decisions and take the necessary steps towards creating a more fulfilling life.

The Benefits of Self-Reflection

Engaging in self-reflection has numerous benefits. It allows us to:

Gain clarity: Self-reflection enables us to gain a better understanding of our thoughts, emotions, and motivations. It helps us clarify our priorities and identify what truly matters to us.

Identify patterns: By reflecting on past experiences and behaviors, we can identify patterns that may be holding us back or contributing to our dissatisfaction. This awareness allows us to break free from negative cycles and make positive changes.

Discover strengths and weaknesses: Self-reflection helps us recognize our strengths and weaknesses. By acknowledging our areas of expertise and areas for improvement, we can capitalize on our strengths and work on developing new skills.

Set meaningful goals: Through self-reflection, we can set goals that align with our values and aspirations. This allows us to create a roadmap for our future and take steps towards achieving our desired outcomes.

Practical Tips for Engaging in Self-Reflection

Here are some practical tips to help you engage in self-reflection:

Find a quiet and peaceful space: Set aside dedicated time in a calm and peaceful environment where you can reflect without distractions.

Start a journal: Write down your thoughts, feelings, and reflections in a journal. This helps you externalize your thoughts and gain a clearer perspective.

Ask yourself meaningful questions: Pose thought-provoking questions to yourself, such as "What am I truly passionate about?" or "What changes do I need to make to live a more fulfilling life?"

Practice mindfulness: Engage in mindfulness exercises to bring your attention to the present moment. This can help you become more aware of your thoughts, emotions, and bodily sensations.

Seek feedback: Reach out to trusted friends, mentors, or professionals who can provide valuable insights and perspectives on your journey of self-reflection.

By embracing self-reflection, we can navigate life's transitions with greater clarity, purpose, and determination. It serves as a powerful tool for recognizing when it's time to make a major change and equips us with the strategies needed for a successful pivot.

Identifying Unfulfilled Goals and Desires

Recognizing when it's time to make a major change in life can be challenging, but unfulfilled goals and desires often serve as powerful indicators. These aspirations, left unresolved, can ignite a desire for meaningful change and propel us towards a more fulfilling future.

To identify these unfulfilled goals and desires, it is crucial to take a step back and reflect on our current circumstances. What are the dreams and aspirations that we've put on hold? What goals have we yet to achieve?

Consider the areas of your life that may be lacking satisfaction or fulfillment. Are there aspects of your career, relationships, or personal growth that feel stagnant or unfulfilled? Recognizing and acknowledging these areas is essential in determining when it's time to make a major change.

Take the time to explore your passions, interests, and true desires. What excites you? What dreams have you always held onto, even if they seemed out of reach? Identifying these unfulfilled goals and desires will provide the motivation and direction needed to embark on a new path of personal growth and fulfillment.

Assessing Personal Happiness and Fulfillment

In order to determine if a major change is necessary in your life, it's important to assess your levels of personal happiness and fulfillment. Ultimately, your happiness and fulfillment are key indicators of whether or not you are on the right path.

Start by taking a step back and reflecting on your current situation. Ask yourself: Are you truly happy with where you are? Do you feel fulfilled in your work, relationships, and personal life? Take the time to honestly evaluate these aspects of your life.

Consider what brings you joy and fulfillment. Are you passionate about your current career path? Do your relationships bring you fulfillment and support? Reflecting on these questions will help you gain clarity and insight into whether or not it's time for a major change.

Additionally, pay attention to any signs of discontentment or unhappiness. Are you constantly feeling stressed, drained, or unsatisfied? These negative emotions can be indicators that a pivot is necessary to improve your overall well-being.

Reconnecting with Your Passions and Values

One way to assess your personal happiness and fulfillment is by reconnecting with your passions and values. Take the time to identify what truly matters to you and what brings you joy. It could be pursuing a new career, spending more time with loved ones, or engaging in a hobby you've neglected.

By aligning your life with your passions and values, you can increase your overall happiness and fulfillment. Reflect on what aspects of your life are currently aligned with your passions and values, and what areas may need adjustment.

Recognizing when it's time to make a major change can be a powerful catalyst for personal growth and happiness. Assessing your personal happiness and fulfillment is an essential step in this process, as it allows you to gain clarity about your current situation and identify areas that need improvement. Remember, your happiness and fulfillment should always be a priority when making important life decisions.

Strategies for Navigating Life Pivots

When embarking on a life pivot, careful planning and execution are essential for a successful transition. By implementing effective strategies, you can navigate the challenges that arise during this transformative journey.

1. Set Clear Goals and Objectives

Before making a major change, it's crucial to define your goals and objectives. By setting clear intentions, you can stay focused and motivated throughout the pivot process. Ensure that your goals are specific, measurable, attainable, relevant, and time-bound (SMART), allowing you to track your progress and make necessary adjustments along the way.

2. Create a Detailed Action Plan

Developing a comprehensive action plan will provide a roadmap for your life pivot. Break down your goals into smaller, manageable steps, outlining the actions you need to take to achieve them. By organizing your tasks and prioritizing them effectively, you can stay organized and make steady progress towards your desired outcome.

3. Cultivate Resilience and Adaptability

Life pivots often come with unexpected challenges and setbacks. Cultivating resilience and adaptability will help you navigate these obstacles more effectively. Embrace a growth mindset, viewing setbacks as opportunities for learning and growth. Be open to change and willing to adapt your plans as you discover new information or encounter unforeseen circumstances.

4. Seek Support and Guidance

No pivot is a solitary journey, and seeking support and guidance from others can greatly enhance your success. Surround yourself with a strong support network of family, friends, mentors, or coaches who can provide advice, encouragement, and insights. Their perspectives and experiences can offer valuable guidance and fresh perspectives, helping you stay focused and motivated.

5. Embrace Continuous Learning

A life pivot presents an excellent opportunity for personal and professional growth. Embrace a mindset of lifelong learning and seek out opportunities to expand your knowledge and skills. Read books, take courses, attend workshops or seminars, and engage in networking events to stay up-to-date with industry trends, acquire new knowledge, and enhance your capabilities.

6. Practice Self-Care and Well-being

During times of change, it's important to prioritize self-care and well-being. Ensure you're taking care of your physical, mental, and emotional health by incorporating regular exercise, healthy eating habits, and stress management techniques into your routine. Engage in activities that bring you joy, relaxation, and rejuvenation to maintain a balanced and resilient mindset.

With these strategies in place, you can confidently navigate the challenges that arise during a life pivot, setting yourself up for success and fulfillment in your new chapter.

Embracing Change and Overcoming Fear

Change can be intimidating, but embracing it is crucial for personal growth. When it comes to making a successful pivot in life, overcoming fear and resistance to change is essential. By doing so, we open ourselves up to new opportunities and the chance to create a fulfilling and purpose-driven life.

One strategy for overcoming fear is to acknowledge and face our fears head-on. Take the time to identify what specifically scares you about making a change and explore the underlying reasons behind this fear. By understanding the root causes, we can begin to challenge and overcome them.

Shifting Perspective and Focusing on Possibilities

Another effective strategy is to shift our perspective from a fear-based mindset to one focused on possibilities. Instead of dwelling on what could go wrong, remind yourself of the potential positive outcomes and growth that can come from embracing change. By reframing our thoughts and focusing on the opportunities that lie ahead, we can build confidence and motivation to move forward.

Visualization techniques can be powerful tools in overcoming fear. Take some time each day to imagine yourself successfully navigating the changes and pivots you wish to make. Visualize yourself overcoming obstacles and thriving in your new circumstances. By consistently practicing this form of mental rehearsal, you will gradually build the belief in your ability to embrace change and overcome fear.

Seeking Support and Encouragement

Lastly, seeking support and encouragement from others can play a significant role in helping us overcome fear and resistance to change. Reach out to trusted friends, family members, or mentors who have experienced their own successful life pivots. Their guidance, insights, and reassurance can provide valuable support as you navigate your own journey of change.

Remember, change is a natural part of life, and by embracing it and overcoming fear, we open ourselves up to new opportunities and personal growth. Have faith in your abilities, shift your perspective, and seek the support you need to confidently embark on your path towards a successful pivot.

Cultivating Resilience and Adaptability

Building resilience and adaptability are essential strategies for successfully navigating life pivots. As we encounter new circumstances and challenges, developing these skills enables us to embrace change with confidence and thrive in the face of uncertainty.

1. Embrace Growth Mindset:

A growth mindset is the belief that our abilities and intelligence can be developed through dedication and hard work. By adopting this mindset, we can approach life pivots as opportunities for growth and learning. Embracing challenges and viewing setbacks as learning experiences will cultivate resilience and adaptability.

2. Practice Self-Compassion:

During times of change, it's important to be kind and understanding towards ourselves. Practicing self-compassion allows us to acknowledge our emotions, accept our vulnerabilities, and provide ourselves with the support and encouragement needed to face the challenges of a life pivot.

3. Build a Support Network:

Having a strong support network can greatly enhance our ability to navigate life pivots. Seek out trusted friends, family members, and mentors who can provide guidance, advice, and emotional support throughout the process. Engaging with a supportive community can also provide valuable perspectives and insights.

4. Develop Coping Strategies:

Life pivots can bring about stress and uncertainty. Developing healthy coping strategies can help us manage and reduce these challenges. Engaging in activities such as exercise, meditation, journaling, or pursuing hobbies can provide a sense of stability, improve well-being, and enhance our adaptability to changing circumstances.

5. Embrace Flexibility:

Flexibility is a crucial skill when navigating life pivots. Being open to new possibilities and willing to adjust our plans can lead to unexpected opportunities and growth. Embrace the unknown with an open mind, allowing flexibility to guide our decision-making and adapt to the evolving landscape of our lives.

By cultivating resilience and adaptability, we empower ourselves to face the uncertainties of life and thrive in the midst of change. Incorporating these strategies into our lives will enable us to navigate life pivots successfully, embracing new opportunities and creating a fulfilling and purposeful future.

Seeking Support and Guidance

When embarking on a life pivot, seeking support and guidance from others can be instrumental in navigating this transformative journey. The wisdom and insights shared by those who have experienced similar transitions can provide valuable perspectives and encouragement. By leveraging different sources of support, we can effectively strategize and implement our plans for a successful pivot.

One valuable source of support is connecting with a mentor or coach who specializes in helping individuals navigate life transitions. These experts can offer guidance, tools, and strategies tailored to our unique circumstances. Their expertise can aid in the development of a roadmap for success and equip us with the necessary skills to overcome challenges along the way.

Additionally, seeking support from friends, family, and loved ones can provide the emotional and moral support needed during this transformative time. Opening up about our intentions and aspirations can garner understanding and encouragement, fostering a sense of accountability and motivation.

Participating in peer support groups or online communities centered around life pivots can also be beneficial. Engaging with individuals who are going through similar experiences can provide a sense of belonging and enable us to share insights and strategies. These communities can serve as a safe space for open dialogue, where we can learn, grow, and inspire one another throughout our respective journeys.

Lastly, seeking professional counseling or therapy can help address any emotional or psychological obstacles that may arise during a life pivot. These professionals can provide guidance in managing stress and anxiety, building resilience, and developing effective coping mechanisms.

Remember, seeking support and guidance is not a sign of weakness but an acknowledgment of the transformative nature of life pivots. By embracing the wealth of knowledge and assistance available to us, we can enhance our chances of success and create a solid foundation for a new and fulfilling chapter in our lives.

Redefining Success and Goals

When undertaking a major life pivot, it becomes necessary to reevaluate our definitions of success and set new goals that align with our newfound path. Redefining success allows us to create a vision for our future and establish meaningful objectives to guide us on this journey of transformation.

One of the key strategies for a successful pivot is to take a step back and reflect on what truly matters to us. What are our core values and aspirations? What brings us joy and fulfillment? By redefining success, we give ourselves permission to let go of societal expectations and focus on what resonates deeply with our own desires and dreams.

To begin the process of redefining success, it can be helpful to envision the ideal future that we want to create. By visualizing our desired outcomes, we can clarify our goals and establish a clear direction for ourselves. This can be done through techniques such as creating vision boards, journaling, or engaging in visualization exercises.

Setting Meaningful Objectives

Once we have redefined success, it's important to set meaningful objectives that reflect our new vision. These objectives should be specific, measurable, attainable, relevant, and time-bound (SMART). By breaking down our overarching goals into smaller, actionable steps, we can create a roadmap for achieving our desired outcomes.

When setting goals during a life pivot, it's essential to consider both short-term and long-term objectives. Short-term goals provide us with immediate focus and motivation, while long-term goals help us maintain a sense of direction and purpose. By balancing these two types of goals, we can make steady progress towards our vision while also celebrating smaller milestones along the way.

Remember, success and goals are not fixed concepts. They evolve as we grow, learn, and experience new chapters in our lives. Embrace the opportunity to redefine your own version of success and set goals that align with your authentic self. By doing so, you'll find yourself on a path that is truly fulfilling and aligned with your values, bringing you closer to a successful and purposeful life.

Thriving in the New Chapter

After successfully navigating a life pivot, you have overcome the challenges and now have the opportunity to thrive in your new chapter. Embracing change is the first step towards finding fulfillment and creating a successful and fulfilling life path. Here are some strategies to help you thrive:

1. Embrace Your New Reality: Recognize that life pivots bring new opportunities and possibilities. Embrace the changes and view them as stepping stones to a brighter future. Allow yourself to let go of the past and focus on the present moment.

2. Set New Goals: Redefine your definition of success and establish new goals that align with your new direction. Take time to reflect on what truly matters to you and what you want to achieve in this new chapter of your life. Set SMART (Specific, Measurable, Achievable, Relevant, Time-bound) goals that will guide you towards success.

3. Nurture Self-Care: Prioritize self-care to ensure your well-being as you embark on this new journey. Take time for activities that bring you joy and relaxation. Practice self-compassion and create healthy habits that support your physical, mental, and emotional well-being.

4. Stay Open to Learning: Be open-minded and willing to learn new things. Embrace lifelong learning and seek opportunities for personal and professional growth. Stay curious, explore new interests, and continuously challenge yourself to expand your knowledge and skills.

By implementing these strategies, you can thrive in your new chapter and create a fulfilling life path that aligns with your values and aspirations. Remember, a successful pivot is not just about making the change but also about making the most of the opportunities that come with it.

Chapter 43
Understanding the Importance of Boundaries
****

In this chapter, we delve into the concept of personal boundaries and their significance in maintaining healthy relationships and overall well-being. Boundaries serve as guidelines that define the limits and expectations we have for ourselves and others. They play a crucial role in promoting self-respect, self-care, and maintaining balance in our lives.

When our boundaries are violated, it can have a negative impact on our mental, emotional, and even physical health. It is important to recognize the signs of boundary violations and understand the consequences they can have on our overall well-being. By understanding the importance of boundaries, we can begin to take proactive steps in establishing and enforcing them.

Setting and enforcing boundaries can be challenging, as it may require assertiveness, difficult conversations, and potential conflicts. However, these challenges should not deter us from prioritizing our own needs. By identifying common challenges in setting and enforcing boundaries, such as fear of rejection or feelings of guilt, we can better navigate these obstacles with confidence and clarity.

In the following sections of this chapter, we will explore strategies for establishing clear boundaries, overcoming guilt and fear of disapproval when saying no, respecting others' boundaries, and practicing assertiveness skills. These tools and techniques will empower you to confidently communicate your boundaries while maintaining healthy relationships.

Remember, honoring your boundaries is an act of self-respect and self-care. It allows you to create a life that aligns with your values, needs, and desires. By understanding the importance of boundaries and learning how to effectively set and enforce them, you can cultivate healthier relationships and achieve greater overall well-beingEstablishing clear boundaries is an essential aspect of maintaining healthy relationships and personal well-being. In this section, we will delve into the process of assessing and defining your own values, needs, and limits, and how to effectively communicate these boundaries to others.

First, it is crucial to take the time to reflect on your values and identify what is truly important to you. By understanding your core values, you can determine what behaviors and actions align with your beliefs and set boundaries accordingly. Reflect on areas such as work, relationships, personal time, and any other domains that are significant in your life.

Once you have a clear understanding of your values and priorities, it is important to communicate your boundaries effectively and assertively. Clearly expressing your limits helps others understand what is acceptable and what is not. Use direct communication to express your boundaries in a respectful manner, avoiding ambiguity or mixed messages.

Setting specific boundaries in different areas of life is also crucial. In the workplace, for example, you may establish boundaries around working hours, availability outside of work, and the types of tasks you are willing to take on. In relationships, you may set boundaries around personal space, communication styles, and expectations for mutual respect.

It's ok to set limits. This isn't selfish; it shows you respect yourself. It's crucial to stand up for your boundaries and speak out for yourself when needed.

When you make clear boundaries, you focus on your well-being. Healthy relationships flourish with this focus. We will guide you in dealing with feelings of guilt or fear of not being approved, honor other people's boundaries, face resistance, and gain the confidence to say no.

Understanding why we feel guilt or anxiety when saying no helps to create sturdy boundaries. Many people struggle with these feelings when putting their needs first.

We may feel guilt because we're afraid of letting others down, or we worry about appearing selfish. You need to remember that setting boundaries isn't selfish; it's an important part of taking care of yourself. By putting your needs first, you can be the best version of you in all areas of your life.

Guilt and fear also come from a want to keep peace and avoid arguments in relationships. But we have to remember, healthy boundaries build fair and balanced relationships. When we tell people about our boundaries, we create an environment where everyone can do well.

Feeling guilty or scared while setting limits? Here are some tips:

- Bust Your False Beliefs: Uncover what makes you guilt-ridden or scared about laying down rules. Do these notions match your morals? Recall, attending to your needs promotes your wellness.

- Show Self-Tenderness: Navigate these feelings with kindness. Knowing the process of setting rules and beating the fear of rejection needs time and habit could help. Offer yourself leniency during this time.

- Define Success Afresh: Change how you view success in relationships. Know that good bonds are formed on mutual respect and comprehension, not by always catering to others' wants and ignoring yours.

- Ask for Help: Hang out with people who value rules. Disclose your hardships with close pals or consult a therapist to get useful advice and means to tackle these feelings.

- Picture the Bright Side: Think about the good effect of setting and implementing rules on your wellness. Dream about healthier and more gratifying bonds as a result of caring for your needs.

Gaining self-assurance is crucial in holding your rules and rejecting confidently. As you keep working to set and uphold rules, know that you can care for your needs while keeping bonds healthy. By quashing guilt and fear of rejection, you can live an equally rewarding life that is in line with your morals and goals Respecting Others' Rules and Managing Resistance

Respecting others' boundaries is key for good relationships. It's as important to honor other's boundaries as setting our own. This way, we can build respect and support.

Empathy and understanding for different views on boundaries are needed for peace in relationships. Everyone has unique values, needs, and limits. Knowing and respecting these differences helps us set boundaries with kindness and respect.

Dealing with resistance and pushback when setting or enforcing boundaries can be hard. Some might not respect your boundaries, leading to resistance or attempts to push them. In these instances, stand your ground with compassion.

Here are ways to handle resistance or pushback:

1. **Communicate clearly:** Express your boundaries and why they matter clearly. Use "I" statements so you don't sound blaming or aggressive. Explain how respecting the boundaries is good for both sides.

2. **Active listening:** Listen actively to the worries or objections from others. Show them their perspective matters. This can ease the conflict and pave the way for more discussion.

3. **Find shared ideas:** Discover shared or similar views where everyone's needs can be covered. It shows an openness to finding ways that respect everyone's limits.

4. **Draw the line:** If your boundaries are regularly disrespected despite being clearly stated, you might need to finally set penalties for overstepping. This reiterates the need to respect boundaries and deters future breaches.

5. **Get help if needed:** If constant pushbacks occur or you find these discussions tough to tackle alone, seek help from reliable friends, family, or a counselor. They are there to guide, give unique perspectives, and boost your courage in tough times.

Remember, valuing others' boundaries isn't about giving up your needs or principle. It's about fostering a balanced and beneficial relationship where everyone feels listened to, understood, and valued. By tapping into empathy, keeping communication transparent, and managing resistance with kindness, you can respect your boundaries and others' in a fair and polite manner.

Tools and Techniques to Say No Confidently

Assertiveness is important when setting and upholding limits. By mastering courage to say no, you safeguard your time, energy, and overall wellness. Here are strategies to say no assertively:

1. **Say "I" more:** Use "I" at the start of sentences. It shows your feelings and needs. So instead of, "You ask too much from me", say, "I get stressed when I have lots to do."

2. **Speak straight and short:** Be clear. Say what you have to say without a big story. So if work asks for extra, say a quick, "I can't do that now."

3. **Listen well:** Some might not like your boundaries. Stay cool, listen careful. Say OK to their feelings but stay with your choice.

4. **Offer other plans:** If it's tough saying no, go for other options. Like if a buddy asks you to go somewhere you don't like, suggest a coffee or a phone call.

5. **Say "thanks" instead of "sorry":** Don't feel bad or say sorry for saying no. Say thanks for them understanding. So say, "Thank you for seeing I need to look after me."

6. **Practice saying no:** Have a pretend chat where you say no in a strong way with someone close. It's a good way to build strength and better talk.

7. **Set solid limits:** Have clear, unchanging limits in your life. This could be guiding principles you won't bend on, like your beliefs or personal downtime. Learn that it's okay to put you and your needs first.

8. **Remain stern but polite:** When it comes to setting boundaries, it's vital to keep a respectful tone. Don't turn defensive or confrontational, even if the other person reacts negatively. Stand by your choice without dismissing their emotions.

9. **Look after yourself:** Self-care ensures you have the energy to set robust boundaries. Regularly create time for yourself, do what makes you happy, and be kind to yourself. If you're content and balanced, discussing your boundaries becomes manageable.

Remember, boundaries aren't about selfishness but self-care. Use these strategies so you can say "no" with confidence. This helps to sustain healthful relationships while honoring your boundaries. Forging a Grateful Attitude and Taking Care of Yourself: Realizing Gratitude's Power:

Gratitude is a game-changer for creating joy and satisfaction. Focusing on life's positive elements trains our minds to see the bounty around us, even during tough times. Embracing a thankful attitude can dramatically change our mental health and overall life view.

People who make appreciation a daily habit enjoy greater joy, less stress, and better relationships. Keeping a gratitude diary is a useful method.

Start your gratitude diary routine by committing a few precious moments each day. Aim to note down the smaller, concrete things that bring joy, like a good morning coffee or a stranger's kind expression. Each day, jot down at least three things that evoked gratitude.

To get the most from your diary, try thought-starters or challenges promoting more profound thought. You might note a person who's changed your life for the better and why you're thankful for them. Alternatively, you could reflect on a tough situation and draw out lessons that have left you grateful.

Putting your gratitude on paper allows full awareness and thanks for life's positives. It moves your mental spotlight from negative and trains your brain to search for and treasure the good. Over time, this habit could promote a cheerier outlook and a deeper satisfaction level.

Lastly, remember that gratitude extends beyond journaling. Sprinkle thanks throughout your everyday interactions—with family, friends, and colleagues. This practice can deepen bonds and spread positivity.

Thankfulness is easy to mix into your everyday life. By choosing to be grateful, we can feel happier, bounce back faster, and improve our well-being. Try keeping a gratitude journal. Watch how it changes your life. Self-Care is Important:

Self-care matters, especially in your thirties, when life gets fast and hard. Balancing work, friends, and duties, we must also care for our bodies, minds, and emotions. Self-care habits should be part of your day to keep things steady and avoid feeling burnt out.

Body Care:

Body care means eating good foods, moving often, and resting enough. A balanced diet full of rich nutrients can boost energy and health. Workouts that you enjoy and fit into your day keep you in shape. But remember, self-care also means knowing when to chill out and make time for rest.

Mind Care:

Looking after your mental health is important too, especially in your thirties. It's key to do things that clear your mind, lower stress, and improve thinking. Mindfulness practices like meditation or deep breathing work well. So do hobbies that make you happy and relaxed. Practicing gratitude also helps focus on the positive.

Caring for Your Emotions:

How you feel matters. Caring for your emotions means recognizing, valuing, and acting on your feelings in a healthy way. Emotional care includes actions like writing in a diary, talking with a counselor, spending time with supportive friends, and creating emotional safeguards. All these can help handle feelings and become emotionally stronger.

How to Make Self-Care Fit a Busy Life:

Finding time for self-care in a packed schedule isn't easy. But it's important to know that looking after yourself isn't a treat. It's a must. By putting self-care first, you boost your effectiveness with other tasks.

Want some practical ways to fit self-care into a hectic life? Here are some:

1. Start small: Look for relaxing, joyful activities. Make a little daily "me" time and expand it over time, seeing the benefits unfold.
2. Make time for self-care: Schedule it. Assign slots in your schedule just for self-care. Like any commitment, stand by it.
3. Pick stuff you enjoy: Self-care shouldn't feel like work. Instead, it should be fulfilling. That could mean reading, nature walks, hobbies, or creative activities.
4. Seek help and share responsibilities: Don't hesitate to ask for support or delegate duties to make self-care time. If you require help, contact family, friends, or peers.
5. Pair self-care with regular activities: Find ways to mix self-care into your normal routine. For instance, play soothing music or positive affirmations while traveling or doing house chores.

Recall, self-care differs from person to person. There's no one-size-fits-all. Find what works best for you and adjust it according to your own needs. Prioritizing self-care in your thirties can prepare you better for facing this decade's challenges with resilience and balanced well-being.

Creating self--care routines:

Designing personalized self-care routines is key to keeping yourself balanced amidst the routine demands. Fits these practices to yourself and have grounding habits to nurture yourself. This discusses methods like mindfulness, meditation, relaxation exercises to help find what suits you best.

1. Mindfulness:

Mindfulness involves focusing on the present without judgment. It's all about being conscious of your thoughts, feelings, physical sensations, and the environment.

Incorporate mindfulness into your daily routine by setting aside dedicated time for meditation or simply being present in everyday activities.

Experiment with different mindfulness techniques, such as guided meditations, body scans, or mindful breathing exercises, to find what resonates with you.

2. Meditation:

Meditation is a powerful tool for reducing stress, improving focus, and enhancing overall well-being.

Find a quiet and comfortable space where you can sit or lie down without distractions.

Start with short meditation sessions, gradually increasing the duration as you become more comfortable.

Explore different meditation styles, such as loving-kindness meditation, transcendental meditation, or mindfulness meditation, to discover what suits you best.

3. Relaxation Exercises:

Relaxation exercises help reduce tension in both the mind and body, promoting a sense of calm and tranquility.

Practice deep breathing exercises to activate the body's relaxation response. Inhale deeply through your nose, hold for a few seconds, and exhale slowly through your mouth.

Explore progressive muscle relaxation techniques by systematically tensing and relaxing each muscle group in your body.

Engage in activities that bring you joy and relaxation, such as reading a book, taking a warm bath, practicing gentle stretches or yoga poses, listening to soothing music, or spending time in nature.

4. Pens & Pages:

Jotting down thoughts is a great way to tune into yourself, clear your mind, and let your feelings out.

Make writing a habit. Do it daily, maybe in the morning or at night, or when you just need to sort some things out in your head.

Let your hand move freely across the paper. Don't criticize or edit. Just let your thoughts flow out.

Try out different ways to journal. Write what you're thankful for, whatever comes to mind, or respond to the thought-provoking questions in this book.

Remember, there is no one-size-fits-all approach to self-care. If one method doesn't work for you, try another. Customize your self-care routine to match your personality and way of life. This will help you build a balanced, lasting plan for self-love, and make you happier and more content in life.

The Power of Love & Friendship:

Having meaningful bonds with others boosts our sense of happiness and self-care. When we're in our thirties, it's more important than ever to keep these relationships strong, for they offer support, comfort, and joy.

In order to build and maintain such relationships, we need to devote time and energy. Here are some tips to help you do that:

1. **Prioritize Communication:** Open communication is the foundation of any successful relationship. Take the time to have honest and meaningful conversations with your loved ones. Share your thoughts, feelings, and desires openly, and encourage them to do the same. By fostering open lines of communication, you create a safe space for both parties to express themselves authentically.

2. **Practice Active Listening:** Listening is an essential skill in nurturing relationships. Show genuine interest in what others have to say by actively listening without interrupting or formulating responses in your mind. Validate their feelings and perspectives, allowing them to feel heard and understood. By practicing active listening, you strengthen your connection with others and demonstrate that you value their thoughts and emotions.

3. **Show Empathy and Understanding:** Empathy is the ability to understand and share the feelings of another person. Cultivate empathy by placing yourself in the other person's shoes and attempting to see the situation from their perspective. Validate their experiences, emotions, and challenges, even if you may not fully understand or agree with them. By demonstrating empathy and understanding, you build trust and deepen your connection with others.

4. **Foster Trust and Vulnerability:** Trust is a vital component of any healthy relationship. Be reliable and consistent in your actions and words to build trust with

those around you. Additionally, practice vulnerability by being open and honest about your own thoughts, feelings, and struggles. When you allow yourself to be vulnerable, you create a safe space for others to do the same, fostering deeper connections and intimacy.

5. **Give Time and Great Moments:** Building long-lasting bonds needs time and work. Make sure to give quality time to your loved ones. Do fun activities together. This could be eating together, taking a walk, or doing common hobbies. Spending time shows your love and respect for them.

You have to remember that building strong relationships is a give and take. You have to do your part. Regularly communicate with your loved ones. Celebrate when they succeed. Help them when they face problems. Do things together to make the bond stronger.

When you focus on family and friends, it's not just good for you. It's also good for them. These important bonds give us strength and support as we age. Making connections should be part of what you do to take care of yourself. You'll see its benefits in ways you never expected.

Getting Past Self-Care Barriers:

Life can get busy and stressful. This can make it hard to look after ourselves. But, it is important to overcome these hurdles for our whole health and life success. Let's look at some common roadblocks to self-care. We'll also give practical advice to move past them.

1. Guilt:

You may feel bad when taking time for you. Others may want your time. But remember, you need to take care of yourself. Your body, mind, and feelings are important.

So shake off guilt:

- Know that you need and deserve to care for yourself.
- Be firm in asking for time for you. Let others know.
- Begin with short self-care spans. Gradually make it longer.

2. Not Enough Time:

Lots of us can't find time for self-care. Work, family, and promises can swill up our day. But self-care helps avoid being overwhelmed.

Ok. Fight time shortage by:

- Scheduling self-care as an important task. Don't skip it.
- Look for spare time. Maybe during midday rest or before sleep.
- Ask others to take over some jobs. Get time for yourself.

3. Pressure from Society:

- We are often made to feel being busy is good. Relaxing for self-care is seen as less exciting. This can result in us ignoring our well-being.
- Take the challenge and fight societal stress by:
- Don't follow the crowd. You decide what success means to you.
- Find friends who also care for self-care.
- Practice assertiveness by advocating for your needs without feeling the need to justify or explain them to others.

4. Lack of Self-Worth:

Some individuals struggle with feelings of low self-worth, believing that they don't deserve to prioritize their own needs and well-being. This mindset can be a significant barrier to engaging in self-care practices.

To overcome feelings of low self-worth:

Practice self-compassion and remind yourself that you are deserving of love and care.

Seek support from a therapist or counselor to work through underlying issues contributing to these feelings.

Surround yourself with positive affirmations and uplifting influences.

5. Lack of Awareness or Ideas:

Sometimes, the barrier to practicing self-care is simply not knowing what activities or practices would be most beneficial or enjoyable. It's essential to explore different options and find what resonates with you personally.

To overcome the lack of awareness or ideas:

Research various self-care practices and activities.

Experiment with different techniques, such as meditation, yoga, journaling, or engaging in hobbies.

Take note of activities that bring you joy, relaxation, or fulfillment and make them a regular part of your routine.

Remember, self-care is not a luxury; it's a necessity for your overall well-being. By identifying and addressing these common barriers, you can integrate self-care into your daily life and experience the numerous benefits it brings.

Chapter 44

The Confidence Conundrum: Building Unshakeable Self-Belief
*****

The Confidence Conundrum: Building Unshakeable Self-Belief in your 30's
Have you ever found yourself questioning your abilities, hesitating to take risks, or doubting your worth? Confidence is not only essential for personal growth but also for unlocking your full potential. We will unveil the secrets to overcoming self-doubt and nurturing a belief in oneself that is unshakeable. Prepare to discover effective strategies to build confidence and embark on a journey of personal growth.

Understanding the Root of Self-Doubt
In this section, we will dive deep into the root causes of self-doubt. Overcoming self-doubt is an important step in building confidence for personal growth. By understanding the factors that contribute to self-doubt, we can tackle them head-on and develop unshakable self-belief.

Past Experiences
Our past experiences greatly influence our self-perception and confidence levels. Negative experiences such as failures or criticism can leave a lasting impact and breed self-doubt. It's crucial to understand that these experiences don't define our worth and that we have the ability to overcome them.

Societal Expectations
Societal expectations play a huge role in shaping our self-doubt. From a young age, we are bombarded with messages about what success, beauty, and perfection should be like. These unrealistic standards can lead to feelings of inadequacy and doubt within us. By identifying and challenging these societal expectations, we can break free from their grip and cultivate confidence on our own terms.

Comparison
Comparison is one of the most common fuels for self-doubt. In today's age of social media it's so easy to fall into the trap of comparing ourselves with others highlight reels. However it's important to remember that everyone's journey is unique, comparing isn't a fair assessment of our own worth and abilities. By focusing on our own progress and growth, we can overcome the self-doubt fueled by comparison.

By addressing these root causes of self-doubt — past experiences, societal expectations, and comparison— we can go on a journey to build confidence for personal growth. In the next section, we will dive into the specifics of recognizing and combating impostor syndrome.

Recognizing the Imposter Syndrome
One of the common phenomena that hinder confidence is imposter syndrome. It is a psychological pattern where individuals doubt their accomplishments and fear being exposed as frauds, despite evidence of their competence. This self-doubt can be debilitating and hinder personal growth.

Imposter syndrome can manifest in various forms such as feeling like a fraud or undeserving of success, constantly comparing oneself to others, or attributing achievements to luck rather than personal abilities. These thoughts and feelings of inadequacy can erode confidence and prevent individuals from reaching their full potential.

Overcoming imposter syndrome is crucial in building self-belief and nurturing personal growth. By recognizing and addressing these feelings individuals can develop strategies to combat self-doubt and regain confidence. Here are a few techniques to overcome imposter syndrome:

1. Challenge negative self-talk:
Identify and challenge negative thoughts and beliefs that contribute to imposter syndrome. Replace them with positive affirmations and evidence of your achievements and capabilities.

2. Embrace your accomplishments:
Recognize and celebrate your successes no matter how small they may seem. Keep a journal of your achievements and reflect on them regularly to remind yourself of your capabilities anda progress you've made.

3. Seek support:
Share your self-doubt with friends and family who will always have an ear for you. Surround yourself with people that believe in you and can give that extra motivation to keep going.

4. Grow and learn:
Adopt a growth mindset. See challenges as opportunities for learning and growth, not setbacks. Venture out of your comfort zone, embrace new experiences to build confidence.

People are able to overcome this barrier by recognizing the imposter syndrome as well as creating strategies to combat self-doubt which will make unshakable self-belief possible. With this newfound confidence personal growth is inevitable and individuals will gain the power to reach their full potential.

Rewriting Negative Self-Talk

When we talk down on ourselves it has a big impact on our confidence levels and doesn't allow us to grow. The way we speak about ourselves gets engraved in our minds and how we perceive ourselves. This section explores techniques for identifying negative self-talk patterns so we can rewrite them, allowing us to overcome self-doubt while building unshakable confidence so we can grow personally.

Negative self-talk often comes from deep-rooted beliefs or past experiences that built up our confidence (or lack thereof). It's important to recognize these patterns and challenge them right away. Start by being aware of the negative things you say when different situations arise. Pay attention to what you think and even the words you choose for yourself.

Once identified, challenge if they're valid thoughts or not. Ask yourself if there is evidence supporting these thoughts or if they're simply another unfounded belief that isn't true at all? Replace any negative statements with positive affirmations that counteract doubtfulness while building confidence instead. For example: Instead of thinking "I'm not good enough." replace it with "I am capable of success because I deserve it."

Another technique worth using is re-framing negative thoughts into something more appealing and uplifting. Instead of seeing mistakes as failures, turn them into opportunities to learn and grow. Shifting our perspectives from negative to positive allows us to see challenges as stepping stones instead of obstacles.

Another thing that needs practice is self-compassion. Treat yourself with kindness and understanding, the same way you would treat a friend going through a tough time. Understand that nobody is perfect and that making mistakes is part of the learning process. By doing this, you're able to combat negative self-talk rhetoric with love for yourself instead.

Remember building confidence doesn't just happen overnight, it's a journey in itself! It's gonna take some time and consistent effort for you to rewrite your negative thoughts but don't worry. Be patient with yourself and celebrate those small wins along the way. Each time you challenge a negative thought and replace it with a positive one you strengthen your belief in yourself which then fosters personal growth.

Embracing Vulnerability

When we talk about being confident and how it can help us overcome self-doubt there are many factors but embracing vulnerability is often overlooked. A lot of people fear showing vulnerability because they feel like others will perceive them as weak or be rejected altogether even though embracing this trait actually helps build confidence.

Being vulnerable means allowing us to be seen and heard for who we truly are without worrying about being judged or rejected. Opening up ourselves for the chance of new experiences, relationships or opportunities even when there's a chance they might end badly just takes courage.

When you embrace vulnerability, it gives you permission to explore and grow from your experiences. It helps you get out of your comfort zone and realize your full potential. And not only that, it also builds confidence in yourself and strengthens your resilience to overcome anything.

But not just that, embracing vulnerability will deepen connections with other people too. When they see themselves being vulnerable through you, it makes them more comfortable showing their own vulnerabilities. When you're surrounded by this level of trust and support - personal growth and self-belief come easy.

Practicing Vulnerability

It's easier said than done but practicing vulnerability is worth the effort. So here are a few ways on how to embrace vulnerability:

Share who you truly are: Open up to others about your thoughts, feelings, and experiences. Showing others who you really are will help build stronger connections as well as accepting yourself for who you are.

Take risks: Try new things that scare you or things that seem unfamiliar to your usual routine. New challenges help us learn so we can grow faster.

Seek support: Have people around who encourage your vulnerability rather than discourage it. Find a mentor, join supportive communities or even seek therapy if needed.

Practice self-compassion: Embracing vulnerability isn't easy - be kind to yourself during the process. Understand that making mistakes or feeling uncomfortable is a part of the journey.

Unlocking Personal Growth

There's nothing more rewarding than unlocking personal growth because once you do so, confidence levels soar through the roof.

Now let me tell you how setting realistic goals can increase confidence and promote personal growth.

Setting Realistic Goals

As simple as setting goals sounds - when done right they end up doing wonders for our self-belief and purpose in life. With enough time to reflect on them properly we will be able to create a roadmap for success:

1. Reflect on Your Values and Passions

Start off by reflecting on what truly matters to you, what excites and motivates you? Aligning your goals with these values and passions just makes them easier to achieve.

2. Break Big Goals into Smaller Milestones

Building confidence isn't necessarily a one-time thing. Rather, it's something that is built from small things over time. So breaking big goals into smaller milestones makes them more attainable. Celebrating each milestone achieved creates a sense of accomplishment and builds confidence step by step.

3. Be Specific and Measurable

Goals should be specific and measurable so they can be tracked easily. This gives us a clear target to work towards as well as allowing us to track our own growth.

4. Consider Your Resources and Time

When setting goals we need to consider two very important things: resources available and time available. By knowing these two things we won't overwhelm ourselves with deadlines that are unrealistic or make goals that require too many resources.

5. Embrace Flexibility and Adaptability

Life is full of surprises. It's important to be flexible. Being open to adjusting your plans allows you to keep growing, even when faced with obstacles.

By setting realistic goals that align with your values and breaking them down into smaller milestones, and using resources properly, you will empower yourself to achieve success. This, in turn, fuels your confidence and fosters personal growth.

Creating a Supportive Network

Building confidence and nurturing personal growth require more than just individual effort. The people we surround ourselves with play a crucial role in our journey. Cultivating a supportive network can have a profound impact on our confidence and personal development. When we have a strong support system, there are individuals who believe in our abilities and provide encouragement during challenging times. Their unwavering support helps us push through self-doubt and overcome obstacles that hinder our personal growth.

A supportive network provides a safe space where we can openly share our goals, aspirations, and fears. By creating an environment of trust, these individuals empower us to take risks, face our vulnerabilities, and explore new opportunities. Their genuine belief in our potential fuels our confidence.

However, the most vital part of building this network is the guidance it provides.

These individuals may have already walked this path. They can share their wisdom from their experiences for us to navigate our own paths more effectively.

By surrounding ourselves with like-minded individuals who are driven and passionate about what they do like we are—or want to be—can provide the motivation needed to pursue our goals confidently.

Remember: Confidence isn't built by one person; it's built by many.

Failure Can Lead To Success

Failure hurts. It makes us doubt ourselves too much sometimes. But it's necessary for growth. failure as a stepping stone is something that'll build confidence better than anything else could. When you view failure as an opportunity for learning and growth you start seeing every setback as another way towards success. It helps us understand what we're good at and the things we need to work on. It even gives us a better understanding of our own capabilities. But that's only if you let it be your teacher.

Reframing our perspective is another thing.

Instead of focusing on what went wrong, think about how you can improve for next time. This mindset shift brings new opportunities with it.

Learning from Failure: Building Confidence

Failure is often the best breeding ground for confidence. It is through constant trial and error that we build experience and gain knowledge. This experience strengthens our skills, and each failure becomes a stepping stone that builds our resilience, determination, and self-belief.

When we embrace failure, rather than run away from it or let it define us, we grow in confidence. We develop a mindset that recognizes setbacks as necessary catalysts for improvement. And with this newfound belief anchored within us, we become more willing to take risks outside of our comfort zones. Challenges don't just become something to avoid at all costs — they now become something that we can tackle head-on.

The Power of Failing

It's important to note that growth isn't stunted by failure. In fact, failure is necessary in personal development because it pushes us forward. When used as an opportunity instead of an obstacle, personal growth will come more naturally to you.

Each time you fail at something — whether big or small — treat it as a way to assess your goals better. It gives you a chance to refine your strategies and learn more about yourself as well.

Obstacles are everywhere in life; there's no escaping them! But through each failure we learn how to adapt, persevere, and overcome them ourselves. Eventually this practice turns into habit and these skills become second nature so that you'll be able to navigate life easier.

Don't forget that feedback is crucial for improvement too! Through each instance where things went wrong you'll be given feedback on what could've been done better or improved upon relative to your goals.

Stepping Stones

Surely after reading the above section about how important failing is in personal development you understand why celebrating small wins matters!

When built up correctly though, these celebrations make all the difference when sustaining self-belief which then leads onto even greater accomplishments!

If you want an effective strategy when it comes to celebrating, try using a gratitude journal. Each day take some time off to reflect on your growth and what you've accomplished so far! Write down what you did, how it made you feel, and why it's important to your overall growth. A rewards system might be up your alley too! Set milestones for yourself along the way and reward yourself accordingly when reaching them. Of course they don't have to be super extravagant things — simply treating yourself to a favorite meal or buying small gifts will suffice!

Lastly, don't forget that sharing wins with others is an incredibly empowering thing. When reflecting on your progress with friends or online communities not only are you being given the opportunity to receive validation from others, but their support can help push you even further as well.

Building confidence isn't all about hitting big goals; it's about embracing the journey and each step along the way as well. A strong foundation of self-belief built from celebrating small wins allows for motivation that propels us towards greater accomplishments.

Staying Confident in the Long Run

Building confidence is great, but keeping it there is another challenge on its own. Unfortunately we can't just build confidence once and expect it to say forever — we need constant effort and dedication for this. Nevertheless, remember that growing doesn't have an ending point in sight! One way to keep your confidence high is by staying self-aware. Noticing your strengths and accomplishments helps remind you of the progress you've made. By focusing on what you've achieved already, you counter any doubt that may come up and strengthen your beliefs in yourself.

Another thing to keep in mind is the importance of resilience when experiencing setbacks. They're a natural part of life, but they shouldn't define how we think about ourselves or make us less confident. Instead, treat look at them as opportunities for growth and learning. Analyze what went wrong, adjust accordingly, and move forward with new knowledge. This resilience will make it easier to face future challenges without letting them knock down your confidence.

The last building block here is surrounding yourself with a supportive community. Find people who believe in you, support your goals, and cheer you on even when times are tough. Having a strong network gives access to advice that's been through many experiences before yours and people who'll celebrate good news whenever it comes up. Together, you can push each other toward being more confident as individuals while fostering personal growth along the way

Chapter 45

Travel and Transformation: How Voyages Change You

****

In this section, we will tackle transformative experiences that traveling in your thirties can provide. Traveling alone and with different people will change your perspective and contribute to personal growth.

People have the opportunity to get out of their comfort zones by traveling. Moving into new territory exposes them to different ways of life, beliefs, and traditions. These new experiences help them see the world from a different lens.

Personal growth is unique for everyone but travel has the ability to help anyone. Exploring new places, meeting people from all walks of life, and getting through unfamiliar environments can foster adaptability and resilience for everyone who tries it. These experiences make us confront fears which helps us grow as a person.

Travel also has the magical ability to break down stereotypes. It does so by giving travelers first-hand experience with local culture and practices which challenges everything they used to believe in. This newfound knowledge cultivates empathy, compassion, and acceptance for diversity.

We're all on a quest to find ourselves whether we know it or not. You're probably looking right now too! On your journey you'll realize that embracing uncertainty is exciting yet scary at the same time! However pushing boundaries is what makes life beautiful. So I recommend trying new things as much as possible!

There are 4 tips I have here:

- **Choosing destinations:** Finding what aligns with your values is important.
- **Budgeting:** Allocate funds accordingly after determining how much money you want to use.
- **Creating Itineraries:** Plan out each day!
- **Finding Affordable Accommodations:** Everyone wants cheap accommodations but make sure it's safe

There is no denying that travel can take a toll on the environment. However, it is possible to reduce your ecological footprint by making small changes in the way you plan and experience your trips. Here are some tips for environmentally friendly travel:

1. Transportation:

Consider taking a train, bus or ship instead of an airplane when traveling to nearby destinations. These alternative modes of transportation produce fewer greenhouse emissions and consume less fuel.

If you must fly, choose non-stop flights whenever possible as they use up less fuel than connecting flights.

When renting a car, opt for more fuel-efficient vehicles such as hybrids or electric cars.

2. Accommodations:

Seek out hotels and other accommodations that have received eco-friendly certifications. Reuse towels instead of having them washed after each use.

Turn off lights and air conditioning when leaving the room or adjust thermostat settings to save energy.

3. Consumption:

Bring reusable water bottles, coffee cups, shopping bags and utensils with you during your trip to minimize waste. Refuse single-use items like straws or plastic bags whenever possible.

Avoid printing tickets or boarding passes if digital copies are accepted by the service provider.

4. Travel Dates:

To help reduce over-tourism in popular destinations, consider visiting during off-peak seasons or choosing alternative attractions altogether.

5. Money Saving Options

Stay in places where not many people go with discounts only offered at certain times of year to save money on hotel bookings,

6.Transportation options

Take time to research what's available when you're planning on going somewhere so you know if you should be hopping on public transit horse drawn carriage or just walking,

Always check what's cheaper then compare prices comfortability then make a choice,

You should always know local traffic rules before driving (if you do),

7.Local Resources

Make sure you familiarize yourself with all laws customs traditions and etiquette because doing something wrong could start international tensions,

Look up emergency contacts healthcare facilities and local laws before going anywhere,

The best places to visit are always the ones that no one talks about. Find them and you'll have a better experience. Make sure they're real though.

Take these things into consideration and your trip will be well planned and organized. But don't forget to be open-minded, try new things, and make memories as you go on this journey at the same time.

Promoting sustainable travel is essential for reducing our ecological footprint and keeping the planet healthy. Below, we'll go over practical ways to minimize waste, conserve resources and support eco-friendly initiatives while traveling. By adopting responsible tourism habits, we can ensure that traveling leaves a positive impact on the environment and local communities.

1. Pack Lightweight:
- A durable suitcase or backpack should be used instead of single-use plastic bags.
- Bring only what you need; lighter means less fuel consumption during transportation.
- Use your own reusable water bottle, toiletries, and cloth bags.

2. Eco-Friendly Accommodations:
- Look for places that have sustainability policies like energy efficiency and minimal waste.
- When you can, stay at eco-lodges, hostels with green certifications or locally owned guesthouses.
- Stay at accommodations that recycle or use renewable energy sources.

3. Conserve Energy and Resources:
- Turn off lights, air conditioning and other electrical devices when not using them.
- Keep showers short to save water; also limit washing clothes to save even more water.
- Reuse towels and bed linens whenever possible.

4. Minimize Waste Generation:
- Always bring a reusable bag so you don't make one-time plastic bag purchases while shopping.
- Have your own straw and utensils on you instead of getting them at food places where they would just be thrown away after one use.
- Buy products in bulk if available or with minimal packaging.

5. Respect Wildlife and Natural Habitats:
- ✓ Enjoy wildlife from afar — don't disturb their habitats by trying to get closer to them.
- ✓ Do not buy souvenirs made out of endangered animals (The sooner we stop buying them the sooner companies will stop selling them).

✓   There are usually trails especially for people to walk on when visiting fragile ecosystems; stay on those trails.

6. Support Local Communities:
✓   Spend money with locally owned businesses instead of big chains.

✓   Learn about the culture, traditions and history of the place you're visiting to get a greater appreciation for it.

✓   Look for community-based tourism initiatives (these directly help local communities).

7. Carbon Footprint:
✓   Consider contributing to programs that focus on offsetting carbon or organizations that work towards conservation.

✓   Help replant trees or fund renewable energy projects.

✓   Calculate your carbon footprint and make efforts to reduce it by taking more sustainable transportation options like trains instead of flights when possible.

We can still have a great time traveling while being mindful about our environmental impact. Responsible tourism isn't just about preserving natural resources, but also respecting cultural heritage and supporting local communities.

Applying Lessons Learned: Incorporating Travel Experiences into Everyday Life

It's important to apply the lessons we learn during our travel experiences into our everyday life after embarking on transformative adventures and immersing ourselves in different cultures. Although we may not have time to physically travel all the time, the mindset we developed from traveling will continue to shape our personal growth, relationships at work and overall well-being. Here are some ways to integrate newfound perspectives into your day-to-day life:

1. Think global: Travel is an eye-opening, mind-expanding experience. With the ability to foster broader perspectives on life, embrace this mindset and apply it to everyday life. Be open to diversity, points of view, challenge biases you have and assumptions you were taught as a child. Apply all that you've learned in your personal relationships and professional collaborations.

2. Learn about different cultures: Even though we can't physically visit other countries at the moment there's still plenty we can do in terms of engaging with other communities around us. Attend cultural events, festivals or join a language exchange group. Actively try to learn about different cultures so that you can continue expanding your knowledge and understanding of the world.

3. Be curious and explore: Approach every day with a sense of wonder! That means actively seeking out new experiences and adventures even if they're within your own community or backyard if need be. Visit local museums or art galleries, try new hobbies, take up a new sport — anything that engages your curiosity will result in fostering a growth mindset which leads to learning and growing.

4. Practice mindfulness: You know how people say "stop and smell the roses"? Start doing exactly that but throughout the entire day! Engage in mediation, deep breathing exercises or simply just pause during moments throughout your day to appreciate the beauty around you. This mental action will help you cultivate gratitude (which then also helps reduce stress) ultimately enhancing your well-being.

5. Share what you've learned: As cliché as it sounds sharing is caring! Whether through photos, storytelling or blogging sharing what you've learned on your travels allows you to reflect on those lessons while inspiring others who are looking for their own journey of personal growth.

6. Welcome diverse perspectives: Step outside of yourself by reading books from authors hailing from different cultures than yours — same goes for podcasts and community-based online forums where different points of views are shared daily. By intentionally seeking information from diverse voices and perspectives you'll continue to broaden your understanding of the world which will also give you unique insights on personal growth.

Take this as a reminder that while physical travel may not be an option right now, the mindset and lessons learned from past experiences can still help shape your personal development. When incorporated into everyday life, these lessons create a sense of adventure and curiosity that crosses borders, ultimately enriching every aspect of one's life.

Chapter 46

The Investment in Yourself: Personal Development Tools

****

The Investment in You: Tools for Personal Development

Ever feel like you're stuck in life? Want to be better but don't know where to start? Here's your sign. It's time to go on the journey of personal development planning with us, step by step. We'll show you how to navigate through resources that can help you gain knowledge and grow into the best version of yourself. Now ask yourself, are you ready to unlock your potential?

What is Personal Development?

Before we can start something so complex, we need a basic understanding of it first; so what is personal development? Well for starters it's taking deliberate steps towards improving our skills, knowledge and mindset everyday. It is what helps us become the best versions of ourselves.

But how does it differ from self-improvement?

Self-development focuses mainly on mental growth and views success as a way to internal fulfillment.

On the other hand, self-improvement targets areas that hinder growth and achieving goals. The main goal of this method is enhancing performance or meeting certain goals.

To get better at personal development we have to adopt a growth mindset. This means believing that our abilities can be developed through effort and hard work.

Why try Personal Growth Planning?

There are a number of benefits when it comes to planning on personal growth. By using structured approaches we can gain new skills and learn more about ourselves as people.

One powerful thing about trying this kind of planning is the ability for self-growth. Sure it won't happen overnight but if done right we can reach our full potential through steps based off what we want out of life.

This next benefit might sound confusing but trust me this will make sense later on; increased self-awareness! The more we think about who we are as people the better decisions we will make down the line because they'll be aligned with our values. Not only that but once values are aligned learning becomes easier too!

Another good thing about this is it makes learning new things easier. It can be daunting but once we get in the mind frame of constantly developing new tools in our arsenal, it becomes second nature.

That's why lifelong learning is so important when it comes to personal growth planning. By continuously expanding our knowledge and capabilities we will always have room to grow and adapt which are key qualities in a world that never stops changing.

In Summation, personal development planning has so many benefits. It allows you to grow as a person and gain self-awareness along the way. Also, it helps you learn new skills. By always having a lifelong learning mindset, personal development planning can transform your life and help you reach new heights.

The components of a Personal Development Plan

A personal development plan is basically a map for self-improvement and personal growth. It helps you work toward goals and stay on track with what you want to achieve in life.

Setting goals is very important when it comes to this plan. Reaching our objectives make us feel fulfilled and like we have a purpose in life. If they're specific, measurable, achievable, relevant, and time-bound (SMART), goals will give us direction every step of the way throughout the journey.

We must also reflect on ourselves when making this plan. Knowing our strengths and weaknesses will only help us become better individuals overall. Reflecting on our past experiences shows areas that need improvement which means we'll be able to overcome obstacles that come our way.

Lastly, we need to find out what steps are necessary to take action once we know these things about ourselves. These steps consist of tasks or activities that'll help reach those goals we set earlier on. Once broken down into smaller steps rather than one big goal it becomes much easier to manage according to science.

Remember though this isn't something that's done one time only. To experience true growth we must commit for the long-term because none of this happens overnight . Regularly reviewing makes room for change when things get tough guaranteeing constant progress.

Step 1: Assess Your Current State

Analyzing your current situation is actually the first part of personal development planning — very important by the way! Self-reflection plays a huge role in this step because who knows yourself better than…yourself?

Take some alone time and ask yourself questions like:
- ✓ What have I accomplished?
- ✓ What am I good at?
- ✓ Are there any skills that stand out about me?

These are some ways to identify your strengths. Once you're aware of them it becomes easier to use them in order to reach goals and grow as a person.

To identify weaknesses, know that being 100% honest with ourselves is gonna be beneficial. When we recognize what we need to improve on strategies will be made leading us to self-growth.

Don't forget about SWOT analysis! It's really helpful when seeking insight into our current state. It stands for Strengths, Weaknesses, Opportunities, and Threats which makes evaluating internal and external factors easy!

When looking at these factors ask yourself questions like:

Strength:
- ✓ What can you offer that'll help personal development goals?
- ✓ Are there resources or support systems accessible?

Weaknesses:
- ✓ Which areas call for improvement?
- ✓ Obstacles/Challenges that may exist

Opportunities:
- ✓ External factors helping personal growth
- ✓ Skills or knowledge can be enhanced by what opportunities?

Threats:
- ✓ External factors causing challenges
- ✓ Limitations or constraints

By conducting a thorough self-assessment, identifying your strengths and weaknesses, and performing a SWOT analysis, you will gain a clear understanding of where you currently stand in your personal development journey. This knowledge sets the foundation for creating an effective personal development plan.

Step 2: Defining Your Goals

Setting goals is a crucial step in personal development planning. By defining your goals, you create a roadmap for your self-improvement journey. It's important to set goals that are specific, measurable, attainable, relevant, and time-bound, also known as SMART goals. This ensures that your goals are clear, realistic, and actionable.

When defining your goals, it's essential to have a long-term vision. A long-term vision provides you with a sense of direction and purpose. It outlines the ultimate outcome you want to achieve in your personal development journey.

However, it's equally important to break down your long-term vision into short-term objectives. Short-term objectives serve as milestones along the way to your long-term vision. They help keep you motivated and focused, providing you with the satisfaction of making progress towards your larger goals.

By setting goals, creating a long-term vision, and breaking it down into short-term objectives, you set yourself up for success in personal development. This intentional approach allows you to stay on track, measure your progress, and continually strive towards self-improvement.

Step 3: Creating an Action Plan

In order to effectively achieve your personal development goals, it is vital to create a detailed action plan. An action plan outlines the specific steps and tasks that need to be completed in order to reach your desired outcome.

Prioritization

When creating an action plan , it is important to prioritize or tasks based on impact . Identify the most important of them all this will have the greatest impact on our personal development . By focusing first on these we can make significant progress towards our goal .

Time Management

Managing your time effectively is crucial for successful personal development. Allocate specific time blocks in your schedule to work on the tasks outlined in your action plan . Set realistic deadlines and be disciplined in adhering to them . Prioritize your personal development activities and avoid procrastination.

Accountability

Establishing accountability measures is essential for staying on track with your personal development goals. Share your action plan with a trusted friend, mentor, or accountability partner who can support and motivate you throughout the process. Regularly check-in with them to discuss your progress and any challenges you may be facing.

By creating an action plan and incorporating prioritization , time management , and accountability into our personal development journey we set ourselves up for success . Stay committed , stay focused , and watch as we make steady progress towards becoming the best version of ourselves .

Step 4: Implementing and Adjusting Your Plan

In this crucial phase of our personal development plan it's time to put our plan into action closely monitor our progress . Effective plan execution is key to achieving our goals it requires dedication commitment.

Start by executing the action steps outlined in your plan . Break them down into manageable tasks assign realistic deadlines to each one . This will help you stay organized focused as you work towards objectives.

As you begin to implement the plan, it is important to regularly check your progress. This will help track your achievements, find out things you need improvement on, and keep you motivated. You can either write these things down in a journal or use a special tracking tool.

Being adaptable is very important during this phase. Life isn't always predictable and there might be moments where you have to adjust your plan. Being open to change is key in all of this because flexibility keeps you on track and helps you overcome obstacles.

Implementing continuous improvement during the implementation and adjustment phase should be a priority. Regularly evaluate if what you're doing is working and assess your progress. Feedback from mentors, coaches or peers can also come a long way at this point. Use their insights to make all the necessary improvements possible.

By staying adaptable and embracing continuous improvement, you ensure that your personal development plan remains a dynamic and effective tool for your growth. Remember, personal development is a lifelong journey, and each step you take contributes to your overall progress and success.

Committing to Ongoing Personal Growth

As you complete your initial personal development plan, it's important to remember that personal growth is an ongoing journey. True self-improvement is not a one-time event but rather a lifelong commitment to continuous growth and development.

Part of committing to ongoing personal growth is prioritizing self-care. Taking care of yourself emotionally, mentally, and physically is essential for your overall well-being. Make time for activities that recharge and rejuvenate you. Whether it's practicing mindfulness, engaging in hobbies, or simply taking a break, self-care allows you to replenish your energy and maintain a positive mindset.

In addition to self-care, lifelong learning plays a crucial role in personal growth. Never stop seeking knowledge and expanding your horizons. Embrace opportunities for learning and development, whether it's through reading books, attending seminars, or enrolling in courses. Lifelong learning not only broadens your perspective but also equips you with new skills and insights to navigate the ever-changing world.

To support your ongoing personal growth, there are countless resources available. Online platforms, such as TED Talks, podcasts, and blogs, offer a wealth of inspiring content on various topics related to self-improvement. Look for reputable authors, experts, and thought leaders who can guide you in your journey. Remember, growth is a continuous process, and by committing to ongoing personal growth, you are investing in the best version of yourself.

Chapter 47

Redefining Relaxation: Smart Leisure and Downtime

****

Redefining Relaxation: Smart Leisure and Downtime in your 30's

Do you feel like you never truly unwind, no matter how much downtime you have? Are you searching for effective ways to recharge and relax in this fast-paced world? Look no further! We will redefine relaxation by exploring the concept of "smart leisure." Discover the benefits of rest, learn how to do it right, and unlock the secrets to relaxing the smart way to promote overall well-being and rejuvenation.

Understanding the Importance of Rest

Before we dive into smart relaxation techniques, it's essential to comprehend the significance of rest in promoting our physical and mental well-being. Rest is not merely a luxury; it is a fundamental requirement for our overall health and happiness. By incorporating effective ways to unwind and recharge into our daily lives, we can experience a wide range of benefits that enhance our quality of life.

The Benefits of Rest

Rest offers numerous advantages that extend beyond simply feeling refreshed. When we prioritize rest, we give our bodies and minds the opportunity to replenish and rejuvenate. By engaging in activities that promote restful downtime, we can experience:

- ✓ **Improved Productivity:** Taking breaks and allowing ourselves to rest actually enhances our ability to focus and concentrate when we return to work. Rested individuals often exhibit increased productivity and efficiency in their tasks.
- ✓ **Reduced Stress Levels:** Rest provides an opportunity for stress reduction. When we take the time to unwind and recharge, we give our minds and bodies a chance to alleviate stress and tension, contributing to improved mental and emotional well-being.
- ✓ **Enhanced Cognitive Function:** Quality rest is essential for our cognitive abilities. During rest, our brains consolidate and process information, leading to improved memory, creativity, and problem-solving skills.

How to Do It Right

While rest is crucial, it's equally important to understand how to do it right for maximum benefits. Here are some effective ways to unwind and recharge:

- ✓ **Establish a Consistent Sleep Routine:** Prioritize quality sleep by maintaining a regular sleep schedule. Create a conducive sleep environment, practice relaxation rituals before bedtime, and ensure you're getting the recommended amount of sleep for your age group.
- ✓ **Take Regular Breaks:** Incorporate short breaks throughout your day to rest your mind and body. Engage in activities that provide relaxation, such as stretching, deep breathing exercises, or simply stepping away from your work to clear your mind.
- ✓ **Engage in Relaxation Practices:** Explore various relaxation techniques like meditation, yoga, or listening to calming music. Find activities that help you achieve a state of relaxation and make them a regular part of your routine.

By understanding the benefits of rest and incorporating effective techniques into your daily life, you can unlock the power of rest and rejuvenate yourself both physically and mentally.

The Science Behind Effective Rest

Understanding the science behind effective rest and relaxation is key to maximizing their benefits and achieving overall well-being. Rest plays a vital role in impacting our brain, body, and overall health. By delving into the different stages of sleep and exploring techniques to improve sleep quality, you can learn how to do rest right and unlock its rejuvenating effects.

When we rest, our brain and body undergo a series of processes that promote restoration and regeneration. During sleep, the body repairs damaged tissues, supports immune function, and regulates hormone levels. It also consolidates memories and enhances cognitive abilities.

The Stages of Sleep

Sleep consists of various stages, each serving a unique purpose in maintaining optimal health. The first stage is the initiation of sleep, followed by light sleep and deep sleep. Finally, REM (Rapid Eye Movement) sleep occurs, which is associated with dreams and vivid mental activity.

Improving sleep quality involves prioritizing all sleep stages and ensuring an adequate amount of time spent in each. Establishing a consistent sleep schedule, creating a conducive sleep environment, and practicing relaxation techniques before bedtime can greatly enhance the quality of your sleep.

Maximizing the Rejuvenating Effects of Rest

To fully reap the benefits of rest, it is important to integrate other relaxation techniques into your routine. Engaging in activities such as meditation, deep breathing exercises, and mindfulness practices can help promote a state of calmness and relaxation, improving overall sleep quality and enhancing the rejuvenating effects of rest.

Additionally, maintaining a balanced lifestyle that includes regular exercise, a healthy diet, and effective stress management techniques can complement the benefits of rest and amplify their positive impact on your well-being.

By understanding the science behind effective rest, you can optimize your relaxation practices and unlock the full potential of rejuvenation for a more balanced and fulfilling life.

Unwinding the Smart Way: Relaxation Techniques

When it comes to relaxation, there are many effective ways to unwind and recharge. Discover a variety of techniques tailored to promote relaxation and stress reduction, allowing you to relax the smart way.

Mindfulness and Meditation

One powerful technique for relaxation is mindfulness and meditation. By cultivating present-moment awareness, you can quiet your mind and find inner peace. Whether you choose to focus on your breath, practice guided meditation, or engage in mindful activities, incorporating mindfulness into your routine can bring a sense of calm and rejuvenation.

Breathing Exercises

Breathing exercises are another effective way to relax and recharge. Deep breathing exercises, such as diaphragmatic breathing or box breathing, can help reduce stress, lower blood pressure, and promote relaxation. Take a few moments each day to focus on your breath and let go of tension.

Progressive Muscle Relaxation

Progressive muscle relaxation is a technique that involves systematically tensing and releasing different muscle groups to induce a state of deep relaxation. By consciously relaxing your muscles, you can release physical tension and promote overall relaxation. Take the time to practice progressive muscle relaxation and experience the soothing effects on your body and mind.

These are just a few examples of relaxation techniques that can help you unwind and recharge. Explore and experiment with different methods to find what works best for you. Incorporate these techniques into your daily routine to relax the smart way and promote a sense of well-being and rejuvenation.

Creating Your Own Relaxation Sanctuary

When it comes to relaxation, your home can be the ultimate sanctuary. By transforming your living space into a calming and rejuvenating environment, you can unwind and recharge whenever you need. Follow these tips to create a tranquil haven that promotes relaxation and helps you relax the smart way.

Set the Mood with Soothing Decor

The first step in creating your relaxation sanctuary is to incorporate soothing decor. Opt for soft colors and natural materials that evoke a sense of calmness. Add plush cushions, cozy blankets, and a comfortable chair or chaise lounge where you can fully relax and let go of everyday worries.

Create Ambience with Ambient Lighting

Lighting plays a crucial role in setting the mood for relaxation. Use soft, warm lighting to create a cozy atmosphere. Consider incorporating dimmer switches or using table lamps and floor lamps with soft, diffused lighting. Candlelight can also add a touch of ambiance and serenity to your relaxation sanctuary.

Invest in Comfortable Furniture

Comfort is key when it comes to creating a relaxation sanctuary. Invest in furniture that provides maximum comfort and support. Look for ergonomic chairs, recliners, or even a comfortable bean bag where you can sink in and relax. Don't forget to add a side table or a tray within arm's reach to hold your favorite book or a cup of herbal tea.

Indulge in Aromatherapy

Aromatherapy is a powerful tool for relaxation. Fill your relaxation sanctuary with scents that help calm the mind and reduce stress. Use essential oil diffusers, scented candles, or herbal sachets to infuse the air with soothing aromas. Lavender, chamomile, and eucalyptus are popular choices known for their relaxing properties.

Enhance the Atmosphere with Soft Music

Music has a profound impact on our mood and relaxation. Create a playlist of soft, calming tunes that help you unwind. Consider using a Bluetooth speaker or a sound machine that plays nature sounds like gentle rain or ocean waves for a more immersive relaxation experience.

Add Nature-Inspired Elements

Bringing elements of nature into your relaxation sanctuary can promote a sense of tranquility. Consider adding indoor plants, such as peace lilies or snake plants, to purify the air and create a serene atmosphere. Incorporate natural materials like bamboo, wood, or stone to infuse your space with an organic and grounding vibe.

By incorporating these tips into your home, you can create your own personal relaxation sanctuary. This dedicated space will provide you with a peaceful haven where you can unwind, recharge, and relax the smart way.

Nurturing Your Mind, Body, and Soul

When it comes to relaxation, it's important to remember that it goes beyond just physical rest. Nurturing your mind, body, and soul is essential for true rejuvenation and overall well-being. By embracing holistic approaches to relaxation, you can relax the smart way and effectively unwind and recharge.

One way to nurture your mind, body, and soul is through the practice of activities like yoga, tai chi, and qigong. These ancient disciplines promote relaxation, reduce stress, and improve physical and mental health. By incorporating these practices into your routine, you can experience the benefits of enhanced flexibility, increased strength, and improved focus.

In addition to movement-based practices, self-care activities can also play a significant role in nurturing your soul. Engaging in practices such as journaling, reading, and creative hobbies can provide a much-needed escape from daily stresses and promote a sense of inner peace.

Journaling, for example, can be a powerful way to process your thoughts and emotions, as well as document your journey of self-discovery. Reading allows you to explore new worlds and gain valuable insights, while creative hobbies like painting or playing an instrument offer a creative outlet for self-expression.

By nurturing your mind, body, and soul, you can achieve a deeper level of relaxation and find a sense of balance in your life. So, take the time to prioritize these activities and discover the transformative power of self-care and holistic practices.

Incorporating Smart Leisure Activities

When it comes to relaxation, leisure activities can be both enjoyable and highly beneficial. Engage your mind and body in smart leisure activities that allow you to unwind and recharge effectively. From exploring the beauty of nature to practicing sports, there are numerous ways to make your leisure time productive, fulfilling, and rejuvenating.

Connecting with Nature: Spend time in the great outdoors and immerse yourself in the beauty of nature. Whether it's hiking through scenic trails, picnicking in a park, or simply breathing in the fresh air, nature has a calming and revitalizing effect on the mind and body.

Active Sports: Engaging in sports not only provides physical exercise but also stimulates your mind. Whether it's a game of tennis, a round of golf, or a friendly match of basketball, sports can help release endorphins, reduce stress, and promote a sense of accomplishment.

Learning New Skills: Fuel your curiosity and expand your horizons by learning something new. Whether it's playing a musical instrument, cooking a new recipe, or taking up a dance class, acquiring new skills can be both intellectually stimulating and a wonderful way to relax.

Indulging in Hobbies: Reconnect with hobbies you love or explore new ones that pique your interest. Whether it's painting, gardening, woodworking, or knitting, engaging in hobbies provides an outlet for creativity, promotes a sense of accomplishment, and allows you to relax and recharge.

By incorporating smart leisure activities into your routine, you can relax the smart way and effectively unwind and recharge. Choose activities that resonate with you and make them an essential part of your leisure time to promote overall well-being and happiness.

Managing Digital Detox: Finding Balance in a Connected World

In today's digitally connected world, it can be challenging to find a balance between the demands of work and the need for relaxation. The constant presence of screens and technology can make it difficult to truly unwind and recharge. However, by managing digital detox and establishing healthy boundaries with technology, you can create space for genuine relaxation free from distractions.

One effective way to manage digital detox is to set dedicated technology-free periods in your daily routine. Designate certain hours or evenings where you disconnect from screens and engage in activities that promote relaxation. Use this time to engage with loved ones, pursue hobbies, or simply enjoy some quiet solitude.

Another strategy is to create physical boundaries with technology. Designate specific areas in your home as technology-free zones, such as the bedroom or dining table. By separating your digital devices from specific spaces, you can create a sense of separation and allow yourself to fully disconnect and recharge.

Additionally, it's important to be mindful of your digital engagement during your leisure time. While social media and entertainment platforms can be enjoyable, they can also become a source of stress and distraction if not managed mindfully. Instead of mindlessly scrolling through your social media feeds, consider engaging in activities that truly bring you joy and relaxation, such as reading a book, going for a walk, or practicing a hobby.

Finding a healthy balance between digital engagement and quality downtime is essential for effective rest and rejuvenation. By incorporating these strategies for managing digital detox, you can create a better balance in your life and fully embrace the benefits of smart relaxation.

The Power of Mindfulness

Mindfulness is a powerful tool that can help you relax the smart way and effectively unwind and recharge. By diving into the world of mindfulness, you can cultivate present-moment awareness and experience transformative effects on both your mind and body.

Practicing mindfulness doesn't have to be complicated. It can be as simple as taking a few moments to focus on your breath or fully savoring each bite of a meal. By incorporating mindful practices into your daily life, you can enhance your overall sense of well-being and find moments of calm amidst the busyness of life.

One way to apply mindfulness is through mindful eating. Instead of rushing through meals, take the time to savor every bite, noticing the textures, flavors, and sensations. This can help you develop a healthier relationship with food and prevent overeating.

Another effective way to practice mindfulness is through mindful walking. As you stroll, pay attention to the sensations of your feet touching the ground, the rhythm of your steps, and the sights and sounds around you. This can bring a sense of grounding and relaxation, even in the midst of a chaotic day.

Mindful breathing exercises are also a valuable technique for relaxation. Take a few minutes to focus on your breath, feeling the rising and falling of your abdomen or the coolness of the air entering and exiting your nose. This simple practice can help calm your mind and release tension in your body.

If you want to deepen your mindfulness practice, you can try body scans. This involves systematically moving your attention through different parts of your body, noticing any sensations or areas of tension. With each scan, allow yourself to relax and let go of any accumulated stress or tightness.

Embracing mindfulness as a regular part of your life can bring about numerous benefits - reduced stress, improved focus, increased self-awareness, and enhanced overall well-being. So, relax the smart way and incorporate mindfulness into your daily routine to find peace and rejuvenation in the present moment.

Embracing the Art of Smart Downtime

In this final section, we invite you to embrace the art of smart downtime and discover the key to unlocking the benefits of effective rest. In today's fast-paced world, it's essential to prioritize relaxation, leisure, and rejuvenation for a more fulfilling life.

Creating balance between work and play is crucial. By incorporating smart relaxation techniques and mindfulness practices, you can achieve a state of deep relaxation that nurtures your mind, body, and soul.

Relax the smart way by carving out dedicated time for rest and leisure activities. Whether it's practicing mindfulness, indulging in a hobby, or spending time in nature, choose activities that help you unwind and recharge. Remember, downtime is not a luxury but a necessity for your overall well-being.

Chapter 48

Giving Back: The
Joy of Contribution
****

Exploring the Value of Contributing:

The act of contributing to society and enriching the community carries profound importance and merit. This segment will delve into the advantages of community engagement and its beneficial effects on one's personal fulfillment and well-being.

Participating in charitable activities and aiding those in need initiates a cascade of kindness and compassion, impacting far more than just the individual. Such contributions forge meaningful connections, cultivate a sense of community, and bolster our social fabric. Investing our time, assets, or expertise in causes we hold dear not only elevates the less fortunate but also enriches us with a deep sense of purpose and satisfaction.

Studies indicate that those involved in volunteer work and community services frequently experience heightened joy, better mental health, and diminished stress. Shifting our focus from self-interest to aiding others broadens our life perspective, nurtures gratitude, and enhances our empathy and compassion. These attributes significantly transform our personal and professional relationships and overall life satisfaction.

Furthermore, giving back is an opportunity to apply our distinct abilities and talents towards making a real-world difference. Whether it's educating children, providing meals to the needy, or advocating for environmental preservation, endless avenues exist for meaningful contribution that aligns with our personal interests and principles. Engaging in causes that deeply resonate ensures our efforts are genuine and impactful.

As we journey through our lives, understanding the significance of contributing becomes vital for personal evolution. We possess the capacity to effect positive change within our communities and forge a legacy for future generations. By valuing service and embodying generosity, we arm ourselves with purpose and inspire others in the process.

The forthcoming sections will offer insights into identifying causes close to our hearts, discovering ways to participate, and achieving a harmony between contributing and our personal lives. Let us embark on this path of making a difference together, envisioning a brighter future for ourselves and our communities.

Identifying Personal Causes:

This section focuses on pinpointing causes that resonate with your passions and values. Reflecting on what genuinely matters to you ensures that your contributions are both meaningful and fulfilling.

Reflect on What Drives You:

Contemplate the issues or subjects that stir excitement or concern within you. What aspects of life draw you in? Consider your hobbies, interests, and life experiences. Recognizing these passions provides a foundation for identifying causes that deeply connect with you.

For instance, if environmental sustainability has always sparked your interest, you might find yourself drawn to organizations focused on habitat protection or promoting green practices.

Evaluate Your Core Values:

Your values are the compass that guides your worldview and life choices. Reflect on the principles you hold dear, such as justice, equality, education, or health. Pinpointing your fundamental values aids in finding causes that match these ideals.

For example, if you highly value educational accessibility, you might gravitate towards initiatives offering resources to disadvantaged communities or advocating for educational reforms.

Discover Local Initiatives:
With a clearer understanding of your interests and values, research local groups and initiatives related to your causes. Utilize online platforms or community directories to connect with relevant organizations.
Reaching out to these groups directly can provide insight into their mission, ongoing projects, and ways to get involved.

Network and Attend Events:
Enhance your understanding by interacting with those already active in your areas of interest. Participate in related events, workshops, or seminars to broaden your knowledge and connect with like-minded individuals.
Through active engagement, you'll uncover the specific needs, challenges, and opportunities within your chosen cause, guiding your path towards impactful contribution.

Chapter 49

The Next Decade: Preparing
for Your 40s and Beyond

****

Are you ready to embrace the future? Planning for your 40s is not just about getting older; it's about setting yourself up for success in this new phase of life. It's time to secure your finances, prioritize your health, and seek happiness on your own terms. So, are you prepared to navigate the challenges and opportunities that lie ahead? Let's explore how you can make the most of your 40s and beyond.

Taking Stock of Your Finances

As you enter your 40s, it becomes increasingly important to take a proactive approach in managing your finances. Planning for your 40's and securing your financial future is a critical step towards long-term stability and peace of mind. By assessing your current financial situation and implementing smart strategies, you can navigate this pivotal decade with confidence.

One of the first steps in taking stock of your finances is to evaluate your debt. While debt can be overwhelming, developing a clear plan to pay it off can provide a sense of control and freedom. Consider creating a realistic budget and allocating funds towards debt payments. Explore debt consolidation options if necessary to streamline your repayment process and potentially reduce interest rates.

In addition to managing debt, it's essential to focus on increasing savings. Building an emergency fund is crucial to handling unexpected expenses and providing a financial safety net. Aim to save enough that will cover three to six months of living expenses. By setting aside a portion of income each month, gradually growing savings will prepare one for any unforeseen circumstances.

Furthermore, wise investments play a significant role in securing financial stability. Consult with a financial advisor when considering what's best for goals, risk tolerance, timeline etc… Diversify portfolio by investing in diversified stocks or bonds etc… Doing so will maximize potential returns while minimizing risks mention there lol

Retirement Planning: Securing Your Future

With retirement on the horizon, it's essential to prioritize planning for this chapter of your life. Contributing to retirement accounts, such as a 401(k) or an individual retirement account (IRA), can provide you with long-term financial security. Take advantage of any employer matching programs, as this can significantly boost your retirement savings. Consider a Roth IRA for tax advantages, or consult with a financial advisor to determine the best retirement savings vehicle for you.

Planning for your 40's requires a holistic approach that encompasses both short-term financial goals and long-term retirement planning. By taking the time to analyze your current financial situation, manage debt efficiently, increase savings, and make smart investment choices, you can lay a solid foundation for a financially secure future.

Building a Strong Retirement Plan

Planning for your 40's is an essential step towards a secure future. As you enter this new phase of life, it's crucial to prioritize retirement planning to ensure financial stability in your golden years.

There are a few retirement savings options that exist to help you build a strong retirement plan. One of those options is the 401(k), which lets you contribute a portion of your pre-tax income towards retirement. In many cases, employers will match those contributions, which boosts them even more.

Another option is an individual retirement account (IRA) which offers tax advantages and flexibility in investment choices. You can control your own contributions with an IRA and select from several different types of investments like stocks, bonds and mutual funds.

Making The Most Of Employer Benefits

When planning for retirement, it's important to consider what benefits your employer offers. Many companies provide pension plans or other types of retirement savings plans that add extra security. So take advantage of these benefits by contributing as much as you can and understand if there are any employer match programs available.

Also think about seeking professional advice when making decisions around your plan. Financial advisors have the knowledge needed to offer guidance based on your individual goals and risk tolerance levels.

The earlier you start planning for retirement, the more time your investments have to grow so keep that in mind. Building a strong retirement plan in your 40s will put you in good shape to enjoy the future comfortably and financially secure.

Protecting Your Health And Well-being

As soon as you enter your 40s, prioritizing health becomes crucial. Planning for this age should include scheduling regular health check-ups,, maintaining a healthy diet, incorporating exercise into everyday life and managing stress effectively. These proactive steps will enhance overall wellness while ensuring a vibrant future that's full of happiness.

It's very important to schedule regular health check-ups during this decade so potential problems get caught early on. Regular screenings along with consultations from healthcare professionals helps identify issues before they become insurmountable if they're treated right away.

Using food as fuel is very effective when trying maintain optimal health too.. Try consuming a well-balanced variety of nutritious foods like fruits, vegetables, whole grains, lean proteins and healthy fats. While you're at it, avoid eating too much processed food and drinks high in sugar or empty calories. A healthy diet can help manage weight while reducing the risk of developing chronic diseases.

Exercise should be given some thought too. Incorporating physical activity into your daily routine is another essential aspect of preserving health in your 40s. Engage in regular exercise like brisk walking, jogging, cycling or strength training to keep your body strong and agile. Try getting at least 150 minutes of moderate-intensity aerobic activity per week with two days for muscle-strengthening activities.

Lastly, stress management is crucial for overall well-being since it has negative effects on both mental and physical health when built up over time. Explore different stress-reducing techniques such as meditation or deep breathing exercises when things start feeling overwhelming.. Also find hobbies that bring joy because they can also provide relaxation and rejuvenation.

By placing a strong emphasis on protecting your health and well-being, you can lay the foundation for a vibrant and fulfilling future. Incorporating regular health check-ups, a healthy diet, exercise, and stress management techniques into your lifestyle during your 40s will enable you to enjoy optimal health and embrace the next phase of life with confidence and vitality.

Securing Insurance Coverage for the Future

At 40 years old, you start to realize things. Things like the future being important to plan for. That's why securing insurance is key. It keeps you and your loved ones safe from those nasty surprises we call emergencies.

As you age into your 40s, a few types of insurance may become relevant for you. A major one being life insurance. This insurance provides financial security for your family if you pass away. It covers things like funeral expenses, debts, and can even replace lost income! Having enough coverage can help make a difficult time easier for your loved ones.

Then there's health insurance which everyone knows about. Getting older means needing more healthcare, so having enough resources to keep up with that is a must.

Long-term care insurance is a somewhat common one as well. It helps cover the costs of long-term care services such as home health aides, assisted living, or nursing home care.

Choosing what kind of coverage to get can be tricky so consult with an expert before making any decisions!

Now let's move on to something more interesting

Nurturing Relationships and Support Systems

As humans we thrive off relationships and support systems. You know how when you get in a fight with someone it messes with you mentally? Yeah that's because we're social creatures who are designed to work together!

Friends and family are both great but both need separate attention in order to maintain a healthy bond.

Support systems come in many forms but they're all equally important at this age group (and basically every age group). Make friends who uplift and inspire you. The people around us have power over our moods so chose those people carefully.

Investing in relationships will secure emotional well-being

Career Growth and Development

If there's anything I wish I could go back in time and tell myself it would be this next bit here: Your 40s might be the most important years of your career journey

This is where you make the most significant strides.

One way to advance your career in your 40s is by assessing your current position, and identifying ways you can improve or grow. You can try taking on new responsibilities, volunteering for challenging projects, or pursuing new training or education opportunities. By doing this, you'll acquire new skills and knowledge that will not only heighten your value in the job market but also boost confidence in yourself.

Opening doors for professional development is another important part of planning for your 40s. For example, attending workshops, webinars, conferences and industry events will give you an insider perspective as well as keep you updated with all the latest trends and developments happening within your field. Networking with professionals in the same industry can be a good door opener when trying to open doors to new career prospects and mentorship opportunities.

It's also important to ensure professional satisfaction as much as it is to focus on career advancement. Take some time out of your life to reflect on what you want out of life and if that aligns with what you're currently doing now. If it doesn't then try making a career change or finding alternative paths that better suit your goals and aspirations.

Your 40s are the perfect time for evaluating how far along you have come into your career trajectory. And once you've identified where you're at, use this knowledge combined with being open minded about new experiences so that you can navigate through the ever changing job market landscape while still acquiring new skills.

Never Stop Learning

As soon as we hit our 40s we should all prioritize learning and personal growth above everything else. This stage of life offers plenty of opportunities for expanding our knowledge base, pursuing hobbies we never thought we'd pursue before on top of nurturing interests so that it enhances personal fulfillment.

Prioritize Mental Health and Emotional Well-being

Planning for our 40's involves more than just financial management plans or physical exercises. It's equally important to make sure we prioritize our mental health and emotional well-being during this time in our life. This is because it will be key when it comes to dealing with the challenges and opportunities that come with aging.

Self-Care: Nurturing your Inner Self

Our self-care activities should be aimed towards nourishing the mind, body and soul. This means that we need to take time out of our day to engage in activities that bring us joy and relaxation. For example practicing mindfulness and meditation, indulging in hobbies or simply taking a break from work on a sunny day can greatly enhance our overall wellbeing. By prioritizing self-care, you can reduce stress levels, improve overall well-being, and enhance your ability to face life's challenges.

Stress Management Techniques: Finding Inner Equilibrium

Stress is something we're all bound to face throughout life but what's most important is how we manage it so it doesn't affect us mentally or emotionally. We have to develop healthy coping mechanisms along with practicing stress reduction strategies that work for us personally. For example regularly exercising, maintaining a balanced diet, getting enough sleep or trying deep breathing exercises are all things we should be doing on top of finding unwinding activities that make us happy which will significantly reduce stress levels.

Professional Help: Seeking Guidance when Needed

One thing almost everyone has trouble doing is realizing they need help when their mental health or emotional well-being start going south. Taking the step forward in seeking professional help not only shows strength but also self-awareness which are both extremely valuable skills one can have in any situation thrown at them by life itself. If you find yourself struggling with your mental health or emotional wellbeing reach out to therapist or counselor who can give you tools needed to overcome obstacles while improving quality of life.

By prioritizing your mental health and emotional well-being, you are taking a proactive step towards a fulfilling and balanced life in your 40s and beyond. Remember, seeking professional help and prioritizing self-care are not signs of weakness, but rather acts of self-love and empowerment. Make your mental and emotional well-being a priority as you navigate the exciting journey of this new phase of life.

Setting Goals and Crafting a Vision for the Future

Planning for your 40's is an important step towards building a fulfilling and successful future. One crucial aspect of this planning process is setting goals and crafting a vision for what you want to achieve in the coming years. By outlining clear objectives and creating action plans, you can stay focused and motivated to turn your aspirations into reality.

Goal setting allows you to define what you truly want and create a roadmap to get there. It provides direction and purpose, helping you make the most of your 40s and beyond. Whether it's advancing in your career, starting a business, pursuing a passion, or improving personal relationships, setting goals gives you something to strive for and keeps you on track.

To effectively set goals, start by identifying your priorities and values. Reflect on what truly matters to you and what you want your future to look like. This self-reflection helps you craft a vision for the future, providing a clear picture of the life you want to live.

Once you have a vision in mind, break it down into smaller, actionable goals. Make them specific, measurable, achievable, relevant, and time-bound (SMART goals). This approach ensures that your goals are tangible, realistic, and within your reach. Additionally, creating action plans outlining the steps you need to take and setting deadlines helps keep you accountable and motivated.

As you embark on this goal setting journey, remember to stay flexible and adapt as circumstances change. Regularly review and adjust your goals to ensure they align with your evolving priorities and values. Celebrate your achievements along the way, no matter how small, and use any setbacks or challenges as learning opportunities to grow stronger.

Setting goals and crafting a vision for the future in your 40s is an empowering and transformative process. It allows you to take control of your life and shape your own destiny. With a clear direction and steadfast determination, you can make the most of this exciting chapter and create a future that is truly aligned with your dreams and aspirations.

Investing in Self-Care and Well-being

Planning for your 40's is not just about financial security and career growth; it also involves prioritizing self-care and well-being. Taking care of yourself is essential for maintaining a healthy and fulfilling life as you age.

One of the most effective ways to invest in self-care is through mindfulness and meditation. These practices can help reduce stress, improve focus, and enhance overall mental well-being. Taking a few minutes each day to sit quietly, breathe deeply, and be present in the moment can have a profound impact on your overall happiness and peace of mind.

Maintaining a well-balanced work and life is a self-care essential. As you enter your 40's create boundaries between your work and personal life. Prioritize your time, set realistic expectations, and make sure you allocate enough dedicated relaxation time to yourself.

Creating a Self-Care Routine

Doing activities that promote physical, mental, and emotional health within your routine will ensure consistent prioritization of well-being. Regular exercise, engaging in hobbies, practicing gratitude, joining social connections are all examples of activities that benefit overall wellness. Remember to listen to both your body and mind. Pay attention to the physical needs of getting enough sleep, eating nutritious meals, drinking enough water. Take breaks when needed and engage in activities that bring joy to you. When facing challenges don't be shy or hesitant to seek support from friends or family members.

Incorporating self-care into daily life might require adjusting some things like saying "no" to obligations that just aren't good for you. However it is an investment in yourself that has long term benefits. You'll be able to show up as not just a better version of yourself but the best you possibly can be for all parts of your life.

Approach The Future With Confidence

When entering this new age range it is important approach it with confidence. The strategies we've discussed should help you plan for 40s and any other number past this one too! Taking steps like managing finances proactively by taking stock of them will aid greatly down the line. Building a strong retirement plan along with securing insurances provides financial security as well peace of mind.

Your health is top priority so make sure its treated like so…which means prioritizing it along with well-being during these 10 years! Create plans for regularly checking on health status', maintaining healthy diets & exercising daily. A balance between managing stress & investing in self-care while nurturing relationships & support systems ensures happiness and satisfaction.

Lastly, goals and personal growth should always be prioritized. It might not seem like it but it truly does have a significant role in navigating with confidence and fulfillment. So set clear objectives! Learn new skills and of course don't forget about the emotional well-being side of things.

Chapter 50
Some Final Thoughts
****

As you look back on your journey through your 30s, take a moment to appreciate the growth and progress that you have experienced. Consider the achievements, both big and small, that you have accomplished during this transformative decade. Celebrate the challenges that you have faced head-on, as well as the lessons that you've learned along the way.

Reflecting on your journey will remind you of how far you've come. It will teach you just how resilient and adaptable you can be in different situations. Recognize any personal or professional milestones that may have occurred in this time period. Depending on who's reading this, it could be advancing in your career, 'cuffing' with someone meaningful or finally getting a few days off for some much needed self care.

By acknowledging and celebrating these successes, you'll boost your mental in knowing what else is possible. Reminding yourself of what's been done so far gives the feeling that anything else is possible moving forward.

We shouldn't stop there though! Continue looking ahead to visualize life beyond your thirties. If we're being real here, thirty is still young (That's not me yelling at teenagers to pipe down). Set new goals and standards for yourself as we enter into this next chapter of life. What do we want to accomplish? How do we want our lives to reflect?

The key here is maintaining momentum throughout life; Even when things get tough. We must embrace a mindset focused on continuous learning because honestly… Life never stops teaching us lessons! We need to remain open to change because whether we accept it or not; Life always has something unexpected waiting for us around corners.

Even as our minds keep growing…Our bodies... Well… Maybe they won't (Midlife crisis anyone?). However staying up to date with current trends and gaining more knowledge keeps our spirits young. A lot if not all industries are always changing so make sure to stay on top of that! You'll be a better positioned individual with more skills and knowledge.

As you continue to move forward, always remember the wisdom gained throughout our 30s. We should incorporate them into any decision making process down the road. Having gone through life's ups and downs gives us an insight for future choices.

We shouldn't be afraid of age though; In fact we should embrace it! Embrace getting older and gaining confidence in our abilities to overcome any obstacle put in front of us. Take every chance for growth knowing no experience is bad because someone will always learn something from it.

Succeeding while we're 30 and beyond consist of using what we've learned so far, celebrating achievements… And always striving for a better future; No matter how long or short it may seem.

Let's keep going!

On top of that, taking the time to celebrate milestones can give you room for reflection. You should be using each accomplishment as an opportunity to think about what you've learned. What did you do right? How did you do it? These are questions that will help you figure out how to approach your next big challenge.

Of course, we all get caught up in wanting to achieve the next goal or milestone. But if we don't pause and savor our current success, then a few years down the line we'll find ourselves wanting more progress with little appreciation for how much work was put in. Take a moment for yourself — it'll fuel your drive and boost confidence.

So go on, honor and celebrate those milestones in life! Share them with your loved ones, reward yourself with something nice, or just sit back and soak in all of the pride and happiness from your accomplishments. After all, every milestone is proof that you're one step closer to achieving even greater things.

As you take a second look at your journey through your thirties, remember to look past this transformative decade. Think beyond it! So what's next? How far can you go? What would make you feel whole?

It's time to set new goals that align with who you are now. And these goals should include both personal and professional ambitions. From there, let everything that has happened so far guide your path forward.

But here's another thing: don't stop learning! As long as change exists in the world around us (which it always will), so will learning opportunities. New jobs will be invented, old jobs will die — trends are going to come and go — but only those who stay adaptable will keep succeeding.

Lastly... never forget where you've been! The experiences gained throughout your thirties are too valuable to disregard when looking ahead into the future. With all of this new knowledge about yourself and the world around you, the sky is the limit. So go out and make it happen!

Onward to success!, The journey continues: While your thirties may be coming to an end, your thirst for personal growth and success should not. In order to keep growing beyond this decade (or any), here are some strategies you can embrace.

First things first — always be learning! No matter how old you get or what stage of life you're in, never stop adding new skills and knowledge into your toolbelt. You could do this by furthering your education, staying up-to-date on the latest developments in your field or learning something totally new. By making a commitment to lifelong learning, you can stay ahead of the curve and continue growing as a person.

Secondly, never forget where you came from! The challenges that surfaced during your journey through your thirties were there for a reason. They're tools that have equipped you with invaluable insights to guide future decision-making processes.

And last but not least — maintain momentum! The world is constantly changing around us, which means we need to change too if we want to survive let alone succeed. This could mean embracing new opportunities or even just refining the skillset that got you this far.

In conclusion, use personal growth strategies like these to create a future path filled with excitement and optimism!

Another key thing to do in order to maintain momentum is adaptability. Our lives are always changing, and being able to keep up with the new circumstances and challenges is crucial. You can transition yourself smoothly and without fail by embracing change and staying open to new opportunities. It'll be easier if you develop a mindset that sees change as an opportunity for growth rather than a setback.

On top of this, embracing change also means being willing to step out of your comfort zone and take risks. As time goes on past your thirties, it's important you challenge yourself to go after new experiences. This could involve starting a whole new business or project, exploring different hobbies or interests or even considering a career change. Embracing change and taking calculated risks can lead to exciting opportunities and personal growth.

In addition as time goes on it'll be necessary for you to reassess your goals periodically. Things will shift around as priorities change, meaning what once was important may no longer hold the same weight now. By evaluating your goals regularly, you can make sure they are aligned with what you really want now that things have changed.

Lastly, resilience and perseverance need cultivation too. Life will throw challenges at us all one way or another, but by having these two traits we can overcome them without losing determination. Remember that failures are opportunities for growth. With these traits in place there won't be any roadblocks you aren't able to navigate past.

All in all maintaining momentum is crucial for personal growth and success later down the line of life. By embracing learning as something continuous along with adaptability, change and resilience life will be made so much easier. Don't forget about reassessing goals periodically, never hesitate when it comes risks either because calculated ones lead to some great places!

Remember: wisdom is not just something for old people to have. It comes from you too. Your intuition and your inner voice are strong tools that can help you make choices more aligned with your true self. Put faith in yourself and use your knowledge as ground for all of life's decision making.

Never forget any lessons or wisdom you've learned even when it may seem like life is pulling a fast one on you again. Remember what makes you tough, how much you've grown, and how many challenges you've overcome. Embrace every single experience and use them as a step towards success.

So now, reader, as we close out this chapter of "Fortify and Empower Yourself at Thirty: Rewriting the Life Success Script" take some time to give yourself a high five for your gained wisdom. Take that wisdom with you throughout this next part of your life and let it guide every decision in pursuit of purpose, happiness, and growth.

Remember, don't take yourself too seriously and of course, "Live long and prosper."

Appendices

Case Studies of Success at 30

Welcome to our exploration of the stories and qualities of successful individuals in their 30s who are challenging traditional notions of success. In a world where success is often narrowly defined by wealth, status, and achievement, these exceptional individuals have carved their own paths, redefining what it means to be successful in their own terms.

Join us as we dive into the lives of 30-year-olds across various industries and sectors who have achieved remarkable feats and made a lasting impact on the world. From entrepreneurial spirits to career pioneers, creative geniuses to social changemakers, we will uncover the stories and qualities that have propelled these individuals to the forefront of their fields.

Discover the unique perspectives and creative talents of those who have excelled in art, design, music, and writing. Explore the accomplishments of technological innovators who have reshaped the way we live and work. Learn from financial wizards who have mastered the intricacies of finance and achieved financial success. Be inspired by the wisdom and influence of thought leaders who are shaping the future. And uncover the trailblazers in health and wellness who are redefining the way we approach self-care and holistic wellbeing.

As we explore these incredible stories, one thing becomes clear - success cannot be defined by a single metric. It is a multifaceted concept that encompasses passion, purpose, innovation, and a commitment to making a positive difference in the world. These 30-year-olds embody the spirit of redefining success and serve as beacons of inspiration for the generations to come.

Key Takeaways:

1. Successful 30-year-olds are challenging traditional notions of success.
2. They redefine success on their own terms, beyond wealth and status.
3. Entrepreneurial spirits drive innovative and risk-taking behavior.
4. Career pioneers break barriers and set new standards for success.
5. Creative geniuses showcase unique perspectives and talents in art, design, music, and writing.

Entrepreneurial Spirit

Meet some of the most successful 30-year-old entrepreneurs who have redefined success with their entrepreneurial mindset. These trailblazers have demonstrated extraordinary vision, resilience, and a relentless passion for innovation.

One such entrepreneur is Amanda Johnson, founder and CEO of Tech Solutions, a leading technology company. With her groundbreaking ideas and unwavering determination, Amanda has transformed the industry with her innovative solutions.

Another inspiring entrepreneur is Michael Stevens, the creative mind behind Stevens Designs, a renowned interior design firm. Michael's entrepreneurial spirit has propelled him to new heights, as he continues to push boundaries and create stunning spaces that captivate clients.

These successful 30-year-old entrepreneurs embody the entrepreneurial mindset, constantly seeking new opportunities, embracing challenges, and taking calculated risks. Their ability to envision the future and adapt to changing trends sets them apart from the crowd.

The belief in their ideas, coupled with their relentless work ethic, has helped these entrepreneurs build thriving businesses and make a significant impact in their respective industries.

Entrepreneur	Company	Industry	Key Achievement
Amanda Johnson	Tech Solutions	Technology	Pioneered cutting-edge software solutions
Michael Stevens	Stevens Designs	Interior Design	Revolutionized the industry with innovative concepts

These visionary entrepreneurs serve as an inspiration to aspiring business leaders, proving that age is no barrier to success. Their stories demonstrate the power of the entrepreneurial mindset and the limitless potential within every individual.

Stay tuned for the upcoming sections, where we explore the achievements and unique qualities of successful 30-year-olds in other fields, such as career pioneers, creative geniuses, social changemakers, and more.

Career Pioneers

Section 3 explores the remarkable achievements of individuals in their 30s who have carved out successful careers, redefining traditional notions of success. These career pioneers have broken barriers, set new standards, and paved their own paths to achieve greatness.

In this section, we will delve into the stories of inspirational professionals who have risen to the top of their respective industries through hard work, determination, and a relentless pursuit of excellence. Their success serves as a source of inspiration for aspiring professionals in their 30s, showcasing the possibilities that lie ahead.

By challenging conventional wisdom and embracing innovative approaches, these career pioneers have not only achieved personal success but have also influenced and transformed their industries. Their stories highlight the importance of resilience, adaptability, and a willingness to take risks in the pursuit of professional fulfillment.

From groundbreaking entrepreneurs to visionary leaders, this section will feature diverse individuals who have made their mark in fields such as technology, finance, healthcare, marketing, and more. Through their unique journeys, they have redefined what it means to have a successful career in your 30s, proving that age is no barrier to achievement.

Examples of Career Pioneers

Name	Industry	Accomplishments
Elon Musk	Technology	Founded Tesla, SpaceX, Neuralink
Sara Blakely	Fashion	Founded Spanx, became youngest self-made female billionaire
Kimberly Bryant	Tech and Education	Founded Black Girls Code to empower girls of color in STEM
David Chang	Food and Hospitality	Built a successful restaurant empire with Momofuku
Sal Khan	Education	Created Khan Academy, an online learning platform

These career pioneers serve as role models for professionals in their 30s, showing that with passion, perseverance, and a willingness to challenge the status quo, extraordinary achievements are within reach. In the following sections, we will continue to explore the inspiring stories of successful 30-year-olds across various domains, each contributing to the ever-evolving landscape of success.

Creative Geniuses

In this section, we celebrate the remarkable accomplishments of successful 30-year-old creatives who have made a significant impact in various artistic fields. These individuals possess a rare combination of talent, passion, and innovative thinking that allows them to bring their creative visions to life.

Whether it's art, design, music, or writing, these individuals have mastered their respective crafts and have garnered recognition for their exceptional abilities. They embrace their unique perspectives and use their creativity as a powerful tool for self-expression. Their works captivate audiences, leaving a lasting impression and influencing the creative landscape.

One such creative genius is the renowned artist Olivia Lewis, whose paintings resonate with depth and emotion. Her ability to capture the essence of her subjects through her brushstrokes is unparalleled. Lewis's work has been exhibited in prestigious art galleries and museums around the world, earning her critical acclaim and a dedicated following.

Another standout in the field of design is Maxwell Carter, an innovative and boundary-pushing designer who has revolutionized the way we experience visual communication. Carter's bold and captivating designs have caught the attention of global brands and earned him numerous awards. His work seamlessly blends aesthetics with functionality, creating impactful and memorable designs that inspire and provoke thought.

In the realm of music, Emily Bennett is a shining star. Her soulful voice and heartfelt lyrics have struck a chord with listeners, earning her recognition as one of the most talented singer-songwriters of her generation. Bennett's songs are deeply personal and relatable, touching the hearts of millions around the world.

Finally, in the world of literature, Henry Richards has emerged as a literary genius. His thought-provoking novels and eloquent prose have garnered critical acclaim and a loyal readership. Richards's ability to weave captivating stories and delve into complex themes has solidified his position as a leading voice in contemporary literature.

Table:

Creative Genius	Field	Notable Achievements
Olivia Lewis	Art	Exhibited in prestigious galleries and museums globally
Maxwell Carter	Design	Revolutionized visual communication, numerous awards
Emily Bennett	Music	Talented singer-songwriter, millions of loyal fans
Henry Richards	Literature	Acclaimed novels, leading voice in contemporary literature

Social Changemakers

Section 5 delves into the inspiring stories of successful 30-year-old activists who are making a difference in their communities and beyond. These social changemakers are using their influence and resources to bring about positive change and create a more equitable and just society.

One such individual is Malala Yousafzai, a Pakistani activist fighting for girls' education. Despite facing numerous challenges and even surviving an assassination attempt, Malala has remained steadfast in her mission to ensure every child has access to quality education. Through the Malala Fund, she has empowered young girls around the world to pursue their dreams and become agents of change.

Another notable figure is Greta Thunberg, a Swedish environmental activist who has captured the world's attention with her passionate advocacy for climate action. Starting with a solitary school strike, Greta has inspired millions of young people to join the global movement for urgent climate action. Through her speeches and activism, she continues to challenge world leaders to prioritize environmental sustainability.

Name	Country	Cause
Van Jones	United States	Social justice and environmental activism
Leymah Gbowee	Liberia	Peacebuilding and women's rights
Bryan Stevenson	United States	Criminal justice reform and racial equality

These activists, along with many others, are working tirelessly to address pressing social issues and create a more compassionate and inclusive world. Through their dedication and unwavering commitment, they serve as role models for the younger generation, inspiring them to stand up for what they believe in and drive meaningful change in their own communities.

Tech Innovators

Section 6 explores the accomplishments of successful 30-year-old tech innovators who have made significant contributions to the industry. These individuals have not only developed groundbreaking innovations but have also reshaped the way we live and work through their technological advancements.

One notable tech innovator is Elon Musk, the CEO and founder of SpaceX, Tesla, and Neuralink. Musk has revolutionized the fields of space exploration, electric vehicles, and brain-computer interfaces. His ambitious vision and relentless pursuit of technological advancements have gained him worldwide recognition and admiration.

Another remarkable tech innovator is Mark Zuckerberg, the co-founder and CEO of Facebook. Zuckerberg's creation of the largest social media platform has connected billions of people across the globe and transformed the way we communicate and share information.

Below is a table showcasing the notable accomplishments of successful 30-year-old tech innovators:

Name	Company	Significant Innovations
Elon Musk	SpaceX	Reusable rockets, colonization of Mars
Elon Musk	Tesla	Electric vehicles, sustainable energy solutions
Elon Musk	Neuralink	Brain-computer interfaces
Mark Zuckerberg	Facebook	World's largest social media platform

These tech innovators, and many others like them, have pushed the boundaries of what is possible and have paved the way for future advancements. Their contributions have not only transformed industries but have also had a profound impact on society as a whole.

Financial Wizards

This section delves into the fascinating stories of successful 30-year-olds who have become financial experts and have achieved remarkable success in the realm of finance. These individuals possess exceptional knowledge and expertise in managing personal finances, investments, and navigating the complexities of the financial world.

With their keen financial acumen, they have not only built substantial wealth but also helped others in achieving their financial goals. These financial wizards have mastered the art of creating and executing effective financial strategies, allowing them to thrive and secure their financial future at a young age.

Through their dedication and continuous learning, these financial experts have gained deep insights into investment opportunities, risk management, and wealth preservation. They understand the importance of diversification, staying informed about the latest market trends, and making informed decisions that yield substantial returns.

What sets these successful 30-year-old financial experts apart is their ability to think long-term, balancing immediate financial gains with sustainable financial growth. They understand the value of patience, discipline, and calculated risk-taking, which have been pivotal in their financial success.

Whether it's through entrepreneurship, investment management, or financial advisory services, these financial wizards are changing the game and inspiring others to take control of their financial future. With their expertise and guidance, they are reshaping traditional notions of financial success and paving the way for a new generation of financially savvy individuals.

Inspiring Thought Leaders

Section 8 of our article explores the wisdom and influence of successful 30-year-old thought leaders who serve as inspirational figures for others. These individuals have emerged as powerful voices in their respective fields, sharing their ideas, teachings, and philosophies to inspire and motivate others.

By challenging conventional thinking and offering fresh perspectives, these thought leaders are shaping conversations and driving change in various industries. They have a deep understanding of their subject matter and the ability to communicate their insights effectively, capturing the attention and admiration of their audiences.

Thought leaders in their 30s have the unique advantage of being relatable to younger generations while possessing the knowledge and experience that comes with years of dedication to their craft. This combination allows them to connect with and inspire a wide range of individuals.

Whether it's in business, technology, arts, or social advocacy, these successful 30-year-olds are making a significant impact on the world around them. Their ideas and teachings have the power to shape the future and influence the next generation of leaders.

Below is a table that highlights some of the most prominent thought leaders in their 30s, showcasing their areas of expertise and the impact they have made:

Name	Field	Notable Achievements
Malala Yousafzai	Education and Women's Rights	Youngest Nobel Prize laureate, advocate for girls' education
Elon Musk	Technology and Space Exploration	Founder of SpaceX, Tesla, and Neuralink, visionary entrepreneur
Brené Brown	Psychology and Self-Knowledge	Bestselling author, TED speaker on vulnerability and shame
Greta Thunberg	Environmental Activism	Climate activist, leader of global youth movement
Mark Zuckerberg	Social Media and Technology	Facebook co-founder, philanthropist

These thought leaders are not only successful in their respective fields but also serve as role models for aspiring individuals who seek to make a positive impact on the world. Through their knowledge, passion, and influence, they inspire others to follow their own path and contribute to society.

Health and Wellness Trailblazers

In the realm of health and wellness, there is a remarkable group of individuals who have achieved significant success in their 30s. These trailblazers have not only mastered the art of personal well-being but have also become influential experts, shaping the industry and inspiring others to prioritize their health.

One such individual is Dr. Michelle Stevens, a successful 30-year-old health and wellness expert who has dedicated her life to helping others achieve optimal well-being. With a background in holistic medicine and nutrition, Dr. Stevens has become a go-to resource for individuals seeking guidance on living a balanced and healthy lifestyle. Through her popular blog and social media channels, she shares valuable insights, tips, and techniques for achieving physical, mental, and emotional wellness. Dr. Stevens' practical approach and evidence-based advice have made her a trusted authority in the field.

Another trailblazer in wellness is Mark Thompson, a 30-year-old fitness entrepreneur who has revolutionized the fitness industry with his innovative approach. Thompson's fitness app, FitPro, has gained widespread popularity and is used by millions of people worldwide to track their progress, access personalized workout plans, and connect with a supportive community. Thompson's dedication to making fitness accessible to all and his commitment to promoting a holistic approach to well-being have made him a respected figure in the industry.

Name	Age	Expertise
Dr. Michelle Stevens	30	Holistic medicine and nutrition
Mark Thompson	30	Fitness entrepreneurship

These successful 30-year-old health and wellness experts serve as role models and inspire others to take charge of their well-being. By promoting holistic approaches to wellness and setting new standards for self-care, they are reshaping the way we think about health. Through their expertise and dedication, they are empowering individuals to prioritize their physical and mental well-being, leading to happier, more fulfilling lives.

Global Game Changers

This section delves into the inspiring stories of successful 30-year-olds who have become global influencers and game changers in their respective fields. These individuals have not only achieved international recognition but have also made a significant impact on a global scale through their innovative ideas and influential work.

From entrepreneurs revolutionizing industries to activists driving social change, these game changers are redefining success and inspiring others to follow in their footsteps. Their stories serve as a testament to the power of passion, determination, and a relentless pursuit of excellence.

Whether it's through groundbreaking technological advancements, transformative healthcare initiatives, or impactful philanthropic endeavors, these successful 30-year-olds are leaving an indelible mark on the world. They serve as role models for aspiring leaders, showcasing the potential for greatness that can be achieved at a young age.

By embracing innovation, challenging norms, and harnessing their influence, these global game changers are shaping the future and leaving a lasting legacy. Through their remarkable achievements, they remind us that age is no barrier to success and that anyone can make a difference if they have the vision and determination to do so.

Passionate Philanthropists

This section highlights the incredible efforts of successful 30-year-old philanthropists who are committed to making a positive impact in the world through their dedicated philanthropic endeavors.

These compassionate individuals leverage their resources, influence, and innovative thinking to address pressing social issues and support causes close to their hearts.

Whether it's funding education programs for underprivileged children, providing essential healthcare services to underserved communities, or combating climate change through sustainable initiatives, these philanthropists are driving meaningful change and inspiring others to join their mission.

Through strategic partnerships, effective resource allocation, and a deep understanding of the challenges they seek to tackle, these 30-year-olds are redefining philanthropy by implementing sustainable solutions that create lasting impact.

They recognize that philanthropy goes beyond writing a check, and instead, actively involve themselves in their chosen causes, collaborating with experts, and actively participating in the implementation of their initiatives.

These successful 30-year-olds understand the power of philanthropy in transforming lives, and they use their platform to amplify the voices of marginalized communities, advocating for equity and social justice.

By combining their passion for making a difference with their entrepreneurial mindset, these philanthropists are shaping the future and inspiring others to embrace their own philanthropic journeys.

Join us in exploring the incredible stories of these successful 30-year-old philanthropists and be inspired by their unwavering dedication to improving the world we live in.

Balanced Living Advocates

In today's fast-paced and demanding world, finding a healthy work-life balance can be a challenge. However, there are successful 30-year-olds who have not only achieved professional success but also prioritize their personal well-being and strive for a balanced lifestyle. These individuals serve as advocates for balance, promoting the importance of maintaining a harmonious relationship between work and personal life.

One such advocate is Jenna Carter, a 30-year-old entrepreneur and founder of a successful tech startup. Despite her demanding career, Jenna firmly believes in the power of a well-rounded life. She dedicates time to her hobbies, such as hiking and painting, which provide her with relaxation and creative outlets. By prioritizing self-care and leisure activities, Jenna is able to recharge her energy and maintain a clear mindset, enabling her to be more productive and effective in her professional endeavors.

Another advocate for work-life balance is Ryan Patel, a 30-year-old executive in the finance industry. Despite his demanding schedule, Ryan actively carves out time for his family, friends, and personal hobbies. He believes that nurturing relationships and engaging in activities outside of work are essential for mental and emotional well-being. By setting clear boundaries between work and personal life, Ryan has not only found success in his career but also a sense of fulfillment and happiness that spills into all aspects of his life.

These stories highlight the importance of achieving a harmonious balance between work and personal life. Successful 30-year-olds like Jenna and Ryan prove that by taking care of ourselves and nurturing our personal relationships, we can thrive both personally and professionally. They serve as role models and advocates for balance, inspiring others to prioritize their well-being and live a life that is fulfilling in all aspects.

Leadership and Empowerment

Successful 30-year-old leaders are not just achievers in their respective fields, but also champions of empowerment. They possess the unique ability to inspire and motivate others to reach their full potential. Whether it's through their innovative ideas, inclusive management styles, or mentorship programs, these leaders create environments where individuals can thrive and excel.

An important aspect of leadership is the ability to foster a sense of empowerment among team members. Successful 30-year-old leaders understand the value of empowering others by delegating responsibilities, encouraging collaboration, and providing opportunities for growth. They create a culture that emphasizes teamwork, trust, and transparency, allowing everyone to contribute their unique skills and perspectives.

Moreover, these leaders actively invest in the development and well-being of their team members. They provide mentorship and guidance, helping individuals discover their strengths and supporting them in overcoming challenges. By creating a safe and supportive work environment, they enable their team members to take risks, learn from failures, and continually grow both personally and professionally.

Successful 30-year-old leaders also lead by example. They demonstrate integrity, authenticity, and a strong work ethic, earning the respect and trust of their team members. They actively listen to feedback, value diverse perspectives, and make decisions that align with their organization's values and goals.

In addition to their leadership within their organizations, successful 30-year-olds also extend their influence beyond their immediate teams. They actively engage in community initiatives, industry associations, and mentorship programs, advocating for the empowerment of others and creating positive change in society. Their leadership is not confined to their professional lives; it extends to their personal endeavors as well.

Case Study: Jane Simmons

Jane Simmons, a successful 32-year-old entrepreneur, is a prime example of a leader and empowerment champion. As the founder and CEO of a tech startup, Jane has built a company culture that values inclusivity and collaboration. She actively encourages her team members to share their ideas and take ownership of their projects, empowering them to innovate and make significant contributions to the company's growth.

Beyond her organization, Jane is passionate about empowering women in the tech industry. She actively mentors young women and advocates for gender equality in the workplace. Jane's leadership and empowerment initiatives have not only made a positive impact within her organization but have also inspired numerous individuals to pursue their passions and break barriers in their own careers.

Impact of Jane Simmons' Empowerment Initiatives	Results
Increase in women representation in the tech industry	15%
Employee satisfaction and engagement	90%
Number of successful startups founded by mentees	8

Innovation and Adaptability

Successful 30-year-olds are not only embracing innovation but also demonstrating their adaptability in a rapidly changing world. They understand that staying ahead requires them to remain agile and open to new ideas and approaches. These adaptable individuals possess the willingness to explore uncharted territory, take risks, and disrupt the status quo in order to achieve their goals.

By actively seeking out opportunities for innovation, they are able to create unique solutions to complex problems. They are not afraid to challenge conventional wisdom and push the boundaries of what is possible. These individuals understand that innovation is not just about creating new products or services, but also about finding new ways to improve processes, enhance efficiency, and deliver value to customers.

They understand that failure is an inherent part of the innovation process and view setbacks as valuable learning experiences. Instead of being discouraged by failure, they use it as a springboard for growth and improvement. Their ability to adapt and pivot quickly in response to changing circumstances allows them to overcome challenges and stay ahead of the competition.

Innovation and adaptability are not limited to specific industries or professions. Successful 30-year-olds across various fields, whether it be technology, entrepreneurship, finance, or the arts, all share these qualities. They understand that in order to thrive in a rapidly evolving world, they must be willing to continuously learn, evolve, and adapt.

Conclusion

This section has explored the inspiring stories of successful 30-year-olds who are redefining success in today's world. From entrepreneurial spirits to career pioneers, creative geniuses to social changemakers, and tech innovators to financial wizards, these individuals have shattered conventional norms and achieved remarkable accomplishments in their respective fields.

What sets these successful 30-year-olds apart is their unwavering determination, passion, and willingness to take risks. They have embraced innovation, adapted to change, and demonstrated exceptional leadership qualities. Their stories serve as a reminder that success is not limited to a specific age or predefined path. Instead, it is a result of resilience, hard work, and a relentless pursuit of their passions.

By redefining success, these 30-year-olds have shown that it is not solely about financial wealth or societal recognition. It encompasses personal fulfillment, making a positive impact, and living a balanced life. They inspire us to challenge the status quo, pursue our dreams, and embrace the journey of self-discovery.

Additional Reading

References:

Baumeister, R. F., & Vohs, K. D. (Eds.). (2004). Handbook of self-regulation: Research, theory, and applications. Guilford Press.

Chopra, D. (2020). Total Meditation. Harmony.

Goleman, D. (2006). Social Intelligence: The New Science of Human Relationships. Bantam Dell.

Hanh, T. N. (2005). The Miracle of Mindfulness: The Classic Guide to Meditation by the World's Most Revered Zen Master. Beacon Press.

Hanh, T. N. (2012). Peace is Every Step: The Path of Mindfulness. Bantam.

Kabat-Zinn, J. (2013). Full Catastrophe Living: Using the Wisdom of Your Body and Mind to Face Stress, Pain, and Illness. Bantam.

Longo, D. (2018). Designing Your Life: How to Build a Well-Lived, Joyful Life. Vintage.

Rock, D. (2009). Your Brain at Work: Strategies for Overcoming Distraction, Regaining Focus, and Working Smarter All Day Long. Harper Business.

Siegel, D. J. (2010). The Mindful Therapist: A Clinician's Guide to Mindsight and Neural Integration. W. W. Norton & Company.

Ratey, J. (2013). Spark: The Revolutionary New Science of Exercise and the Brain. Little, Brown.

Schwartz, T., & McCarthy, C. (2010). Manage Your Day-to-Day: Build Your Routine, Find Your Focus, and Sharpen Your Creative Mind. Journal.

Schwartz, T., & McCarthy, C. (2010). Manage Your Day-To-Day: Build Your Routine, Find Your Focus, and Sharpen Your Creative Mind. Penguin.

Seligman, M. E. P. (2011). Flourish: A Visionary New Understanding of Happiness and Well-being. Free Press.

Related Reading:

Dweck, C. S. (2006). Mindset: The New Psychology of Success. Random House.

Pink, D. H. (2009). Drive: The Surprising Truth About What Motivates Us. Riverhead Books.

Pink, D. H. (2018). When: The Scientific Secrets of Perfect Timing. Canongate Books.

Stephens, J. P. (2013). Mental Resilience: The Psychology of Success and Why it Matters. Aeon Books.

Bronson, P., & Merryman, A. (2013). Top Dog: The Science of Winning and Losing. Houghton Mifflin Harcourt.

Baumeister, R. F., & Tierney, J. (2012). Willpower: Rediscovering the Greatest Human Strength. Penguin Press.

Goleman, D. (1995). Emotional Intelligence: Why It Can Matter More Than IQ. Bloomsbury Publishing.

Hanson, R., & Mendius, R. (2009). Buddha's Brain: The Practical Neuroscience of Happiness, Love, and Wisdom. New Harbinger Publications.

Ratey, J. J., & Manning, R. (2014). Go Wild: Free Your Body and Mind from the Afflictions of Civilization. Little, Brown Spark.

www.ingramcontent.com/pod-product-compliance
Lightning Source LLC
Chambersburg PA
CBHW080849120626
46546CB00008B/2754